READINGS IN
THE THEORY OF
INDIVIDUAL PSYCHOLOGY

READINGS IN
THE THEORY OF
INDIVIDUAL PSYCHOLOGY

Edited by
Steve Slavik
Jon Carlson

Routledge
Taylor & Francis Group
New York   London

Published in 2006 by
Routledge
Taylor & Francis Group
270 Madison Avenue
New York, NY 10016

Published in Great Britain by
Routledge
Taylor & Francis Group
2 Park Square
Milton Park, Abingdon
Oxon OX14 4RN

Printed in the United States of America on acid-free paper
10 9 8 7 6 5 4 3 2 1

International Standard Book Number-10: 0-415-95168-2 (Hardcover)
International Standard Book Number-13: 978-0-415-95168-5 (Hardcover)
Library of Congress Card Number 2005008176

Library of Congress Cataloging-in-Publication Data

Readings in the theory of individual psychology / Steve Slavik and Jon Carlson, editors.
    p. cm.
  Includes bibliographical references and index.
  ISBN 0-415-95168-2 (hardbound)
  1. Adlerian psychology. I. Slavik, Steven. II. Carlson, Jon.

BF175.5.A33R43 2005
150.19'53--dc22   2005008176

Taylor & Francis Group
is the Academic Division of Informa plc.

Visit the Taylor & Francis Web site at
http://www.taylorandfrancis.com

and the Routledge Web site at
http://www.routledge-ny.com

To all those who have benefited, who continue to benefit, and who will benefit from Adler's theory.

Contents

About the Editors

Jon Carlson, PsyD, EdD, is Distinguished Professor in the Division of Psychology and Counseling at Governors State University (Illinois) and psychologist at the Wellness Clinic in Lake Geneva, Wisconsin. He holds a certificate of psychotherapy from the Alfred Adler Institute and edited the *Journal of Individual Psychology* for several years. He has authored 38 books, 140 professional journal articles, and developed over 200 professional video/DVD programs.

Steve Slavik has a master's degree (1991) from the Adler School of Professional Psychology in Chicago and another in Hispanic studies from the University of Victoria (2004). Currently he works in private practice as an individual and marriage counselor in North Vancouver, BC, and acts as a supervisor for master's-level counseling students. He has a number of publications in professional journals, is coeditor with Jon Carlson of *Techniques in Adlerian Psychology*, and is the editor of the *Canadian Journal of Adlerian Psychology*.

Contributors

Alfred Adler
Heinz L. Ansbacher
Margaret L. Bass
Mark H. Bickhard
Amy L. Brinkerhoff
Linda Campbell
Earl W. Capron
Ann W. Carns
Michael R. Carns
Fern Clemmer
Richard L. Coleman
James W. Croake
William L. Curlette
Paul N. Dixon
Rudolf Dreikurs
Thomas E. Edgar
Brian Lee Ford
Jane Griffith
Fred J. Hanna
Trevor Hjertaas
Jack Huber

Thor M. Johansen
Roy M. Kern
Richard Royal Kopp
Donald N. Lombardi
Guy J. Manaster
Alfred E. McWilliams, Jr.
Erik J. Melchior
Al Milliren
James G. Murphy
Paul R. Peluso
Regine Seidler
Christopher Shelley
Michael J. Stasio
Alan Stewart
Mark H. Stone
Donald A. Strano
Tony Testerment
C. Edward Watkins, Jr.
Mary Streppa Wheeler
Joanna White
Wes Wingett

Preface

As soon as a scientific system is offered to the world, it appeals to individuals, both laymen and scientists, with a trend of mind similar to that of the author of the system and provides them with a scientific foundation for an attitude towards life which they had achieved previously.

Alfred Adler (1956, p. 197)

Adler's greatest contributions seem to rest in the many practical and straightforward ways of dealing with others in psychotherapy and counseling, including both a direct method of understanding human behavior and effective strategies and techniques. His pragmatic approach appeals to practical people and, therefore, within the ranks of Adlerian adherents, the practitioner has become well represented. In fact, the practical ideas and methods are so clearly useful and effective that little research into the basic concepts and methods, or into their effectiveness, has been required. Therefore, only minimal attention has been paid to making Adler's theory precise, and even less has been paid to researching his ideas.

One problem seems to be that before any additional research can occur, the theory needs to be clearly and effectively articulated. It is surprising that, although the call for research into Adlerian theory occurs periodically, no commonly agreed on definitions of fundamental Adlerian concepts have been published that identify possible ways to make the concepts amenable to research. Neither has any summary and integration into theory of established results become available in print. Further, no general discussion of the possible aims for research and possible methods of research suitable to Adlerian psychology has been published.

We hope that by publishing this volume such considerations can begin to be addressed. In regard to theory, the fundamental issue described in a number of the invited essays included in this volume is how issues specific to individuals can be addressed by research methods that use statistical and group methods, and how the results of such methods can be useful to practitioners who have individuals before them. Stated in another way, how can a "psychology of understanding" be studied using current "objective" methods? As will be seen in several of the essays included in this volume, many of the fundamental concepts and relationships of Individual Psychology depend on the specific meanings that individuals attribute to events. How, then, is a researcher, who is looking for a general rule, to assess both the significance of the event to an individual and the individual's movement in response to it? The issue has not been addressed generally in Adlerian research, nor have instruments or methods that take this subjectivity into account been devised.

With the publication of this volume, we hope to promote the discussion of such issues. Herein, we have brought together some of the best theoreticians as well as some of the classic articles on Adlerian theory. Our hope is that, with this beginning, others will follow to clarify Adlerian concepts and to devise ways to make them amenable to assessment and measurement in objective fashions, or else to devise ways to assess them that take into account their subjectivity.

Steve Slavik and Jon Carlson

Reference

Adler, A. (1956). *The Individual Psychology of Alfred Adler: A systematic presentation in selections from his writings* (H. L. Ansbacher & R. R. Ansbacher, Eds.). New York: Basic Books.

I
Introduction

CHAPTER 1

Models, Theories, and Research in Individual Psychology

STEVE SLAVIK

In 1974, the then-editor, Ray Corsini, asked readers of the *Journal of Individual Psychology* the question, "Were you to suggest some objective nomothetic studies within Individual Psychology, which one would you feel [was] particularly important?" (p. 37). Although not uniformly, the responses tended to endorse research in "the practice of Adlerian psychotherapy" (p. 37) or in the verification of the effectiveness of Adlerian methods. William Pew summarized the trend well:

> We need longitudinal studies, long term follow-up of individual, couple, group and family counseling and therapy. We need studies of attitudinal and behavioral changes resulting from participation in family education centers and marriage education centers. We need studies which prove the efficacy of Adlerian principles in the classroom. We need verification of the efficacy of Adlerian child-rearing techniques. (p. 42)

Since then, except for studies in parent education effectiveness (Berrett, 1975; Burnett, 1988; Croake & Burness, 1976; Croake & Glover, 1977; Frazier & Mathes, 1975; Freeman, 1975; Gordon-Rosen & Rosen, 1984;

Hinkle, Arnold, Croake, & Keller, 1980; Krebs, 1986; McKay & Hillman, 1979; Mullis, 1999; Newlon, Borboa, & Arcinega, 1986; Todres & Bunston, 1993, Urban, 1991; Wiese, 1989), little research has been done in these areas. In 1999, Watkins and Guarnaccia stated that we still "need studies of Adlerian counseling and psychotherapy.... They are few, far between, and hard to find" (p. 226). Nonetheless, we would point out that as little as has been done in outcome and efficacy research, correspondingly little has been done in research in the basic concepts and principles of Individual Psychology (IP). For example, where is research related to the connection between apperception and perception? Where is research concerning the relation of apperception to memory, or between encouragement and change in apperception? What is the relationship between social interest and courage? How can we operationalize the concept of activity? How would we measure "standing still" or "retreating"? Can we assess personality characteristics as *methods*, rather than as traits? Is social interest a personality characteristic, a method of dealing with others, a property of activity, or a momentary state?

These, and many other questions, remain untouched, perhaps because the concepts are still vague and ambiguous. In many cases, little or no discussion has transpired in Adlerian literature with the purpose of clarifying the concepts and suggesting research questions and methods. Again, as recently as 1999, Watkins and Guarnaccia could recommend that Adlerian researchers and theorists "continue to refine definitions and quantification measures where needed. Where concepts have been left undefined and unquantified, research has been minimal.... Let us begin to define and quantify the undefined and unquantified" (p. 227). It is the purpose of the present volume, in some cases, to begin and, in other cases, to continue such a process. The ultimate goal is to provide a theory of IP with some empirical support.

As well, we want to open more definitely the idea that since Adlerian thinking is an "understanding" psychology that attempts to understand the relationships of psychological events by placing them in their psychological context (Ansbacher & Ansbacher, 1956), phenomenological methods are appropriate in its study. A distinction common in current phenomenological studies is that between the *phenomenological attitude* and *phenomenologically derived knowledge* (McCabe, Capron, & Peterson, 1991; Thorne, 1997). The former is represented by the respect a therapist or researcher holds in entering the world of others and requires an acknowledgment of the extent to which a therapist or researcher prejudices the understanding of another by his or her own attitudes. The latter is empirical and verifiable knowledge with origins in phenomenological observation and investigation. While IP is generally taken to be a phenomenological psychology (Ansbacher &

Ansbacher, 1956; Mosak & Maniacci, 1999), the focus of this attribution is generally on the practice of Adlerian psychotherapy. Little attention is given to phenomenologically derived knowledge of individuals and of relationships among individuals. We would like to see more phenomenological studies of the basic concepts of IP. The idea of "activity" readily comes to mind. All Adlerian therapists have some kind of idea of "standing still," "withdrawal," and "moving forward," which could be put to use in such a study.

Theories and Models

To open our discussion, we distinguish between theories and models. By theory, we mean a set of propositions that relate well-defined and accepted concepts of the theory to one another. These concepts are operationally related to methods or instruments used to identify or measure their incidence. In addition, a body of evidence, determined through the use of the methods or instruments, is said to support the propositions of which the theory is comprised. This evidence provides support to the theory through its accuracy and precision. Another way to state this is that of Cacioppo, Semin and Berntson (2004): "A general scientific hypothesis that has a body of empirical support constitutes a scientific law, and a logically closely interconnected set of scientific laws constitutes a scientific theory" (p. 215). In their sense, no comprehensive theory of IP has yet been developed.

By a model, we mean a system of statements describing a certain domain, detailing "the way things work" within the domain, with no presumption of supporting evidence, nor even necessarily of consistency and clarity in the use of the concepts. Models may range from a very informal statement of "on the face of it, this is how it seems to me," to a more formal analysis of the terms used and the domain discussed. Models are more likely judged by their scope or range, rather than by their accuracy and precision. That is, if a model includes and relates the important elements of the domain, it is considered adequate. In Adler's writings, we find three important models: one of personality, one of pathology, and one of therapeutic practice.

However, before we discuss IP in particular, it would be well to describe theories, models, and their interactions in a broader way. Within the field of counseling and psychotherapy, one finds a number of models, including those of:

- personality
- normal and abnormal functioning
- personality change or personal change
- effective therapeutic practice
- models of the therapeutic process and outcome

As well, research presently exists in all of these areas, leading to more or less extensive theory development. In some cases, research also guides model building, and vice versa.

The relationship between a theory and a model is not always simple, but will be of some importance in this collection of essays, so we will devote a little attention to it. *Prima facie*, one might think that a model, given sufficient evidence, is transformed into a theory. Yet, such is seldom the case. Models frequently are ambiguous, with poorly defined terms, and often they make no provision, except perhaps anecdotal, for evidence. At the same time, however, a model gives the theorist both constraints regarding the meaning of terms and ideas regarding relationships of concepts, that is, regarding hypotheses.

Models certainly guide theorists and researchers. As Nagel stated in 1961, a model serves "as a guide for setting up the fundamental assumptions of a theory, as well as a source of suggestions for extending [or restricting] the range of their application" (pp. 108–109). A model has considerable value because it suggests relationships that the experimenter may seek to verify and the theorist to describe. Such conceptual adjustment works in the other direction as well, since theory enables models to be corrected. Theory incorporates accuracy and precision into a model, giving rise to revision of the model, particularly regarding the concepts and the range or circumstances of their application. A noted example of the interaction between model and theory in IP occurs with the concept of birth order, where the idea of actual birth order has had to be replaced by that of psychological birth order.

However, the interaction between a model and a theory derived from it is not fully described with clarifying how they may be used to modify one another. Given the greater formality of a theory and its dependence on evidence, almost of necessity the theorist will require the lesser formality of the model to generate possibilities for expansion of theoretical propositions (hypotheses) and subsequent research. Equally important, models may suggest ways in which or points at which concepts may be usefully operationalized (Nagel, 1961). For example, if in the IP model of personality, *lifestyle* were taken to be the consistency of behavior of a person, across situations, lifestyle might be assessed through a diagnostic procedure, similar to diagnosis utilizing *DSM-IV* (APA, 1994). Any consistency running through a variety of behaviors might allow the definition of a general motive (Ajzen, 1988). In further research, such a diagnostic procedure might be a useful assessment tool in the study of the relationship between lifestyle and activity level. Yet, this type of identification and assessment might be of little value in studying how memory conforms to lifestyle, where both practice and the model might suggest using a method to assess lifestyle in terms of convictions. Thus, models—and practice based on models—suggest appropriate ways to identify and measure or otherwise assess concepts, depending on the pathway of study. For those who tend to accept the IP model as a *given*, rather than as a model, these ways may be obscured.

A danger that might arise from too literal a dependence on a model is to assume the indispensability for theory of certain concepts within the model. Some concepts within a model may be too general or ambiguous to allow for measurement, or may not be necessary in a theory. Three that come to mind for Adlerian thinking are the existence of a creative self, the childhood origins of feelings of inferiority, and—dare we say?—social interest itself. The first two may be inessential concepts in an Adlerian theory since they are universal assumptions in the model and a theory can be formalized without them. The third is perhaps redundant (and this will be explained below). Another danger of too literal a reliance on the model of IP is to assume that theorists need to attend to the practice directives of the model in formalizing or testing the theory. The practice of psychotherapy can be treated independently of the more fundamental concepts of the model. If this distinction is not made clearly, one might think that the foremost purposes of empirical study in IP are process, outcome, and effectiveness research. However, the focus in this book is on the fundamental concepts of the model and their relationships, rather than on outcome research. The same applies to the broader-reaching study of democratic family or social processes, the life tasks, or developmental models. Important and interesting as they are, work in these areas might benefit from studies in the more basic concepts of Adlerian thinking.

In sum, models and theories serve independent purposes. The model in IP serves to conceptualize and guide practice and to provide an intuitive basis for theorizing; theory seeks to guide research and research seeks to verify the usefulness of concepts and to test hypotheses. Accordingly, two important criteria for evaluating theory are whether concepts are useful in discriminating ostensibly important elements of the domain and in providing explanatory power to the theory. Concepts must identify the important elements or events of the domain on which the theory focuses, and they must be robustly related to other concepts in ways that allow explanation of the events of the domain.

The Logical Structure of the Individual Psychology Model of the Person

In Adler's writing, we find the understanding that individuals are indivisible "units related to inside and outside problems" (1937, p. 776). Adler further suggested that these individuals express themselves "in movement and direction toward a successful solution of outer and inner confrontations ... [and,] as in physics we cannot measure any movement without relating it toward another space. ... This other space is the social organization of mankind" (1937, p. 776). That is, people constantly undertake problem-solving activity within a social field, aimed at the solution of inner and outer problems. However, the basic conception of the person as a unit embedded in the social organization of mankind rests on other concepts in Adler's thinking:

1. The unity of the individual, which Adler has called the life style, depends on a master plan (Shulman, 1985), a creative model of what one takes oneself to be.

2. All psychic processes—such as apperception, thinking, dreaming and memory—*conform to* the plan and the unity is a consequence of such subordination. An individual becomes somewhat like a hologram, in which any psychic production contains all important information regarding one.

3. In particular, *apperception* is the perception of one's capacities and the environment "as if" they were resources or deficiencies, opportunities or obstacles to one's master plan.

4. Likewise, *activity* and its level are consistent with the master plan. Activity can be evaluated only in terms of direction and intensity within a social field. As Huber (1975) has described the concept of activity, "Adler presents a picture of man as constantly moving [and], ... as with any moving object, it is necessary to state where that object is moving to make any meaningful statement.... Man's degree of activity is analogous to a measure of speed and man's degree of Social Interest ... is analogous to a measure of the direction of movement" (p. 66).

5. In order to account for the master plan, Adler imputed a *creative self* or an inherent creative power to the individual. The idea of what one takes oneself to be is an active creation of the individual not only in his or her early circumstances, but throughout life.

6. The master plan, in turn, rests on or is composed of beliefs or *life style convictions* about oneself, others, and the nature of the social world.

7. The master plan arises through the mediation of the creative self as a *compensation* for a *felt inferiority.* Thus the motivation for the unity of the individual is a felt inferiority, from which the person attempts to escape through his or her compensatory life style.

Other concepts depend less on the creative self than on the idea of a person's embeddedness in a social world. The social world provides the "space" within which a person moves and, as well, provides the context within which direction of movement finds meaning (Kohler, 1947).

8. In order to distinguish forward from backward movement in life, Adler used the concept of *social interest,* a quality belonging to activity or, perhaps, to the person.

9. An *inferiority complex* is the presentation of the self as weak or inferior, in order to excuse oneself in a retreat from tasks of living. This complex may result, at least in part, from the *family constellation* in which the child originally found him or herself. A *superiority complex* is "an exaggerated attempt to act as if one were not feeling inferior and then acting that way" (Mosak & Maniacci, p. 82). As Mosak and Maniacci point out, it is akin to the inferiority complex, except it requires the presentation of the self as superior without making the effort to be so. Both complexes represent *overcompensation* rather than successful *compensation* for an inferiority feeling.

10. *Organ jargon* refers to the reciprocal influences of the mind and the body in which the master plan of the individual is expressed in bodily functioning. Instances of organ jargon typically present (and excuse) an individual's hesitation to move forward or his or her standing still.

Other concepts further help to account for the systematic behavior of the individual.

11. *Pessimism* is the conviction that anything one does will turn out badly.

12. *Discouragement* is the reluctance to try to solve problems and to better oneself, resulting in the avoidance of challenges which, if faced successfully, could increase one's social interest.

13. *Encouragement,* the antidote to discouragement, is the process of recognition by oneself or others of one's abilities and strengths, enhancing the willingness to try something new.

Ambiguity in Individual Psychology

This model of personality is rife with metaphor and, therefore, difficult to formulate rigorously. It is important to keep in mind that one purpose of a theory is to explain observable events in terms of concepts and relationships that have been shown to be useful and verifiable, respectively. We can mention a few difficulties or questions that come to mind, both in regard to usefulness of concepts and to their possible relationships.

1. The person is said to be a unit or to have a unitary personality. What are the criteria by which one can be said to be a unit? How could one tell if a person were not a unit? How can an individual fail to be a unit? If one cannot fail, or if there are no "nonunitary" personalities, the concept seems rather meaningless. That is, its use adds no discriminatory power or explanatory power to a theory. By way of contrast, what entities are not unities?

2. Is life style measurable nomothetically? Is it not, above all, an idiographic concept? What explanatory power does a nomothetic concept of life style have?

3. Psychic processes conform to a master plan. What does "conform to" mean here? How could one tell if they failed to conform? What are the criteria by which one can judge that they conform? Are there degrees of conformity? If a person's psychic productions resemble a hologram, how can such resemblance be demonstrated or measured? What personality element oversees the construction and what processes are involved in the creation of conformity?

4. If activity is a central concept in Adlerian thinking, how can we define it so that the two components of intensity and direction are clear? What kind of measure can be devised for activity that considers both aspects? How is activity related to behavior?

5. A creative self forms the master plan. Where is the creative self? Is it the same as adult creativity? Is a "creative" adult more able to change his or her master plan than one who is not creative? What other capacities does the creative self have? Perhaps the idea that the creative self forms a master plan begs the question: a creative self may need all the capacities of an adult to form a master plan, including a goal. What is the relationship of the creative self to convictions?

6. The master plan rests on convictions. How do we identify and confirm the existence of convictions? How are convictions related to other psychic processes such as thinking or memory? How are convictions related to the regulation of activity or to the generation of emotions? How are convictions related to inferiority feelings or to an inferiority complex? Given the idea that convictions frame and guide one's movement in life, are the notions of inferiority and superiority necessary?

7. What evidence exists for a "felt inferiority" and its childhood origin? How would we measure a felt inferiority? How will we relate it to a master plan? Will we want to relate it through the intensity of the feeling or through the content of the inferiority? How can we define how and verify that a lifestyle "compensates" for a felt inferiority?

How do we differentiate empirically a compensation from an over-compensation?

8. Is the inferiority complex another name for a certain type of life-style? How do we identify an inferiority complex? Likewise, how do we identify a superiority complex? Is the concept of overcompensation redundant? What explanatory power do these concepts contain that is not already available in that of lifestyle?

9. How is apperception different from perception? What are their relationships? If individuals always "apperceive," how can we define "perception" and is the contrast useful, even if definable? How might one measure the "level of apperception"? How is apperception related to life style, to the master plan, or to convictions? With change of convictions, how does apperception change?

10. Are pessimism and discouragement redundant concepts? That is, are they encompassed by particular convictions and descriptive of convictions—or are they additional qualities of the person or of his or her activity or life style? Do the concepts add anything to the explanatory power of the theory not already contained in that of life style convictions? If we could measure pessimism and discouragement, what are we measuring? What individual methods of operation or coping styles do the concepts name or describe? Can we operationally differentiate praise from encouragement? How would we measure the effectiveness of encouragement in therapy?

11. What is social interest? Has Adler's original idea seemed not to be amenable to research? Is the concept of social interest perhaps redundant in an Adlerian theory? If the notion of social interest exists in order to help us define the direction of movement of an individual (i.e., either as toward others or away from others), perhaps it is unnecessary because the movement itself is primary and carries a direction in itself. If social interest is a useful, independent construct, is it a quality of a person (a method of operation) or of his or her activity (a state)? Are there socially interested people, or actions? Do lifestyles "have" social interest? Is it part of the set of convictions people hold, or is it part of activity? In general, who or what has social interest? What is the concept intended to explain?

These and other questions arise when thinking about how to formalize the model of IP and about how to clarify the concepts and relate them to other concepts.

This Book and Its Contents

We have used, very loosely, two criteria in selecting the topics discussed in this volume. First, we thought the topics should be fundamental concepts of Adler's personality theory. Second, some early and recent statements of the concepts needed to be available. Clearly, however, we were not strict in adhering to these criteria. We were much clearer in inviting essays to discuss the topics.

The task we set for invited essays was formidable: to produce (1) a commentary on the original concepts of Adlerian theory and on the extant discussion and clarification ("history") of these concepts in order to make them amenable to research; and (2) a summary and critique of current research, if any exists. However, the ultimate focus of the invited essays is neither on the history nor on current research. The focus is to use the history and current research to offer suggestions regarding new ideas for research on the topics, including new and better ways to measure or examine the concepts and their possible relationships with other constructs. In short, we were looking to produce a text that attends to the original ideas of Adler, that offers a critique of current research, and that offers new ideas or directions.

This book includes two or more reprinted articles (where possible) discussing basic Adlerian concepts: an early, original statement, and another, more or less current statement. The latter may be a summary of current research and issues. These are prefaced by invited essays with three goals.

First, they provide a commentary on the history of the discussion about and clarification of selected basic Adlerian concepts, from their original statement by Adler (and others) to their current definition and operational definitions in current research (if any). The aim is to show how current research hits the mark or fails to hit the mark of the original concept. Questions that may be considered include:

- Has there been a discussion that clarifies the concept?
- Is the concept ambiguous and is further clarification needed?
- Is the current definition appropriate to the original intent?
- If not, what is the consequence?
- Is there an operational definition or means of identifying or measuring the concept that facilitates research?

Second, the essays provide a brief critique of current research on the topic. This critique may consider questions such as:

- Is current research in line with the original concept?
- If no, why not?

- If yes, what questions need addressing within the current conceptual framework?
- Does current research indicate that either the concept or the research direction needs reformulation? That is, do robust research results indicate that the concept and its relationships are well defined and useful? Or do weak results indicate that it is not well defined, not well operationalized, or not useful as a construct?

The purpose of this section is not to provide a summary of research; rather, it is an assessment of how current research may be useful in the support or reformulation of Adlerian theory.

Third, and most important, the essay provides new ideas concerning the clarification and operational definitions of the concept, related to the original definition of the concept. It also provides ideas regarding research methods that might prove effective, and suggests new research questions. The goal here is open-ended and we asked for original and creative thinking in an overview of where research might effectively go.

References

Adler, A. (1937). Psychiatric aspects regarding individual and social disorganization. *The American Journal of Sociology, 42*(6), 773–780.

Ajzen, I. (1988). *Attitudes, personality and behaviour*. Milton Keynes, UK: Open University Press.

American Psychiatric Association (1994). *Diagnostic and statistical manual of mental disorders*, 4th edition [*DSM-IV*]. Washington, D.C.: Author.

Ansbacher, H. L., & Ansbacher, R. R. (1956). Individual Psychology in its larger setting. In H. L. Ansbacher & R. R. Ansbacher (Eds.), *The Individual Psychology of Alfred Adler: A systematic presentation in selections from his writings* (pp. 1–20). New York: Basic Books.

Berrett, R. D. (1975). Adlerian mother study groups: An evaluation. *Journal of Individual Psychology, 31*(2), 179–182.

Burnett, P. C. (1988). Evaluation of Adlerian parenting programs. *Individual Psychology, 44*(1), 63–76.

Cacioppo, J. T., Semin, G. R., & Berntson, G. G. (2004). Realism, intrumentalism, and scientific symbiosis: Psychological theory as a search for truth and the discovery of solutions. *American Psychologist, 59*(4), 214–223.

Corsini, R. (1974). Individual Psychology today and tomorrow, as seen by the editors of this journal. *Journal of Individual Psychology, 30*, 9–42.

Croake, J. W., & Burness, M. R. (1976). Parent study group effectiveness after 4 and after 6 weeks. *Journal of Individual Psychology, 32*(1), 108–111.

Croake, J. W., & Glover, K. E. (1977). A history and evaluation of parent education. *Family Coordinator, 26*, 151–158.

Frazier, F., & Mathes, W. A. (1975). Parent education: A comparison of Adlerian and behavioral approaches. *Elementary School Guidance and Counseling, 10*, 31–38.

Freeman, C. W. (1975). Adlerian mother study groups: Effects on attitudes and behavior. *Journal of Individual Psychology, 31*(1), 37–50.

Gordon-Rosen, M., & Rosen, A. (1984). Adlerian parent study groups and inner-city children. *Individual Psychology, 40*(3), 309–316.

Hinkle, D. E., Arnold, C. F., Croake, J. W., & Keller, J. F. (1980). Adlerian parent education: Changes in parents' attitudes and behaviors, and children's self-esteem. *The American Journal of Family Therapy, 8*(1), 32–43.

Huber, R. J. (1975). Social interest revisited: A second look at Adler. *Character Potential, 7*, 65–77.

Kohler, W. (1947). *Gestalt psychology: An introduction to new concepts in modern psychology.* New York: Liveright.

Krebs, L. L. (1986). Current research on theoretically based parenting programs. *Individual Psychology, 42*(3), 375–387.

McCabe, A., Capron, E., & Peterson, C. (1991). The voice of experience: The recall of early childhood and adolescent memories by young adults. In A. McCabe & C. Peterson (Eds.), *Developing narrative structure* (pp. 137–173). Hillsdale, NJ: Erlbaum.

McKay, G. D., & Hillman, B. W. (1979). An Adlerian multimedia approach to parent education. *Elementary School Guidance and Counseling, 14*(1), 28–35.

Mosak, H. H., & Maniacci, M. P. (1999). *A primer of Adlerian psychology: The analytic-behavioral-cognitive psychology of Alfred Adler.* Philadelphia, PA: Brunner/Mazel.

Mullis, F. (1999). Active parenting: An evaluation of two Adlerian parent education programs. *Journal of Individual Psychology, 55*(2), 225–232.

Nagel, E. (1961). *The structure of science: Problems in the logic of scientific explanation.* New York: Harcourt, Brace & World.

Newlon, B. J., Borboa, R., & Arcinega, M. (1986). The effects of Adlerian study groups upon Mexican mothers' perception of child behavior. *Individual Psychology, 42*(1), 106–113.

Shulman, B. H. (1985). Cognitive therapy and the Individual Psychology of Alfred Adler. In M. J. Mahoney & A. Freeman (Eds.), *Cognition and psychotherapy* (pp. 243–252). New York: Plenum.

Thorne, S. E. (1997). Phenomenological positivism and other problematic trends in health science research. *Qualitative Health Research, 7*(2), 287–293.

Todres, R., & Bunston, T. (1993). Parent education program evaluation: A review of the literature. *Canadian Journal of Community Mental Health, 12*(1), 225–257.

Urban, T. A. (1991). A case study of the effects of an Adlerian program on parent attitudes and child-rearing techniques. *Dissertation Abstracts International, 52,* A4218.

Watkins, C. E., Jr. & Guarnaccia, C. A. (1999). The scientific study of Adlerian theory. In R. W. Watts & J. Carlson (Eds.), *Interventions and strategies in counseling and psychotherapy* (pp. 207–230). Philadelphia: Taylor & Francis.

Wiese, M. J. (1989). Evaluation of an Adlerian parent training program with multiple outcome measures. *Dissertation Abstracts International, 50,* A3538.

II
General

CHAPTER 2

Introduction to Adlerian Psychology: Basic Principles and Methodology

AL MILLIREN and FERN CLEMMER

Dr. Alfred Adler was born in a suburb of Vienna in1870; he died in 1937 at the age of 67 in Aberdeen, Scotland, while on a lecture tour. He graduated from the medical school of the University of Vienna and established his medical practice in 1895. In 1902, Adler served for a brief period as a general physician in the Hungarian army. Later that same year, Sigmund Freud invited him to attend the early Wednesday evening Vienna Psychoanalytic Society meetings. It appears that these were "invitation only," closed meetings attended by those whom Freud selected. Adler was a central part of this group for approximately nine years, even serving as president in 1910. Adler came to disagree with Freud during these later years, particularly over the role that sexual and social factors played in individual development and motivation (Milliren, Newbauer, & Evans, 2003).

Freud couched his theory in terms of biological, sexual, and aggressive drives. It was Adler's view that we are social beings, that human behavior and motivation make sense only in the social context. The difference with Freud became so intense that in 1911 a split came about. One might say that it was a fairly bitter divorce that never healed. Adler then started coffee house style meetings in Vienna. Anyone was invited to come and attend. If you walked in off the street, you could sit with the group and participate. Adler's open meetings, as opposed to Freud's closed ones, shows a major difference between the two men, the one being more socially oriented and the other more exclusionary.

Out of that early development, Adler founded the Society for Individual Psychology and began lecturing about and consulting from his new psychology or theory of personality, Individual Psychology. The term *individual* derives from the Latin word *individuum*, meaning whole. From this holistic perspective, Adler encouraged those interested in psychology to think in terms of the whole individual or personality rather than parts. Adler never made divisions as Freud did in terms of id, ego, and superego.

Holism is an assumption of Individual Psychology, meaning that all aspects of a person connect to all other aspects of that person. The only way to understand a system, including a human being, is to understand that entire system. The whole cannot be understood by examining parts in isolation from the whole system.

Adler cautioned that less attention be paid to people's words than to how people move through the world. He often spoke of people voting with their feet. "It's not what you say, as much as what you do in this world that tells us what you're about." Intention is not nearly as important as the act.

Adler's psychology was a phenomenological psychology. It is not what we experience that makes a difference, it is how we experience that experience. It is our interpretation of the event, not the event itself. When we're talking with clients or students and trying to work with people, we don't focus on what went on. Our concern is with what they think about what went on and what they chose to do with it.

Adlerian psychology has a positive, optimistic view of the world: It sees us as creating our own private logic and, in effect, creating our own patterns for achieving success in the world. The fact that we can create these patterns also means that we can change them when they don't work for us. No one is a victim except in his or her own mind. We need to think in terms of people moving forward with resilience rather than being stuck in some kind of pathology.

Adler taught that we need to learn to understand emotions through their purpose. We use emotions. Think about a morning when you were running a little late. If you didn't get a little anxious, you wouldn't get to work on time. You needed that anxiety or discomfort to get you moving. On some occasion or another, you may have been done an injustice. If you didn't become angry, you might not have done anything to resolve it. If you didn't have feelings of attraction, you would never move toward people. Emotions exist to serve a purpose; they do not run us. Dreikurs called emotions "the kind of gasoline that runs our car." It helps us move toward something. Without emotions, we might not move.

Social Embeddedness

Individual Psychology is founded on the premise that human striving involves the community as well as the individual—we are *socially embedded.*

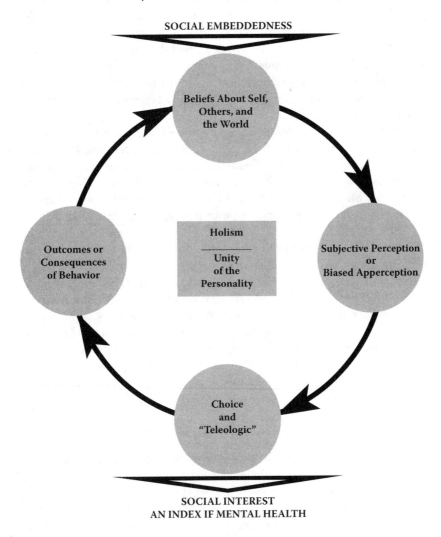

Fig. 2.1 Model of Adlerian personality development.

People's lives and contributions flourish when they feel they belong to the community as equals. Adler (1956) strongly believed in this fundamental need to cooperate with and contribute to the welfare of society. We are, after all, social beings.

It is also out of that social embeddedness that we discover who we are. The way people respond and relate to us influences what we believe about who we are, how others are, and the way in which the world should treat us. Very early on, newborns begin to make sense out of interactions. You smile, they burp, you smile again and they go, "Oh, this is good!" Sometimes they get that gas smile and we respond as if it were a real smile. By virtue of that response they think, "Wow! This is pretty neat."

As they grow a little older, they look around the family and everybody is bigger than they are. Everyone knows so much more. Everyone is stronger and tells them how to do things better. Almost inevitably, they begin to develop some inferiority feelings in response to being smaller, weaker, less logical, or not as quick on their feet. They feel "less than." Adler called this a "felt minus" position. Sometimes they find other small people who feel less. As they grow up with those feelings, and their peers also have those feelings, everyone comparing themselves with stronger, smarter folks and comparing their coping skills with life's insurmountable problems, they see that they have some work to do. Compensating for universal feelings of inferiority generates a striving for perfection, significance, and security—a "perceived plus."

Kopp (1982) holds that the way individuals choose to engage in that striving for significance and security depends on several things. First, it depends on a sense of identification with other human beings. Second, it depends on the person's self-ideals, what he wishes to express or become. Third, it also depends on the person's definition of security, significance, and success. Fourth, the way the person has trained him- or herself in cooperative behavior patterns is important. Finally, Kopp's fifth consideration is what he calls the person's conjunctive attitudes and feelings toward others. Due to a unique combination of these variables, each person has a personal way of striving or thriving.

Beliefs

As Adler (1956) explained, behavior is influenced by our beliefs. *Beliefs about self, others, and the world* form the foundation of our private logic, which in turn, colors our view of the world. These beliefs are often in some kind of nonword form—intuitions, affective states, or visual representations. We acquire a nonlanguage understanding of the world early in life.

What are these nonword forms of thinking? When my dog "thinks" I am ready to leave the house, she lies down in the middle of the hall, where she anticipates that I will pass. When I head down the hall and get about six feet away, she rolls over on her back as an invitation to scratch her on the belly. She is not lying there thinking, "As soon as he gets here, I'll roll over and he'll scratch me." Still, she understands that, in some way.

It is difficult to manipulate these nonword beliefs in order to change them, so putting them into words makes the beliefs manageable and changeable (Messer, 2000). One of the reasons counseling is so powerful is that part of counseling is helping people put words to the beliefs they hold. We may never attach language to some of that until someone sits down with us and says, "Hey, could it be that this is going on for you?" And we have a recognition reflex and say, "Oh!"

Out of our social situation, we develop beliefs. If we were going to formalize those beliefs, they would be in terms of, "I am ...."; "Others are ...."; and "The world is ...." Of course, we don't classify them as such while we are creating these beliefs, but it is an easy way for us to make an academic account of them. Thus, *we* decide. The *pampered child*, for example, may develop beliefs as follows:

I *deserve to be cared for.*
Others *will take care of me.*
The world *owes it to me.*

A few years ago, an undergraduate student commented, "I am like a worm in an apple. And, as long as there is plenty of apple, I'm OK." He didn't have to do much, just hang out. Of course, he had to take what was there since he didn't allow himself other choices! But for him, the situation was satisfactory. We develop a system of beliefs that helps us navigate in the world.

Subjective Perception

Beliefs influence our perceptions. Adler indicated that perception and other behavior "springs from opinion" (1956). *Subjective perception* is the way we create how we see things. Beliefs or opinions about self, others and the world color and are in turn colored by subjective perception or *biased apperception.*

Dewey (1971) defined family atmosphere as parents' characteristic pattern of behavior that they teach to their children as a standard for social living. A child responds to situations according to the personal outlook on life created in this family atmosphere. Family climate can only influence the development of one's personality because the individual interprets the meaning of the family atmosphere through a self-crafted lens of his or her own "biased apperception" or "private logic." People develop self-images and figure out how folks are supposed to act based on their subjective perceptions of how people act in their families. The reality of how the family acted matters far less than the child's *experience* of their actions. From this biased position, the child decides how to respond to similar experiences in the future. The person is a meaning-creating organism. "We experience reality always through the meaning we give it ... as something interpreted" (Adler, 1931, p. 3).

So, beliefs influence perception. If we believe, for example, that we are not capable, then everything we see, in terms of the way the world is going, will look as if it is difficult. If we think we are stupid, everything will *seem* complicated. Many children approach school thinking that they cannot do well there. Everything they are asked to do is perceived as being too difficult, no matter what it is. You will hear the way they "burn their bridges ahead of them" when they say, "This is too hard!" This often occurs when they haven't even started. They are already gearing up to find the difficulty. These are children whose core beliefs are that they are incapable of being successful.

Each child wants to find a psychologically significant place in the family and, ultimately, in the community at large. What are the contributors to the child's sense of a psychological place? It's partly where each child finds him- or herself in the family structure, that is, his or her birth position. It's partly the family atmosphere, that is, morals, values, opinions, communication styles. Even more than that, the psychological place found by a child is influenced by how that child *perceives* the situation as well as by the decisions, plans, promises, and conclusions the child *draws from those perceptions* (Adler, 1927; Ferguson, 1984).

Perception leads to the third element in the cycle shown in Figure 2.1. We can be creative about what we want to do in terms of our behavior. We have beliefs that influence how we perceive the world and those beliefs structure the decisions we make about how we are going to do things. Although we have choices about our behavior, those choices are often limited by the perceptions we hold.

Choices

Adler said that life was movement. Behavior is always a choice. Individual decision making derives from the private logic and from the individual's creativity. That's why so many techniques in Adlerian psychotherapy are designed to help people become aware of their early decisions (Shulman, 1971). Adlerian counseling also asks clients to reevaluate attitudes they drew from a "child's perspective" and that, from an adult perspective, might call for change (Dreikurs, 1967; Kopp, 1982; Mozdzierz, Macchitelli, & Lisiecki, 1976).

Some of our choices of behavior happen so quickly that we really pay no attention to the underlying decisions we make. For example, you go in the bathroom, and because you have done it for years, you automatically flip on the lights. You know exactly where the switches are. You don't stop to think about them because that pattern is ingrained. However, you begin to discover the choices and the thinking that you do when you go to a strange bathroom where the switches are not in the accustomed position. If the old patterns don't work, you start changing your pattern. That's when you discover you have choices and that you have to process what you do.

Everything that we do serves a purpose. What we do is aimed at getting somewhere, accomplishing something. This is a key concept of Adlerian Psychology—the "teleologic" of behavior. Instead of unfolding in inevitable, patterned potentialities or being pushed along by instincts and drives, a person *strives toward* chosen ideals and goals (Maddi, 1978). For example, a person might be seen as striving for perfection. This kind of "wheel-spinning" may find expression in the fictional final goal of the lifestyle (Kopp, 1982). For example, a child, early on, might have decided, "I must do everything perfectly in order to have a place in this family." Perfection might become the person's fictional, final goal—fictional because perfection is unobtainable, final because it dictates the goal of one's behavior.

As Adler's theory developed, his emphasis on the *direction of the striving* replaced his earlier focus on inferiority feelings and compensations. He said that the main problem of psychology is to comprehend "the direction-giving, pulling forces and goals which guide... movements" (Adler, 1964, p. 216).

Making and acting on a "healthy" choice of behavior displays a sense of worth as well as the "courage to be imperfect." A positive choice is a risk and may even be a bit frightening. Impaired functioning, according to Individual Psychology, involves "choosing the past." When people have been discouraged, their movement or life style manifests safeguard mechanisms that may sabotage positive decision making while protecting against the anxiety or fear of being proven worthless (Adler, 1956).

In the family atmosphere, movements toward goals form relational patterns. These relational patterns—along with personal goals, private logic, attitudes, and family atmosphere—produce the blueprint for living (Dinkmeyer, 1989) referred to as life style. If an older child in a home where responsibility is valued, for instance, chooses to take care of younger siblings, that child is likely to become responsible. If that child chooses not to take care of siblings and rebels, and thus acts against taking responsibility, the child's life style and personality will form in a different direction.

The creative power of life is expressed through the development, pursuit, and achievement of goals. Such power is *teleological*. Understanding the goal enables us to see the hidden meaning behind acts and see them as parts of the whole. "Goals reflect core values, reinforce an image of the ideal self, compensate for inferiority feelings, guard against pain, provide meaning in the present, and promote hope for the future" (Griffith & Graham, 2004, p. 26). They emerge in response to life challenges and develop into one's philosophy or style of life.

Outcomes

Choices lead to *outcomes* or *consequences*. Life involves adaptation to the social environment. Adaptation uses creative trial and error—trying things and repeating what works (Campbell, 1974; Popper, 1965). Every choice has consequences. "Assuming responsibility for the choice amounts to accepting the definition of self that ensues from it" (Maddi, 1978, p. 188). The choices of behavior, dreams, thoughts, feelings, even memories protect the definition of self and serve one's fictional final goal. A child "strives to develop along a ... direction fixed by the goal which he chooses for himself" (Adler, 1956, p. 187).

Choices lead to outcomes, all of which confirm our beliefs about ourselves, such as beliefs of inferiority. Some inferiority feelings are exaggerated or intensified. The "inferiority complex" describes the attitude of one who maintains that he or she is out of solutions or is not equal to perceived challenges (Adler, 1964). A compensatory goal in response to an inferiority complex guides the search for security and significance, compensates for feelings of inadequacy, and protects self-esteem. Controlling, getting, opposing, and martyrdom are compensatory life style goals (Adler, 1956, 1964, 1969).

Everything we do is designed to lead us somewhere. Some goals are immediate, some are long term, but everything we do is aimed at obtaining something useful for us. Typically, whatever we get leads us back to the beliefs that we hold and the cycle continues. This cycle of beliefs, perceptions, choices, and outcomes is self-reinforcing unless somebody or something interrupts it. The life style stabilizes at about five years of age, after which the child's "attitude ... is usually so fixed and mechanized that it proceeds in more or less the same direction for the rest of ... life" (Adler, 1956, p. 189). Unless a change in life style is produced by artful intervention or by the individual's recognition of fault and errors (Adler, 1966), the direction persists.

Holism

Adler (1927) emphasized the principle of holism, the idea that everything connects to everything else about the person. We each function as a complete system wherein each element influences all others. This leads to the concept of the *unity of the personality*. If you get the right pieces of information, you can have a complete picture of a person.

Adler wanted to hear some recollections of early childhood experiences. Then he wanted to know the child's perceived situation in the family, conclusions the child drew from perceptions of his place in the family, the sociopsychological configuration of the family, and the family atmosphere. He thought that with those clues, along with some information about the private logic that developed from the child's choices and outcomes, he could get a glimpse of the core of an individual's personality and could understand how that individual dealt with the world.

How the person dealt with the world, his or her modus operandi or "way of going about going about," along with the person's opinions, conclusions, and cherished values, are the foundation and description of that person's *life style* (Lombardi, 1993). Life style is the creative response to early experiences that influences perceptions of self and the world, emotions, motives, and actions (Adler, 1927). If we understand a person's life style, it means that we understand that person's private logic, beliefs, purposes, and ways of belonging in the family and society. That's why we call it holistic.

Strauch (2003) emphasizes the holistic nature of life style. He found some similarities between the holistic principles of chaos theory and lifestyle. He sees life style as foreshadowing today's systems theory. Though life style is often erroneously equated with ego, self, or personality, it describes patterns of relating and movement in a person's life more accurately than any traits or qualities (Eckstein & Baruth, 1996). The way chaos theory is often explained, a person can be viewed metaphorically as a physical system. A person's way of going about things might seem chaotic or random. A closer examination, however, could reveal an underlying pattern. This pattern can be seen on three levels: the biological, psychological, and social (Strauch, 2003). Life style is a pattern that guides behavior, thoughts, and feelings, even if these aspects don't seem related at first glance.

Social Interest

Our goal in therapy, counseling, and education is to increase social interest. Simply put, social interest is the capacity to cooperate and contribute. We want people to be able to relate to one another on a horizontal plane as equals and to do what the situation requires. Social interest "means *feeling with the whole* ... under the aspect of eternity (Adler's emphasis). It means striving for a form of community that must be thought of as everlasting … the ideal community of all mankind, the ultimate fulfillment of evolution" (Adler, 1956, p. 142).

In our schools, in our workplaces, and in our families, we still function where someone is the "boss" and others are expected to do what they are told. What might be more effective is family, work, and class meetings with house rules and routines that everyone follows and agrees on from a level of equality.

Think about a time in your life when someone tried to control you. What are the kinds of things you did in response? Did you become defiant and rebel? You can do that noisily by being openly aggressive or you can do it quietly. If you do it quietly, you can be passive/aggressive and maybe forget to do things. You can also passively submit. But do we want folks to be in the habit of submission? Marriages between young people often show abusive characteristics, indicating that unthinking submission is not necessarily a lesson young women need to carry into their adult lives.

What else do folks do to defy? They withdraw, get pregnant, fail school, do drugs, become alcoholic. Most of the things that we classify as "trouble" are the very things that are in response to being overcontrolled. Many of our school administrators, school counselors, and teachers have not quite figured out how to help, rather than control; to lead, rather than to intimidate.

On the other hand, if we do not want to control, we often let things go too far the other way: "I let you do what you want." Instead of being autocratic, parents have become permissive with their children. We are aware of one family where the parents have gone out of their way to support their little girl, but all she can do is whine and complain. And she is 4 years old. She is in charge of the house rules and routine and her parents are resentful. They have some good moments that keep them hooked in, but the child is taking advantage of them and the parents are resentful. Of course, that is no different from the adults in charge doing things their way. What is changed is the direction of who is in charge.

Cooperation

In order to enjoy real cooperation, we need to move away from the mentality of vertical relationships. We want to help people learn how to engage in the give and take of cooperation. Cooperation in our culture is still defined as, "You do what you are told." Most parents who come in to talk about their children begin with something like, "They just don't cooperate." We need to ask them what that means. "Well, when I tell 'em to go to bed, they stay up. They haven't been cooperating!"

There is negative and positive cooperation. If I tell you what to do and you don't do it, that's cooperation in the negative direction. An argument is negative cooperation that often leads to a negative outcome. On the other hand, what might happen if two people decided to have an argument and no one came, or one person walked away before the argument began? There would be no argument. It takes agreeing to play that game. An alternative is to decide not to cooperate in things that you find destructive.

We need to begin to see others as equals. Some of us may know more than others, may have been around more, may have more experience than others, but that does not change the equal value of people or the social equality that we need to have. A primary difficulty with most institutions is that we have not figured out how to manifest that level of cooperation.

We need to work with people rather than against them. The goal should be to help people reach a level at which they start working *with* others. Very often that is the first thing that an educator, counselor, or therapist gives people. They offer a relationship of equals while people learn to cooperate. For some, it may be the first time in their lives that they've been in a relationship in which they haven't been told what to do or told someone else what to do.

Contribution

We can do things that contribute to and for members of the group. Contributions do not have to be big deals. Did you hug anybody this morning, kiss them, smile at them, be friendly? Those are all contributions. We can make those contributions every day. Little things make a big difference for the group as a whole. If you are not working for the good of the group and with people, then mental health deteriorates, because the only way to feel like an important individual in this world and to have a place of significance is to be with people and for them. We need, from infancy forward, to help people learn social interest.

We would not have survived had it not been for others. We are helpless at birth; we can do nothing for ourselves. In order to survive, we almost require contact with other human beings. In fact, marasmus is a condition seen in infancy—a withering away from lack of contact. Children will not always make it without someone to hug and to hold them.

The efforts of a person in a helping profession are most effectively aimed at helping others increase their cooperation or increase their contribution. If you are not looking at helping from that perspective, you are probably not being very helpful. We surely don't want to assist people to move in the other direction. We don't want them not to cooperate and not to contribute. People who are emotionally healthy do not want that direction for themselves. Mentally healthy people find ways to cooperate, contribute, and build relationships. These are the efforts that allow them to enjoy life and feel good about their choices and about the identity they may have chosen. These are the efforts through which we find our happiness.

Research

Some researchers have developed short cuts to catch a glimpse of life style. Interview formats for evaluating life style include the Kern (1982) BASIS-A Lifestyle Scale, the Children's Lifestyle Guide (Dinkmeyer & Dinkmeyer, 1977), and the Life-Style Inventory (Shulman & Mosak, 1988).

Some studies have investigated the links between lifestyle/personality attributes and certain behaviors. Axtell and Newlon (1993), looking at life style themes of women expressing symptoms of bulimia, found that a few of those themes were the need to please, perfectionism, and excessively high standards. Barrett (1981) found that life style themes of inferiority and being controlled were found in three case histories of individuals expressing anorexia nervosa symptoms. Laser (1984) found that early memories of men and women with obesity described experiences in which they were the center of attention (Mosak's "getter," 1995) or in which they tried to exert, or were successful at exerting, their power over situations or people (Mosak's "controller," 1995). Allen (1971) describes research in the field of psychophysiology and social psychology that validates life style as a construct.

Several researchers have explored the application of sandtray to the assessment of lifestyles (Aoki, 1981; Segal, 1990; Sjolund & Schaefer, 1994; Sternberg, 1996). Sweeney, Minnix, and Homeyer (2003) use the life style approach with sandtray, a technique associated with play therapy for children, but which seems to be appropriate for clients of all ages who present issues not easily addressed with talk therapy. People can develop a concrete representation of their life and the way they do things in the sand. Discussing the things they place in the sand may be more productive than trying to make language describe the sometimes abstract problems they face. Others use sandtray for evaluation and facilitation in couples con-joint therapy.

Wheeler, Kern, and Curlette (1993) developed the Life-Style Personality Inventory (LSPI) to assess similarities across individuals' life styles. Their inventory has 164 statements beginning with, "When I was a child, I." Respondents answer each item on a Likert scale, and the instrument is scored on seven life style themes and a social-interest index (Wheeler & Acheson, 1993). Based on research with the LSPI, Wheeler and her colleagues (Curlette, Wheeler, & Kern, 1997) developed the Basic Adlerian Scales for Interpersonal Success—Adult form (BASIS-A) Inventory to replace the original LSPI. The BASIS-A measures five life style themes: Belonging/Social Interest, Going Along, Taking Charge, Wanting Recognition, and Being Cautious. Five additional scales help to interpret results: Harshness, Entitlement, Liked by All, Striving for Perfection, and Softness. The life style themes and scales of the BASIS-A Inventory offer a quick way to identify some key elements of life style and a promising tool for life style research.

Belangee, Sherman, and Kern (2001) looked at relationships between life style/personality attributes (e.g., introversion, need for approval, distrust, and perfectionism) and eating disorder symptoms and behaviors by using the BASIS-A Inventory and the Eating Disorder Inventory-2 (Garner, 1991). Belonging/Social Interest from the BASIS-A was negatively correlated with Interpersonal Distrust from Garner's (1991) Eating Disorder Inventory. Wanting Recognition from the BASIS-A was positively correlated with Perfectionism and Drive for Thinness. Being Cautious (BC) was positively correlated with Perfectionism.

Implications for Counseling and Therapy

The central, circular portion of the model gives us a quick view of how we might go about working with our students and clients. Basically we have four choices. First, we can help them change their thinking. This appears to be the primary place where Adlerians work in their educational and therapeutic efforts. The focus is on helping people discover and gain insight, awareness, and understanding of the nature of their movement through the world. The objective is to help them change their beliefs through some form of cognitive restructuring. If a person changes his or her thinking, then what he or she is doing will change.

Since the process of change is holistic, we could conceivably move to the bottom of the cycle and help our students/clients change what they are doing. If you teach a person to do a different thing for themselves, then maybe their beliefs will change. When you start doing something new, and start acting differently, you start to think differently about yourself. Try on some new behavior and thinking can change. So we could work on either end. Mind or body doesn't matter. It's all connected.

We also have interventions at the perception juncture to the right of the cycle. Fritz Perls and the Gestaltists were helping people change perceptions. They worked on awareness and one's ability to be more conscious of what's going on around. You may know folks who walk through the world with no sense of where they are or what is going on or who is there, especially in relationships. They say and do things without seemingly caring about how they impact someone else.

We could also move to the left side of the model where the counselor/therapist can manipulate outcomes. In many respects, it is what we do when we recommend encouragement as a kind of "universal intervention." However, managing outcomes is difficult at best! One of our Depression-born parents would always watch for sales in the newspaper. He had more toilet paper when he died than a person could use up in two years. But, since he was a Depression child, part of his thinking was, "You never know where the next thing will come from, so you take advantage of it now." He had canned goods that were out of date and in bad shape. Nevertheless, he bought more and more because he was still operating out of the premise that if you do not get it now you may never have the chance later. In all the years, no one was able to stop the excessive shopping. It remained his way of contributing and he believed that he was doing the sensible thing.

Adler (1927) wrote that there must be some private, unique scheme or reason in everyone that influences behavior and decisions. He invented the term *private logic* to describe the subjective schemas developed from choices and the perceptions of the outcomes of those choices. An individual's private logic may only make sense to the individual and may even go against what others believe to be common sense.

Thus, we have four ways to intervene with people. Our preference is to help them understand what is going on for them, how they are moving through the world, because many times when you shed light on that, they begin to change other areas in their lives. Once you realize that part of your thinking makes no sense, you start adjusting the things that you do. When you change your frame of reference, sometimes you have more choices and can select more useful forms of behavior. On the other hand, if we change a specific behavior, that may be enough; and in some cases it may be all that is necessary. We have a cycle or wheel of opportunities for intervention, and we can interrupt it at any point in order to help others make useful changes.

Conclusion

In summary, we think in terms of seven basic principles. The first is *social embeddedness*, the source from which we draw conclusions about self, others, and the world. Second, we have the conclusions or *beliefs* themselves. Third, we have a creative, *perceptual* part that allows us to look at the world in whatever way our beliefs direct. That influences the third part of the picture, our *choices*. And, obviously, those choices lead to *outcomes* which, more than likely, reinforce the held *beliefs*. The *holistic* process is what binds these elements together. Counselors can intervene at any point in the cycle because, according to systems theory, making an intervention at any point will affect the whole system. In order to be effective, interventions should always be focused on enhancing the individual's capacity for cooperation. The overriding question should be: Have our efforts enhanced the student's or client's *social interest?*

References

Adler, A. (1927). *Understanding human nature.* New York: Greenberg.

Adler, A. (1931). *What life should mean to you.* New York: Capricorn Books.

Adler, A. (1956). *The Individual Psychology of Alfred Adler: A systematic presentation in selections from his writings* (H. L. Ansbacher & R. R. Ansbacher, Eds.). New York: Basic Books.

Adler, A. (1964). *Superiority and social interest: A collection of later writings* (H. L. Ansbacher & R. R. Ansbacher, Eds.). New York: Norton.

Adler, A. (1969). *The science of living.* New York: Anchor Doubleday.

Allen, T. W. (Ed.). (1971). *The Counseling Psychologist* (Vol. 3). Beverly Hills, CA: Sage Publications.

Aoki, S. (1981). The retest reliability of the Sand Play Technique: II. *British Journal of Projective Psychology & Personality Study, 26* (2), 25–33.

Axtell, A., & Newlon, B. (1993). An analysis of Adlerian life themes of bulimic women. *Individual Psychology, 49,* 58–67.

Barrett, D. (1981). Early recollections of anorexia nervosa patients: Reflections of life style. *The Journal of Individual Psychology, 37,* 5–14.

Belangee, S. E., Sherman, M. F., & Kern, R. M. (2001). Exploring the relationships between life-style personality attributes and eating disorder symptoms and behaviors in a nonclinical population. *Journal of Individual Psychology, 59*(4), 461–474.

Campbell, D. T. (1974). Evolutionary epistemology. In P. Schilpp (Ed.), *The Philosophy of Karl Popper* (pp. 10–52). La Salle, IL: Open Court.

Curlette, W., Wheeler, M., & Kern, R. (1997). *The BASIS-A Inventory technical manual.* Highlands, NC: TRT Associates.

Dewey, E. (1971). Family atmosphere. In A. Nikelly (Ed.), *Techniques for behavior change* (pp. 41–47). Springfield, IL: Thomas.

Dinkmeyer, D. (1989). Adlerian psychology. *Psychology: A Journal of Human Behavior, 26*(1), 26–34.

Dinkmeyer, D., & Dinkmeyer, D. (1977). Concise counseling assessment: The children's lifestyle guide. *Elementary School Guidance and Counseling, 12,* 117–124.

Dreikurs, R. (1967). *Psychodynamics, psychotherapy, and counseling.* Chicago: Alfred Adler Institute.

Eckstein, D., & Baruth, L. (1996). *The theory and practice of life-style assessment.* Dubuque, IA: Kendall/Hunt.

Ferguson, E. D. (1984). *Adlerian theory: An introduction.* Chicago: Adler School of Professional Psychology.

Garner, D. (1991). *Eating Disorder Inventory-2 professional manual.* Odessa, FL: Psychological Assessment Resources.

Griffith, B. A., & Graham, C. C. (2004). Meeting needs and making meaning: The pursuit of goals. *Journal of Individual Psychology, 60* (1), 25–38.

Kern, R. M. (1982). *Lifestyle scale.* Coral Springs, FL: CMTI Press.

Kopp, R. R. (1982). On clarifying basic Adlerian concepts: A response to Maddi. *Journal of Individual Psychology, 38* (1), 80–89.

Laser, E. (1984). The relationship between obesity, early recollections, and adult life-style. *Individual Psychology, 40,* 29–35.

Lombardi, D. (1993). Antisocial personality disorder and addictions. In L. Sperry & J. Carlson (Eds.), *Psychopathology and psychotherapy: From diagnosis to treatment* (pp. 405–427). Muncie, IN: Accelerated Development.

Maddi, S. (1978). Existential and Individual Psychology. *Journal of Individual Psychology, 34*, 182–190.

Messer, M. M. (2000). *Anger intelligence: An introduction to anger therapy.* Chicago, IL: The Anger Institute.

Milliren, A., Newbauer, J., & Evans, T. (2003). Adlerian counseling and psychotherapy. In D. Capuzzi & D. Gross (Eds.), *Counselling and psychotherapy: Theories and interventions* (3rd ed., pp. 91–130). Upper Saddle River, NJ: Pearson.

Mosak, H. H. (1995). Adlerian psychotherapy. In R. J. Corsini & D. Wedding (Eds.), *Current psychotherapies* (pp. 51–94). Itasca, IL: Peacock.

Mozdzierz, J., Macchitelli, F., & Lisiecki, J. (1976). The paradox in psychotherapy: An Adlerian perspective. *Journal of Individual Psychology, 32*, 169–184.

Popper, K. (1965). *Conjectures and refutations.* New York: Harper & Row.

Segal, I. (1990). Sandplay: A validation study of sandplay as a projective technique. *Dissertation Abstracts International, 51*(6-B), 3146–3147.

Shulman, B. (1971). Confrontation techniques in Adlerian psychology. *Journal of Individual Psychology, 27*, 167–175.

Shulman, B. H., & Mosak, H. H. (1988). *Manual for life style assessment.* Muncie, IN: Accelerated Development.

Sjolund, M., & Schaefer, C. (1994). The Erica Method of sandplay diagnosis and assessment. In K. O'Connor & C. Schaefer (Eds.), *Handbook of play therapy. Vol. 2: Advances and innovations* (pp. 231–252). New York: Wiley.

Sternberg, A. (1996). Psychological assessment of the child patient using sandplay. *Dissertation Abstracts International, 57*(3-B), 2166.

Strauch, I. (2003). Examining the nature of holism within lifestyle. *Journal of Individual Psychology, 59*(4), 452–460.

Sweeney, D. S., Minnix, G. M., & Homeyer, L. E. (2003). Using sandtray therapy in lifestyle analysis. *Journal of Individual Psychology, 59*(4), 376–387.

Wheeler, M., & Acheson, S. (1993). Criterion-related validity of the Lifestyle Personality Inventory. *Individual Psychology, 49*(1), 51–57.

Wheeler, M., Kern, R., & Curlette, W. (1993). *The BASIS-A Inventory.* Highlands, NC: TRT Associates.

CHAPTER 3

Fundamentals of Individual Psychology

ALFRED ADLER

Individual Psychology is concerned with "normal" and "abnormal" man in his uniqueness, and his aptitude for society, love and vocation. The areas of investigation are: the understanding of human nature (*Menschenkenntnis*), education, work, vocation, and psychotherapy.

The capacity of the human organism for achievement, its connectedness with the earth, with human beings, and with the other sex, are the given preconditions which we recognize. Only the first of these appears alterable. We recognize as variable functions the attitude the individual takes toward the community, the kind and amount of his work achievement, and his attitude toward the other sex, and we evaluate these by their ultimate usefulness for the community. Thus we arrive at the conclusion that the I-Thou relationship, the productivity for the community, and the relationship of the sexes are never private matters but problems of the community, and that erroneous solutions, as they arise from inadequate preparations in early childhood, offend against the absolute truth and have detrimental results for those who carry them out.

Goal Striving and Self-Consistency

Such assertions had, of course, to be justified in the correctly understood peculiarity of the human psyche, in the study of which Individual

Psychology has arrived at many new insights. One of these is that the human psyche is closely connected with the motor apparatus which serves through appropriate movements to overcome, to attack, and to ward off the difficulties of the environment. The psychological organ is first of all an organ of attack and defense, to make the future favorable for the person.

This can be accomplished, even imagined or understood, only if we assume a goal which stands firm under all circumstances: to gain security and superiority over attacks from outside by nature and man. As the concrete portion of this goal the following may take a prominent place: the tempting tasks of self-preservation and drive satisfaction; striving for power, wealth, dominance, godlikeness; or, corresponding to our outdated cultural ideal, the masculine role of a hero.[1]

This goal, gained in early childhood, dominates the movements of the psyche and the body, and collects all innate and acquired powers into a self-consistent personality. It forms the self-consistent life plan, and runs right through all expressive movements and symptoms like the uniqueness of an artist through his creations. Only when we have recognized this, the individual's action line, when we regard each one of his phenomena in the light of the whole personality, the connection of the part with the core of the personality, can we understand the significance, the meaning, the value, and the necessity of each phenomenon.

Likewise, character traits strike in us an understanding note only when we leave them in the context of the entire line of movement of the person. Thus we have learned that modesty may be bragging, that a critical attitude and the depreciation tendency may be a feeling of weakness. Laziness, indolence, loss of interest, absent-mindedness, and inclination to waste time are always found in people who no longer believe in themselves or in the productiveness of their performance; and nervous symptoms appear always when an imminent decision threatens to lead to defeat. We shall expect timid considerations and counterarguments in those whom we know to have had previously a hesitating attitude. We have always found that waywardness is connected only with cowardliness in life. It begins, once the individual has lost hope, and left the side of generally useful achievements. The remaining activity is useless, as primarily in neurosis, or harmful, as in criminal careers. Likewise we have been able to show that cases of sexual perversion (homosexuality, fetishism, sadism, masochism, etc.), and neurosis, originate not in primary drives, nor in experiences, but in that they banish the sex drive to the remaining field of action once the norm has been excluded through distrust in their own power.

Inferiority Feeling and Compensation

All these and other phenomena we have observed take place simultaneously in all the known relational systems. They follow the main line of movement in the direction of a fulfillment, of an aspired superiority over existing difficulties, and they also always are related to the community and its traditional lawfulness regarding fellowmanship, work, and love. All human behavior is at every point a reply to these three great questions of humanity and at the same time an attempt at compensation for a feeling of inferiority. We assume, then, a general inferiority feeling in man from which arises the striving to overcome all hostile forces. The entire development of mankind, its worthwhile and its mistaken attempts, characterize this course. And even in this mass-psychological consideration we find a compelling correction in the rule of social interest and its aim toward the common weal.

This inferiority feeling—compensation relationship appears to us to be the deepest mechanism yet found in all psychological life. It is so deep-seated and so much the master of all movements that no one, not even our critics, can think or object, except in line with this dynamic: inferiority feeling—compensation.

Individual Psychology starts with the understanding for the child's inferiority feeling. Its stimulation arouses all powers, the entire psychological movement, to force compensations, or to push in that direction. The necessity to superordinate a goal to every movement brings into all psychological movement a plan which leads to a self-consistent organization of the personality. All abilities and drives are subordinated to this life plan. Efforts to make reflexes, a drive, the constitution, or sexual libido the starting point of psychological research are in vain—except for revealing the trivial sequence of cause and effect, separated out from the context of the personality. One can discover the meaning and significance of such research, that is, its usefulness for psychology and *Menschenkenntnis*, only if one subsumes under the openly observable facts, secretly or unconsciously, the life plan found by methods of Individual Psychology. This means that one inquires into the way, the intention, the wherefore of these facts.

The development of the young child's life plan is decisively influenced by the evaluation of his organs. The greater the innate inferiority of an organ the more clearly will the striving for compensation set in, often leading to overcompensation. We can speak of balanced compensation when the outcome proves adequate to man's cosmic and social connectedness. This can happen through greater achievement and an increased growth spurt, or through the stepping in of another supporting organ. The effect of training is always also involved. In addition, we always find characteristic psychological efforts arising from the distress of the threatened life and the child's increased weakness and insecurity which are encountered on the path to perfection. This is one of the roots of increased creative power for which Individual Psychology has brought about such clear understanding. The mightily increased training of a weaker organ (alimentary tract, sense organ, organ of movement, etc.) leads to new movements and devices, technically superior because more differentiated; sharpens attention and interest; and in favorable cases leads to a stronger grasp of the coherence between man and his surroundings, and continuously lends the individual who has remained victorious the strong courageous feeling of great competence. Elsewhere we have described in detail how visual, accoustical, and motor types may arise from such constitutions, who are particularly capable of earning a good living. Also, Alice Friedmann and I have shown that a large number of left-handed children within our right-handed culture are put at a disadvantage, but under favorable circumstances, through a continuous training of the poorer right hand, can attain better achievements than the right-handed.

Origins of Mistaken Goals

In any case, increased insecurity causes a mood or despondency in the child which leads first of all to low self-esteem. This psychological situation can never mean a point of rest. From it originate increased movement, haste, and impatience. A whole sequence of other character traits are strongly evoked from the total psychological growth-material and lead one to infer a whipped-up life plan and an extremely high goal. Normal successes of life are no longer enough, but specially great successes, concealments, safeguards, pretenses, and excuses are needed to quiet the deepened inferiority feeling. "To be more than others" becomes the maxim of life, or at least to appear to be more; to be everything or nothing, hammer or anvil! All these are errors on the way to an art of living and fellowmanship which necessarily lead to conflicts. Stormy ambition at the beginning of the course regularly creates a counterweight of extreme caution from which arise the greatest inhibitions. Every test and decision becomes a terrible threat to the laboriously maintained equilibrium. This type is most frequent. We find him well protected by an excuse or a symptom of nervous disorder, not at the front of life, but somewhere in the hinterland, way below the average and the achievements which he could have attained. Where he should prove himself, he shows somehow the hesitating attitude.

There are four great questions of life which, although schematized, encompass all the relationships of life; the social relationship to fellowmen, the question of occupation, the question of love, and the attitude toward art and creative endeavor (*schöpferische Gestaltung*). In these four questions there is always an unsolved remainder, or one of the questions, in a less happy and exaggerated way, is made the focus of life. Such children require a special method of education; such adults, a re-education along the lines of Individual Psychology.

Children who are brought up harshly, without love and warmth, grow up in a similar depressed situation [as cases of organ inferiority], and meet with similar difficulties. In their case the extremely important function of the mother (or a substitute) has been lacking, which would have given the child the experience of a trustworthy partner who is a fellowman and would have mediated to him the Thou and its relationship to the I. In this relationship the child matures into a social being, develops his social interest, and learns to comprehend himself as a part of all of humanity.

Here one sees again the total inadequacy of the Freudian conception of this relationship as libidinous (Oedipus complex), since a sexual tie would never lead toward community, but always again to other sexual ties or to the repression of sexuality. Incidentally, Freud is presently already about to change his conception in accordance with ours.

This second type of child (often illegitimate) finds himself in an oppressive, hostile world, which can easily obstruct for him the straight path of making himself useful to the community, as in the first type. In all human relationships he will reveal a tendency toward isolation, and will not easily be won for togetherness, nor for working together.

The third type of person less suited, more poorly prepared for life and work, comes from the enormous circle of pampered children. Here the mother's function, mentioned above, has turned out to be too strong. The tie becomes so overpowering that nobody but the mother, no situation but the motherly one is readily accepted. Here, too, the development of fellow-manliness suffers, but so also does the development of the child's abilities, because the mother with her care and guardianship stands everywhere as an obstacle in the way. The entire form of life of the child will now adjust to this symbiosis and is in bad shape for other situations. Thus there is no room for the development of self-esteem and initiative. In all independent achievements a nostalgic grasping for help and relief will appear. The whole conduct of life reveals a serious inferiority feeling.

Fear of Failure and Its Consequences

The above three situations essentially have in common the acquisition of an increased inferiority feeling, a higher and more rigid guiding goal, and a life style more or less in contradiction to the demands of life. Such demands always make themselves known loud and clear as soon as the individual enters a new situation, different from the previous one, for which, due to his life style as well as his highly raised expectations, he is not properly prepared. At first it may be failures which scare him. Later his growing discouragement, the concretization and confirmation of his serious inferiority feeling, prevent him from coming closer to a solution of his life problems. This inhibition forces a change in the old goal-direction. Now the password is no longer superiority, but prevention of a visible or felt defeat.

The new goal presents a new form of life in sharply delineated features. Since due to fear of failure everything must remain unfinished, all striving and movement turn into pseudo-activity which, at least on balance, takes place on the useless side. The individual becomes unsocial or neurotic, or both at the same time. His uselessness, because he has lost the belief in distinguishing himself on the useful side, can grow to a point where he becomes punishable, i.e., by laws through which the community seeks to protect itself against erroneous developments.

While the individual is still in school such errors are usually inability, laziness, and all the phenomena of opposition to learning, at times, however, also trembling ambition and overzealous striving in which fear of the future discloses itself. When there is stronger inhibition of activity, we find at the onset of discouragement the alleviating circumstances of nervous phenomena, sham movements through which the individual, seized by the hesitating attitude, does *as if* he were doing something. In social, occupational, and love life, arguments against progressive development constantly arise. Incidents happen which are disastrous or are immensely exploited, and a continuous change of the point of attack testifies to the spuriousness of the initiative.

In such a hopeless mood, in the continuous fear of a disgracing defeat, usually in excessive dependency on the opinion of others, the right thing is often dropped and the wrong thing seized upon. Such people often describe themselves as haunted by misfortune, or born under an unlucky star. They are full of superstitions, because those who have lost the belief in themselves always believe in something else. They not only praise pessimism as the only concept of life worthy of man, but they also act accordingly. Thus they never arrive at the development of their powers because they employ them only in a half-hearted way. If they fail in a task, they consider their pessimism justified and do not understand that their deficiency is due to their inadequate confidence. A real increase in strength and a proper training, as well as good results, are always owed to an optimistic philosophy of life. This is of course more easily available to him who is rightfully convinced of his equal value and equal potential for success, in line with others.

Rational Approach to Education and Psychotherapy

The developments described above take place not according to a recognizable causality, but at the urge of necessity, under the compulsion of a final goal. In the understanding or concretization of this goal the possibility of errors on the part of the child, a quite subjective factor, must always be taken into account. Such errors are obviously enough underestimation of the self and easily occurring discouragement, as well as overestimation of others. We aim to remove such errors through conversation, explanations, words and thoughts, to change the person who has become asocial into a fellow man. We are convinced of a much higher achievement potential for our protégés than they themselves and probably also other schools of psychology are. This justifies our claim to be taken as a rational method of education and psychotherapy.

At the same time, the strong emphasis on psychological dynamics, on the significance of social interest, and on the striving for power should remove us from the strange prejudice that Individual Psychology is an intellectualistic doctrine.

The experiences of a child or an adult alter nothing on his action line once it is established, nor on his goal. However, both are interpreted and concretized according to his experiences. Experience can make one clever only to the extent that it enables him to bring his actions into a better form, to express his goal in a way which better corresponds to reality. In psychosis, the breaking off from the four problems of life is almost complete, and the logic of human living-together, "which binds us all," is given up as interfering with the flight from the community. Here the final goal usually shows itself in an unveiled, uncritical form: to be the Kaiser, God, Jesus, and the like. Within the community and the approximate range of normality, it is possible that ambition, a critical attitude, over-sensitivity, etc. can exist as suspicious signs of such a goal setting. But an excessive sensitivity reveals the underlying inferiority feeling, and disturbs development, since contradictions and conflicts with the true demands of life develop spontaneously and give rise to nervousness as a safeguarding form of life.

A true alteration of the form of life, the life line, and the life plan seems possible only through the growing understanding for these coherences, in a rational manner, then, only through Individual Psychology insight into the misleading goal.

To accomplish such a task, be it through education or Individual Psychology treatment, to transplant the goal of children or adults into the area of the generally useful, it is necessary to know or to recognize the early childhood situation in which the psychological configuration and form were born.

Personality Unity and Appraisal

Through our network one can with some practice easily succeed in discerning from all the expressive movements the secret melody of a person. This is especially the case if we take into consideration his posture (also in sleep), outward bearing, and handwriting, as further indicators of the core of the personality. We also wish to point out that we appreciate what is new in our view and often contradictory to other views, and thus we can understand the resistance of sometimes even very meritorious investigators, which, however, is slowly receding.

A stronger resistance is offered against our findings regarding the limited significance of feelings, of pleasure and displeasure, and of their intensity as the causal explanation of actions. When my goal is fixed, then only those feelings will stir which fit into my scheme. Accordingly, feelings are no arguments, but only the betraying signs of my approval or disapproval of a present task.

Also, regarding the problem of will, we can follow only to a certain point the wonderful theoretical considerations of psychologists. We are convinced that, contrary to general theory, the visibility and duration of a willed act is in strict contrast to the expected action. Not only does nothing happen during the volitional act, but very often the prominence of will is followed by a remarkable inactivity. This holds primarily for practical life. It seems to be one of the cultural devices of our time that the will is so often presented for the deed.

In our contextual view we find a large number of movements and values in a new and clearer light. Take, for instance, doubt. If one accepts the necessity of psychological movement, and with this the obligation to participate in the external world, then we find that doubt, while it lasts, is a concealed but easily deciphered "no," a standing still.

The pursuit of this and similar problems has yielded a further accomplishment of Individual Psychology, namely advancing the understanding of bodily forms of expression, the language of the organs, the utilization of affects, character traits, and nervous symptoms. We find that very often these contrast with the thinking, feeling, and willing of the individual in their [negative] social significance and dependency on a goal of superiority or of quitting, or of both. Whatever has been designated as conscious, unconscious, preconscious, etc., is always shown to be in accord with the personal action line, and to possess social activity.

The self-consistency of the physical and psychological attitude of a person is also explained by the dominating role of the final goal, and we understand why it is usually not difficult to recognize at first glance a pampered child, or one raised without love, a teacher, a physician, an actor, a scientist. [As mentioned,] even sleep posture often coincides directly with the action line—fearful people like to pull the covers over their heads, or curl up like a hedgehog on the defensive; presentable people, who wish to appear big, cannot stretch themselves enough, etc.

Also dream life and fantasies depend on the action line: they are connected with a present problem, are seeking, as though going over a bridge, to coordinate it with the final goal, and thus to solve it individually. Associations and the entire current of thinking and understanding are subject to the same trend.

We consider very important our results in examining earliest childhood recollections. Whether genuine or made up, they are unusually close to the birth of the personality and illuminate for us the situation during the formation of the self.

We attribute equally great significance to the child's fantasies of occupational choice; they are clearly expressed, even though clumsy, concretizations and verbalizations of the striving for significance, power, and superiority. One can easily recognize in them the kind and extent of activity; usually infer the quality and depth of the inferiority feeling; and often find clear traces of a training for a later occupation. Accordingly, the problem of occupation becomes clear to us as a very deeply experienced concern of the whole personality. Occupational choice as well as practice mirror for us the whole personality of the individual.

Masculine Protest and Equality

Our theory of the masculine protest is in full accord with all the findings of Individual Psychology. It is nothing other than the concretization of a striving for power that is necessarily enforced through the social underestimation and undervaluation of woman in our culture. The automatic connection of the concept of power with that of masculinity allows girls only an open or concealed striving for equality with man, or a substitute of *seeming* equality.

Womanliness is experienced like an inferior organ from which there grows a strong compensatory striving. If it is possible to steer this trait toward the generally useful side, valuable achievements come of it, in the form of equal rights and progress. Otherwise the outcome is whipped-up, over-heated endeavor which leads to collapse and prevents the solution of life problems; or it is paralyzing cowardliness and embittered resignation with equally defective end results, usually with the appearance of neurotic disorders. This old process of fermentation creates much fruitless dissatisfaction in the soul of a woman; disturbs her social feeling; prevents her from fully developing her worth and her abilities in the production process, in art, and in science; and diminishes her aptitude and inclination for love, marriage, and motherliness. Disturbances in sexual contact are in the last analysis often to be traced to this evil of the devaluation of woman. Among the worst of these consequences are deficiencies in sexual behavior, perversions, and prostitution. The tragedy of this condition against which we must fight with all our resources in school and at home is increasingly recognized more clearly, thanks to our explanations. But it can be removed only in the context of the logic of human living-together, and with a strong foundation of equal value for all.

Conclusion

Our understanding of the relationships between man, earth, community, and bisexuality—as well as our establishment of the unity of the personality within these limits—keeps us from a one-sided belief in an eternally unshakeable wisdom and understanding. Individual Psychology claims no more for itself than to be taken as a theory which does justice to the present condition of civilization and to our present knowledge of man and his psychological conditions, and which does so better than other contextual theories.

Yet we consider decisive: the influence of the mother in the family as the one who prepares the way for social interest; the influence of the school in correcting the errors in upbringing made by the family; and the removal of economic oppression of one class by another and one nation by another.

In our numerous educational guidance clinics we act in accordance with these thoughts. Our educational measures appear to us as currently the best prophylactic interventions against waywardness, childhood problems, neurosis, and psychosis.

Two great difficulties—the superstition of the heredity of mental disorders, and the talent delusion—seem at present to be surmounted, and gradually room becomes available for the understanding of the fundamental significance, in the origin of the above failures, of errors in education and world philosophy.

Bibliography[2]

Adler, A. The practice and theory of Individual Psychology (1920). Paterson, N.J.: Littlefield, Adams, 1963.

Adler, A. The neurotic constitution (1912). New York: Moffat, Yard, 1917.

Adler, A. Das Problem der Homosexualität (1917, 1926). Leipzig: Hirzel, 1930.

Adler, A. Die andere Seite: eine massenpsychologischc Studie über die Schuld des Volkes. Wien: Heidrich, 1919.

Adler, A. Study of organ inferiority and its psychical compensation: a contribution to clinical medicine (1907). New York: Nerv. Ment. Dis. Publ. Co., 1917.

Adler, A., Furtmüller, C., Wexberg, E. (Eds.) Heilen and Bilden: Grundlagen der Erziehungskunst für Ärzte und Pädagogen. 2nd ed. Munich: Bergmann, 1922.

Appelt, A. Stammering and its cure. London: Methuen, 1929.

Schulhof, Hedwig. Henrik Ibsen: der Mensch und sein Werk im Lichte der Individualpsychologie. Reichenberg: Spiethoff, 1923.

Rühle-Gerstel, Alice. Freud und Adler: elementare Einführung in die Psychoanalyse und Individualpsychologie. Dresden: Am andern Ufer, 1924.

Naegele, Otto. Der Erziehungsgedanke im Jugendrecht. D. Oestreich (Ed.) Entschiedene Schulreform. Vol. 48. Leipzig, 1925.

International Society for Individual Psychology. Questionnaire for Individual Psychologists. In A. Adler. Social interest: a challenge to mankind (1933). New York: Capricorn Books, 1964. pp. 299–306.

Rühle, O. Die Seele des proletarischen Kindes. Dresden: Am andern Ufer, 1925.

Kanitz, O. F. Das proletarische Kind in der bürgerlichen Gesellschaft. Jena: Urania Verlag, 1925.

Schwarz, O. (Ed.) Psychogenese und Psychotherapie körperlicher Symptome. Wien: Springer, 1925.

Künkel, F., & Künkel, Ruth (Eds.) Mensch und Gemeinschaft; kleine Schriften zur Individualpsychologie. Berlin-Dahlem, 1927.

Wexberg, E. (Ed.) Handbuch der Individualpsychologie (1926). Amsterdam: Bonset, 1966. 2 vols.

Wexberg, E. Ausdrucksformen des Seelenlebens. Celle: Kampmann, 1928.

Internationale Zeitschrift für Individualpsychologie, 1926, 4.

Adler, A. Various papers. In A. Bethe et al. (Eds.), Handb. norm. pathol. Physiol. Vol. 14(1). Berlin: Springer, 1926.

References[3]

Adler, A. The psychology of power (1928). J. Indiv. Psychol., 1966, 22, 166–172.

Adler, A. Les idées fondamentales de la psychologie individuelle. Rev. Psychol. concrète, 1929, 1, 89–101.

Adler, A. Grundbegriffe der Individualpsychologie. In F. Giese (Ed.) Handwörterbuch der Arbeitswissenschaft. Vol. 1. Halle: Marhold, 1930. Columns 2428–2437.

Adler, A. The Individual Psychology of Alfred Adler. Ed. by H. L. & Rowena R. Ansbacher. New York: Basic Books, 1956.

Adler, A. Superiority and social interest: a collection of later writings. 2nd ed. Ed. by H. L. & Rowena R. Ansbacher. Evanston, Ill.: Northwestern Univer. Press, 1970.

Ansbacher, H. L. Life style: a historical and systematic review. J. Indiv. Psychol., 1967, 23, 191–212.

Rom, P. Concrete psychology: the work of Georges Politzer. J. Indiv. Psychol., 1969, 25, 101–105.

Notes

1. In another paper of this period Adler added an alternative to "the typical ideal of our time," which would be required by social feelings, namely, "that of the saint, purified, to be sure, from fantastic clinkers originating from superstition" (1).—Ed. note.

2. In this brief bibliography as of 1926 supplied by Adler, the German originals have been replaced by the English translations, and some individual papers by the later collective work into which they were gathered.—Ed. note.

3. These references pertain to the editorial comments.—Ed. note.

CHAPTER 4

An Introduction to Individual Psychology

RUDOLF DREIKURS

The Community Feeling

What forms the character of a human being? What makes a man act as he does? What forces govern all the activities of the human mind? These are the fundamental questions which psychology tries to answer. So many people are now exploring them and there are so many theories that we are apt to feel confused. Some people assume that the life of each individual is determined by the experiences and desires of his ancestors (Jung). Others regard the Psyche as the battlefield of the most various instincts, corresponding to various forms of the sexual instinct (The Psycho-Analysis of Freud). Many think that the most complicated behaviour patterns are the outcome of the automatic action of certain reflex mechanisms, which are built up and maintained by habit (The Reflexology of Bechterev). Others look upon man with all his functions as the mere product of his environment, which through the medium of education directs his behaviour (The Behaviourism of Watson). A number of other theories have been advanced by different pioneers in order to explain psychic phenomena. The leading idea of the Individual Psychology of Alfred Adler is found in his recognition of the importance of human society, not only for the development of individual character, but also for the orientation of every single action and emotion in the life of a human being.

There are certain species that cannot exist without close contact with their kind. Man belongs to these. Nature has not fitted him to fight single-handed. He is not equipped in the same way as other animals for the struggle for existence. He neither has weapons of attack in the form of sharp teeth, great physical strength and powerful claws, nor is he able to defend his life by extraordinary swiftness or inconspicuous smallness. It seems that men formed herds exactly like other herding animals simply because this was necessary in order to preserve existence.[1]

Most of us have no adequate idea of the extent to which man nowadays depends on co-operation with his fellow men. We have only to think of the thousands of people whose labor we employ each day, or need only consider how many people have co-operated to provide our houses, clothing, food, and a thousand other necessities of our daily lives. For centuries man has lived in more or less close social relations with his fellow men and has adapted himself to a system of division of labor and mutual assistance. During infancy the human child is one of the most defenceless creatures in the world. He cannot find his food without help, nor even walk alone. In exercising all his functions he depends on the co-operation of others.

The question now arises: *to what extent* can living in a closely knit community form the character of an individual? It might seem, as the Psycho-Analysis of Freud maintains, that human instincts adapt themselves only incompletely and faultily to the reality of close social relationships, and that the human Psyche is indeed at the mercy of incompatible demands—the need for adjustment to the community, and the needs of innate instincts. Nevertheless, observation shows that not only among men, but also among animals, close social relationships, with the very delicate adjustment to the claims of others which is involved in such relationships, decisively affect the nature and characteristics of species, and even enable some individuals to revolt against laws of nature which otherwise prove generally irresistible. All living creatures feel a compulsion to maintain life, which causes them to seek food, and a desire to propagate themselves, which finds its fulfillment in love. And yet under certain circumstances men refuse to obey their natural instincts. Children may choose to starve themselves if they think such tactics are the best they can adopt in a struggle with their parents. Prisoners starve themselves as a form of protest. Thousands upon thousands of people who wish to evade the claims of a love relationship suppress every sexual emotion. Man has tamed his natural instincts and subordinated them to his attitude to his environment, and we find that the bees go to even greater lengths. They have reduced the sexual instinct—otherwise an all-powerful instinct, dominating the whole sphere of nature—to a precisely ordered function, which they regulate in accordance with the needs of their commonwealth at any given moment. They not only command means enabling them to decide arbitrarily whether they will produce males or females, but they can also allot the sexual function to certain individuals and later deprive them of it. Thus even creatures like bees, who live in the most closely knit communities known to us, can reverse generally valid biological laws. This supports Alfred Adler's view of the importance of society for the development of individual character among human beings.

When we observe people we find that the nature, character and actions of an individual are determined by the experiences he encounters in the community within which he grows up. Here we seem to approach Watson's theory of Behaviourism, according to which man is the mere product of his environment. But if we look deeper we find that in addition to the influence of environment another vitally important circumstance remains to be considered. Different people respond in different ways to the same experiences and influences. Man does not merely react. He adopts an individual attitude. The attitude adopted depends on the impressions the individual forms in early childhood. Environment is indeed a determining factor. Yet this environment is not the individual's real environment but merely his environment as it appears subjectively to him. Therefore the decisive factor for the development of character is not the influence of environment, but the attitude to environment which the individual takes up. Man develops his characteristic behaviour—his character—solely by opposition or support, negation or affirmation, acceptance or non-acceptance.

Man's urge to adapt himself to the arbitrary conditions of his environment is expressed by the community feeling innate in every human being. Its roots go centuries deep. But this innate social characteristic, which is common to all, must be developed if the individual is to be qualified to fulfil the complicated demands of the community in which the civilized adult lives.

The human community sets three tasks for every individual. They are: work, which means doing useful work, friendship, which embraces social relationships with comrades and relatives, and love, which is the most intimate union with some one of the other sex and represents the strongest emotional relationship which can exist between two human beings.

These three tasks embrace the whole of human life with all its desires and activities. All human suffering originates from the difficulties which complicate the tasks. The possibility of fulfilling them does not depend on the individual's talents nor on his intelligence. Men of outstanding capacity fail where others with far inferior powers achieve relative successes.

It all depends on community feeling. The better this is developed and the happier the relationship between the individual and the human community, the more successfully does he fulfil the three life tasks, and the better balanced his character and nature appear.

The community feeling is expressed subjectively in the consciousness of having something in common with other people and of being one of them. People can develop their capacity for cooperation only if they feel that in spite of all external dissimilarities they are not fundamentally different from other people. A man's ability to co-operate may therefore be regarded as a measure of the development of his community feeling.

A specific example will help us to visualize the situation more clearly: A man becomes a member of a group, a club, a political party or some other association. His community feeling expresses itself subjectively in his consciousness of membership. Expressed objectively it will show how far he is able to co-operate in life. On his community feeling depends how soon he makes contact with others, whether and to what extent he can adapt himself to others, whether he is capable of entering into other people's feelings and of understanding other people. A man who thinks only of himself, of how he is to uphold his own dignity and of the part he means to play, is sure to cause trouble within his circle of friends and acquaintances.

Readiness to co-operate, which is one of the characteristics of a good comrade, is tested most rigorously in difficult situations. Most people are perfectly willing to co-operate so long as everything is to their liking. It is much more difficult to remain a good comrade in an uncongenial situation. If the tie which binds a man to a community is weak, he will easily break away as soon as anything he does not like happens. The stronger his feeling of membership, the more surely will he remain loyal to the community, even when he cannot enforce his own wishes. We never find conditions which entirely conform to our wishes in any human relationship, be it friendship, the family, love or work. Sooner or later, therefore, we are bound to become involved in critical situations, and the way we behave then will show whether we are community minded or not.

Another characteristic of the good comrade is his readiness to demand less than he offers. Nowadays most people brought up in large towns are spoilt children, who measure their happiness and satisfaction only by what they get. This is a grave error, for which thousands pay in unhappiness and suffering. People who make it their object to get as much as possible are always clutching emptiness. They are insatiable. Only a rare and brief moment of attainment rewards months or years of covetousness and ambition. None but those who can seek their happiness as a part of the whole, that is to say, in the contribution they themselves can make to the community, can feel satisfied with themselves and their lives. The community feeling therefore is expressed by willingness to contribute without thought of reward.

We shall have a sufficiently reliable criterion as to whether any given action takes into account the needs of the community, if we observe to what extent the action is objective. Objective action implies suitable and right behaviour in any situation. It is impossible to prescribe how anyone should behave in this or that situation. Every situation involves a special and very complicated set of circumstances, and no one can say beforehand how they should be handled. The crucial questions are:—Have the rules of community life been mastered? Is the individual ready to subordinate himself to them? If so, he will know more or less the right course to adopt in any situation, no matter how difficult, because he will be able to regard his problems objectively. He will never be baffled if he can subordinate ego-centric wishes to the objective needs of the community.

In spite of the apparent chaos of present-day social relationships we have rules to guide us. These rules are clear to everyone even though they have never been definitely formulated. Each person becomes aware of the relentless logic of life as soon as he tries to escape it. Success or failure is the answer given by the community to fulfillment or non-fulfillment of the life tasks.

Frequently a man whose contacts with the community are superficial appears to be consistently successful, while another who always seemed to have adapted himself sufficiently to the needs of the community may suddenly break down. The explanation is that the strength of the community feeling is not always put to the proof. If a man is spared by favorable circumstances from undergoing rigorous tests, he may easily give others the impression of being able to solve every problem. He is like a pupil who for some time escapes examinations. His knowledge is taken for granted. If a man has to endure great hardships his lack of training for life will be revealed more quickly. But sooner or later everyone has to show how far his community feeling has developed. This moment decides whether his life can be happy or not. Therefore disaster and misfortune are not inevitable causes of suffering and discouragement, but test situations, which prove whether people are ready to co-operate. While one accepts defeat, another keeps a brave heart. He never loses his feeling of comradeship with other people and in the end he wins through.

Yet the community feeling does not mean, as misrepresentations of the teachings of Alfred Adler often incorrectly state, simply a feeling of belonging to a certain group or class of people, or benevolence towards the whole race. Sometimes the interests of various groups conflict. (This is the dilemma of a workman on strike, who may hesitate between his family's welfare and the need for solidarity with his fellow workers.) In such perplexing situations the community feeling causes us to see that the interests of the super-ordinate group, which are justified on the ground of objective needs, have the first claim on us. We certainly want to do what we can to help men to found a community embracing the whole human race, to whose interests all the special interests of individuals and groups would be subordinated. But in practice we are still a long way from realizing this ideal. The community feeling has no fixed objective. Much more truly may it be said to create an attitude to life, a desire to co-operate with others in some way and to master the situations of life. Community feeling is the expression of our capacity for give and take.

Finality

Clearly the attitude adopted by the individual to the problems of community life could not determine the development of his character were he driven from the beginning in a certain direction by inherited tendencies. If instincts and other innate forces governed his behaviour at every juncture, only a certain adaptation and modification of his personality in response to the conditions of his environment would be possible. It is found, however, that all the characteristics of the individual, and indeed his whole personality, are developed by the attitude he adopts to his environment in early childhood. Actually the personality is developed in this way only if human soul-life is teleologically orientated. In other words, the object which the individual pursues in his actions is the decisive factor. We must admit this if we believe that his attitude to his environment consistently determines all his actions, and the sum of his actions—his personality.

But are we justified in rejecting causality, the law which was hitherto thought to determine the mental development of all human beings, in favor of the view of finality, which prefers to stress the fact that the individual can select from a great variety of ways and means? We now find that quite apart from psychology, science in general is becoming concerned to an ever increasing degree with this much debated problem—causality or finality.

Probably the Neo-Vitalists were the first to assume that the question of use was the decisive law governing all forms of life. They reached their assumption after studying the evolution of species and organs, and above all the biological processes of the body. In their view all symptoms of illness and all pathological changes are not effects produced by some harmful agent, but weapons for defeating it. The classical example of this is inflammation, the "purpose" of which is to destroy the invading bacteria by multiplying leucocytes. Similarly every biological change is understood solely in the light of the purpose it is intended to accomplish.

Quite apart from such biological trains of thought, Alfred Adler stresses the fact that all living things move, and that every movement must have a goal. So, according to Adler, all living things seek a goal. With regard to man in particular, Alfred Adler declares that it is impossible for us to understand his behaviour and actions unless we know their goal.

This teleological mode of thought, which appears to contradict all our accustomed beliefs, formerly met with the keenest opposition from science, and was frequently rejected as unscientific. The last great development of the natural sciences in particular was based on acceptance of the doctrine of causality, which regards every occurrence as the simple effect of a certain cause. The theory that a connection other than that between cause and effect may be at the root of any observed occurrence is extremely difficult to grasp, yet Individual Psychologists are now experiencing the great satisfaction of seeing it accepted by what is surely one of the exactest sciences, Physics. Although this repudiation of the law of causality made it possible to ascertain the boundaries of causality only in the realm of the smallest atom, it involved such a fundamental change in the laws of thought that the violence and frequency of the debates on the subject among students of physics are understandable. This overthrow of causality in another field at the same moment is an apparent coincidence, but has many parallels in the history of the development of human thought, and there can be no doubt that it contributed to the great advance made in the field of psychological research.

When an individual acts in a certain way we naturally ask why he does so. This indeed was the only question asked by psychology before Alfred Adler. In the early days of psychological research people tried to find a purely mechanical and material explanation for all actions. They believed that impressions were transmitted to the body through the sense organs, and then indirectly—through a reflex or brain process—a certain action was liberated. Freud was the first to discard the theory that human actions are governed by physical laws, and emphasized the need for the acceptance and recognition of purely spiritual laws for man, but even he was misled by the principle of causality, and looked to the past for the explanation of all human actions. He declared that all former psychic experiences were reserves of certain psychic energies, and therefore must be recognized as compulsive factors, which necessarily produce a certain result.

The principle of causality, whether it was handled by materialists or by Freudians, was never particularly useful or practical. The subtler the methods employed by the former in tracing the springs of man's actions, the more chaotic was the picture in which they sought to reproduce multitudinous sense irritations and reflex channels, and to prove that man is governed by purely physical laws. On the other hand, as a result of Freud's attempt to find a law of energy embodying his discovery that man was dominated by a psychic force, rash theories were advanced. These theories could never be verified in practical life. They could only be demonstrated in the special atmosphere of a psychoanalyst's consulting room. The next step was to discover an entirely different law of movement for human beings.

Adler made a remarkable discovery when he found the motive force of every human action in the goal of the action. This discovery is fully confirmed by personal experience, as far as the normal life of a healthy human being is concerned. Objections could only be raised with regard to some human actions which appear to be useless and senseless and to be performed against the agent's wish, or at least without his wish. Far from rousing opposition, however, Adler's views as to the purposive quality of even these aberrations are supported by the observations of almost all famous psychiatrists, including some who otherwise have very little to say in favor of Individual Psychology, such as Wagner-Jauregg, Bonhöffer, Kahn, etc. It is true that they go only a little way in accepting the teleological law. They do not recognize the importance of the tendency betrayed at the beginning of apparently unwilled actions except in connection with outbreaks of hysteria and neurosis which follow accidents. But if they make only these exceptions, they admit by implication that even when a man does not consciously recognize the fact that his actions have a certain goal—even when he feels that he performs them against his own will—his actions may still have a goal.

The phenomenon of the unconfessed goal is closely connected with the problem of consciousness, which requires a more detailed discussion than it can receive in this chapter. Here we will limit ourselves to observing that it may not be very obvious to an ordinary man that all his actions have a goal; so that a situation in which he feels as if he is being driven first one way and then another by conflicting wishes, and is not clear as to what he really wants, may give him the impression that the human mind is the battlefield of various instincts and impulses, and that the resulting action is to be attributed to the victory of the strongest instinct. Nevertheless, since we regard the human being as an undivided personality, we judge not only the resulting action, but also the previous hesitation as a consistent and reasonable "action," serving its particular purpose as effectively as a simple unfettered expression of will may serve a different purpose. This subject will be discussed at greater length in the personality.

It is obvious from everything that a human being does, that he has the power to orientate towards a certain environment, for ultimately his action and inaction are decided solely by the question of "which way?" He is not driven through life by his past, but impelled to go forward into the future—and the force that impels him is not an external force. He moves of his own accord. All his actions, emotions, qualities and characteristics serve the same purpose. They show him trying to adapt himself to the community. Character is not determined causally by equipment or instincts. Neither is it formed by environment, which would bring us back once more to causal determination. Belief in finality is based on belief in the "creative power," which enables a man to seek his goal as he judges best. Man acts far more than he reacts. At this point Individual Psychology comes into contact with the views of Bergson, who recognizes the essential indetermination of every living substance in his theory of the "élan vital."

The Spoilt Child

From the very first day of his life the human child has a place in a community with which he has to make contact in order that the necessities of his life may be satisfied. His first way of communicating with his surroundings is by screaming. He cries for his mother to come when he feels hungry or experiences any discomfort, and no matter how small the infant, his screaming is regulated according to the parents' behaviour.

From the very outset the infant has certain social functions to perform. This makes some kind of discipline essential. The infant's first task is feeding. It is comparatively easy to train a healthy child to perform this task, that is to say, to teach him to co-operate satisfactorily with the mother. Every child will, of course, offer some resistance to the first attempt to fix regular feeding hours. He will scream at other times, but if the parents are sensible and patient, they will not allow this to deter them from enforcing their system. The child will soon give up screaming, and within a few days will automatically accustom himself to regular feeding hours and even exhibit a certain degree of satisfaction in keeping them. So for the first time in his life he adapts himself and co-operates with others as a member of the community.

Unfortunately at this early stage serious mistakes are very frequently made. From motives of false pity overanxious parents try to "spare the poor little thing" in every possible way. "Oh, he'll accustom himself to regular hours later on when he's stronger." It is very natural for the parents of a child who is delicate or ill to feel extremely concerned. By the doctor's advice possibly even these parents will attempt to teach a child regular habits, but if the child has some difficulty in learning to suck, and regularly loses strength during the first days of his life, they will not have the heart to "let him go hungry" when he cries to be fed. The result is that discipline is disregarded.

The older the child grows the more difficult it becomes to teach him disciplined habits. Each day strengthens his resistance to any change from irregular hours, once he has grown accustomed to them. At the same time the steady development of his lung powers becomes more and more patent. Then, as irregular hours prevent him from thriving the mother's anxiety increases. But the more she tries to establish an orderly régime, the more the child screams, and after a shorter or longer period of hesitation the mother gives way. The child thus makes his first important discovery—that he can get his own way by screaming, or at least make his mother take him up and rock him in her arms or give him something to pacify him. (Freudians make the fatal mistake of regarding the child and the whole of mankind as obedient to the "pleasure principle," so that every frustration must be the counterpart of a "pleasure ideal." They forget that this applies only to people who have not become happy members of the community. Pleasure may be derived even from discipline, if it appears reasonable, and after all, pleasure simply expresses acceptance.)

The result of the various forms of spoiling and pampering is that the child grows up in a hot-house atmosphere and enjoys artificial privileges, which exempt him from the natural discipline of community life. He need not submit to the rules which apply to all the other members of the first community he encounters in life—the family. Special precautions prevent him from knowing any discomforts. Artificial warmth envelopes him. He need not earn recognition by any achievements of his own. Pity and indulgence shield him from all the disagreeable consequences of his actions. He never learns to put up with anything he does not like. Somebody is always ready to help him and spare him the necessity of making any effort. Over great anxiety holds him back from encountering dangers which spell risk and demand courage.

Parents who spoil a child make it very difficult for the child to become a useful member of the community. Most of us are spoilt children. This is not the less true because many of us do not feel at all as though we had ever been spoiled. For every attempt to spare the child the necessity of submitting to necessary communal discipline must result in the child's disliking discipline, in his adopting a hostile attitude towards it, and ever afterwards resenting even the modicum of discipline which has to be maintained wherever people live in a community. (In this connection Freud speaks incorrectly of the "destruction of instinct" which' civilization inevitably involves.)

Whenever a child is spoilt a time always comes when at last an attempt is made to discipline him. The child naturally resists this. He cannot see why something which he was hitherto allowed to do should suddenly be forbidden once and for all. He does not feel that order is a wise law, enabling people to live together in a community, but that it is a mere parental whim. Frequently, therefore, all that sticks in the memory of spoilt children is the struggle with the parents, who for their part generally make use of highly unsuitable methods to achieve by force an object that could have been realized without any difficulty at all, if they had previously shown less weakness.

The only safe rule for ascertaining how much spoiling a child has had and the degree of hostility to discipline this has engendered is provided by asking to what extent the child is aware of being spoiled. A child is particularly alive to the situation if, being the only child in the family, he alone is pampered and allowed to dictate to the other members of the family and regulate their lives, as if they existed merely to minister to his wants. He will not regard his pampered childhood in the same light if later on he has to live in very uncongenial surroundings. This alone shows that the child himself is fully responsible for the meaning he attaches to the parents' behaviour, and for the attitude to his past which he adopts in consequence.

Snubbing

Sooner or later the spoilt child feels frustrated and realizes that a right which he believes he is justified in claiming is being curtailed. Spoiling actually amounts to disregard of the child's right to become independent and to learn at an early age what the requirements of life are. Usually spoiling is far less the result of consideration for the child, as the parents assert, than of consideration for their own feelings, because they cannot bear seeing the child wear out his strength, suffer in any way or get into difficulties. Doting parents deprive the child of other vital rights. These are the parents who cannot allow a young child to sleep regular and sufficient hours, merely because they want to dandle him, or because visitors coming to the house want to admire him. The desire to parade a child in front of visitors encroaches on his right to play with other children. Excessive anxiety deprives him of his right to freedom of movement.

The child is frustrated and deprived of his rights in a particularly flagrant manner if the parents interfere with discipline and make disturbances from no motives of love for the child, but solely out of regard for their own interests. If excessive love often makes it difficult for the child to become a happy and useful member of the community, as much may certainly be said of unkindness, which denies that the child has a place of his own in the family. Children whose parents hate them because they came into the world unwanted are often denied their rights in a very shameful way. Sometimes parents turn away from a child because she is a girl instead of the boy they had been hoping to have, or because they see a certain resemblance between the child and some one they dislike. Sometimes a parent has a spite against a stepchild. The parents' unkindness is always felt more keenly by the child if he is very much indulged by another person, who probably acts from some motive of compensating justice.

Snubbing always arouses resistance. Often the child's resistance or obstinacy may appear to have been destroyed by beatings or by other measures of force adopted by his elders. But under cover of even the most abject submissiveness the child will still achieve his object—retreat from the community, evasion of all the implications of communal life. Such is the effect produced on the child if he only thinks he is hated. Not infrequently the child misjudges the parents' behaviour. He may believe that they care little for him, even when this belief is not justified in reality. On the other hand the child will not want to retreat into himself if he fails to observe that his parents really hate him, and remains unaware of being snubbed.

The Inferiority Feeling and Striving for Significance

We have seen how both spoiling and snubbing may hinder the child from becoming a useful member of the community. We must now discover what factor comes into play in the mind of the spoilt child and the snubbed child alike. How can experiences so different from each other as spoiling or snubbing have the same effect—that of disturbing the community feeling innate in every human being?

When we examine this paradox more closely we find that whether the child is spoilt or snubbed, he always develops a feeling of his own relative inferiority, which causes him to resist the rules of the community and to adopt a hostile attitude to the community. The behaviour of all children and all adults establishes the general validity of the following law: The natural community feeling of every human being reaches its limits when feelings of inferiority arise.

A diagram may make the situation easier to grasp.

The individual tries to get himself accepted by the community (C). He therefore moves along the line a—b, that is to say, if no obstacle checked his advance towards the community he would move along this straight line towards C. Man would only act and develop in response to the conditions of his community. The force ruling his actions and psychic life would be undisturbed community feeling.

But we have seen that difficulties may prevent the child from becoming a happy and useful member of the community. He imagines that the community is a hostile world and feels unable to cope with it. It seems to him that the community repulses him and tries to force him down (in the direction shown by the line b—c in our diagram).

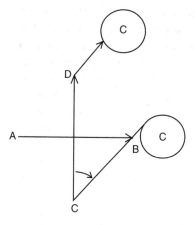

Fig. 4.1 Figure

In the minds of children, and later also of adults, all ideas of being repulsed are inevitably connected with the subjective feeling of being "less" than other people. It is immaterial whether the child accepts the superiority of others as a result of spoiling, because he underestimates his own strength and regards his dependence on the superior strength of others as something to be taken for granted, or whether as the result of snubbing he has come to believe that the superior power of others will always be victorious. Invariably the child imagines that the contrast between his power and the power of other people means that the other people are "worth more" than he is.

The child resents this feeling of being low down in the scale, and very soon all his actions show that he is moving in a new direction. In response to his innate community feeling he persists in trying to get himself accepted at any cost by the community. But as he assumes that his value is too small or his strength inadequate, he thinks that he can reach the community only by first climbing to a higher position. Consequently, as already stated, he moves in an entirely new direction, shown in our diagram by the line c–d. Any person who labours under a sense of inferiority always tries to obtain power of some kind in order to cancel the supposed superiority of other people. His feeling of inferiority impels him to strive for significance.

It should always be remembered that the inferiority feeling is a subjective feeling. The inferiority may exist only in the imagination of the individual when he compares himself with others. The inferiority feeling is in a very deep sense quite independent of a man's true value, because when he compares himself with other people he gives them fictive values. Anyone who doubts his own value always over-estimates the capacities of other people. Therefore neither the absence nor the presence of inferiority feelings is any index to a man's real value. Some extremely valuable and successful people suffer acutely from inferiority feelings. On the other hand we may not be able to find a trace of an inferiority feeling in a lunatic. An individual's estimates of his own value, which find expression in inferiority feelings, are based entirely on his personal attitude to the community and to other people. That is to say, they are founded on his own opinions. He plays the role of both prosecutor and judge at his own trial. The low value he assigns to himself often appears to be connected with actual failures, but there can be no doubt that anyone who believes that his failures prove his lack of value deceives himself. Very frequently people come to entirely wrong conclusions about their own successes or failures. Often a man disparages everything valuable that he has done, and attaches far too much importance to a completely senseless failure. In the end all failures turn out to be not so much the causes of inferiority feelings as inevitable consequences of such feelings. As surely as people expect little of themselves they meet with failures.

People betray their inferiority feelings and their consequent desire for significance in an endless variety of ways. Whenever we observe human mistakes and faults (which we only regard as mistakes and faults because they violate the rules which enable people to live in a community), we shall always find a feeling of inferiority causing the individual to renounce the direct line of approach to the community. Every fault, whether it is a defect of character, or a single instance of mistaken conduct, grows out of evasion of some social task. People evade social tasks in order to conceal their own deficiencies and to avert a dreaded failure.

There are two chief modes of evasion. On the one hand people may run away from their opportunities, avoid making decisions, limit their sphere of action and try to gain time or set a distance between themselves and other people. We all take out several of these "insurance policies" during our lives. Our object is to conceal a feeling of inferiority either from others or from ourselves. On the other hand, people may try to deflect the line they take in an upward direction. They try to gain special significance by achievements in some particular field. If they can do so by means of useful achievements they will perhaps appear to be perfectly capable of adapting themselves to the community, although their deepest impulses were fear of the community and a tendency to retreat. Sometimes, indeed, fear is the incentive for outstanding achievements, which contribute to human progress and the development of culture. It is only when a man does not seek success in the form of useful achievement, or undervalues contributions he can make to the community because his need for personal significance is too great, that he acts in response to his will-to-power without regard for anything useful and wastes his strength "on the useless side of life." He despises his fellow-men, his environment and life itself, and sets his heart on achieving meretricious successes at any price, even at the price of his own suffering. The martyr's role of suffering is a particularly clear example of the way in which a man appears to reverse real circumstances in a struggle with a powerful regime, since the helpless martyr triumphs over the brute force of those who are actually more powerful than he.

Disparagement of others and of life itself may be expressed in a number of ways. Sometimes it is displayed openly in dissatisfaction with everything or extremely cutting criticisms. Equally often it poses as goodwill towards men. Extravagant idealism or exaggerated moral tenets and ethical principles set up such high standards for other people that they necessarily appear small and worthless. Disparagement of reality is also expressed in fantasy and melancholy, and most frequently in daydreams, which relegate every-day-life and the present moment entirely to the background.

These capacities for taking cover and finding a fictive increase of power receive their training in childhood. A spoilt child in particular quickly succeeds in converting his feeling of inferiority into a strong desire for significance. It is easy enough for him to play a special rôle, since he enjoys importance by the mere fact of his existence, even though he has no useful achievement to his credit. He is most afraid of not being noticed, because he thinks this means he is no longer important. He claims every minute of his mother's attention. He tries to stop her talking to grown-ups and other children, and insists on her sitting with him while he is going to sleep. But if he feels that he has not sufficiently safeguarded his weak position, or believes that it is being threatened in some way, he adopts stronger measures. He behaves naughtily, retreats into shyness, refuses to eat and gets into tempers or panics. In brief, he employs all the tricks of a cunning little animal in order to make the grownups do what he wants them to do. The spoilt child with an inferiority feeling always tries to tyrannize in some way over other people, especially if he happens to be an only child or the youngest of a family.

So spoilt children develop various characteristics, by means of which they try to overcome their feeling that they have no value for other people. The deficiency or supposed deficiency they feel most keenly is their most vulnerable spot. Often they are timid because they magnify dangers and consequently try to give them a wide berth. A child who feels that his own strength is inadequate grows to need support. He tries to make other people his slaves; he lacks firmness of character; he becomes unruly and easily gets tired, with the result that the grownups themselves have to carry out his tasks if only for the sake of peace and quietness. Instead of finding happiness in successful achievements, he looks for cheaper sources of satisfaction; he becomes frivolous, idle, and pleasure-seeking, and escapes into fantasies and daydreams.

A child who gets the impression that people neglect and hate him tries to revenge himself for his feeling of helpless frustration by giving them as much trouble as he can. There is nothing very attractive about the head-strong, grimy child who knows just how to touch the grown-ups in their weak spots and, of course, uses his knowledge to protest against their treatment of him. He behaves wilfully at school and becomes generally unpopular with his teachers. His fondness for giving the grown-ups unpleasant shocks may even encourage him to develop criminal tenden-cies, for a perverse wish to be disagreeable is a common motive for lying and stealing.

It would be necessary to quote individual case histories in order to prove that all faulty behaviour in childhood and adult life alike is the result of unsuccessful attempts to overcome feelings of inferiority in misguided ways. Yet we know that the inferiority feeling is a driving force which pro-duces the most various travesties of asocial conduct, because all impulses directed against the community vanish in proportion as the inferiority feeling diminishes and the individual learns to estimate his own value more correctly. Once a human being declares war on the community, peace cannot be restored until he has found a correct standard of values.

Organ Inferiority

Organ inferiority affords a particularly plain example of the part played by inferiority feelings and the way they may develop or be overcome. Any organ or organ system in the human body may be affected by an organ inferiority.

By organ inferiority is meant not an absolute defect but a relative weak-ness of an organ as compared with the functions of other organs, so that subjectively the individual experiences difficulty in exercising his func-tions. Now, since the use of functions constitutes the child's principal task in the community, anything which seems to make it harder to regulate his functions also gives him the impression of being worth less than other people—that is to say, gives him a feeling of inferiority. Some examples will probably make this clearer.

An organ inferiority which affects the alimentary tract does not in the least mean that the digestive organs are unhealthy. It is true, however, that if a child is delicate all the functions of the digestive organs are more labo-riously regulated and more easily disturbed than they are in a healthy child. It is more difficult to get the delicate child to eat regular meals and he easily falls into irregular ways with regard to defecation. He therefore finds it more difficult to be an orderly member of the community and to acquire habits of cleanliness. All the child's difficulties confirm his belief that it is too hard for him to regulate the functions of the digestive organs, though the other people who are older have no difficulties of any kind.

All physical disturbances in the exercise of functions can operate as organ inferiorities. A child with eye trouble may grow up inattentive. An inferiority of the uro-genital organs may lead to difficulties in the control of the bladder function. An extremely delicate constitution, which curtails the length of time that can be spent in physical exertions or stoutness accompanied by un-gainliness and clumsiness are resented and rated as organ inferiorities. Similarly a child may resent being unusually small—in fact, anything which gives him the impression that he is of less value physically than other people.

Relative unskillfulness of the right hand in a child who is born left-handed may also have the effect of an organ inferiority. When this child tries to learn to shake hands in the ordinary everyday way with the right hand, he will experience considerable difficulty. He will then be inclined to exaggerate his incapacity for learning to do things correctly.

At this juncture a vital question presents itself for consideration: What is the outcome of organ inferiority or what response does it evoke? There are two diametrically opposed ways of dealing with this as with all other situations involving psychological difficulties. The decision is simply a question of more or less courage. Does the child allow the difficulties resulting from an organ inferiority to discourage him or not? On this depends the course he subsequently takes. An organ inferiority is never static. It is not something that merely exists. Rather it operates dynamically through the final use to which it is put.

Let us consider in more detail the very common organ inferiority of constitutional lefthandedness. The child experiences difficulty in using his right hand. The grown-ups find fault with him and scold him. The child gradually loses faith in himself and becomes careless and clumsy. When he has to learn to write he writes badly. Nobody realizes that because he has been left-handed from birth he naturally finds it difficult to use his right hand. He is always being reminded of his extraordinary carelessness and clumsiness. If owing to excessive spoiling the child has lost faith in his own capacities at a very early age, he will regard every difficulty which crops up as insurmountable and give up trying to acquire manual dexterity because he is clumsy with his right hand.

Among children who have become extremely discouraged the organ inferiority of the right hand may easily produce permanent defects in the exercise of important functions. These children will always be clumsy. Their handwriting will be bad. They will have hard work in making up their minds to perform manual tasks and consequently they will tend to become slovenly. As a result of being lefthanded (a peculiarity which is not always very evident) a child may even have difficulty in learning to read. So difficulties viewed in a spirit of growing discouragement produce various defects.

The child may respond in this spirit to organ inferiorities of the alimentary tract or of the bladder. Great difficulty is experienced in regulating the functions of the digestive organs and the child develops dirty habits. If he is severely punished he will become bad-tempered. If his parents show anxiety he will take advantage of his difficulties to get more attention. In short, the child will retreat further and further from a courageous solution of his difficulties, and his feeling of inferiority will grow in proportion.

But this is not the only way of responding to an organ inferiority. If the child has not become discouraged he treats his difficulty very differently. He observes it and tries to overcome it. He pounces most eagerly on his greatest difficulties and tries to excel chiefly in activities in which these difficulties seem calculated to hamper him. He wants to master his difficulties and the requirements of life at the same time. And success is within his reach. Such a child later accomplishes outstanding achievements in the very field where he at first encountered difficulties. The early clumsiness of lefthanded children gives place to special dexterity, which, as often as not, finds expression in artistic productions. Children with organ inferiorities of the alimentary tract persevere in their efforts to gain control and mastery of these functions until they become extremely fastidious and methodical. Frequently a special value attached both to eating and defecation replaces the original difficulties.

These responses to difficulties all confirm a fundamental law for overcoming inferiority feelings, which was already stated by implication in the previous chapter.[1] Whenever an attempt is made to compensate for an inferiority feeling, this is never done by way of actual compensation, but always in the sense of overcompensation.

The reason for this is clear. If anyone makes great efforts so as not to be worth less than others in a certain field he lives in constant dread lest he should find that he is, and that other people will know it also. And even when he has already become as expert as other average people, he will still be afraid lest there should be someone who excels him. So he is continually drawn towards the goal of perfection, which is never attainable in practice.

Everyone who, instead of being discouraged, tries to overcome organ inferiorities, obeys this law of overcompensation. Very musical people are often found in families where defects of hearing are remarkably common, and artistic people in families with all kinds of defects of eyesight. So we begin to understand a fact which at first seems very perplexing—namely, that geniuses, artists and great men often exhibit unmistakable signs of organ inferiority in the very field of their outstanding achievements. Examples of famous musicians whose hearing was impaired by constitutional organ inferiorities like Franz and Smetana, famous orators whose speech organs were affected by certain weaknesses in early life like Demosthenes and Viktor Adler, famous painters with defective eyesight like Manet and Lenbach, and famous writers who combined a romantic imagination with defects of eyesight like Karl May and Jules Verne, can be multiplied at will and clearly prove that frequently an organ inferiority provides the incentive for artistic achievements. It is by no means the only incentive for undertaking the special training which necessarily precedes any outstanding achievement. No doubt there are many reasons why a child endeavors to achieve a special success in a special field; yet constitutional organ inferiority provides a stimulus which, far from being rare, is extremely common.

The presence of a constitutional organ inferiority cannot, however, be deduced from its consequences, that is to say, from defects or from overcompensation. It is justifiable to speak of an organ inferiority only when it has been sufficiently proved that there was a constitutional defect which rendered the exercise of a function difficult. Proof is furnished chiefly by the family anamnesia, i.e., when organic disorders of a certain organ system occur extremely frequently among the nearest relatives. Suspicion that an organ inferiority exists may be confirmed by a number of other indications, such as birthmarks, the development of feverish skin disorders in that part of the body which is nearest to the organ thought to be affected by an inferiority, or by subsequent organic deterioration of the organ; for instance, by the appearance of tumours, or by otosclerosis when organ inferiority of the ear is suspected. There are several signs that betray latent lefthandedness—as for example, a steady preference for using the left hand for performing small unimportant actions, like clapping, cutting cards, etc.

On the other hand, we should not, of course, hold an organ inferiority responsible for every difficulty encountered in the use of a certain organ. It is indeed true that as a human being develops, any disturbances in the normal performance of functions are most likely, *ceteris paribus*, to make common cause with an organ inferiority. That is why disturbances of functions are so often used to reinforce resistance or become modes of evasion.

A child can just as well use his organs (as, for example, his digestive organs) to promote a disturbance, even when they are entirely free from organ inferiorities. The only safe guide is to see whether by these means he achieves his object, that is to say, whether other people and, above all, his parents, submit to the disturbance. Any healthy organ can be trained to promote a disturbance; and under some circumstances even a secondary functional disturbance, for which the way has been prepared by sufficient training, may later lead to relative overcompensation. For example, children who hungerstrike without the stimulus of organic defects may later attach importance to eating plentiful meals.

This human tendency to overcompensate for inferiority feelings plays a most important part in the history of mankind. Just as an organ inferiority may lead to the performance of outstanding artistic achievements in a particular field, so every endeavour to rise higher, and every achievement which promotes the development of the race and advances civilization, is the outcome of the wish to ease a gnawing feeling of inferiority. All human beings experience moments of anxiety or at least are troubled on account of the insufficiency of the body, which is felt like an organ inferiority. For the human body is not only little fitted to endure the material hardships of life. It is also subject to illness and death. Man knows the cosmic laws of origin and dissolution. He perceives his own smallness in the universe and is aware of the anguish which is inherent in everything that lives. Besides, as children we have all felt small and inferior as compared with the grownups, and we are all impelled to over-come difficulties. Extreme physical defencelessness not only apparently caused men, as already noticed, to form communities, but also led to the development of the human intellect. In compensation for inadequate physical strength, man acquired the capacity for using powerful forces outside his own person, such as stones, weapons, animals, the forces of nature and machinery.

In the life of an individual also the feeling of inferiority may become the incentive for achievements which, while they help him to go forward and develop more fully, also promote the advance and higher development of the whole race. The inferiority feeling ends in retreat and self-frustration only when the individual has become so discouraged that he no longer relies on achievements "on the useful side of life."

Heredity and Equipment

The observations concerning the importance of organ inferiority in general and the implications of overcompensation in particular which Alfred Adler made when he began his investigations formed the foundation on which the whole structure of Individual Psychology was later erected, and at the same time provided an entirely new standard for rating the importance of hereditary equipment.

Laws of heredity come into force wherever life is handed down from generation to generation and there can be no doubt that they are applicable in a very real sense to human beings. Man has from birth many natural propensities, capacities and weaknesses like any other animal, but he is fundamentally different from all other animals in that the part played in his development by a community life gives him a mastery over his "natural equipment" such as has never hitherto been observed even among animals living in the closest of communities.

The previous chapter dealt with the technique of this mastery. Let us now look more closely at the question of equipment.

It is obvious that if a certain function of the body falls into disuse it becomes increasingly difficult to exercise it. Any capacity may go to waste for want of training in childhood. The most valuable talent—amounting even to capacity for outstanding artistic achievements—is useless to a child who neglects and indeed probably refuses to train it out of spite against his parents. The same applies to a gift for mathematics or manual dexterity—in fact, to any capacity for achievement in any field. All human methods of achievement are extremely complicated and cannot be mastered without training. If training is neglected abilities remain undeveloped. It is not even enough to have a special talent.

Thus it becomes clear that what determines the way in which the personality finally develops is "not the equipment we bring with us, but the use we make of it."[2] By the interplay of neglect and training each individual forms his capacities and qualities as his individual position within the community demands. He is free from the restrictions of causal determinism as represented by his equipment.

Therefore what a man has become is in no way indicative of the quality of the equipment he had at the outset. In every individual we see only the phenotype, from which we can deduce little about the genotype. With man we cannot as with other animals learn much from the study of a series of generations, not only because the series we are able to observe are generally too short, but also because in every separate case the significance of psychological phenomena can be understood only through a course of psychological analysis which covers a limited space of time, that is to say, only by observing what is going on at the present moment, and not by looking back to ancestors.

Scientific investigators find it easier to deal with man's physical inheritance. But it is necessary to be cautious in discussing even this subject, as processes which appear to be purely physical may be changed in individual cases by psychological factors. In most accounts of the connection between physical structure and character the physical factor generally, though not always, takes precedence. Character and physical structure do indeed affect each other in turn, but a man's psychic personality, just as much as his innate capacities and the physical conditions of his life, represents material for him to utilize when choosing his personal objective.

Man also exercises choice in his response to the so-called "instincts," which appear to govern him like all living creatures. These are primarily the instinct for self-preservation expressed by hunger, and the instinct for continuing the race, expressed by love. These inborn urges appear to dominate all animals with the exception of those living in very close communities, like ants, bees, men and their domestic animals. Among these, as has already been shown, numerous examples may be observed of complete control gained over the urges of hunger and love. So long as these and other instincts are amenable to reason we have no ground for assuming that our actions are arbitrarily determined by our instincts. Only when our actions are contrary to common sense do we appear to have any argument for the alleged supremacy of "instincts."

Upon closer examination, however, unreasonable behaviour usually proves to be the outcome of hostility to the order established by the human community. In themselves hunger and sexuality are forces without direction. The individual personality alone sets a goal before the "instincts" and gives them a special content. Hunger then becomes appetite and sexuality becomes love. All the complications and conflicts involved in the "satisfaction of the instincts" arise in this way. The complications are not indications of the strength of the "instincts" but give expression to individual proneness to create problems. Hunger allows comparatively little scope for the attainment of personal motives—thirst practically none. Hence they can be more easily satisfied. But many personal objectives may be concealed beneath love and other instinctive emotions.

The Family Constellation

The theory that each person has an innate individuality from birth appears to find confirmation in the fact that children in the same family are different from each other. It is indeed admitted by those who uphold this theory that the parents' behaviour can influence the child's attitude, and through this the development of his character, but they say that the parents treat all the children alike and that therefore the differences between the children must be attributed to their equipment.

Upon closer examination, however, it is found that each child has an essentially different position in the family and must see all the circumstances of his childhood in an entirely different light. Besides, in practice the parents never treat two children alike, but behave very differently to each. There may be a difference in the affection they feel for the children, and there certainly will be in the opinions they hold about them. At this point it might be useful to suggest briefly some points of view which are characteristic of the different children in a family.

Let us begin with the eldest child. The outstanding fact of his childhood is that at first, though only for a limited period, he was the only child. While he is the only child he is likely to get far too much spoiling. He is the center of attraction and the special object of his parents' care. Then he suddenly finds himself in the thick of a tremendous experience. A brother or sister is thrust upon him. Even if the first child is already a few years old he is hardly ever able to gauge the situation correctly. He notices only that another child now continually monopolizes his parents, especially his mother, who devotes herself to him, and lavishes any amount of time and care on him. He readily believes that the newcomer will rob him of her love. He cannot know, of course, that he was once looked after by his mother in exactly the same way and that all the care she bestows on the second child does not mean that she loves him more. So, feeling that he has been set aside, the eldest child frequently shows understandable jealousy when another child is born, even if before the birth of this child he longed for a brother or sister.

If the mother can make the elder child aware of his undiminished value by pointing out to him his importance as the elder and therefore more advanced child, and so enlist his will to co-operate, he will adapt himself to the new situation with comparative ease. But the parents may not understand what is going on in the elder child's mind and may grow impatient over his unfounded jealousies and ailments. If, as is most probable, they then take the younger child under their protection in order to defend him against the elder child's overbearing conduct, the elder child may easily give up trying to win good opinions by making himself useful, as he probably could do, but becomes obstinate and tries to take up his parents' attention by resorting to every possible trick that naughtiness can suggest to him.

Even if under the most favourable circumstances two children of the same parents manage to live together in apparent harmony they may become involved in a rivalry which, though not always openly declared is none the less deadly. The elder child tries either to preserve his superiority or, if it is already endangered at least to prevent the younger child from attaining superiority. The older the second child becomes and the greater the part he takes in activities which formerly appeared to be the prerogative of the elder child, the more reasonable seems the latter's fear of being overtaken and surpassed. He endeavours in every way to safeguard his superior position as the elder and more advanced child.

What has been said about the first child suggests the situation which the second child meets. He never loses sight of the brother or sister who has got a short start of him. He fully realizes that the elder child is endeavoring to impose his superiority on him. He resents the imputation that he is less important. He regards everything the other child can do and he himself cannot do as an indication of his own inferiority. So every second child tries to catch up to the first child. This explains why second children are generally much more active than first children, whether they choose the line of useful achievement or naughtiness.

The outcome of the rivalry between the first and second child depends mainly on the help each child gets from others. The one who has the parents on his side is, of course, in a stronger position. Occasionally also an elder child, like Esau in the Bible, may renounce his birthright because he simply gives up trying to hold his position against the attacks of the younger child. The child who emerges victorious from the struggle is more likely to be successful throughout the remainder of life than the other, who will always accept defeat too easily. The duel between the two first children generally decides the whole subsequent course of their lives.

As frequently observed, however, one child is not always victorious in everything and the other defeated in everything. One achieves superiority in one province and the other in another. When this happens we have the plainest proof that the development of individual character is determined even in the smallest detail by the attitude to environment adopted in childhood.

It is not too much to say that we usually find a fundamental difference both as regards nature and character between the first two children. This becomes easy to understand if we remember that each of the two tries to achieve superiority in the very field where the other encounters difficulties. The younger child in particular develops an almost uncanny power for detecting the elder child's weak points and proceeds to win praise from parents and teachers by achieving brilliant successes where the other has failed. When there is keen rivalry and only a slight disparity of ages between two children of the same parents, we often find that later on at school each does particularly well in subjects in which the other does badly. If one child is puny and ailing the other grows up robust and hardy. If one is exceptionally clever at lessons the other tries to win recognition by success in something else. A child whose rival is very attractive in appearance will probably try to impress people with his intelligence or courage; but obviously it would be impossible to enumerate all the variations produced by this preference for antithesis.

The antithesis often seems to be based on inherited capacities, especially if each of the children appears to take after a different parent. But a child's psychological attitude can make the physical likeness to one parent more pronounced. A certain similarity may result from imitation of this parent's facial expressions, gestures, attitudes and peculiarities of speech; for a characteristic cast of features is gradually formed by constant repetition of the same facial movements.

To a far greater extent, however, similarity of nature and character is the outcome of the child's special training. It is true that we cannot tell beforehand why the child should imitate this particular parent. We can only be wise after the event. Often the child tries to acquire the characteristics of the parent whose ally in family quarrels he has become. He seizes on these characteristics because he hopes to reach the goal of superiority by evincing like the parent who is his ally a definite character as against the other members of the family. Actuated by the same desire to gain power, many children imitate the parent with whom they are in direct conflict.

Freud fully recognizes the importance of this situation for the formation of a child's character. But while in his eyes it is indicative of a very complicated development of the Ego-ideal, which makes the feared and hated parent a secret object of love, Individual Psychology has a very simple explanation to offer. The parent who counters many wishes and is very severe is the child's conception of power. This explains why children imitate the parent they fear. They merely wish to have this parent's power. So we are able to formulate the only fundamental law governing the development of the child's character: *he trains those qualities by which he hopes to achieve independence or even a degree of power and superiority in the family constellation.*

In a large family of children the conflict between the first and second child is repeated under some form or other lower down in the family, but it generally tends to be less fierce. Consequently children who come in the middle of a family usually develop more balanced characters. The third child frequently sides with one of the two elder children. Often two children lower down in the family treat each other as rivals like the first and second children.

The youngest child has a special rôle to play. Not merely one child, but all the other children are ahead of him. All the other members of the family spoil him and regard him as the little one. He generally develops characteristics which make it likely that other people will help him to shape his life, such as helplessness, a winning nature and whimsicality. But youngest children often prove very clever if their smallness becomes an impulse for outstanding achievements.

A boy in a family of girls and vice-versa one girl in a family of boys is in a special position. These children will form a characteristic appreciation of their rôles and will develop qualities which help them to play these rôles.

They often overestimate the importance of the rôle of their own sex, because this represents the essential difference between themselves and all the other children. Naturally the importance they attach to the rôle played by their own sex also depends on the value attached to it within the whole family and above all on the value attached by the parents to their own sex rôles, with the possible superiority of either the father or the mother.

So it becomes understandable why people adopt a certain attitude to their fellow beings in childhood, and why above all they get a definite idea of themselves. We must now try to see why a line of conduct which was reasonable and understandable in childhood is pursued throughout the rest of life.

The Life Plan and the Life Style

At birth the child encounters an unknown world and a mode of life which he has to learn. Above all he has to learn the rules of the human community, to perform functions and master the tasks set by life. At first the child sees only that part of life and of the human community which is bound by his environment, the family in which he is living. To him this environment means "life" and the members of the family seem to be "the human community" and he attempts to adapt himself to them.

He seeks to maintain himself within this concrete community by means of a variety of acquired accomplishments, characteristics, modes of behaviour, capacities, and artifices. The difficulties he encounters have been outlined in previous chapters. If we now examine the situation more closely we find that the child is bound to get the impression that the difficulties he personally experiences are the absolute difficulties of life. He does not realize that the other people round about him are involved in conflicts of an entirely different nature. His growing intelligence prompts him to overcome the difficulties of his position, so far as this appears possible, unaided and alone.

This explains why every individual by the time he is four to six years old has developed a definite character and why any fundamental change of character after the fourth to sixth year is hardly possible. Character is therefore simply the manifestation of a certain plan which the child has evolved and to which he will adhere throughout the rest of his life.

A child's life plan does not grow out of a certain peculiarity nor out of isolated experiences, but out of the constant repetition of certain difficulties, real or imagined, which he encounters. Each individual will find out special ways and means which appear to be serviceable for his special plan. Out of the individual's special life plan develops the life style which characterizes him and everything he does. His thoughts, actions and wishes seize upon definite symbols and conform to definite patterns. The life style is comparable to a characteristic refrain in a piece of music. It brings the rhythm of recurrence into our lives. Everyone offers the stoutest opposition to any attempt that is made for whatever reason to change his life style.

So we can understand why an only child becomes timid if he feels that to be alone and unaided is the greatest hardship in life—a difficulty which cannot be surmounted, and why he betrays himself at every turn if he rates his importance in the community in terms of the recognition and consideration he gets. We can understand why the eldest child of a family may live in constant dread of being supplanted and why a second child may always feel at a disadvantage. It also becomes clearer why in later life these people continue to behave as though they were still living in the same situation as in childhood.

In addition to the difficulties encountered within the family circle, the child's social environment plays an important part in fixing the life plan. The family's position in the community may cause the child to conclude that community life involves certain social and economic dangers. Social conditions may determine the ideas he forms about his position in relation to his comrades and playmates—in short, in relation to all his fellow beings. In order to contend with all these dangers he tries to evolve a definite plan.

An imaginary example may make the situation plainer. Let us picture a child growing up in a colony of thieves. He learns that if he is to maintain himself at all he must keep a careful watch on his property, distrust others and defend himself against their depredatory tendencies. Later on he is able to leave the colony and live in the ordinary world where thieves do not compose the entire population. But he continues to behave as before, because his chief fear in life is to become the victim of a thief. He does not believe the assurances other people give him that this fear is excessive, and is always looking out for incidents which appear to justify his behaviour. Whenever anything is stolen he feels triumphant. If on the other hand he hears of an honest finder who has given up his find, he is inclined to dismiss the report as untrue and say that he is not simpleton enough to believe such a fantastic story. And if sooner or later it becomes impossible for him to doubt a person's honesty, he gets out of his dilemma in another way. This man, he says, must certainly be crazy—at least, he is different from normal people.

Probably, however, his companions will appeal to his better nature and tell him that he really must give up his unreasonable mistrust. He may then try to prove that he is broadminded and actually give his confidence to some person; but it is practically certain that the first person he trusts will turn out a thief—partly because people of this type have been familiar to him from childhood and he feels secretly at home with them, and partly because he can turn the incident to account as an irrefutable argument: "There now, you see what happens if I believe what you say!" After this he can continue to practice without let or hindrance the rules of conduct he learned as a child and hold the wickedness of other people responsible for all the disagreeable experiences he goes through in consequence.

This obviously imaginary example of a single peculiar circumstance exaggerated out of all proportion to the real conditions of life illustrates firstly the importance of the life plan. Secondly it shows that it is possible to persist in the course first chosen only by grossly misrepresenting facts encountered later. We are forced to regard everything we see and all our experiences from a biased standpoint if we wish to preserve intact the mistaken ideas about life and ourselves which we formed as children. The private brand of logic which each person evolves appears to justify his mistaken behaviour, and prevents him from seeing that most of the difficulties and disappointments in his life are the logical consequences of mistakes in his life plan.

Notes

1. It is a well-known fact that birds fitted to share the struggle for existence and to rear their young in pairs, gather together in flocks before undertaking the difficult task which a long journey involves. Likewise weak, defenceless animals form herds in order to organize a better defence. The formation of a community is a very effective way of preserving existence, and therefore it is often adopted, but it is not the only way. Animals similar to those living in communities are also frequently found leading a solitary mode of existence.
2. Alfred Adler.

CHAPTER 5

On Clarifying Basic Adlerian Concepts: A Response to Maddi

RICHARD ROYAL KOPP

Comparisons between Individual Psychology and other schools of thought help to clarify the fundamental principles of Individual Psychology. Maddi (1978) calls attention to points of similarity and difference between Existential and Adlerian theory. Some of his conclusions are inaccurate, however, and convey an erroneous view of Individual Psychology. The points at which Maddi misinterprets Individual Psychology will be identified and discussed in this paper. Maddi's conclusions will be re-evaluated in light of these corrections.

Future Orientation: Life Plan versus Life Style

Maddi accurately points out that Individual Psychology views the person as a meaning-creating organism. "We experience reality always through the meaning we give it; not in itself, but as something interpreted" (Adler, 1958, p. 3). Maddi also notes that Individual Psychology emphasizes directionality and the future in contrast to the past as a basis for explaining behavior. However, these concepts seem insufficiently used in Maddi's analysis. One source of difficulty is that Maddi uses Adler's phrase "life plan" (Adler, 1959) in referring to Adler's conceptualization of personality.

Adler began using "life style" in place of "life plan" in 1926 (Ansbacher & Ansbacher, in Adler, 1969, p. xvi) in order to emphasize the individual's style of implementing this plan in everyday life (Ansbacher, Note 1). This shift in terminology placed even greater emphasis on the direction of the striving and the method of movement. Maddi's use of the earlier term seems to contribute to several difficulties in his analysis.

Maddi sees clearly an important subtlety in Individual Psychology, one which views the person as striving toward ideals, and not as unfolding in inevitable, patterned potentialities or as being pushed along by instincts and drives (Maddi, 1978, p. 184). His observation that Individual and Existential Psychologies are similar in their future orientation would be strengthened, however, if he were to emphasize the striving for perfection and significance which finds individual expression in the fictional final goal of the life style instead of emphasizing the "life plan." Adler's mature theory emphasizes the direction of the striving and gives a subordinate role to inferiority feelings and their compensations (Ansbacher & Ansbacher, in Adler, 1956). Adler states, "The main problem of psychology is to comprehend the direction-giving, pulling forces and goals which guide all other psychological movements" (Adler, 1930, 1973, p. 216). The similarity to Sartre's "pull toward an as yet unformulated future" (Maddi, 1978, p. 184) is striking.

Inferiority Feelings, Compensation, and Choice

Observing that inferiority feelings are a given in Individual Psychology but that they reflect a decision in Existential Psychology, Maddi concludes that personal choice is emphasized more in Existential Psychology than in Individual Psychology. Maddi's premise is inaccurate, however. First, Adler identifies two kinds of inferiority feelings: universal feelings of inferiority and exaggerated feelings of inferiority (Adler, 1958). Both types of inferiority feelings give rise to compensatory strivings. Choice plays a crucial role in this compensatory process.

Universal Feelings of Inferiority

Universal feelings of inferiority are indeed a given of human nature, as Maddi suggests. They are biologically and anthropologically given and rooted in our physical limitations, which in turn demand that we form social units in order to survive. Biologists (Darwin, 1915) and anthropologists (Kropotkin, 1914; Leakey & Lewin, 1977; Montagu, 1966) have supported this thesis.

Seemingly there is no decision at the biological level. Decision making plays a crucial role, however, when we consider the compensatory striving of the organism in response to these biologically based feelings of inferiority. Compensating for universal feelings of inferiority generates a striving for perfection, significance, and security in harmony with other fellow human beings in order to overcome shared problems. Yet the particular expression of the striving in an individual depends on (a) a sense of identification with others; (b) personal self-ideals toward which the individual strives; (c) personal definition of security, significance, and success; (d) specific cooperative behavior patterns in which the individual has trained him/herself; and (e) conjunctive attitudes and feelings toward others which facilitate this movement. Each of these factors involves an individual's decision-making and meaning-creating processes. As such, they reflect, and indeed require, choices (often unconscious) which the individual makes.

Exaggerated Feelings of Inferiority

The second type of inferiority feelings are those which are exaggerated, intensified, and personalized. Adler called this the "inferiority complex" which "describes the attitudinal stand of a person who thereby expresses that he is not in a position to solve an existing problem" (Adler, 1935). This "attitudinal stand" reflects nonconscious choices made during childhood which form the basis of the style of life. In Adler's words, "I am convinced that a person's behavior springs from his opinion. We should not be surprised at this, because our senses do not receive actual facts, but merely a subjective image of them" (Adler, 1956).

Although it is true that Individual Psychology views the individual's decision making capability within an evolutionary context in which some "decisions" are made at the level of natural selection and species adaptation, it is clear that individual decision making is a basic and pervasive quality of the life style and of the individual's creativity. As we have seen, this is true for both universal and exaggerated feelings of inferiority. This is why so many techniques in Adlerian psychotherapy are designed to help the client confront current decisions (Shulman, 1971) and re-evaluate current choices in order to make changes (Dreikurs, 1967; Mozdzierz, Macchitelli, & Lisiecki, 1976).

Social Interest and "Choosing the Future"

Maddi's suggestion that Individual Psychology may not elaborate the personal aspects of growth to the degree that Existential Psychology does seem accurate. The two positions complement each other in this regard. Individual Psychology adds a crucial dimension to the growth process which is absent in Existential Psychology, that is, the special context in which personal growth occurs. For Individual Psychology, choosing the future—the unpredictable and unknown—is not the primary component of healthy choice. While future choice may be associated with all healthy choices, one could choose the future in an unhealthy way. For example, one could choose to jump off a bridge or to play Russian roulette, thus demonstrating a willingness and desire to "tolerate the unknown and the unpredictable." Most of us would agree that these would not characterize healthy choices, primarily because they are potentially destructive to oneself or others and because they do not contribute to the individual or to the common welfare.

Choice, specifically choosing the unknown and the unpredictable, is inevitably present in healthy compensation for inferiority feelings. It has been noted that we all strive toward goals which compensate for inferiority feelings. The compensation is healthy, according to Individual Psychology, if it contributes to others as well as to oneself. This is often referred to as "meeting the needs of the situation." Conversely, striving for personal superiority over others in order to compensate for exaggerated and intensified feelings of inferiority is maladaptive and not a healthy choice. Individual Psychology and Existential Psychology would appear to have a point of agreement here: Socially interested compensatory striving in a task-oriented direction expresses a willingness to encounter the unknown and therefore risk failure. The new behavior which risks failure attests to the sense of worth of the individual and models the courage to be imperfect. This is healthy functioning. Analogously, maladaptive functioning, according to Individual Psychology, would involve "choosing the past," a movement characterized by safeguard mechanisms which protect against "basic anxiety," the fear of being proven worthless (Adler, 1956). This movement expresses a conviction that a failure in life's marketplace would be taken as a defeat—proof to all that one is of little value and has no place among one's fellow humans.

In summary, although it is true that a "future orientation" is present in healthy choices and a "past orientation" is present in unhealthy choices, neither orientation is the sole defining characteristic of these directions. The social context and social interest are important for understanding healthy and maladaptive behavior. This distinguishes Individual Psychology from Existential Psychology and from most other psychological systems.

The Social Context and Choice

Individual Psychology emphasizes the social context, as Maddi notes. However, Maddi's suggestion that "concrete, conventionally defined goals" and "socially-defined roles" characterize compensatory striving in Individual Psychology is incorrect. Maddi concludes that life-style goals are conventionally defined, giving only limited occasions for decision making and in routine actions and conventional meanings. These erroneous conclusions are based on Maddi's argument that "if felt inferiorities are universal and conditioned socially, then goals couched in terms of socially-defined roles are to be valued as compensatory efforts" (Maddi, 1978, p. 190). The important role of individual choice in compensating for inferiority feelings has already been discussed. Unfortunately, Maddi, like many others, presumes that social embeddedness implies social conditioning, a "dedication to the pursuit of socially-sanctioned roles" and pursuit of "behavioral stability" (Maddi, 1978, p. 190). An examination of the nature of the compensatory goal, social role, life style, and social embeddedness will further support the contention that Maddi's conclusions are in error.

The Compensatory Goal embodies the direction of an individual's law of movement. It represents the individual's personal, subjective answer to the questions "For me, where does security and significance lie? How can I compensate for my feelings of inadequacy so that I can safeguard my self-esteem?" Controlling, getting, opposing, and martyrdom are examples of compensatory life style goals (Adler, 1935, 1956, 1969; Mosak, 1959, 1971, 1973). Two points are important here. First, goals themselves are chosen by the individual in response to that individual's perception of his or her early environment. The choice represents the individual's finding of a psychological role in the family (in contrast to Maddi's "conventional role") in the family. Thus choice plays an essential part in the emergence of an individual's life style goal. The choice is made without awareness, much like the choice which occurs in the developing of one's "fundamental project" (Maddi, 1978, p. 183). Note that one's choice is limited, not by convention, but by the fact that early life style choices limit future directions. We will discuss this in greater depth below.

The Social Role

Maddi uses becoming an excellent physician to illustrate a typical goal. Desiring to become a physician is not a life style goal, however. Rather, it is an example of a concrete goal, one which is consciously set. It is also a social role, an occupation. Other occupations exemplify still other social roles. Roles of mother or father and roles related to group affiliation such as religion, nationality, or gender are also examples of social roles. Any single role can express several life style goals, depending on the purpose for which the role is pursued. On the other hand, any particular life style goal might be expressed through a variety of social roles. Mosak's (1968) description of how the same behavioral symptoms can express several goals and how several behaviors can serve a particular life style goal expresses the same point.

To illustrate, let us take Maddi's example of the excellent physician. The purpose of filling this social role could be to contribute to society by alleviating sickness and suffering. Perhaps the choice of becoming a physician expressed a striving to overcome a sense of inadequacy in the face of death; Adler saw his own career choice in medicine as a compensatory attempt to overcome his fear of death (Bottome, 1957; Mosak & Kopp, 1973). Yet other possibilities exist. Becoming a physician could express a striving for control over others or for prestige. Here, the same social role serves a goal of neurotic superiority by striving to elevate oneself over others. Thus, it is the style in which the social role is filled, and not the role itself, which defines the nature of the compensatory striving.

We noted above that different roles can serve a particular lifestyle goal. For example, a direction other than becoming a physician could have been chosen to compensate for a fear of death. Some such compensatory choices (like that of becoming a physician) would express some measure of social interest: becoming a nurse, for example, or perhaps an undertaker. Other compensatory directions, however, would reflect an exaggerated and intensified feeling of inadequacy and helplessness in the face of death. These compensations would constitute a withdrawal from life through neurotic or psychotic safeguarding strategies. One could develop a morbid preoccupation with death or attempt to defeat death by hallucinating that one is God in order to achieve imagined immortality. Here, again, we see that it is the style and purpose of filling a social role, not the social role itself (as Maddi suggests) which characterizes the compensatory striving for significance and security. Also it is clear that the social context does not determine individual choice in Individual Psychology.

Social Embeddedness in an Evolutionary Perspective

Maddi's misinterpretation of life style goals as "conventionally-defined," and his notion that these goals encourage "routine actions and conventional meanings" ignores an often misunderstood dimension of social interest: Socially interested attitudes and behavior must be viewed from the perspective of evolution. Adler found that many followers and observers of Individual Psychology make

the mistake of understanding what we call community as a private circle of our time, or a larger circle which we should join. Social interest means much more. Particularly, it means *feeling with the whole, sub specie aeternitatis,* under the aspect of eternity [Adler's emphasis]. It means a striving for a form of community which must be thought of as everlasting.... It is never a present-day community or society, nor a political or religious form. Rather, the goal which is best suited for perfection would have to be a goal which signifies the ideal community of all mankind, the ultimate fulfillment of evolution. (Adler, 1933)

It follows that choices conforming to present social norms are not necessarily in the social interest. It is the current "needs of the situation," functioning as an approximation of the ideal community of mankind, which are the only real criteria for assessing socially interested behavior and attitudes. Since society can never be certain which is the correct ideal and which path can best reach it, there can be no concrete, fixed definition of social interest. Yet, the parameters of social interest are relatively clear and stable: increased freedom for all, an opportunity for people to live a life of contribution, feeling a sense of community with others and a sense of dignity and worth for oneself. Martin Luther King Jr.'s civil disobedience in the sixties is considered to be an excellent example of nonconforming dissenting behavior which is in the social interest (Ansbacher, 1968).

Clearly, the movement of individuals and groups toward psychological and social goals which are in the social interest requires neither conventionality nor routinism. On the contrary, socially interested movement increases choices and opens new directions for the individual and for the ever-larger social units of which one is a part. It seems evident, therefore, that social embeddedness and social interest never determine individual choice.

Consciousness, Determinism, and Choice

Although it is true that Adler rejected Freud's idea of the structural unconscious with its determinism, nonconscious[1] processes play a central role in Individual Psychology. For example, the basic convictions of the life style, including the goal, are nonconscious. Maddi is correct, however, when he points out that consciousness, specifically conscious choice reflecting responsibility for one's behavior and intentions, plays an important role in Individual Psychology. Yet his characterization of Individual Psychology is misleading in that he implies that most or all human processes are conscious according to Individual Psychology. In actuality, his examples of these conscious processes, "safeguard mechanisms," "fictional finalisms" and "life plans," each function outside of awareness. Adler defined unconscious as "not understood" (Adler, 1956). Safeguard mechanisms, usually neurotic symptoms or aggressive or distancing behavior, "serve an unconscious, hidden function" (Ansbacher & Ansbacher, in Adler, 1956, p. 263). Any character trait "will be wholly or partly 'in the unconscious' depending on what the self-consistency of the personality requires" (Adler, 1956, p. 267). Fictional finalisms and life plans similarly are "carried on in the darkness of the unconscious" (Adler, 1956, p. 78; Ansbacher & Ansbacher, in Adler, 1956, p. 88).

Despite Maddi's suggestion that Existential Psychology emphasizes personal choice more than does Individual Psychology, his characterization of Existential Psychology's position on choice and determinism is equivalent to Adler's "soft determinism." The Ansbachers (in Adler, 1956) point out that

> Although the objective factors of heredity and environment, organ inferiorities, and past experiences are utilized by the individual in the process of forming his final goal, the latter is still a fiction, a fabrication, the individual's own creation. Such causality corresponds to "soft" determinism, that is "determinism from the inner nature of life," as contrasted to "hard determinism from external pressures alone" (William James, according to Murphy, 1947.) (In Adler, 1956, p. 89)

Maddi's interesting discussion of Existential Psychology and determinism captures a different, yet entirely consistent, aspect of "soft determinism." The creativity of the individual contributes some level of "free" choice. It is not totally free according to Individual Psychology, but neither is it totally determined by external factors. Maddi states that, for Existential Psychology,

> The initial choice made by a person is regarded as free in the sense of being undetermined. But as soon as the choice is made, it has consequences, e.g., others respond to the person in particular ways, certain alternatives are no longer available, and the person may begin to think of himself in particular ways. Assuming responsibility for the choice amounts to accepting the definition of self that ensues from it. (Maddi, 1978, p. 188)

This is precisely true in Individual Psychology as well. As the child strives to develop, he "strives to develop along a line of direction fixed by the goal which he chooses for himself" (Adler, 1956, p. 187). Thus, although "the origin of the law of movement is attributed to the 'free creative power' of the child" (Ansbacher & Ansbacher, in Adler, 1956, p. 188), the life style stabilizes at about five years of age, after which the child's "attitude to his environment is usually so fixed and mechanized that it proceeds in more or less the same direction for the rest of his life" (Adler, 1956, p. 189). One can change one's life style, however, "by the individual's own recognition of his faults and errors" (Adler, 1937). These statements contradict Maddi's conclusion that Existential Psychology emphasizes choice more than Individual Psychology. Instead, both Individual Psychology and Existential Psychology emphasize personal choice and individual freedom within a causal framework of "soft determinism."

Summary

In this paper the author presents a critique of Maddi's comparative analysis of Individual and Existential Psychologies. The present discussion agrees with Maddi's view that Individual Psychology sees persons as creating meaning, orienting themselves toward the future, exercising conscious choices, and striving toward ideals. It is argued that Maddi (1) misinterprets Individual Psychology's concept of inferiority feelings, failing to note the different types of inferiority feelings and their implications, and erroneously concluding that inferiority feelings limit individual choices; (2) relies on "life plan" instead of the later "life style," which emphasized the role of choice in personality development and functioning; (3) views compensatory striving as conventionally defined and socially determined, ignoring the role that subjectivity, choice, behavioral style, and purpose play in this striving; (4) ignores the fact that socially interested attitudes and behavior can increase choice; and (5) misconstrues "safeguard mechanisms," "fictional finalisms," and "life plans" as conscious instead of nonconscious processes.

The present author agrees with Maddi that both Existential Psychology and Individual Psychology are future oriented and that Existential Psychology, more than Individual Psychology, emphasizes personal aspects of growth. Contrary to Maddi's conclusions, however, both Existential Psychology and Individual Psychology emphasize personal choice and individual freedom within a causal framework of "soft-determinism." Individual Psychology holds that social interest characterizes healthy choices. It is argued that this social-evolutionary dimension is absent in Existential Psychology.

Reference Note

1. Ansbacher, H. Personal communication, 1973.

References

Adler, A. Complex compulsion as part of personality and neurosis. *Paper read at the Vienna Association for Individual Psychology,* 1935. In H. Ansbacher & R. Ansbacher (Eds.), *Superiority and Social Interest.* Evanston, III.: Northwestern University Press, 1964.

Adler, A. *The Individual Psychology of Alfred Adler* (H. Ansbacher & R. Ansbacher, Eds.). New York: Harper & Row, 1956.

Adler, A. *What life should mean to you* (1931). New York: Capricorn Books, 1958.

Adler, A. *The practice and theory of Individual Psychology* (1927). Totowa, N.J.: Littlefield, Adams & Co., 1959.

Adler, A. *The science of living* (1929). New York: Anchor Doubleday & Co., 1969.

Adler, A. *Superiority and social interest* (H. Ansbacher & R. Ansbacher, Eds.) (3rd ed.) New York: Viking Press, 1973.

Darwin, C. *The ascent of man.* London: Murray, 1915.

Dreikurs, R. *Psychodynamics, psychotherapy and counseling.* Chicago: Alfred Adler Institute, 1967.

Kropotkin, P. *Mutual aid.* Massachusetts: Porter Sargent, 1914.

Leakey, R. & Lewin, R. *Origins.* New York: Dutton, 1977.

Maddi, S. Existential and Individual Psychology. *Journal of Individual Psychology,* 1978, 34, 182–190.

Montagu, A. *On being human.* New York: Hawthorn, 1966.

Mozdzierz, J., Macchitelli, F., & Lisiecki, J. The paradox in psychotherapy: An Adlerian perspective. *Journal of Individual Psychology,* 1976, 32, 169–184.

Shulman, B. Confrontation techniques in Adlerian psychology. *Journal of Individual Psychology,* 1971, 27, 167–175.

Notes

1. I use the term "nonconscious" instead of "unconscious" to differentiate Adler's concept from Freud's conceptualization.

CHAPTER **6**

Adler's Organ Jargon

JANE GRIFFITH

Sometimes the mouth lies or the head does not understand;
but the functions of the body always speak the truth.
(Adler, 1956, p. 434)

Adler's concept of "organ jargon" provides both a framework and a technique for understanding and working with clients and patients who exhibit physical symptoms, whether or not the symptoms are predominantly organic or functional. Although Adler may not have originated the idea, he made it his own by carrying it forward, and, like the inferiority complex, "organ jargon" came to be associated with him. According to M. Robb, an Individual Psychologist writing in 1932, Georg Groddeck coined the term. Robb reports Groddeck as saying, "Illness is not merely a burden to be lifted, but is a ... declaration." This is the essence of organ jargon.

In 1933 Adler (1956) wrote that bodily functions "speak a language which is usually more expressive and discloses the individual's opinion more clearly than words are able to do.... The emotions and their physical expressions tell us how the mind is acting and reacting in a situation which it interprets as favorable or unfavorable" (p. 223). In 1934, Adler (1956) extended this understanding, writing that "someday it will be proved that every organ inferiority may respond to psychological influences and speak the organ language …. It is essential to understand this physical speech, which I have called "organ jargon" (pp. 308, 310).

Carruthers (1932), an Individual Psychologist, also understood somatic symptoms as manifestations of Life-Style, both as it is outwardly expressed and as it is inwardly experienced. He foreshadowed the findings of contemporary researchers when he hypothesized that involuntary (out of conscious awareness) somatic "gestures" can ultimately lead to organic disease. He explained that while physical symptoms may initially be functional, if the pattern of expression (jargon) continues, the organ undergoes "crystallization," resulting in organic illness.

The assumptions of Adler and his colleagues have been borne out (see Selye, 1976; Friedman & Rosenman, 1974); therefore, it is even more important than they theorized for therapists to understand and make use of organ jargon in their work with clients who somatize.

Organ Selection

The organ expressing the Life-Style will be particular to the individual.

1. It may be a genetically inferior organ, whose weakness and susceptibility make it "available" to the person.
2. It may be "modeled" after a person in the client's family of origin (such as "everyone in my family has allergies" or "my sisters and my mother all have stomach trouble"). There may be a congruence between the inferior organ and the family practice of expressing attitudes and feelings by means of it.
3. The organ may have an important symbolic value to the client (heart trouble may signify disappointment in life or love; breast cancer may be related to the loss of the parenting role in mid-life).
4. The organ may be "chosen" because it is "fashionable" (premenstrual syndrome and eating disorders may be "in," while migraines and irritable bowel syndrome may soon be passé).

The Unconsciousness of Organ Selection and Jargon

The client does not know why he or she has the physical symptom or illness and is only aware that he or she suffers. It would not be to the person's advantage to be conscious of the symptom selection or its purpose. Dreikurs (1967) clarified this when he wrote that "consciousness is not required for most human functions, be they physical or psychological…. [It] would often serve to impede rather than to assist" (pp. 63–64). Indeed, to continue to make use of the symptom, the client *must* remain unaware. Dreikurs (1977) explained: "Symptoms are chosen without conscious realization on the part of the patient. He remains completely unaware of what he is doing…. Otherwise, the symptom would lose its whole value and significance as an alibi or as an excuse" (p. 188).

Organ Jargon and Life-Style

Our understanding of the jargon will elude us unless we understand the person and make valid connections between the person's convictions and fictions and the symptom. As Dreikurs (1967) put it, "An organ can never 'speak its dialect' unless the individual permits it to 'speak'—unless he has a use for this symptom in his life-plan, in the pursuit of his fictive goal" (p. 28).

As holistic thinkers, Individual Psychologists know that Life-Style is revealed in any movement of the person, whether the behavior takes the form of thought, feeling, or action. A physical symptom is a behavior; it is part of the person's general line of movement, consistent with the Life-Style and in line with the person's striving toward a subjectively conceived goal of superiority or mastery. Adler (1956) stated that "the nature of psychogenic disease will remain unclear as long as the guiding characteristic of striving toward above has not been brought out" (p. 109).

The Jargon as a Solution

The jargon is not only a statement and a declaration, it is a solution; it is an imperfect solution, to be sure, but a solution, nonetheless. As Robert L. Powers (1983) expresses it, "Clients do not come to us with *problems*. We all have the same problems: how to earn a living, how to make friends, how to have a satisfying sexual relationship. Each of us has *solutions* for these problems according to our own Life-Styles. In psychotherapy, we address the client's *faulty* solutions."

While the solution is faulty, it is, in Dreikurs' (1977) terms, "The best and most effective answer the patient has found so far in regard to his needs in the situation" (p. 188). It is to the client's advantage for the therapist to respect the symptom as an ingenious response to what the client perceives to be an otherwise insoluble problem. Adler (1956) led the way: "We look upon symptoms as creations, as works of art" (p. 330). Once the client understands that the symptom is his or her own creation that has functioned as a solution, he or she will also be able to respect it. Having understood and respected the behavior, the client is free to reconsider, reorient, and retrain him- or herself.

Organ Jargon and Self-Esteem

It is the therapist's and client's task to uncover the meaning of the "jargon." It may be that the client's Life-Style does not allow for direct expression in the situation. The person may believe that clear, unambiguous movement would jeopardize his or her rehearsed place among others at home, at work, or in his or her social group. Why does "place" need to be safeguarded to the extent of physical suffering? Powers (1984) explains it this way: "To have a place among others is a primary necessity for our survival during the long period of infancy and childhood. Having a place is, in fact, 'a matter of life or death.' The biological necessity for place equates, in the mind of a symbol-using animal, with 'face,' or self-esteem; therefore, for the human being, self-esteem can be a 'matter of life or death.'" When we are willing to suffer pain for the sake of self-esteem, it is because self-esteem is more important to us than comfort. It is linked to our subjective assessment of our significance and what is required of us to maintain it (for example, "I'd rather die than be named a coward"). We generate symptoms when our significance is challenged and our Life-Style allows us no other possibility for meeting the challenge. Adler (1956) wrote, "All neurotic symptoms have as their object the safeguarding of the patient's self-esteem and thereby also the style of life" (p. 262). The symptom, therefore, may be thought of as if it were "an honorable way out" for the client.

What Is Organ Jargon?

The "jargon" or statement made by the organic symptom conveys the client's assessment of him- or herself, others, and the situation. We have numerous body-related metaphors that may provide the clue. Some are listed here, together with typical symptoms. It is the task of the therapist to help the client use his or her own words to translate the symptom's language. This list is intended to assist therapists in thinking in terms of organ jargon.

aching arm: I have such a burden. I'm his or her right arm. I'm carrying too much of a load.
aching back: Get off my back. I have no backbone. I'm leaning over backward for him or her. It bends me out of shape. I take it all on my back. I'm saddled with this load.
aching neck: It's a pain in the neck. I'm too stiff-necked to give in on this.
aching shoulders: I carry the world on my shoulders. I'm shouldering too much.

acne: I want to break out. I can't face it. I'm boiling over.

allergies: I'm so sensitive. I'm too rash. I can't tolerate any more. I've reached my limit on what I can stand.

anorexia: I have no appetite for it. I can't choke it down. You can't force it down my throat.

arthritis: I can't stand it. I'm freezing up. I'm rigid. I can't bend on that. I can't change. I can't give up my position. I'm hardened to the situation.

arthritis in hands: I can't handle this.

asthma, emphysema: It's smothering me. I feel suffocated by it.

blisters on hands: It's too hot to handle.

bowel irritation: I'm full of shit. I want to get free of this. I want to get clean or clear of this. It's a pain in the ass.

constipation: It turns me off. I don't give a shit. I'm shut out. I'm uptight about it. I won't yield on this. I won't give myself up to this. I won't give of myself.

fatigue: I'm tired of this. It wears me out.

frequent urination: Piss on it. I'm pissing my life away.

headache, migraines: I'm going to blow my top. I'm going to explode.

heart trouble: I haven't the heart for it. It makes me heavy-hearted. I'm broken-hearted.

impotence: Go screw yourself. I'm shrinking from you. I can't get it up. I don't have what it takes.

inattention, agitation: I'm strung-out, scattered. I can't get myself together. I've got to get going. I can't sit still for it.

indigestion: I have a hard time accepting this. I'm sour on it. I'm belly-aching about it.

nausea, bulimia: It makes me sick. It's nauseating. I can't stomach it. I want to throw up. What I'm forced to take in is disgusting.

obesity: I'm putting up a barrier between myself and others. Don't get close to me. I've got a wall around me so I won't get hurt.

stumbling, clumsiness: I can't stand on my own two feet. Don't lean on me. Don't count on me. I can't find my way.

ulcers: It's eating me up inside.

The Use of "Organ Jargon" with Clients

When you introduce the concept to clients, you will find that they usually enjoy it and will work with you to find expressions or statements that "fit." Adler (1956) wrote, "Behind the [symptom] … lies something more, something personal and entirely individual" (p. 330). It is the idiosyncratic meaning of the symptom that we strive to uncover. Organ jargon has the benefit of keeping therapy light. Adler (1956) wrote that he "always found it an immense advantage to keep the level of tension in the treatment as low as possible" (p. 346); discussing organ jargon assists the therapist in this goal.

If the jargon is not forthcoming by means of the introductory discussion, you may be able to elicit it by asking the client to describe the symptom in terms of figures of speech. Prompt him or her with sentence stems: "It's like…" "It's as if…" "It makes me feel…" You may also use one or more of the following questions. These are offered only to prompt and guide conversation, not as a sequential "questionnaire." They are based on a formula that the therapist attempts to unfold: symptoms express attitudes and have social consequences that reveal private logic.

1. Note and discuss the physical signs (that is, observable indications of the symptom).
2. What are the symptoms? Describe them as to:
   a. location
   b. intensity
   c. duration
   d. size, weight, density
   e. shape
   f. color

Exploration of any one of these aspects of the symptom can prompt or reveal the jargon. In this connection, it is helpful to ask the client to draw a picture of the symptom, or to ask the client to "be" the organ, using the gestalt technique.

3. Are there any accompaniments to the symptom?
   a. emotional
   b. behavioral
   c. sensory
4. When did you first notice this symptom?
   a. Where were you?
   b. Who was there?
   c. What happened?
   d. How did you feel (affect)?

The setting may provide the "situation" you are seeking. "Who was there?" may reveal the "target" person against whom the symptom is being directed or for whose "benefit" it is being generated. To ask what happened may tell you the "challenge." The feeling tone will reveal the person's evaluation.

5. What else was going on in your life at the time? How did you feel about it? If the situation in number 4 doesn't provide the jargon's meaning, this may reveal the exogenous factor and the jargon.

6. Have you noticed a pattern? When has the symptom:
   a. recurred or intensified?
   b. disappeared or abated?
7. What happens as a consequence of the symptom? Who is most affected?
   a. in the family
   b. at work
   c. among friends or in the community
8. Can you see any way in which these consequences could be useful, beneficial, preferable, or desirable to you in your situation? Here we are concerned to discover the justification in the private logic for the unconscious willingness to suffer. As stated above, people are willing to suffer for some more significant private value connected with self-esteem; for example, to gain or maintain the position as the "good" person or the one who is victimized and therefore deserves special consideration, or to safeguard against the loss of such a position.
9. Let's try to imagine how *someone else* might gain these "benefits" without this symptom. It is impossible for the client to imagine him- or herself operating any other way, since we can only do what we have learned how to do. Therefore, we must call upon the person's common sense by asking the person to imagine others in the same situation, especially others they admire, and to draw out several scenarios. You will most likely get answers like, "Well, my sister would just say, 'I'm not going to put up with that!' And she wouldn't either! But *I* can't do that."
10. What would happen if you used one of these approaches to gain these "benefits"? Here we want to identify those ideas, values, judgments, and convictions that argue against the common sense and direct, symptom-free movement, and also uncover how the person's "place" would be jeopardized by behavior other than maintenance of the symptom.

Limits to What the Therapist Can Do

The counselor will have already taken a complete history of the client, perhaps will have completed a Life-Style Assessment, and will have asked The Question (to differentiate between whether the symptom is predominantly organic or functional). The counselor will also have ensured that the client is getting appropriate medical attention for the symptom. For while the therapist and client search for the symbolic meaning of the symptom, its function in terms of the Life-Style, and to master new ideas and operations, the symptom is inflicting physical damage that must be interrupted.

As Carruthers (1983) wrote, "The foundations of the disease by which we die have been laid earlier in life through our habits of thought, feeling, and of action."

We believe that every physical symptom or illness has psychological meanings, but we do not profess that organic damage may be cured solely through psychotherapy. "The limits of curability by psychological treatment are determined by the extent to which the functional unity of the individual has been broken up so that organic changes of an irreparable nature have set in" (Crookshank, 1933).

References

Adler, A. (1956). *The Individual Psychology of Alfred Adler.* H. L. Ansbacher & R. R. Ansbacher (eds.). New York: Basic Books.

Carruthers, J. (1932). Organic disease and affective life. *Individual Psychology Medical Pamphlets, 4,* 40–49.

Crookshank, F. (1933). Individual Psychology and health. *Individual Psychology Medical Pamphlets, 9,* 46–55.

Dreikurs, R. (1967). *Psychodynamics, psychotherapy, and counseling.* Chicago: Alfred Adler Institute.

Dreikurs, R. (1977). Holistic medicine and the function of neurosis. *Journal of Individual Psychology, 33*(2), 171–192.

Friedman, M. & Rosenman, R. (1974). *Type A behavior and your heart.* New York: Knopf.

Powers, R. L. (1983, 1984). Personal communications.

Robb, M. (1932) Organ jargon. *Individual Psychology Medical Pamphlets, 4,* 61–67.

Selye, H. (1976). *The stress of life.* Rev. ed. New York: McGraw-Hill.

III
The Creative Self

CHAPTER 7

The Creative Self

MARK H. STONE

Those familiar with Individual Psychology know that Adler specified three main tasks in life—friendship, love, and work. However, in a paper published in the *Handbook of the Science of Work* (Giese, 1930) and reprinted as *Fundamentals of Individual Psychology* (Adler, 1970), Adler specified a fourth task as follows:

> There are four great questions of life which, although schematized, encompass all the relationships of life; the social relationship to fellowmen, the question of occupation, the question of love and the attitude toward art and creative endeavor [*schöferische Gestaltung*]. (Adler, 1930/1970, p. 8)

Ansbacher, who edited this reprint, speculated that the fourth task consisted of an extension of the work task to leisure and hobbies. Yet, no one actually knows what Adler specifically meant by this fourth creative task. He neither defined it further in this paper nor clarified it anywhere else. However, there is an argument for showing that the task of "art and creative endeavor" reaches far beyond what we call the "arts," and past what Ansbacher thought might be an application to leisure and hobbies. What Adler spoke of was the creative endeavor of the self in constructing what he earlier designated as *life line, guiding line,* or one of a host of other similar expressions. I have identified more than 30 such phrases Adler used to explain this idea (Stone, 2001). My argument for this interpretation of what Adler meant by a fourth task is based upon the fact that he indicated every person shows creativity in their solution to the tasks of life by constructing a subjective, personal viewpoint for how to interpret the world, and for how to think and behave. This is what constitutes the *creative self* at work. Another example supporting this position comes from Adler's paper on *Mass Psychology* (1937), where he writes:

> After long-continued study and reflection, I found that one's style of life—acquired in early childhood—is a result of the process of adapting oneself to the evolving structure of one's immediate environment; and that this process of adaptation is effected by relatively inadequate means, *by the creative power of the child* actuated by the evolutionary urge to conquer and surmount obstacles. (p. 114, my emphasis)

Similar statements supporting this position were made by Adler where he opined about "the creative power of the child" (Adler, 1969, p. 6; 1979, p. 187).

Appropriate Methods of Inquiry

Some study is necessary in order to ascertain how to investigate a subjective mode of thinking and behavior, such as an individual's creative power. Conducting a life style assessment is the analytic tool utilized in Individual Psychology to investigate subjective modes of thinking and behaving (Mosak & Shulman, 1971). However, where does this mode of inquiry fall within the broader scope of all research on self-inquiry?

The research modes by which we seek to gain knowledge are summarized in Table 7.1. This table suggests three levels of inference beginning first with the case study, proceeding to retrospective studies and, hence, to the prospective study, the only true experimental condition, also known in biomedical studies as clinical trials. Only the third level provides the true experimental conditions whereby specific hypotheses can be tested using a random selection of subjects and controls that address methodological bias.

The case study mode was the venue of Freud, Adler, and all clinician-theoreticians who have sought to illustrate abstract generalizations by means of individual case examples. The incest motif drawn from Oedipus is the best known example whereby Freud employed a mythic illustration

TABLE 7.1 LEVELS OF INVESTIGATION

Level	Type of Study	Unit of Study	Description of Study	Methodological Strengths	Weaknesses
1	Case Study	One person	Report or personal history	Generate hypotheses	Selection bias, lack of control group
2	Retrospective Study	Collection, database	Group description, aggregate	Generate hypotheses	Selection bias, lack of control, comparison of subgroups
3	Prospective Study	Groups with replications within	Controlled experiment, clinical trials	Test hypotheses, random selection, blind, double-blind control, placebo	

from Greek literature. He also published many case studies including Wolf Man and Dora. Adler is known for the case of Mrs. A and many other cameo illustrations. The elements of such an approach capitalize upon an illustrative individual. They report behavioral observations with a focus on forming generalized conclusions applicable to all persons. Such interpretations, however, are less frequently grounded upon incontrovertible data, but usually focus on an interpretation of data using a special emphasis and rationale for how this information should be interpreted from the writer's (subjective) point of view.

Karl Popper (1963) has addressed this matter, with specific mention of Adler. A substantial quotation from his writing clarifies this important point.

> I found that those of my friends who were admirers of Marx, Freud, and Adler, were impressed by a number of points common to these theories, and especially by their apparent *explanatory power*. These theories appeared to be able to explain practically everything that happened within the fields to which they referred. The study of any of them seemed to have the effect of an intellectual conversion or revelation, opening your eyes to a new truth hidden from those not yet initiated. Once your eyes were thus opened you saw confirming instances everywhere: the world was full of verifications of the theory.... As for Adler, I was much impressed by a personal experience. Once, in 1919, I reported to him a case which to me did not seem particularly Adlerian, but which he found no

difficulty in analyzing in terms of his theory of inferiority feelings, although he had not even seen the child. Slightly shocked, I asked him how he could be so sure. "Because of my thousand-fold experience," he replied; whereupon I could not help saying: "And with this new case, I suppose, your experience has become thousand-and-one-fold...." What, I asked myself, did it confirm? No more than that a case could be interpreted in the light of the theory.... It was precisely this fact—that they always fitted, that they were always confirmed—which in the eyes of their admirers constituted the strongest argument in favor of these theories. It began to dawn on me that *this apparent strength was in fact their weakness.* (pp. 34–35, my emphasis)

Popper's personal reflection clearly illustrates the problem with generalizing from cases selected with a biased and subjective viewpoint. This occurred even with Adler, a theorist for whom we have a special interest and affinity.

Often, many possible explanations for case histories are possible and the problem with theorists dealing with case illustrations is that multiple interpretations are not usually entertained. Yet, if we become perplexed by the differing interpretations possible from behavioral information, we miss the obvious fact that this mode of research inquiry is limited to the generation of hypotheses, as indicated by Table 7.1, and not to the explication of valid conclusions. Hence, the case study approach can only offer deceptively simple interpretations of complex data according to a particular mode of interpretation. This is the point clearly made by Popper. Nevertheless, the case study does offer a rich source of creative exploration by which to stimulate further investigations, and to proffer hypotheses. Even so, generalizations formed from selected case studies are highly suspicious unless more than selected corroborating evidence can be produced.

Methodological Issues in the Study of the Creative Self

Investigation of the creative self poses many methodological problems. Can we even investigate the subjective intricacies of the self by using objective procedures? Windelband (1904) proposed that information might be subclassified as *idiographic* or as *nomothetic.* By idiographic, he meant that data was subjectively oriented, and by nomothetic he indicated that data might be abstracted for its generalities, its "laws," so to speak. Ansbacher called Adler's psychology idiographic par excellence. The major fault of the case study approach is that generalizations made by relying only upon the idiographic mode all too soon become nomothetic! As Popper argued, case study advocates too frequently assume that the illustrative individual is normative for all other persons.

To investigate the creative self we must focus upon the subjective features of the individual, and the uniqueness of each person, but also determine the common elements that might be shared among all persons. Adler proposed that each person, very early in life, creatively constructs a self—designated by a life style—that typifies a mode of interpreting the world in concert with this subjective interpretation. A life style assessment is a case study interpretation. Consequently, it, too, is subject to all the criticisms raised earlier about the case study approach. However, this critique of the case study approach does not relegate this mode of inquiry to the garbage heap. Instead, it should be used with careful recognition that such a mode of inquiry is not normative in and of itself. It may generate hypotheses and it may foster explanations. These will have to undergo further scrutiny before they can be fully acclaimed.

Popper (1972) suggested that we *conjecture* boldly, but that we subject all our conjectures to intense *refutation*. Only those conjectures that survive such rigorous scrutiny should be retained. Even then, they should be continuously subjected to further refutation. His model for addressing conjectures was not to seek proof, but to refute hypotheses until there was a survival of only the fittest of the hypotheses. He further specified that every hypothesis must always be capable of being "falsified" if it was truly to be entertained as a working hypothesis.

Peirce (1940, 1957) had much earlier identified what he considered the only three legitimate modes for making inferences. He added to the well-known modes of deductive and inductive reasoning his creative addition—*abduction*. By abduction, Peirce pointed to an important mode of creative speculation in the process of inquiry. Those who want to consider every harebrained idea that comes along may greet this mode with satisfaction, but this was not the case for Peirce. He wanted abduction reserved for useful speculation that was rich in insight and would lead to productive outcomes.

A modern physicist, Feynman (1965) said exactly the same thing:

> In general, we look for a new law by the following process. First, we guess it. Then we compute the consequences of the guess to see what would be implied if this law that we guessed is right. Then we compare the result of the computation to nature, with experiment or experience, compare it directly with observation to see if it works. If it disagrees with experiment it is wrong. In that simple statement is the key to science. (p. 156)

Adler (1979) offered a somewhat similar statement:

> [Y]ou have to guess, but *you have to prove it* by other signs that
> agree. If you have guessed and the other signs do not agree, you
> have to be hard and cruel enough against yourself to look for
> another explanation. (p. 141, my emphasis)

In *guessing*, the emphasis is placed upon a stochastic or probabilistic guess,
and not upon blind speculation. Guesses are to be entertained as working
hypotheses—abduction according to Peirce. While Adler grasped the
essentials of guessing and refutation in clinical work, he appears to have
fallen victim to Popper's methodological criticism by trying to "prove"
rather than "refute" a hypothesis as the means for obtaining the generalizations required in science.

However, Adler's investigation of the creative self offers a rich palate of
opportunity. He emphasized that each person creatively constructs a self
illustrated by a life style. This creative self is the impetus by which individuals live their lives. These lives may be richly rewarding with friendships,
accomplishments, and satisfaction in love. They may also have little to sustain the self through friends and loving relationships, and little or no
accomplishment. The qualities selected by which one evaluates life determine the degree of satisfaction. To constantly complain about lack of stat-
ure, and ignore one's extraordinary good health is an illustration of how
data can be subjectively used to defend, refute, or ignore any subjective
interpretation about life. Adler's sine qua non for normality was *community feeling*. He argued that normality and wholesomeness as a person was
evident by one's orientation to others, and not to his and her selfishness or
self-aggrandizement.

Investigation of the creative self obligates us to first address operationally defining what we mean by the term, and then align it to investigations
that will explicate the concept. Bridgman (1961), who originated the idea
of operational definitions, described the process as follows:

> In general, we mean by any concept nothing more than a set of
> operations; the concept is synonymous with the corresponding set
> of operations. If the concept is physical, as of length, the operations
> are actual physical operations, namely, those by which length is
> measured; or if the concept is mental, as of mathematical continuity,
> the operations are mental operations, namely those by which we
> determine whether a given aggregate of magnitudes in continu-
> ous.... We must demand that the set of operations equivalent to
> any concept be a unique set, for otherwise there are possibilities of

ambiguity in practical applications which we cannot admit. (pp. 5–6)

Bridgman cautions us not to create concepts that are without operations. That is an important requirement, so we must be able to describe the operations that define the creative self if we are to discuss this concept at all. These operations must be clear and unambiguous. Furthermore, the operations for this concept should not overlap or be confused with those of another.

Operational definitions concerning the creative self should probably include aspects of the soul or psyche as expressed in the Greek sense. Adler (1979) wrote, "the very word 'psychology' means science of the soul." He argued that no psychology worthy of the name could neglect this important area by emphasizing a solely mechanistic view of the person. While Adler's point is evident to any clinician who knows from experience that psychotherapy includes "soul-work," it also opens the door to the vagaries of definition and to a variety of interpretations—some productive, others bizarre. Rank also addressed the importance of the soul in personality, especially in his work *Psychology and the Soul* (1950). However, there are therapists who eschew all but radically "behavioral" techniques, and there are those who will engage even the most outlandish practices. Psychology has had to contend with a wide range of treatment approaches based upon multiple interpretations of the personality and of the role of the self. There is little agreement within the field about what is deemed bona fide, and what is not. Even the recent movement to follow only empirically supported approaches in treatment is not without its critics. These controversies only add complexity to any investigation.

Any attempt to study the creative self must clarify terms, specify hypotheses that are testable, and pursue empirical investigations that will sustain or refute these hypotheses. While the case study can introduce stimulating inquiries by way of abduction or guessing, the crux of the matter rests upon conducting investigations that rigorously test the hypotheses that result from intelligent speculation.

Interestingly, Adler offers some useful models to investigate his theory. These are given in a paper written in 1913 (Adler, 1925). In this paper, he constructs what look like two regression models.[1] While they are not explicit mathematical expressions, they do, nevertheless, embody important aspects of Adler's psychology. The first models what he calls a "schematic picture of the peculiar orientation of neurotics and psychotics" (p. 40) and Adler states it as:

Individual + experience + environment + demands of life = a neurosis.

In this model, Adler says that the neurosis of the individual is said to result from inferiority, heredity, sexual constitution, emotionality, or character. Experiences, environment, and external demands also contribute. The result permits the persons to "take refuge in sickness" (p. 40). Adler argues that this model is a wrong conceptualization for the origination of neurosis. He further states, with no small insinuation against Freud's theories, that "wish fulfillment" and "libido" cannot be considered as causes either.

Adler next presents "a better formula":

Evaluation $(I + E + M)$ + Arrangement (Experiences + Character + Emotionality + Symptoms) = Personality Ideal.

I, E, and M stand for individual, experience, and environment, respectively. He explicates this formula saying:

> In other words, *the only definite and fixed point conceived of is the personality-ideal.* In order to approximate more nearly to his god-likeness, the neurotic makes a tendentious evaluation of individuality, his experiences, and his environment. But since this does not by any means suffice to bring him to his life-line or nearer to his goal, he provides experiences which his previously determined favorable applications made easier—of feeling set-back, deceived, suffering—all of which give him the trusted and desired basis of aggression. That he constructs so much from real experiences and from possibilities and builds just the type of character-traits and affect-preparations that fit into his personality-ideal, follow from the above description and has been discussed by me in detail. In a similar fashion the patient identifies himself with his symptoms, all his experiences taking the form that appears necessary and useful for the heightening of his feeling of personality. Not the slightest trace of a predetermined autochthonous teleology is to be found in this modus vivendi, projected and tenaciously adhered to be means of a self-suggested principal goal. The neurotic life-plan is maintained and teleologically arranged only by the urge toward superiority, by the careful evasion of dangerous-looking decisions, by previously tested wanderings along a few clearly determined lines of direction and the enormously increased safety-net. In consequence, the questions relating to the conservation or loss of psychic energy lose all their meaning. The patient will create just as much psychic energy as will enable him to remain on his path of superiority and express his masculine protest and god-likeness. (Adler, 1925, p. 41)

Adler makes an interesting point in the first sentence, printed in italics in the original paper, where he says, "*the only definite and fixed point conceived of is the personality-ideal.*" Adler conceives of the personality ideal as fixed. Consequently, he specifies the independent variables free to vary in support of the fixed dependent variable—the personality ideal. Adler further describes how the individual "*provokes experiences*" [emphasis in the original] and especially, how the individual "constructs so much from real experiences" to "fit into the personality-ideal." Such constructions are creative ones, albeit not always useful.

Adler's explanation reverses the customary regression equation by making the dependent variable fixed instead of free to vary from the influences of the independent variables. It is the independent variables that are "creatively adjusted" by the individual. Adler further explains that people "build" the variable characteristics as needed in order to fit them to suit the personality ideal. Hence, we arrive at what Adler specifies as the basic model:

Personality-ideal = an evaluation and arrangement of experiences.

Study of the Creative Self

Now we have models that can be tested for their validity. A variety of research studies could emanate from Adler's conception of personality formation and its relationship to mental illness. The creative self can now be investigated. Adler has offered in this early paper an exquisite approach by which to determine the validity of some aspects of his psychology. Gordon Allport (1955) recommended that all investigations of personality utilize both "objective" and "subjective" instruments. He argued that subjective measures should never be used alone, but always in combination with objective ones so as not to rely too much upon self-reports. In any case, perhaps so-called objective methods are frequently no more reliable than subjective self-reports. "Objectivity," if there is any in an objective test, usually results from using less ambiguous methods, and standardized scoring methods, usually lacking in so-called subjective tests. However, objective tests are not automatically immune to bias and subjectivity simply because we name them so.

A mix of insightful speculation and rigorous experimentation must be joined together in order to determine a useful outcome to the questions emanating from Adler's psychology, in this instance—the creative self. Several problem areas stand out.

1. The creative self can only be investigated if it is operationally defined so that the concept or any aspect of it is clearly understood by how it operates.

This task is harder than it appears. We use words, seemingly common and clearly understood, that actually are fraught with ambiguity. Research studies must provide clear, operational definitions about what is being investigated.

2. The investigation should address one of the inferential models suggested in Table 7.1. Comprehensive research programs may use more than one approach, but such investigations should provide a clear explanation of the design(s) used so that every step is understood, and so that the study is capable of being replicated. Methodological bias must be addressed. Campbell and Stanley (1966) introduce some of these issues. Revisions and amplifications are found in texts on research methods and designs (e.g., Isaac & Michael, 1981).

3. The tools used for gathering data need to be chosen with care. They need to be articulated with the concepts under investigation, but they must also meet psychometric standards. Reliability and validity need to be substantiated beyond generalizations. They must specifically relate to the concepts under investigation. Constructing measures must also be addressed (Smith & Smith, 2004).

4. Analysis of data should proceed beyond tests of significance to detailed investigations of both hypothesized and alternate models. Finally, there must be the more substantial investigation of the data (residuals) that do not conform to the hypotheses. Such approaches are part of the general literature on data mining. Studies emanating within Individual Psychology cannot remain ignorant of these matters.

Conclusion

In conclusion, I address the article that served to stimulate this paper—*The Creative Self in Adlerian Psychology* (Edgar, 1985)—and the major points made by the author. He rightly gives prominence to the role of creativity in Adler's psychology. It is this creative power of the person that formulates what we now call life style, and which designates the subjective construction of a unique and personal view of the individual. While clinicians learn the elements of life style analysis, the assessment process itself also contains the subjectivity of the clinician superimposed upon the subjectivity of the client. Can any clarity arise from such a process?

The morass of subjectivity that abounds in this area cannot lead to valid generalization unless we apply some rational criteria by which to compare and contrast data, and by which to determine what is the same and what is different in our observations. *Creativity* is an overworked word that needs more restriction on its use. Bridgman has indicated that we must define the word according to operations and not by subjective appellation. Not everything accomplished merits the title "creative." Wearing your shoes on the opposite foot, your clothes inside out, or your pajamas to school is not creative, but the activities of grade school children celebrating "backwards day." The compensations of many persons in addressing the tasks of life do not merit the designation "creative." They can often be seen as sad and pathetic attempts to cope that lead nowhere. When Adler used the word *creative*, he meant a constructive and ingenious means that humans employ in devising for themselves a subjective view of the self, the world, and how they should act. Adler spoke of that "spark" that impels individuals to movement. If we do not clarify terms, we cannot research this important topic. Feynman (1966) made this point in criticizing the word *energy* for students studying physics. He asked if the word *energy* actually explained anything, or whether or not it was merely an empty definition, a tautology. His test was as follows:

> Without using the new word [energy] which you have just learned, try to rephrase what you have just learned in your own language. Without using the word energy, tell me what you know now about the dog's movement. (p. 15)

Feynman argued that if one could not explain energy without resorting to the word itself, the word only served as a synonym, or empty definition and not an idea. For "creative self" to be a meaningful abstraction, a clear and pragmatic indication of its operations is required without the use of the phrase.

Second, Edgar (1985) rightly addresses the important distinction between group generalities and individual behavior. He offers this example:

> For a large number of slum children in a certain ghetto, all of whom are black and who come from divided homes, one may speculate that 80 percent will not complete high school. Nevertheless, for one child selected from that larger group, accurate predictions based on just heredity and environment simply cannot be made. (p. 337)

The important point to be made from this example does not concern his mention of heredity, environment, or the illustration he has chosen to use, but the fact that group generalizations, however true, are not sufficient proof for instances of individual behavior. A generalization is just what it means; it speaks to the general and not to the specific. While exceptions to the rule do not invalidate the generalization, the rule itself does not dictate the behavior of every individual. This is why the analysis of residuals is so important. We want to know not only how and why a certain hypothesis operates as it does, we also want to know the exceptions to the rule. The answers to these questions serve as a springboard to yet further questions, and the process continues.

Ross Mooney (1956) specified a program for creative research. In his program, he suggests that all outcomes provide

> a better conception of the [person] as a creative being, a better conception of the [person] we would become, and better ways of ordering the behavior and environment toward actualizing the [person] we would become. (p. 266)

Mooney wanted creative research, but he also wanted "more creative science." Good science is creative. It requires explicating the steps to take. Writing elsewhere (Stone, 2004), I have specified *Observing, Scoring, Measuring, Analyzing* and *Applying* as the most essential steps in science. Thus, science progresses by dialogue between the inner world of abstract ideas and the outer world of concrete experience. Ideas are hypothetical guidelines and experience brings them to life.

The answers to all these questions will not be easy to find, the work will be taxing, and the effort must be immense. Emerson (1965) put it well in his poem *The Sphinx* (1841, p. 447),

> Thou art the unanswered question;
> Couldst see thy proper eye,
> Always it asketh;
> And each answer is a lie.

Careful reasoning is the only way to proceed if we are to address the difficult problem of discerning how creativity can be operationally defined, and examined in the context of specific hypotheses. Adler was a strong proponent of reason. Science is the mode of reason and experimentation, insightful theory and the examination of data. The answers we find must not only describe, they must predict. To understand a process fully, we must do more than explain it. To understand a process fully, we must be able to predict a course of behavior that can be verified. That is the difficult task to accomplish in any research program, especially one that seeks to investigate the creative self.

References

Adler, A. (1925). *The practice and theory of Individual Psychology.* Paterson, NJ: Littlefield, Adams.
Adler, A. (1937). Mass psychology. *International Journal of Individual Psychology, 3,* 111–120.

Adler, A. (1969). *The science of living.* New York: Doubleday.

Adler, A. (1970). Fundamentals of Individual Psychology. *Journal of Individual Psychology, 26*(1), 3–16. (Original work published 1930.)

Adler, A. (1979). *Superiority and social interest: A collection of later writings* (H. L. Ansbacher & R. R. Ansbacher, Eds.). New York: Norton.

Allport, G. W. (1955). *Becoming: Basic considerations for a psychology of personality.* New Haven, CT: Yale University Press.

Bridgman, P. (1961). *The logic of modern physics.* New York: Macmillan.

Campbell, D., & Stanley, J. (1966). *Experimental and quasi-experimental designs for research.* Chicago: Rand McNally.

Edgar, T. (1985). The creative self in Adlerian psychology. *Individual Psychology, 41*(3), 336–339.

Emerson, R. W. (1965). The sphinx. In *Selected writings.* New York: New American Library. (Original work published 1841)

Feynman, R. (1965). *The character of physical law.* Cambridge, MA: MIT Press.

Feynman, R. (1966, April 1). *What is science?* Address to National Science Teachers Association, Los Angeles, CA.

Giese, F. (1930). *Handbook of the science of work.* Stuttgart: Institute of Technology.

Isaac, S., & Michael, W. (1981). *Handbook in research and evaluation.* San Diego, CA.

Mooney, R. L. (1956). Groundwork for creative research. In C. E. Moustakas (Ed.), *The self.* New York: Harper (pp. 261–270).

Mosak, H., & Shulman, B. (1971). *Life style inventory.* Chicago: Alfred Adler Institute.

Peirce, C. S. (1940). *The philosophy of Peirce: Selected writings* (J. Buchler, Ed.). New York: Bobbs-Merrill.

Peirce, C. S. (1957). *Essays in the philosophy of science* (V. Tomas, Ed.). New York: Bobbs-Merrill.

Popper, K. R. (1963). *Conjectures and refutations.* New York: Harper Torchbooks.

Popper, K. R. (1972). *Objective knowledge.* Oxford: Clarendon Press.

Rank, O. (1950). *Psychology and the soul.* New York: Barnes.

Smith, E., & Smith R. (2004). *Introduction to Rasch measurement.* Maple Grove, MN: JAM Press.

Stone, M. H. (2001). Adler's psychology of personality*: The Neurotic Constitution. The Canadian Journal of Adlerian Psychology, 31*(2), 10–25.

Stone, M. H. (2004). Steps to science. *Journal of Questioned Document Examination, 12,* 41–46.

Windelband, W. (1904). *Geschichte und naturwissenschaft.* Strassburg: Heitz.

Notes

1. A regression model specifies the hypothesized independent variables thought to influence and produce a selected dependent variable. The general form is Ind Var_1 + Ind Var_2 + Ind Var_3 + ... + Ind Var_n = Dependent Variable.

CHAPTER 8

The Creative Self in Adlerian Psychology

THOMAS E. EDGAR

Adler (1964, p. 142) took a certain pride in keeping a piece of metaphysics in Individual Psychology. At a time when "scientific" psychologists strove to separate themselves from philosophical or metaphysical considerations, Adler maintained an idealistic positivist position. He declared late in his career that

> unfortunately, there are many who have an erroneous view of metaphysics, who would like to see everything eliminated from the life of mankind which they cannot comprehend immediately …Every new idea lies beyond immediate experience. Vice versa, immediate experience never yields anything new. It is only the synthesizing idea which connects the data of immediate experience …. I see no reason to be afraid of metaphysics; it has had a very great influence on human life and development. *We are not blessed with the possession of the absolute truth, and on that account we are compelled to form theories for ourselves about our future and about the results of our actions.* (1964, p. 142, emphasis added)

Clearly Adler has placed the experiencing person at the very center of meaning. The person is, however, not just a passive receiver of experience, but an active participant in giving personal meaning to the empirical data of immediate experience. This creative power of the individual was a major intervening variable in Adler's thought through most of his long and productive career. He essentially developed a psychology with a soul (Adler, 1964).

Adler's psychology became a subjective psychology with the creative self as a central construct. In the dispute between Freud and his followers and Adler and his colleagues, this theme became a central battleground. In this regard Allport (1955) noted:

> Hence the individuality of man extends infinitely beyond the puny individuality of plants and animals, who are primarily or exclusively creatures of tropism or instinct.... Man talks, laughs, feels bored, develops a culture, prays, has a foreknowledge of death, studies theology and strives for the improvement of his own personality. (p. 22)

Given that Allport's speculation is accurate, then Adler (1964, p. 62) was one of those theorists who was a "voice in the wilderness" of the pre-World War I days crying that the self or soul must remain the focal point if psychology is to provide satisfactory explanations.

In proposing the creative self as a major theoretical construct in his theory, Adler introduced a sort of principle of indeterminacy similar to the Heisenberg principle in physics.

Adler (1970) was to claim that the environment and heredity acting together on the child provided only probabilities at most.

> ...consequently the view of those who believe in the causative influence of heredity on the one hand, or environment on the other are as complete explanations of his personality, made untenable by the assumptions of the creative power of the child. The drive (to move toward mastery, perfection) is without direction until it has been incorporated into the movement toward the goal which he creates in response to his environment. This response is not simply a passive reaction but a manifestation of creative activity on the part of the individual. It is futile to attempt to establish psychology on the basis of drives alone without taking into consideration the creative power of the child which directs the drive, molds it into form, and supplies it with a meaningful goal. (p. 414)

For large numbers of persons who were born under similar environmental conditions and with similar genetic inheritance, rather accurate probability predictions may be made. As an example, for a large number of slum children in a certain ghetto, all of whom are black and who come from divided homes, one may speculate that 80 percent will not complete high school. But for one child selected from that larger group accurate predictions based on just heredity and environment simply cannot be made.

One must consider, when trying to predict for one child, the creative power of *that* child. The behavior of that child is certainly influenced by both heredity and environmental conditions. Children (and adults) do tend to draw similar conclusions from similar circumstances. But the one who wishes to predict the future of an individual must know what use that individual has made of his experience. Environment and heredity provide the brick and mortar, but it is the way that the individual has used these materials which we must consider to understand that person. As Adler (1964) declared:

> We concede that every child is born with potentialities different from those of any other child. Our objection to the teachings of the hereditarians and every other tendency to overstress the significance of constitutional disposition is that the important thing is not what one is born with, but what use one makes of the equipment. We must ask ourselves: "Who uses it?" ... To understand this fact we find it necessary to assume the existence of still another force, the creative power of the individual. We have been impelled to attribute to the child a creative power, which casts into movement all the influences upon him and all his potentialities, a movement toward the overcoming of an obstacle. (pp. 176–177)

In the judgment of this writer, this addition of the creative self to Adler's psychology is one of the major reasons that his point of view gained so little acceptance by academic psychologists prior to World War II. The early psychologists were intent upon being "scientific," upon discovering the laws determining human behavior, of modeling psychology upon the "real" sciences such as chemistry and/or physics. With the concept of the creative self firmly in place, Adler's psychology clearly rejected the fundamental assumption of the scientific psychologists, the assumption that behavior was caused by a complex array of external and potentially understandable and measurable factors.

When combined with the need to move toward perfection and mastery, the concept of the creative power of the individual leads directly to the Adlerian construct, the style of life to be discussed else where.

Adler repeatedly returned to the creative self or to human creativity (creativity in the German has been variously translated into English as creative self or creative power) as he continued to develop his point of view.

Perhaps one of the clearest statements of his beliefs concerning creativity and the style of life is given below (Adler, 1964):

> We cannot know in advance what the child will make of all the influences and the experience of his organs. Here the child works in the realm of freedom with his own creative power. Probabilities abound. I have always endeavored to point them out and at the same time to deny that they are causally determining.... Here [in heredity and environment] there are thousands of possibilities in the realm of freedom and of error. Everyone will form an error, because no one can get hold of the absolute truth. (p. 187)

Adler, in placing the creative power of the individual in a central position in his psychology, allied himself with the emerging "third force" in psychology. To the "scientific" psychologist this decision-making power of the individual was written off as a part of error variance or as a nuisance variable. To Adler this power was central to the understanding of the human being; it became in his view an essential characteristic of the person.

References

Adler, A. (1964). The Individual Psychology of Alfred Adler: A systematic presentation in selections from his writings. H. L. Ansbacher & Rowena R. Ansbacher (eds.). New York: Harper & Row.

Adler, A. (1970). Superiority and social interest, a collection of later writings. H. L. Ansbacher & Rowena R. Ansbacher (eds.). Evanston, Ill.: Northwestern University Press.

Allport, G. (1955). Becoming: Basic considerations for a psychology of personality. New Haven: Yale University Press.

IV
Social Interest

CHAPTER 9

In Search of Social Interest

JACK HUBER

My life as a psychologist, both as a researcher and therapist, has been spent primarily in the pursuit of social interest. Consequently, I appreciate the opportunity to present ideas concerning social interest here.

I became interested in Alfred Adler as an undergraduate—I had become a psychology major because I hoped to learn something about human nature. For the most part, my course was a disappointment because of the strong behavioral zeitgeist prevalent during those times. Humans, according to this viewpoint, were little more than automatons, that is, byproducts of their environment. I did have one Freudian professor who gave me more of what I wanted, because, as Bettelheim (1982) has noted, one side of Freud's theory was a type of *seeleanalyse*—a *geisteswissenschaft* rather than a *naturwissenschaft* (a science of the spirit as opposed to a natural science). However, his theory seemed preposterous then and seems preposterous today. Quite simply, all anxiety cannot be traced to a fear of castration.

After receiving my bachelor's degree at Kent State University, I had the good fortune to attend the University of Vermont where I encountered Professor Heinz Ansbacher who introduced me to Adlerian psychology and thus opened the door to understanding the soul of humankind. At the heart of Adlerian psychology is the concept of social interest; this idea has provided for me the stimulus for over 40 years of research.

Who Was Adler?

Although Ansbacher (2004) has cogently argued that Freud taught Adler the art of therapy, as Ellenberger (1970) has also clearly shown, Adler was not a neo-Freudian; in fact, he influenced Freud, as can be seen in the Freudian concept of reaction-formation which is very similar to the Adlerian idea that predates Freud, the transformation of a drive into its opposite (Adler, 1956).[1]

Adler was in actuality an early humanist and it is in this domain that he has left a profound legacy and effect. Rogers' concept of the real and ideal self is very similar to the inferiority–superiority dynamic of Adler. More significant in the classic *Motivation and Personality*, Maslow (1970) uses the term *Gemeinschaftsgefühl* to describe the self-actualized individual.[2]

In addition to an important theoretical contribution, Adler made a significant practical contribution by stressing the importance of primary prevention of mental illness through educational reform and enlightened parenting techniques. To this end, he was well on his way to revising the Viennese school system when he had to flee his home city because of the rise of Hitler (Hoffman, 1994). Today, many who have not heard of Adler know of Dreikurs, one of Adler's early disciples, because of his influential writing concerning parenting and education. Adler wished to heal the world with his message of social interest, and this is captured in the fact that he died as he lived, on a lecture tour, after making a speech about social interest in Aberdeen, Scotland, in 1937.

What Is Social Interest?

The term *social interest* represents the difficulty English speakers have had in translating the German word *Gemeinschaftsgefühl*. Ben Ansbacher (personal communication, 2004) has indicated that his father, H. L. Ansbacher, has stated that *community feeling* would be a more suitable translation than *social interest*. Yet, it seems to me that several ideas are embodied in the German root word, namely, community, doing, and feeling. To give this word justice in English, one would have to say that it means behaving with others in a cooperative and empathic way.

At the very least, the word implies that we are inextricably linked with others and that Moreno's (1934) concept of the social atom is correct; that is, that the smallest meaningful unit in psychology implies at least two people. At the larger end of the spectrum, however, the concept of social interest is indicative of one's relationship to the entire cosmos. Thus, environmental concerns such as pollution and the energy crisis are essentially questions of social interest (Adler, 1964). The key question for all individuals is whether their schema of apperception, their worldview, embodies social interest.

Perception and Selective Attention Behavior

Adler was fond of quoting Seneca who said, *Omnia ad opinionem suspensa sunt,* or as he would put it, "I am convinced that a person's behavior springs from his opinion" (Adler 1956, p. 172). This is to say, one's life style is related to one's fictional (perceptive) system. It follows, therefore, that if one's schema of apperception is imbued with social interest, then the individual's selective attention should be directed toward the human or social aspects of the environment. Building on an early experiment by Stone and Ansbacher (1965), several colleagues and I observed this to be the case. Using double-aspect stimuli, we observed that attention to the social aspect of these stimuli, especially the communication organs of the face (mouth, eyes, and nose) was related to mental health, improvement in therapy, and altruistic behavior such as giving blood (for a review of this work, see Huber, 1977, 1978). Our earlier attempts had good predictive validity, but we were not able to establish concurrent validity with other measures of social interest. However, Groff and her colleagues (Groff, Leeper, Thomson, Huber, & Forsyth, 2001) have found that selective attention to organs of communication in the double-aspect task has a positive correlation with a factorially derived scale of empathy and a negative correlation with a liking for racist jokes.

Phylogeny and Ethology[3]

When I first started teaching about Adler and social interest, my students objected by saying, "What about survival of the fittest?" They thus made me study Darwinian-Spencerian theory. The results of this quest left me with ideas that essentially supported Adlerian theory.

> If we define altruism as being all action which in the normal course of events benefits others instead of benefiting self, then, from the dawn of life, altruism has been no less essential than egoism, yet secondarily, egoism is dependent on it. (Spencer, 1872, p. 20)

> Natural selection will modify the structure of the young in relation to the parent, and of the parent in relation to the young. In social animals it will adapt the structure of each individual for the benefit of the whole community, if the community profits by the selective change. (Darwin, 1871, p. 67)

The legacy of Darwin left its effect on Kropotkin (1902) who, in his book *Mutual Aid,* stated that animals that cooperated were more fit to survive than those that *did not cooperate.*

Since Darwin's and Spencer's time, writers such as Wilson (1975), Trivers (1971), and Hamilton (1964) have struck the same theme, namely, that evolution selects for cooperative, altruistic behavior. Certainly, a great deal of evidence demonstrates that infrahuman species cooperate and benefit from social living. Emlen and Demong (1975), for example, have observed that cliff swallows living in large groups survive better than those in small groups because more there are more eyes to search for food and predators. Masserman and his associates (Masserman, Wichkin, & Terris, 1964), in a fascinating experiment, made an observation consonant with the presence of empathy in animals. He and his colleagues observed that animals that had experienced shock were less likely to shock others for food than animals that had not experienced shock. In a presentation at the meetings of the North American Society for Adlerian Psychology, McVittie and Erwin (2004) presented evidence indicating the presence of a cellular structure in the prefrontal cortex that is operative in human and animals when one is engaged in empathic activity.

Perhaps these cellular structures are active when animals are behaving in the many cooperative ways that have been observed in the field. Elephants have been observed to aid wounded comrades at risk to themselves (Siebenaler & Caldwell, 1956). Howler monkeys make bandages for each other (Southwick, 1963). One of the most interesting discussions of cooperative, socially interested behavior, has been cited by Dethier (1962), who describes the mating behavior of wasps. In order to mate, the male wasp must touch the antennae of the female wasp; short male wasps are unable to do this. But, on some occasions, one male will touch the antennae while another will copulate.

In popular literature, such as *Seabiscuit* (Hillenbrand, 1991), and the dog training manual, *The Dog Listener* (Fennell, 1994), the authors point out that animal behavior must be understood within the animal's social context, because the herd or pack is essential for the animal's survival. Thus, social interest may be, as Adler suggested, an innate potential. This last sentence raises the interesting theological question: in what image are humans created?

Religion and Literature

Adler's psychology was religious in nature because he was trying to answer ultimate questions of an eternal nature. That he was trying to answer ultimate questions is especially true of his feelings concerning social interest, because he regarded these observations to be truths *sub specie aeternitatis*, under the aspect of eternity. Adler felt that all great movements had community feeling at their core.

This is certainly in line with the prime message of Christianity captured in John 15:12, "This is my commandment that ye love one another as I have loved you." The same is true of Judaism where the male child's circumcision, or *Bris*, is his first step toward social living, culminating in the adolescent boy's Bar Mitzvah, a formal ceremony indicating his complete entrance into the community. The ceremony for an adolescent female's entrance into the community is called a Bat Mitzvah. Of interest from an Adlerian perspective is the definition of a *mitzvah*, a good deed toward others pleasing to the sight of God.

Confucianism, too, is permeated with the concept of social interest. A central concept in Confucianism is *Jen* (pronounced ren) the symbol that consists of the symbols for man and two. Like Adler's view of social interest, Confucius (1970) sees *Jen* as an innate aspect of being human; he states, "All men are born good: he who loses his goodness is lucky to escape" (p. 25). *Jen* consists of *Chung*, faithfulness to one's humanity, and *Lu*, empathy. Confucius says of the virtue *Jen* that "it cannot live in solitude; neighbors are sure to grow up around it" (p. 77). Here, Confucius's observations coincide with those of Adler; one who lives with social interest feels at home with others. One who does not live with social interest, however, feels, according to Adler, as if he or she were living in enemy territory, a feeling captured in many great novels such as *The Catcher in the Rye, Frankenstein, The Picture of Dorian Gray*, and *Madame Bovary* to name a few. In all of these works, the protagonists felt as if they were at war with others. Adler (1956) felt that literature taught the profound lessons of nature.

The story of *Frankenstein* is particularly interesting because the so-called monster's good nature, that is, social interest, had to be beaten out of him. Confucius believed, as did Adler, that while society could hinder the development of social interest, it could foster this development through the educational system. Confucius stated that teaching such things as music and ceremony should promote harmonious, that is to say, socially interested living (McGee, Huber, & Carter, 1983).

Were Confucius alive today, I believe that he would agree with Adler that psychotherapy is a form of education promoting social interest through the expression of unconditional social interest on the part of the therapist, or in religious terms, the therapist shows his or her clients grace. This grace, while enlivening and encouraging, is not irresistible. Adler (1956) stated that no one is obligated to his or her symptoms. Yet, no one is obligated to change. Unconditional social interest may be like grace; as Aquinas stated, grace is sufficient for salvation but not irresistible. Perhaps this thought can make the therapist more tolerant and appreciative of his or her clients (Huber, 1987).

Sexual Orientation

Since the 1970s, the psychological community has stressed increased acceptance of alternate sexual orientations. The most significant evidence of this is the removal of homosexuality as a disorder from the *Diagnostic and Statistical Manual of Mental Disorders* (American Psychiatric Association, 1980). In this context, it is no surprise that a storm of protest arose when the *Journal of Individual Psychology* in 1991 republished a "classic article" by Krausz (1991/1948) in which homosexuality is depicted as a compulsion neurosis.

In the spate of many reaction papers to this article, Catherine Hedberg and I (1995) studied the relationship of homosexuality to social interest empirically by employing a 2 x 2 x 2 quasi-experimental design with sexual orientation, gender, and type of helping behavior serving as the quasi-independent variables. We observed the scores of male and female, heterosexual and homosexual individuals either engaged or not in a dramatically prosocial activity, being an AIDS buddy. An analysis of covariance revealed a main effect for type of helping behavior only, with those engaged as AIDS buddies scoring dramatically higher on the Sulliman Scale of Social Interest. These findings were opposed to traditional Adlerian theory because all disorders, including homosexuality, were supposedly related to deficient social interest. Theory, however, is not a fixed thing; to be viable it must change in the face of new evidence. The following vignette indicates Adler was prepared for such an eventuality concerning homosexuality. McDowell (1977) reports:

> I was 22 years old, newly graduated from college.... Among my more rarified clients was a very personable highly intelligent young man of 21, who was living in "sin" with an older man in Greenwich Village. My supervisor commanded me to write up "John's" case history, presenting his problem and asking for Dr. Adler's advice in treatment. I did just that and was granted an interview.

> He glanced down for a moment at my report of "John," which lay on top of a vastly untidy desk, and he looked at me over his glasses.

> "You say this John is a homosexual?"

> "Oh, yes," I replied.

"And is he happy, would you say?"

"Oh, yes," I replied.

"Well," leaning back in his swivel chair and putting his thumbs in his vest. "Why don't we leave him alone? Eh…?" This was doubtless the most profound wisdom he could have shared with me. (pp. 81–82)

Games and Jokes

As mentioned earlier, Adler felt that good parenting and education would promote the development of social interest. While it is true that Adler felt that pampered children were the scourge of the world, it is difficult to think of an experimental analog to test the validity of this assumption. Some years ago, Dana Smith, Sonya Mullis, Beth Turner, and I felt that the prisoner's dilemma game presented a chance to study the effects of pampering. Simply put, with this game, one has the possibility of maximizing one's gain by being selfish, if a competitor is compliant. However, one stands to lose a great deal if both players are selfish. Mathematicians have demonstrated that a cooperative strategy during the game results in the greatest gain for all involved. We observed that if a confederate was always compliant, an opponent acted selfishly. These findings are in accord with the hypothesis that pampering breeds selfishness and low social interest (Smith & Huber, 1986). In a second experiment using the same game, we gave our participants the Sulliman Scale of Social Interest (SSSI). We then divided them via a median split and found that those scoring higher on the SSSI adjusted their game strategy to the behavior of a confederate who either was compliant, selfish, or reciprocal (reciprocity was defined as mirroring the behavior of the subject). However, participants who scored in the bottom half of the SSSI did not change their behavior in relation to the confederates' behavior—they failed to understand the differences in the social situation (Huber, Turner, Mullis, & Howell, 1991).

Most recently, the focus of our research has been on jokes. Using joke categories empirically derived by Forsyth, Altermat, and Forsyth (1997), along with logically derived joke categories, we have observed that liking jokes that depreciate others has significant negative correlations to empathy (Breitbiel & Huber, 1999). Nevertheless, the appreciation for this kind of humor significantly decreases as a student moves from their first to second year of university or college training (Carr, Christman, & Huber, 2000). One exception to this finding stands out, however. Women find jokes that make fun of men as most humorous while the opposite is true of men (Woody, Zivalitch, & Huber, 1993). At the time of writing, we have preliminary findings that specific classroom experiences can combat prejudicial ideas that seem to exist because of the war between the sexes (Woody et al., 1993).

Conclusion

One mark of a good theory is its heuristic value, whether it can lead to good observation and thought. This certainly has been the case for me because Adlerian theory has made me think about and conduct research concerning perception, ethology, religion, sexual orientation, parenting, and humor. Adler's theory has a broad range of convenience; that is, it applies cogently to a great many things.

Aronson (2004) has correctly observed that the findings in social psychology clearly indicate that violence leads to violence. Yet, I believe that the converse is also true, that social interest leads to social interest. This point is brought home to me by the behavior of my grandmother. She left Germany with my father in 1910. Yet, she wrote to her family and friends for the rest of her life. After the war, she sent clothes, candy, and cigarettes to our family in Stuttgart and other parts of Germany. In 1965, when I went to Germany for the first time, I was warmly received by many people because of her love. After a conference of Adlerians held in 2004, my wife, daughter, and I met with my cousin to float down the Rhine River together. If it had not been for my grandmother's social interest, this would not have happened.

References

Adler, A. (1956). *The Individual Psychology of Alfred Adler: A systematic presentation in selections from his writings* (H. L. Ansbacher & R. R. Ansbacher, Eds.). New York: Basic Books.

Adler, A. (1964). *Social interest: A challenge to mankind.* New York: Capricorn.

American Psychiatric Association. (1980). *The Diagnostic and Statistical Manual of Mental Disorders* (3rd ed.). Washington, D.C.: Author.

Ansbacher, H. L. (2004). Concerning the relationship of Freud and Adler. *Journal of Individual Psychology* (in press).

Aronson, E. (2004). The social animal. New York: Worth.

Bettelheim, B. (1982, March 1). Reflections: Freud and the soul. *The New Yorker*, 52–88.

Breitbiel, E., & Huber, R. J. (1999). *Humor: A correlational study.* Poster session presented at the annual meeting of the Eastern Psychological Association, Baltimore, MD.

Carr, A., Christman, H., & Huber, R. J. (2000). *Humor, empathy, and education.* Paper presented at the annual meeting of the Eastern Psychological Association, Baltimore, MD.

Confucius. (1970). *The analects of Confucius* (L. Giles, Trans.). New York: Heritage.

Darwin, C. (1871). *The descent of man.* London: Murray.

Dethier, V. (1962). *To know a fly.* San Francisco: Holden Day.

Ellenberger, H. (1981). *The discovery of the unconscious.* New York: Basic Books.

Emlen, S. T., & Demong, N. J. (1975). Adaptive significance of synchronized breeding in a colonial bird: A new hypothesis: *Science, 188,* 1029–1031.

Fennell, J. (1994). *The dog listener: Learn to communicate with your dog for willing cooperation.* Quill: New York.

Forsyth, G. A., Altermat, E., & Forsyth, P. (1997). Humor, emotional empathy, creativity, and cognitive dissonance. Paper presented at the annual convention of the American Psychological Association, Chicago, IL.

Groff, T. S., Leeper, A. M., Thomson, H., Huber, R. J., & Forsyth, G. A. (2001). *Antecedents and correlates of Gemeinschaftsgefühl.* Paper presented at the annual meeting of the Eastern Psychological Association, Washington, D.C.

Hamilton, W. D. (1964). The genetical evolution of social behavior. *Journal of Theoretical Biology, 7,* 1–51.

Hedberg, C., & Huber, R. J. (1995). Homosexuality, gender, community involvement, and social interest. *Individual Psychology, 51,* 244–252.

Hillenbrand, L. (2001). *Seabiscuit.* New York: Random House.

Hoffman, E. (1994). *The drive for self.* Reading, MA: Addison Wesley.

Huber, R. J. (1977). Selective attention behavior: An empirical approach toward Adler. *Journal of Individual Psychology, 33,* 213–222.

Huber, R. J. (1978). Selektives Aufmerksamkeitverhalten: Eine empirische Untersuchen zu Adlers Hypothese vom Gemeinschaftsgefühl. *Beitrage zur Individualpsychologie,* 74–82.

Huber, R. J. (1987). Psychotherapy: A graceful activity. *Individual Psychology, 43,* 437–43.

Huber, R. J., Lomax, S., Robinson, S., & Huber, P. P. (1978). Evolution: Struggle or synergy. *Journal of Individual Psychology, 34,* 210–20.

Huber, R. J., Turner, B., Mullis, R., & Howell, M. (1991). *Relations between measures of social interest and the prisoner's dilemma game.* Poster session at the annual meeting of the American Psychological Society, Washington, D.C.

Krausz, E. O. (1991). Homosexuality as a compulsion neurosis. *Individual Psychology, 49,* 284–93. (Original work published in 1948.)

Kropotkin, P. (1902). *Mutual aid: A factor in evolution.* Boston: Porter-Sargent.

Masserman, J. H., Wichkin, S., & Terris, W. (1964). "Altruistic" behavior in rhesus monkeys. *American Journal of Psychiatry, 121,* 584–85.

Maslow, A. H. (1970). *Motivation and personality.* New York: Harper & Row.

McDowell, E. H. (1977). In G. J. Manaster, D. Deutsch, & B. J. Overholt (Eds.), *Alfred Adler as we remember him* (pp. 81–82). Chicago: North American Society of Adlerian Psychology.

McGee, V. J., Huber, R. J., & Carter, C. L. (1983). Similarities between Confucius and Adler. *Individual Psychology, 39,* 237–46.

McVittie, J., & Erwin, C. (2004). *How we become who we are: What the new science has to say about Adlerian Psychology—A research summary.* Paper presented at the annual meeting of North American Society for Adlerian Psychology, Myrtle Beach, SC.

Moreno, J. L. (1934). *Who shall survive?* Washington, D.C.: Nervous and Mental Disease Publishing.

Siebenaler, J. B., & Caldwell, D. K. (1956). Cooperation among adult dolphins. *Journal of Mammalogy, 37,* 122–27.

Smith, D., & Huber, R. J. (1986). *Cooperation and pampering.* Paper presented at the annual meeting of North American Society for Adlerian Psychology, St. Louis, MO.

Southwick, C. (1963). *Primate social behavior.* New York: Van Nostrand.

Spencer, H. (1872). *Principles of ethics* (vol. 1). New York: Appleton.

Stone, P. A., & Ansbacher, H. L. (1965). Social Interest and performance on the Goodenough Harris Draw-a-Man Test. *Journal of Individual Psychology, 21,* 178–86.

Trivers, R. L. (1971). The evolution of reciprocal altruism. *Quarterly Review of Biology, 46,* 35–37.

Wilson, E. O. (1975). *Sociobiology: The new synthesis.* Cambridge, MA: Harvard University Press.

Woody, J., Zivalitch, D., & Huber, R. J. (1993). Poster session at the annual meeting of the Eastern Psychological Association, Baltimore, MD.

Notes

1. Many current textbooks refer to Adler as a neo-Freudian.
2. Rogers and Maslow had contact with Adler in New York during the 1930s (Hoffman, 1994).
3. Almost all of the material in this section comes from Huber, Lomax, Robinson, and Huber (1978). This article contains many more references and interesting examples.

CHAPTER 10

Social Interest: A Meta-Analysis of a Multidimensional Construct

MARGARET L. BASS, WILLIAM L. CURLETTE, ROY M. KERN, and
ALFRED E. MCWILLIAMS, JR.

Seeking a definition of social interest and its quantifiable meaningfulness to mental health have constructed measurement instruments and conducted extensive empirical research. The purpose of this research synthesis was to assess how social interest instruments correlate with each other and other constructs in psychology. The benefit would be to provide a basis for the further development of the construct of social interest.

Defining the Social Interest Construct

The multidimensionality of the social interest construct becomes evident when the various definitions are compared (Peterson, 1985): "There appears to be greater agreement among Adlerians (including Adler himself) that social interest is important than there is agreement on exactly what constitutes social interest" (p. 5). Adler wrote in *Problems of Neurosis* that the individual with social interest "feels at home in life and feels his existence to be worthwhile just so far as he is useful to others and is overcoming common, instead of private feelings of inferiority" (Ansbacher, 1991, p. 28). Adler defined social interest, *Gemeinschaftsgefühl* in his native

123

German, by adopting an English quotation, "to see with the eyes of another, to hear with the ears of another, to feel with the heart of another" (Ansbacher & Ansbacher, 1956, p. 135). Others have defined social interest somewhat differently. For instance, Ansbacher (1991) chose "interest in the interests of mankind" (p. 37). Mosak (1991) recommended that social interest be conceptualized as a "hypothetical construct," which implies an inner state broader than a mere descriptive generalization (p. 311). O'Connell's (1991) term, humanistic identification, was an effort to identify social interest in a broader manner to include the affective, intellectual, and behavioral aspects of social relationships. Adler believed that "all failures in life ... were lacking in social interest" (1931, as cited in Tavis, 1990, p. 12) and referred to social interest as "the cornerstone of mental health" (Rareshide & Kern, 1991, p. 464). Ansbacher (1991) wrote that "social interest is the criterion for mental health" (p. 33). Individual Psychology theorists agree that social interest is a broad construct and essential to mental health.

The major translators of Adler's work, Ansbacher and Ansbacher, published *The Individual Psychology of Alfred Adler* in 1956 to present "a systematic and ... authentic form" of Adler's contributions (p. xv). Contributing to the variations in later theorists' definitions may be their reliance on this 1956 translation, as they did not have the benefit of Ansbacher's (1992) revised translation of *Gemeinschaftsgefühl.* After revisiting Adler's writings and reflecting upon the history of the German Adlerians' usage and the English Adlerians' usage of the construct, Ansbacher proposed that community feeling was Adler's prominent usage for the meaning of *Gemeinschaftsgefühl.* Community feeling was defined as encompassing one's feelings toward others and self, inanimate objects, and the present time as well as the future, and it tended toward the metaphysical, the cosmos of the community of mankind. Community feeling was a feeling and a passive state of mind. Interest was the motivational and behavioral process through which action was taken. When action and progress were for the benefit of mankind, they were socially useful and thus evinced social interest. To Ansbacher, "community became then a direction giving ideal" (p. 403) with social interest being "the action line of community feeling" (p. 405).

Problems in measuring social interest. Previous research has indicated that the challenge to constructing an objectively scored instrument capable of measuring social interest is the construct's multidimensionality (Bickhard & Ford, 1976; Mozdzierz, Greenblatt, & Murphy, 1986; Rareshide & Kern, 1991). Five self-report measures of social interest were found which were constructed since the 1970s; however, researchers have concluded that these instruments appear to be measuring different aspects of social interest (Crandall, 1981; Curlette, Kern, Gfroerer, & Whitaker, 1999). Further evidence that social interest is not unidimensional is that social interest instruments tend to have low intercorrelations (Bubenzer, Zarski, & Walter, 1991; Curlette et al., 1999; Hedberg & Huber, 1995; Highlander, 1984; McDougal, 1985).

Contributing to the variability which decreases effect size are measurement problems inherent in instrument construction, such as those related to construct validity (Leak, Millard, Perry, & Williams, 1985). Also, social desirability, the tendency to "fake good," becomes a problem in self-report instruments that inquire about subjective attributes (Cooper, 1992; Leak, 1982; Peterson, Epperson, & Hutzell, 1985; Tavis, 1990). Both construct validity issues and the consequences of "faking good" contribute to obscuring the individual's true score or ability measure. A meta-analysis of research findings concerning the social interest construct provides a statistical summary of the intercorrelations of various social interest instruments, the magnitudes of the correlations between social interest instruments and other psychological constructs, and information regarding its multidimensionality.

Measuring instruments. In his 1961 address at the Tenth Annual Conference of the North American Society for Adlerian Psychology, Rotter (1962) called for the measurement of social interest in an "objectively verifiable or testable form" (p. 4). He acknowledged the difficulty of securing an operational definition of social interest by saying that it would be "unlikely that any one operational definition would please most Individual Psychologists" (p. 8). Developers constructed three pencil and paper, self-report social interest instruments in the 1970s. The Social Interest Index (SII; Greever, Tseng, & Friedland, 1973) included a total score and four subscales designed to measure the life tasks of friendship, love, work, and self-significance. In Sulliman's Scale of Social Interest (SSSI; Sulliman, 1973), measurement of social interest was approached in a "global manner with two subfactors: (a) 'concern for and trust in others' and (b) 'confidence in oneself and optimism in one's view of the world'" (Kaplan, 1991, p. 121). Crandall's (1981) Social Interest Scale (SIS) "was designed to assess a person's interest in the interests or welfare of others" (p. 107).

Success in solving life tasks is dependent upon the individual's lifestyle and the degree of social interest he or she incorporates into the solution. Crandall (1980) observed that social interest is exhibited differently in different situations. Having an interpretation of the individual's lifestyle may provide a broader measure of the influences of social interest on the individual's behavior. Curlette et al. (1999) recommended that "because social interest is such a broad construct, it is advantageous to consider a person's lifestyle in relation to social interest" (p. 69). Two additional instruments included in this study have that capacity.

Developed by Wheeler, Kern, and Curlette (1982), the Life Style Personality Inventory (LSPI) was composed of seven lifestyle themes and a Social Interest Index (LSPISII). The authors found that as research accumulated on the LSPI, the eight themes could be revised and reduced without decreasing the usefulness of the instrument. By combining or eliminating themes from the LSPI, the five themes of the Basic Adlerian Scale for Interpersonal Success—Adult Form (BASIS-A) emerged. The refined instrument included five themes augmented by five additional scales. One of the five primary themes was addressed by the Belonging Social Interest (BSD) scale which focused on feelings of belonging as a child (Curlette, Wheeler, & Kern, 1997).

Overview of Previous Research

Social interest scales have positively correlated with self-esteem (Riggins, 1990), acculturation (Miranda & White, 1993), religious beliefs (Tobacyk, 1983), self-efficacy (Dinter, 2000), psychological well-being and life satisfaction (Rodd, 1994), femininity (Murphy, 1994), coping resources (Kern, Gfroerer, Summers, Curlette, & Matheny, 1996; White, 1989), volunteerism (Hedberg & Huber, 1995), affiliation (Wheeler & Acheson, 1993), social concern (Schneider, 1991), and happiness and sense of humor (Dixon, Willingham, Chandler, & McDougal, 1986). Negative correlations have been found between social interest and hopelessness (Miller, Denton, & Tobacyk, 1986), depression (Earles, 1982; Fish & Mozdzierz, 1991), narcissism (Joubert, 1998), external locus of control (Fish & Mozdzierz; Wheeler & White, 1991), anxiety (Fish & Mozdzierz), substance abuse (Keene & Wheeler, 1994), and abasement, autonomy, and dominance (Wheeler & Acheson). These indicators of adjustment and maladjustment do correlate with social interest in the expected negative or positive directions, but their correlations have remained small to moderate.

On the same sample, correlations between social interest instruments that purport to measure the same construct should be large, but they usually result in small to moderate correlations. Crandall and Biaggio (1984) found the SIS and the SII correlating at .32 for college students. For Australian singles club members, the correlation between the SIS and the SII was .161 (Brough, 1994). Bubenzer et al. (1991) found a negative correlation of .29 between the SII and the SIS in a sample of master's-level counseling students. Peterson et al. (1985) found additional discrepancies when comparing social interest among 36 female prison inmates and 36 female university employees. For inmates the correlation between the SII and the SIS was .059, but for the university employees the correlation between the two instruments was .295. In their study of participants in an alcohol-detoxification treatment program, Mozdzierz et al. (1986) partialed out social desirability from the correlation between SSSI and SIS, which resulted in a value of $r = 2.07$. For sample of nurses, the correlation between the SSSI and the LSPISII was .21 (Riggins, 1990), and, using a sample of parents, Highlander (1984) found the correlation of the SIS and the LSPISII to be .081. In their study of sexual orientation and volunteerism, Hedberg and Huber (1995) found the SSSI and the BSI were related at $r = .211$. Among a sample of college women, Curlette et al.'s (1999) comparison of the SSSI with the BSI had a correlation of .33. The failure of these instruments to have large correlations with each other on the same samples suggests that they may be measuring different aspects of social interest.

Bubenzer et al. (1991) addressed the issue of instruments' measuring specific aspects of social interest by including three social interest instruments, the SII, SIS, and Altman's Early Recollection Questionnaire, in their study. These instruments' small correlations with each other on the same sample led the researchers to conclude "that each instrument was measuring a different dimension of social interest" (p. 128). They did find that the SII scores correlated significantly with personality characteristics representative of social interest, while the other two instruments did not. In their study of inpatient participants in an alcoholism treatment program, Mozdzierz et al. (1986) found the SIS to be weak as a correlate of adjustment, but their findings encouraged them to propose that the SSSI's validity could be "extended to a 'pathological' population" (p. 40). In contrast, Curlette et al. (1999) found no significant difference between the SSSI and the BSI in the ability to predict stress coping resources. Searching for an operational definition has become complicated because social interest is a broad construct, and different instruments do not correlate highly with each other. Thus, it was our hope that this meta-analysis of empirical research studies of the social interest construct of Individual Psychology would provide an impetus for researchers to develop better operational definitions.

Meta-Analysis: Concepts and Practices

The meta-analysis statistical procedure for reviewing and integrating research literature is accomplished by placing primary study results on a common metric "in a quantifiable manner to provide a parsimonious summary" (Matheny, Aycock, Pugh, Curlette, & Cannella, 1986, p. 521).

The conversion of a study's result to a summary statistic which is common across studies enables the analysis of the magnitude of effect across studies to help reveal the cumulative knowledge at present. Meta-analysis has been shown to be useful in guiding future research in regard to theory and practice (Hedges & Olkin, 1985).

The selected effect size statistic for this study was the correlation coefficient. Hedges and Olkin (1985) described the product-moment correlation as a scale free index of effect magnitude. Second, to give greater weight to studies with larger sample sizes, we multiplied each study correlation coefficient by its sample size, and then all weighted correlations were summed. This sum was divided by the sum of all sample sizes to obtain the weighted average effect size (Hunter & Schmidt, 1990, p. 100). This mean effect size is the overall estimate of effect magnitude for the domain or question of interest. Third, the overall mean effect size and the observed variance, the frequency weighted average squared error (p. 100), were evaluated by homogeneity tests to determine whether substantive variables, methodological characteristics, or sampling error were the likely sources of the variability. Nonsignificant homogeneity test results indicate that sampling error probably accounts for the variability. When homogeneity test results are statistically significant, additional testing for subgroups of effect sizes based on other variables is indicated.

Threats to the validity of a meta-analysis include biases at the individual study level such as publication bias, selective reporting, and the file drawer problem. Publication bias is journal editors' preferences for studies finding statistical significance (Hedges, 1990). Selective reporting occurs when study authors do not report statistical information needed to compute effect sizes (Matheny et al., 1986). Researchers themselves threaten validity by choosing not to publish research that does not yield significant or expected results, putting these data in a file drawer rather than submitting them for publication. These factors contribute to a "biased over estimate of effect magnitude" (Hedges, p. 19).

It is preferred in meta-analysis that effect sizes be independent of each other such that only one effect size may be taken per sample. To address this issue, separate meta-analyses were conducted on randomly selected independent effect sizes from each study, in addition to the usual total number of effect sizes available from all studies.

The generalizability of meta-analysis results is limited when the samples used in the original studies entering the meta-analysis are not representative of the general population. Watkins (1994) surveyed the literature from 1981 to 1991 and found 38 social interest articles which included 45 independent samples. He made the observation that two-thirds of the studies were limited to samples of undergraduate or graduate students. Another criticism made by Watkins of the original studies was the lack of specification of subjects' ages or races.

Research Questions

The purpose of this study was to investigate the correlations of social interest instruments with each other and with other correlate variables. In this meta-analysis "correlate variables" is the general term used to describe the collection of all the variables which were related to one or more of the five social interest instruments in the 124 studies. The correlate variables fell into one of four categories: variables from psychological and other tests excluding a second measure of social interest, measures of social interest, subject behaviors, and demographic variables of the participants. Of the total 1,163 effect sizes, approximately 88% were correlations of social interest instruments and instruments measuring variables from psychological and other tests excluding a second measure of social interest. For example, instruments measuring depression included the Minnesota Multiphasic Personality Inventory depression subscale, the Depression Adjective Checklist, the Beck Depression Inventory, and the Multiple Affect Adjective Checklist depression scale. In all, over 250 instruments with more than 300 subscales are represented in this meta-analysis.

The other three categories of correlate variables constituted less than 12% of the effect sizes. Sometimes a second measure of social interest was correlated with one of the five measures in this study. In many instances, the second measure of social interest was not among the five which met the admissibility criteria for studies in this meta-analysis. An example of behavioral variables were alcoholics' behaviors such as length of membership in Alcoholics Anonymous, length of sobriety, frequency of meeting attendance, and number of family members in the 12-step program. Demographic variables of the participants were characteristics such as age, education level, gender, grade point average, and socioeconomic status.

In particular, we asked the following questions:

1. When the social interest construct is measured with different instruments for different correlate variables, does this result in homogeneous correlations? To investigate this question, all the correlations in this meta-analysis were summarized to obtain an overall effect size in two ways. First, a homogeneity test was run on all the effect sizes. Second, a homogeneity test was computed on randomly selected independent effect sizes from each study. These tests were conducted using Hunter and Schmidt's (1990) chi-square test for homogeneity of effect size.

2. What is the value of the average correlation of each of the five social interest scales with the correlate variables? This question was addressed by obtaining the average correlation between each social interest instrument in the meta-analysis and any variable it was correlated with in the studies reviewed. The subgroup of studies on which an average correlation was obtained was called a subgroup meta-analysis. Also, separate tests of homogeneity were calculated for total effect sizes and for randomly selected effect sizes.

3. To what extent do social interest scales correlate with particular measures of different psychological constructs? To examine a social interest instrument's relationship to a correlate variable, a subgroup meta-analysis was run for a particular social interest instrument with a specific correlate variable. This kept the comparison of social interest instruments to each other on the same construct. The inclusion criterion for a correlate variable at this level required it to be represented by at least ten effect sizes from the total number of effect sizes across all instruments. This decision reduced the number of effect sizes from 1,163 to 384 effect sizes (or correlations) which were available in the data set used for the analysis. (The original 1,163 correlations did not provide effect sizes for *all* instruments on all psychological contructs.)

4. What are the values of the average intercorrelations between various measures of social interest? To answer this question, average correlations were found between pairs of social interest instruments.

Both questions 1 and 2 summarize the correlations that exist in the literature based on the variables that authors of the original studies had decided to report. Answers to these two research questions provide general background information or guidelines about typical correlations with social interest instruments. They are general questions that average over many different correlate variables and set the stage or provide a backdrop for interpreting correlations with social interest measures. Questions 3 and 4 are more meaningful because they are more specific; question 3 links to particular constructs and question 4 compares particular instruments.

Method

Literature search procedures. To identify empirical studies for possible inclusion in this study of social interest, the authors made electronic searches of the literature. Databases accessed were PsychLit, PsycFirst, ERIC, Dissertation Abstracts International, Digital Dissertations, and

Medline. References of the retrieved articles from these searches were reviewed to locate additional sources of empirical studies.

Inclusion criteria. Criteria employed to determine inclusion of a study were that the study included scores on one or more of the self-report instruments designed to measure the social interest construct, the SII, SIS, SSSI, LSPISII, and the BSI; that the research had an experimental or quasi-experimental design, and/or the study compared social interest instrument scores with correlated instrument(s); and that the research had been published or reported since 1977. This date was selected based on Watkins's (1983) observation that the study of the social interest construct had increased since 1977. Finally, studies that did not report enough statistical information to estimate effect size were excluded.

Effect size metric. The correlation coefficient was the metric used to describe the shared variance of the social interest instrument and the correlate variable. Many of the correlate instrument scales were scored in the direction that a positive relationship with social interest would have a negative value. To resolve this, the effect size metric was the absolute value of the correlation to allow summary of the magnitude of the relationship regardless of direction. Original study statistical results were converted to correlation effect sizes using formulas found in Rosenthal (1994), Hedges and Olkin (1985), and Hunter and Schmidt (1990). Fewer than 10% of the correlations in this meta-analysis were derived by using conversion formulas involving means, standard deviations, and t-tests. Correlations reported in the primary studies were inserted directly into the meta-analysis data set. Deshpande and Viswesvaran (1992) found no systematic differences in the comparison of correlations calculated from conversion formulas and those reported in the original studies. Hough and Hall (1994) found no significant differences in meta-analysis mean effect sizes when pooled variance or control group variance was used for converting means and standard deviations to effect sizes. In converting mean differences to correlations, calculations were made using the pooled variance as recommended by Hunter and Schmidt (1990).

Mean effect size and observed variance. The effect size mean is the weighted average effect size of all study effect sizes. Each study effect size correlation is weighted by the sample size, summed, and divided by the sum of all sample sizes (Hunter & Schmidt, 1990, p. 100). This weighted average effect size is the mean of subject effect sizes, not study effect sizes, which gives greater weight to studies with larger samples. The observed variance corresponding to the weighted average effect size is the frequency weighted average squared error (p. 100). The square root of this quantity is referred to as SD in the tables. The difference of each study effect size and the weighted average effect size is squared, then multiplied by the study sample size. These totals are summed and divided by the sum of all sample sizes to compute the frequency weighted average squared error or observed variance.

Independence. Because many studies reported correlations on the same sample with one or more social interest instruments and with one or more correlate instruments, these correlations could not be assumed to be independent. To select and report only one effect size correlation from each study would have resulted in a loss of information. We used the following approach to address the issue of independence when multiple effect sizes were available from the same sample. First, an overall mean effect size correlation was computed on the total number of effect sizes available. Then, a second mean effect size correlation was computed with one randomly selected effect size from each sample. When effect sizes were aggregated by social interest instrument, this approach was repeated. When effect sizes were aggregated by social interest instrument and one of the psychological constructs used in research question 3, these effect sizes were deemed independent because a study infrequently contributed more than one measure of the psychological constructs being related to social interest instruments. Only rarely were effect sizes measuring the same correlate characteristic taken from the same sample. In one instance (Tobacyk, 1983), three of an instrument's subscales were combined in a sub-analysis.

Test of homogeneity of effect size. The chi-square test of homogeneity of mean effect size is given in Hunter and Schmidt (1990, p. 112). Rejection of the null hypothesis implies that the observed variance is greater than that expected by chance, indicating that the variation was due to other variables and that further investigation to identify the other variables would be appropriate. When the chi-square test was not significant, the null hypothesis was not rejected, suggesting that the observed variance could be accounted for by sampling error, and no further search for moderators was indicated. As Hunter and Schmidt (1990) have warned with a large number of studies, the power of the chi-square statistic is great, and a Type I error may occur even when the variation across studies may be trivial. Hunter and Schmidt deemed the chi-square's not being significant as strong evidence that there was no variation beyond sampling error.

Analysis and Results

Descriptive study characteristics. Electronic searches using the acronyms of Sll, SIS, SSSI, LSPI, and BASIS-A and the term social interest resulted in a total of 269 references from 1977 or later (see Table 1). Some references were duplicated, as databases overlapped in citing references. Of the 124 studies included in this meta-analysis, 34% were from *The Journal of Individual Psychology,* 10.5% were from other journals, 54.9% were from dissertations, and 0.7% were from unpublished studies. The total number of effect sizes calculated from all studies was 1,163. Of this total 43.4% were from *The Journal of Individual Psychology,* 8.4% from other journals, 48.0% from dissertations, and 0.2% from unpublished studies.

Publication bias. To address the issue of publication bias, we compared mean effect sizes from articles from *The Journal of Individual Psychology (JIP)* and from other journals with mean effect sizes from dissertations. For both JIP and other journals, the total weighted mean effect size was $r = .23$. The independent weighted mean effect size for other journals was $r = .26$, and the *JIP* independent weighted mean effect size was $r = .28$. In comparison, the weighted mean effect size for the total number of effect sizes taken from dissertations was smaller at $r = .22$. For independent effect sizes from dissertations, the weighted mean effect size was $r = .23$. Thus, for this meta-analysis, published articles had larger effect sizes than dissertations; however, the difference in effect magnitude was not nearly as great as differences that other meta-analyses on other topics have found (e.g., Matheny et al., 1986). In general, publication bias did not appear tobe a problem.

Generalizability. To address Watkins's (1994) criticisms of the limitation of samples to college students and the lack of reporting sample age and race, we collected this information from the studies used in this meta-analysis

TABLE 10.1 Number of References Cited by Electronic Databases for Social Interest Instruments

Database	BASIS-A	SIS	Sll	SSSI	LSPISII
Digital Dissertations	12	42	18	8	12
Dissertation Abstracts	8	13	7	5	13
PsycFirst	10	0	3	1	2
PsychLit	2	49	37	9	5
Medline	0	1	2	0	0
ERIC	0	4	6	0	0
Total	32	109	73	23	32

(see Table 2). Concerning sample characteristics, Watkins found that two-thirds of the study samples were college students. In this meta-analysis independent effect size samples included 37.4% college students. The total number of effect sizes had 28.7% of the samples as college students. Race was not given in 58.1% of the independent effect sizes and in 65.75% of the total number of effect sizes. In regard to race, a majority of studies reported a mixed racial sample; however, our observations have been that in the mixed race samples, the majority was White. In conclusion, this collection of primary studies had a greater diversity of subjects than those surveyed by Watkins.

Question 1 results: Meta-analysis of the social interest construct. The mean effect size for the 154 independent effect sizes was r = .253, SD = .155 with a homogeneity test calculated value of 2153 = 674.55, p < 1.0-10. We concluded that the hypothesis of homogeneity of independent effect sizes should be rejected. The mean effect size of the total 1,163 effect sizes was r = .228, SD =.090 with a homogeneity test calculated value of 21162 = 3879.295, p < 1.0–10, which supported rejection of the null hypothesis that sampling error accounted for the observed variance. When the social interest construct is measured in different statistical ways with different instruments for different correlate variables, the results are not homogeneous. This result provides justification for looking at various subgroups of effect sizes which are referred to as subgroup meta-analyses in the following sections.

Question 2 results: Subgroup meta-analyses by social interest instruments. To see how social interest scales correlate with all the correlate variables in the meta-analysis data set, total and independent study mean effect sizes were calculated, and tests for homogeneity were made (see Table 3 & Table 4, respectively). The total overall mean effect size magnitudes for the SII and SSSI were largest (r = .300). The SIS had the smallest mean effect size (r = .171) and the largest number of effect sizes (n = 406). Ironically, the lowest effect size was for the most used social interest instrument, the SIS,

TABLE 10.2 Sample Characteristics for Independent and Total Effect Sizes

Characteristic	Effect Size Independent	Total
Mean age in years	33.9	27.5
Mean education in years	13.9	14.4
College students	37.4%	28.7%
Race not given	58.1%	65.7%

TABLE 10.3 Total Mean Effect Sizes and Homogeneity Tests Results for Each Social Interest Instrument

| Instrument | Total Mean Effect Sizes | | | Homogeneity Test |
	No. (of Effect Sizes)	r	SD	χ^2
SlI	223	.298	.162	737.97*
SIS	406	.171	.123	569.12
SSSI	144	.296	.186	715.60*
LSPISII	127	.202	.161	645.14*
BSI	170	.212	.173	715.27*

Note. $^*p \leq 05$. r is weighted by the number of subjects. SD is the square root of the frequency weighted average squared error (Hunter & Schmidt, 1990, p. 100).

in correlational studies. The homogeneity test value of the SIS did not exceed the critical value and was not statistically significant at the .05 level, so we concluded that the population variance of the SIS was due to sampling error. The other instruments' tests for homogeneity were significant, a result indicating the presence of moderator variables.

Somewhat different results were found in the meta-analyses of independent effect sizes. The instruments with the largest mean effect sizes were the BSI and SII at $r = .351$ and $r = .330$, respectively. Again, the SIS had the smallest magnitude of effect size with $r = .183$. For the SII, SIS, SSSI, LSPISII, and BSI, homogeneity tests were significant, and the null hypotheses were rejected. Because each social interest instrument had at least one homogeneity test which was statistically significant, all the social interest

TABLE 10.4 Independent Mean Effect Sizes and Homogeneity Tests Results for Each Social Interest Instrument

| Instrument | Independent Mean Effect Sizes | | | Homogeneity Test |
	No. (of Effect Sizes)	r	SD	χ^2
SII	33	.329	.155	119.67*
SIS	58	.183	.131	116.69*
SSSI	13	.223	.146	37.64*
LSPISII	21	.224	.182	142.72*
BSI	24	.351	.226	175.84*

Note. $^*p \leq .05$. r is weighted by the number of subjects. SD is the square root of the frequency weighted average squared error (Hunter & Schmidt, 1990, p. 100).

instruments were retained in the search for moderators described in the following section.

Question 3 results: Subgroup meta-analyses of social interest instruments and correlate variables. What are typical correlations for the five social interest instruments with 12 different psychological constructs? The results for each social interest instrument aggregated by correlate variables permitted comparisons of the effect size magnitudes of the individual social interest instrument with specific constructs indicative of psychological adjustment or maladjustment in addition to social desirability (see Table 5). These subgroup meta-analyses were limited to variables having at least 10 effect sizes in the total data set, with the exception of the variable religious immaturity which had 9 effect sizes. Under this criterion of the total 1,163 effect sizes included in the data set, only 384 were included in these subgroup meta-analyses. In the following paragraphs, a brief discussion is provided of the average correlations for social interest instruments for the following psychological variables: empathy, cooperation, social support, locus of control, spirituality, religious maturity, religious immaturity, marital adjustment, narcissism, depression, anxiety, and competition.

On Table 5 the focus can be (a) on comparing average correlations on social interest instruments across a common set of psychological variables or (b) on comparing the magnitude of average correlations of psychological variables with social interest measures. First, in terms of comparing social interest instruments, the SSSI had the highest point estimate on the average correlation with psychological variables on five of the six psychological variables. The BSI had the single highest correlation ($r = 2.71$ with depression), but the study needs replication. The SIS performed poorly compared to the SII and the SSSI except in regard to religious immaturity, where there was a mean effect size of $r = .241$. Furthermore, for measures of religious maturity, the SIS correlation was lower ($r = .192$) than the SIS ($r = .244$). In general, the SIS appeared to correlate the lowest on the psychological constructs measured in this meta-analysis.

For depression the BSI effect size was an outlier needing investigation. This negative correlation of $r = 2.71$ for the relationship between depression and social interest was taken from Miranda's (1994) study of acculturation and mental health among a Latino population. Additional studies among the Latino population by Miranda and White (1993) and Miranda and Umhoefer (1998) reported large correlations between acculturation success and social interest. These social interest effect sizes were taken from samples dichotomized on acculturation instruments with bipolar scales. Miranda (personal communication, November 8, 2000) suggested these results may be a confluence of factors, "i.e., the BASIS-A measuring

TABLE 10.5 Mean Effect Sizes of Social Interest Instruments Aggregated by Correlate Variables

Correlate Variable/ Instrument	Total Mean Effects		Homogeneity Test	
	No. (of Effect Sizes)	r	SD	χ^2
Empathy				
SII	6	.337	.160	10.02
SIS	17	.135	.084	10.46
SSSI	12	.355	.203	138.43*
LSPISII	1	.087	.000	
Cooperation				
SII	2	.136	.027	0.15
SIS	5	.120	.020	1.27
SSSI	5	.428	.093	8.24
BSI	1	.251	.000	
Social Support				
SII	3	.237	.045	1.36
SIS	5	.106	.057	5.25
SSSI	7	.239	.053	7.26
Locus of Control				
SII	1	.158	.000	
SIS	6	.118	.062	4.38
LSPISII	4	.198	.068	3.27
BSI	11	.095	.076	4.24
Spirituality				
SII	7	.297	.127	16.04*
SIS	18	.168	.126	19.53
Religious Maturity				
SII	8	.244	.121	12.03
SIS	8	.192	.158	19.57*
Religious Immaturity				
SII	3	.131	.080	2.03
SIS	3	.241	.034	0.39
Marital Adjustment				
SII	12	.307	.098	10.73
LSPISII	4	.216	.066	3.69

(*Continued*)

TABLE 10.5 Mean Effect Sizes of Social Interest Instruments Aggregated by Correlate Variables

Correlate Variable/ Instrument	Total Mean Effects			Homogeneity Test
	No. (of Effect Sizes)	r	SD	χ^2
BSI	2	.123	.041	0.27
Narcissism				
SIS	7	.255	.093	4.81
SSSI	2	.413	.108	10.58*
LSPISII	1	.017	.000	
Depression				
SII	3	.344	.085	0.81
SIS	7	.148	.074	2.42
SSSI	5	.631	.124	16.61*
LSPISII	7	.346	.343	16.77*
BSI	1	.710	.000	
Social Desirability				
SII	6	.262	.141	6.67
SIS	15	.120	.090	8.54
SSSI	8	.165	.147	18.89*
LSPISII	1	.227	.000	
Anxiety				
SII	3	.291	.077	0.61
SIS	6	.151	.117	5.03
SSSI	6	.210	.235	54.75*
LSPISII	1	.004	.000	
Competition				
SII	7	.162	.082	5.02
SIS	3	.157	.106	2.82
LSPISII	1	.048	.000	

Note. *$p \leq .05$. r is weighted by the sample size. SD is the square root of the frequency weighted average squared error (Hunter & Schmidt, 1990, p. 100).

curvilinear factors, appropriateness of the instrument with minority populations, and/or the norm group's insensitivity to the Latino realities." Miranda recommended cross-validation studies of acculturation and the Latino population using the BASIS-A.

Which of the psychological constructs studied (based on the correlations available in the original studies) appear to have the highest correlations with the social interest scales? Depression appears to be the highest, with both the SSSI and BSI having moderately high correlations. Cooperation has small to moderate correlations with the BSI and SSSI. Narcissism had small to moderate correlations with the SIS and SSSI. Empathy tends to have small correlations with the SSSI and Sll. Other constructs whose measures had small correlations with social interest measures were the following: spirituality ($r = .30$ with Sll), marital adjustment ($r = .31$ with Sll), and anxiety ($r = .29$ with Sll).

Question 4 results: Subgroup meta-analyses of social instrument instruments. To assess how social instruments agree with each other, we calculated 16 effect sizes for various pairs of instruments and ran tests for homogeneity (see Table 6). The variability cannot be explained by sampling error for the relationship of the SII with the SIS and of the SSSI with the SIS. Consequently, this provides statistical evidence that these three, the SII, the SIS, and the SSSI, could be measuring different aspects of social interest. More primary research relating social interest scales to each other is needed before meta-analysis can reasonably help identify the moderator variables or constructs being measured.

To understand further the characteristics of the studies included which compared instruments, we computed the following descriptive statistics. Publication types were evenly divided between *The Journal of Individual Psychology* articles and dissertations. The education of 94.4% of the subjects in the above studies ranged from 14 to 17 years. The median age of all subjects

TABLE 10.6 Homogeneity Tests of Effect Sizes of One Social Interest Instrument with Another

| Instruments | Mean Effect Sizes | | Homogeneity Test | |
	No. (of Effect Sizes)	r	SD	χ^2
SII & SIS	9	.206	.366	36.71*
SSSI & SIS	3	.216	.117	12.35*
SSSI & LSPI	1	.205	.000	
SSSI & BSI	2	.292	.062	3.34
LSPI & SIS	1	.080	.000	

Note. *$p \le .05$. r is weighted by the number of subjects. SD is the square root of the frequency weighted average squared error (Hunter & Schmidt, 1990, p. 100).

was 33 years. Subjects' reported affiliations were college students (22.7%), graduate students (18.2%), and general population (27.3%). Alcoholics represented 4.5% of the total sample. All other sample group characteristics were widely dispersed. Given that 40.9% of the subjects were enrolled in college, which is similar to the validation samples, it would be expected that there would have been larger effect sizes between instruments, and homogeneity would have been achieved, but this convergence did not occur. As noted by the authors in many of the primary studies, different social interest instruments seemed to measure different aspects of the construct.

Relationship to social desirability. The effect sizes with social desirability for the SII and SSSI were r = .262 and r = .165, respectively (see Table 5). Thus, there is some evidence that social desirability may be a minor influence on the scores of the SSSI and the SII.

For the LSPISII, only one study, with a correlation of r = .227 with social desirability, has been conducted. The BSI addresses the issue of social desirability through the respondent's reflecting back to early childhood experiences. The BASIS-A authors believe this method of item presentation "distances the respondent from the present and helps reduce socially desirable responses" (Curlette, Wheeler, & Kern, 1997, p. 16). When using the BSI, Miranda and Umhoefer (1998) reported the procedure of eliminating those subjects from the sample who scored above the 95th percentile on either the Harshness or the Softness scale on the BASIS-A Inventory as a way of controlling for social desirability.

Gender as a Possible Moderator Variable. To see if gender influenced the heterogeneity of the social interest variable across all instruments, an aggregate was made by social interest instrument and the research designs comparing the social interest scores of men and women. For the 39 effect sizes, the homogeneity tests on the SII, SIS, SSSI, LSPISII, and the BSI were not significant, and the null hypothesis was not rejected. Thus, sampling error accounted for the variability between genders (see Table 7). Although there were no differences, in terms of point estimates of magnitude of effect size, the SSSI had the smallest correlation with gender followed by the BSI. The largest correlation was with the SIS, indicating it is the most gender-sensitive of the social interest instruments included in this meta-analysis.

Discussion

The purpose of this meta-analysis was to summarize the correlations of social interest instruments with each other and with other psychological

TABLE 10.7 Mean Effect and Homogeneity Tests Results for Each Social Interest Instrument when Men's and Women's Response Are Compared on Social Interest Instrument Scores

| Instrument | No. (of Effect Sizes) | Mean Effect Sizes | | Homogeneity Test |
		r	SD	χ^2
SII	2	.140	.063	1.97
SIS	17	.204	.094	18.62
SSSI	5	.128	.016	0.17
LSPISII	1	.020	.000	
BSI	3	.118	.029	0.26

Note. No χ^2 results were significant with $p \leq 05$. *r* is weighted by the number of subjects. *SD* is the square root of the frequency weighted average squared error (Hunter & Schmidt, 1990, p. 100).

constructs. The study summarized research findings since 1977, which included at least one of the five pencil-and-paper, objectively scored social interest instruments, the SSI, SIS, SSSI, LSPISII, and the BSI of the BASIS-A. As such, this research synthesis is the most comprehensive survey to date of empirical research on the social interest construct.

Generalizability. Data were collected from 154 independent samples from 124 studies for a total of 1,163 study effect sizes. The total sample size for independent studies was 18,809 individuals. Approximately one-third of the participants were college students when they participated in the studies. The mean age of the sample was early 30s, and the average education level was two years beyond high school. Even though the sample size is large, the results are limited in their generalizability to the general population because of the subjects used in the primary research studies.

Clarifying the construct being measured: Gemeinschaftsgefühl. The most important finding from this meta-analysis was further documenting the low pair-wise correlations between the five instruments that purport to measure the construct of social interest. The average correlations between pairs of social interest instruments ranged from .08 to .22.

Ansbacher (1992) wrote that it was incorrect to substitute "social interest" for "community feeling" in the translation of *Gemeinschaftsgefühl*. Because Ansbacher revised his translation of *Gemeinschaftsgefühl*, it may be worthwhile to reconsider the current efforts to operationalize *Gemeinschaftsgefühl* by clarifying the construct being measured.

An initial step for achieving an operational definition of social interest/ community feeling may be to discuss dimensions for its measurement. To accomplish this goal, recognized authorities could form a panel of experts brought together in conference for the purpose of establishing specific dimensions of the social interest construct. Researchers who have developed instruments could review the status of their research beyond the summaries included in this article to aid in the discussion of dimensions. As the dimensions constituting social interest become clearer, these could form the basic of the operationalized definition of social interest. We do not suggest that there will be only one definition: There has not been a single definition for other major constructs in psychology, such as intelligence or creativity.

Correlations of social interest instruments with psychological constructs. If a researcher were to design a study to correlate a social interest instrument with a psychological variable, a reasonable correlation to expect would be approximately .25. However, particular instruments will correlate higher with particular constructs. For example, in this meta-analysis, the average correlation of the SSSI with depression was .62. Another instance is the correlation of .43 of the BSI with the social support (Curlette et al., 1997, p. 27).

For research question 2, meta-analyses were run on the data grouped by each of the social interest instruments. Both the Sll and the SSSI had the highest total weighted mean effect size at $r = .30$, $n = 223$ and $n = 144$, respectively. The BSI had the highest weighted mean effect size for the independent data at $r = .35$, $n = 24$. The SIS had the smallest weighted mean effect size of all instruments for both data sets. The homogeneity test was not significant for the SIS on the total data set. When effect sizes are grouped by a single social interest instrument and its correlate variables, the meta-analyses results are not homogeneous. The lack of homogeneity implies that it is not reasonable to believe that all correlate variables have about the same relationship with a social interest measure.

For research question 3, when the effect size data were grouped by each social interest instrument and a single correlate variable, homogeneity was achieved most of the time. The Sll had higher weighted mean effect sizes with spirituality, religious maturity, marital adjustment, anxiety, competition, and social desirability. The SSSI had the highest weighted mean effect size with empathy, cooperation, social support, locus of control, and narcissism. The BSI had the highest mean effect size with depression. The SIS's highest mean effect size was with religious immaturity, but it performed least well with empathy, cooperation, social support, spirituality, religious maturity, and depression. Small mean effect sizes are an indication that no single correlate variable as measured by the correlate instruments is synonymous with social interest as measured by any social interest instrument. Most of the homogeneity tests were not significant, so multidimensionality was not likely present at this level of analysis.

Most perplexing was the minimal performance of the SIS. This instrument had a negligible effect size with social desirability as well as with all other indicators except religious immaturity. The SIS did not perform as well as other instruments as a measure of social interest, and the SIS was found to be the most gender discriminating of all the instruments.

Conclusion

Inquiry into the social interest/community feeling construct should be approached in a multidimensional manner. When an existing social interest instrument is used in research or practice, reference should be made to the general or specific aspect of social interest being measured as supported by empirical research. This meta-analysis has shown that there are challenges related to the social interest construct for study of Individual Psychology.

References

References marked with an asterisk indicate studies included in the meta-analysis.

Ansbacher, H. L. (1991). The concept of social interest. *The Journal of Individual Psychology, 47,* 28–46.

Ansbacher, H. L. (1992). Alfred Adler's concepts of community feeling and of social interest and the relevance of community feeling for old age. *The Journal of Individual Psychology, 48,* 402–412.

Ansbacher, H. L., & Ansbacher, R. R. (Eds.). (1956). *The Individual Psychology of Alfred Adler.* New York: Harper & Row, Publishers.

*Arnold, J. (1995). An exploration into the relationship between social interest and self-esteem in undergraduate psychology students (Doctoral dissertation, University of South Carolina, 1995). *Dissertation Abstracts International, 56/06,* B3501.

*Ashby, J. S., Kottman, T., & Rice, K. G. (1998). Adlerian personality priorities: Psychological and attitudinal differences. *Journal of Counseling & Development, 76,* 467–474.

*Bertelson, S. K. (1991). *Clinical correlates of life styles patterns found in psychiatric inpatients.* Unpublished doctoral dissertation, Georgia State University, Atlanta.

Bickhard, M. H., & Ford, B. L. (1976). Adler's concept of social interest: A critical explication. *The Journal of Individual Psychology, 32,* 27–49.

*Boynton, R. D. (1988/1989). Drug addiction, life style personality factors and psychopathology (Doctoral dissertation, Georgia State University, 1988). *Dissertation Abstracts International, 50/03,* A0647.

*Brough, M. F. (1994). Alleviation of loneliness: Evaluation of an Adlerian-based group therapy program. *The Journal of Individual Psychology, 50,* 40–51.

*Brown, D. D. (1988/1989). Aggression and social interest in behavior disordered students (Doctoral dissertation, University of North Texas, 1988). *Dissertation Abstracts International, 49/07,* Al 762.

*Buda, E. M. (1981). Adolescents' perceptions regarding their parents' use of selected Adlerian/Dreikursian childrearing principles and the expression of social interest (Doctoral dissertation, California School of Professional Psychology, 1981). *Dissertation Abstracts International, 42/05,* B2045.

*Bubenzer, D. L, Zarski, J. J., & Walter, D. A. (1991). Measuring social interest: A validation study. *The Journal of Individual Psychology, 47*, 124–135.

*Campbell, M. L. (1998/1999). Measures of control and functioning among mood and anxiety disorders in an outpatient psychological services center setting (Doctoral dissertation, Adler School of Professional Psychology, 1998). *Dissertation Abstracts International, 59/09*, B5073.

*Casey, D. M. (1997/1998). The Basis-A inventory of lifestyle and locus of control: Outpatient substance abusers vs. non-substance abusers (Doctoral dissertation, Adler School of Professional Psychology, 1997). *Dissertation Abstracts International, 58/09*, B5109.

*Chandler, C. K., & Willingham, W. K. (1986). The relationship between perceived early childhood family influence and the established life-style. *The Journal of Individual Psychology, 42*, 388–394.

*Christopher, J. C. (1992). The role of individualism in psychological well-being: Exploring the interplay of ideology, culture, and social science (Doctoral dissertation, University of Texas at Austin, 1992). *Dissertation Abstracts International, 53/12*, A4206.

*Cooper, E. M. (1992/1993). Object relations and defense styles as mediators of stress among older adults (Doctoral dissertation, Columbia University, 1992). *Dissertation Abstracts International, 54/01*, B487.

Crandall, J. E. (1980). Adler's concept of social interest: Theory, measurement, and implications for adjustments. *Journal of Personality and Social Psychology, 39*, 481–495.

Crandall, J. E. (1981). *Theory and measurement of social interest: Empirical tests of Alfred Adler's concept.* New York: Columbia University Press.

*Crandall, J. E. (1984). Social interest as a moderator of life stress. *Journal of Personality and Social Psychology, 47*, 164–174.

*Crandall, J. E., & Biaggio, M. K. (1984). Relations of two measures of social interest to ego defensiveness. *The Journal of Individual Psychology, 40*, 83–91.

*Crandall, J. E., & Kytonen, J. A. (1980). Sex, age, and stress as moderators for the relation between social interest and well-being. *Journal of Individual Psychology, 36*, 169–182.

*Cuff, W. T. (1993/1994). The experience of courage and the characteristics of courageous people (Doctoral dissertation, University of Minnesota, 1993). *Dissertation Abstracts International, 54/10*, B5408.

*Curlette, W. L., Kern, R. M., Gfroerer, K. P., & Whitaker, I. Y. (1999). A comparison of two social interest assessment instruments with implications for managed care. *The Journal of Individual Psychology, 55*, 62–71.

Curlette, W. L., Wheeler, M. S., & Kern, R. M. (1997). *BASIS-A inventory technical manual.* Highlands, NC: TRT Associates, Inc.

*Davidson, K., Smith, N. M., & Jensen, M. C. (1986). Social interest and the library student. *The Journal of Individual Psychology, 42*, 44–49.

*Davis, P. B. (1998/1999). The relationship between family demographic factors, personality, locus of control, and academic achievement in students who have left the family environment in order to attend college (Doctoral dissertation, Georgia State University, 1998). *Dissertation Abstracts International, 59/07*, B3752.

Deshpande, S. P., & Viswesvaran, C. (1992). Is cross-cultural training of expatriate managers effective: A meta-analysis. *International Journal of Inter-Cultural Relations, 16*, 295–310.

*Dinter, L. D. (2000). The relationship between self-efficacy and lifestyle patterns. *The Journal of Individual Psychology, 56(4)*, 462–473.

*Dixon, P. N., Willingham, W. K., Chandler, C. K., & McDougal, K. (1986). Relating social interest and dogmatism to happiness and sense of humor. *The Journal of Individual Psychology, 42*, 421–427.

*Dodd, J. M. (1997). Effects of self-esteem, empathy, and parental bonding on the development of social interest (Doctoral dissertation, University of Missouri, 1997). *Dissertation Abstracts International, 57/08*, B3513.

*Doss, C. R. (1993). Adlerian life styles and the Myers-Briggs type indicator (Doctoral dissertation, University of North Texas, 1993). *Dissertation Abstracts International, 54/05*, A1676.

*Downing, R. (1987/1988). Goals of behavior, social interest, and parent attitudes in an alternative school (Doctoral dissertation, North Texas State University, 1987). *Dissertation Abstracts International, 48/10*, A2541.

*Earles, T. D. (1982). Adlerian life style and clinical depression in mothers of disturbed children (Doctoral dissertation, Georgia State University, 1982). *Dissertation Abstracts International, 43/06*, A1834.

*Edwards, D., & Kern, R. (1995). The implications of teachers' social interest on classroom behavior. *The Journal of Individual Psychology, 51*, 67–73.

*Eidson, C. E., Jr. (1996/1997). Personality similarity between supervisor ratings of subordinates' customer-service work performance (Doctoral dissertation, University of Southern Mississippi, 1996). Dissertation Abstracts International, *57/07*, B4758.

*Emery, W. E. (1998/1999). Coping styles, belonging, and control among a mood and anxiety disorder population (Doctoral dissertation, Adler School of Professional Psychology, 1998). *Dissertation Abstracts International, 59/12*, B6486.

*Evans, W. J. (1996). An investigation into the construct validity of the attitudes about reality scale (Doctoral dissertation, Kent State University, 1996). *Dissertation Abstracts International, 57/ 12*, B7766.

*Farnum, M. K. (1981). Social interest in children (Doctoral dissertation, Northern Illinois University, 1981). *Dissertation Abstracts International, 42/04*, A1487.

*Fish, R. C., & Mozdzierz, G. J. (1991). Validation of the Sulliman Scale of Social Interest with psychotherapy outpatients. *The Journal of Individual Psychology, 47*, 150–153.

*Friedman, S. I. (1983/1984). The effect of Jewish religious education on the moral reasoning and social interest of yeshiva high school students (Doctoral dissertation, Fordham University, 1983). *Dissertation Abstracts International, 44/07*, A2091.

Greever, K. B., Tseng, M. S., & Friedland, B. U. (1973). Development of the social interest index. *Journal of Consulting and Clinical Psychology, 41*, 454–458.

*Hedberg, G, & Huber, R. J. (1995). Homosexuality, gender, communal involvement, and social interest. *The Journal of Individual Psychology, 51*, 244–252.

Hedges, L. V. (1990). Directions for future methodology. In K. W. Wachter and M. L. Straf (Eds.), *The future of meta-analysis* (pp. 11–26). New York: Russell Sage Foundation.

*Hedges, L. V., & Olkin, I. (1985). *Statistical methods for meta-analysis*. Boston, MA: Academic Press, Inc.

*Hettman, D. W., & Jenkins, E. (1990). Volunteerism and social interest. *The Journal of Individual Psychology, 46*, 298–303.

Highlander, D. H. (1984). Adlerian life style, social interest, and depression in parents (Doctoral dissertation, Georgia State University, 1984). *Dissertation Abstracts International, 45/02*, A12516.

*Hornbuckle, D. R. (1992). Counselor mental health: An analysis before and after training (Doctoral dissertation, Georgia State University, 1992). *Dissertation Abstracts International, 53/ 12*, A4210.

Hough, S. L., & Hall, B. W. (1994). Comparison of the Glass and Hunter-Schmidt meta-analytic techniques. *Journal of Educational Research, 87*, 292–296.

*Hsieh, T. T. Y. (1987). Heavenly minded and earthly good: A study of social interest, ethical style, and word spirit orientation among Christians. *Journal of Psychology and Theology, 15*, 144–147.

Hunter, J. E., & Schmidt, F. L. (1990). *Methods of meta-analysis: Correcting error and bias in research findings*. Newbury, CA: Sage Publications.

*Hutner, B. D. (1997/1998). The "BASIS-A inventory" and the "Rorschach InkBlot method": An exploratory correlative study (Doctoral dissertation, Adler School of Professional Psychology, 1997). *Dissertation Abstracts International, 58/10*, B5646.

*Johnston, T. B. (1988). Validation of the life style personality inventory and the prediction of success in treating pain (Doctoral dissertation, Georgia State University, 1988). *Dissertation Abstracts International, 49/06*, B2406.

*Joubert, C. E. (1986). Social interest, loneliness, and narcissism. *Psychological Reports, 58*, 870.

*Joubert, C. E. (1987). Pet ownership, social interest, and sociability. *Psychological Reports, 61*, 401–402.

*Joubert, C. E. (1989). The famous sayings test: Sex differences and some correlations with other variables. *Psychological Reports, 64*, 763–766.

*Joubert, C. E. (1995). Associations of social personality factors with personal habits. *Psychological Reports, 76*, 1315–1321.

*Joubert, C. E. (1998). Narcissism, need for power, and social interest. *Psychological Reports, 82,* 701–702.

*Kaplan, H. B. (1991). Sex differences in social interest. *The Journal of Individual Psychology, 47,* 120–123.

*Keene, K. K., Jr., & Wheeler, M. S. (1994). Substance use in college freshman and Adlerian lifestyle themes. *The Journal of Individual Psychology, 50,* 97–109.

*Keiter, M. H. (1999). An analysis of the nature of the relationship between faculty social interest and students' perceptions of teaching effectiveness (Doctoral dissertation, Pennsylvania State University, 1999). *Dissertation Abstracts International, 60/08,* A2827.

*Kern, R. M., Edwards, D., Flowers, C, Lambert, R., & Belangee, S. (1999). Teachers' lifestyles and their perception of students' behaviors. *The Journal of Individual Psychology, 55,* 422–435.

*Kern, R., Gfroerer, K., Summers, Y., Curlette, W., & Matheny, K. (1996). Life-style, personality and stress coping. *The Journal of Individual Psychology, 52,* 42–54.

*Kern, R. M., Penick, J. M., & Hamby, R. D. (1996). Prediction of diabetic adherence using the BASIS-A inventory. *The Diabetes Educator, 22,* 367–373.

*Knutson, K. A. (1999). An investigation of relationships between school culture and leadership social interest (Doctoral dissertation, Florida Atlantic University, 1999). *Dissertation Abstracts International, 60/06,* A1850.

*Kottman, T., & Ashby, J. S. (1999). Social interest and multidimensional perfectionism. *The Journal of Individual Psychology, 55,* 176–185.

*Kutchins, C. B., Curlette, W. L., & Kern, R. M. (1997). To what extent is there a relationship between personality priorities and lifestyle themes? *The Journal of Individual Psychology, 53,* 373–387.

*Lack, L. C. (1996). An exploration into the relationship between social interest and role-taking empathy (Doctoral dissertation, University of South Carolina, 1996). *Dissertation Abstracts International, 57/03,* A1032.

*Lane, W. D. (1992). Assessing the susceptibility of the life style personality inventory to socially desirable and socially undesirable response sets: A construct validity study (Doctoral dissertation, Georgia State University, 1992). *Dissertation Abstracts International, 53/02,* A407.

*Leak, G. K. (1982). Two social interest measures and social desirability response sets. *The Journal of Individual Psychology, 38,* 42–46.

*Leak, G. K. (1992). Religiousness and social interest: An empirical assessment. *The Journal of Individual Psychology, 48,* 288–301.

*Leak, G. K., & Gardner, L. E. (1990). Sexual attitudes, love attitudes, and social interest. *The Journal of Individual Psychology, 46,* 55–60.

*Leak, G. K., Millard, R. J., Perry, N. W., & Williams, D. E. (1985). An investigation of the nomological network of social interest. *Journal of Research in Personality, 19,* 197–207.

*Leak, G. K., & Williams, D. E. (1989). Relationship between social interest, alienation, and psychological hardiness. *The Journal of Individual Psychology, 45,* 369–375.

*Leak, G. K., & Williams, D. E. (1991). Relationship between social interest and perceived family environment. *The Journal of Individual Psychology, 47,* 159–165.

*Lee, I. (1992). The effect of three forms of individualistic-collectivistic group counseling on Korean clients' social commitment, individualistic-collectivistic orientation, and perceptions of counselor functioning (Doctoral dissertation, George Washington University, 1992). *Dissertation Abstracts International, 53/03,* A722.

*Lingg, M. A. (1990). Adolescent discouragement development of an assessment instrument (Doctoral dissertation, University of North Texas, 1990). *Dissertation Abstracts International, 51/05,* A1510.

*Lockwood, C. T. (1982). Psychosocial adjustment to cancer and its relationship to social interest, dysfunctional beliefs, religious orientation, and selected physical and demographic variables (Doctoral dissertation, West Virginia University, 1982). *Dissertation Abstracts International, 43/03,* B854.

*Logan, E. M. (1990). The relationship of Adlerian life style themes and social interest of level of adjustment in couples (Doctoral dissertation, Georgia State University, 1990). *Dissertation Abstracts International, 51/10,* A3366.

*Logan, E., Kern, R., Curlette, W., & Trad, A. (1993). Couples adjustment, life-style similarity, and social interest. *The Journal of Individual Psychology, 49,* 456–467.

*Maltby, J., MacAskill, A., Day, L., & Garner, I. (1999). Social interest, and Eysneck's personality dimensions. *Psychological Reports, 85*, 197–200.

*Markowski, E. M., & Everett, L. W. (1988). Social interest and mothers of exceptional children. *The Journal of Individual Psychology, 44*, 35–40.

*Markowski, E. M., & Greenwood, P. D. (1984). Marital adjustment as a correlate of social interest. *The Journal of Individual Psychology, 40*, 300–308.

Matheny, K. B., Aycock, D. W., Pugh, J. L., Curlette, W. L., & Cannella, K. A. S. (1986). Stress coping: A qualitative and quantitative synthesis with implications for treatment. *The Counseling Psychologist, 14*, 499–549.

*McDougal, K. B. (1985/1986). Attribution of responsibility: Community attitudes toward survivors of suicide (Doctoral dissertation, Texas Tech University, 1985). *Dissertation Abstracts International, 46/08*, B2788.

*McGreevy, M. H. (1997/1998). Early recollections of life style themes of sex offenders (Doctoral dissertation, Adler School of Professional Psychology, 1997). *Dissertation Abstracts International, 58/07*, B3929.

*McGreevy, M. H., Newbauer, J. F., & Carich, M. S. (2001). Comparison of lifestyle profiles of incarcerated sexual offenders with those of persons incarcerated for other crimes. *The Journal of Individual Psychology, 57*, 67–77.

*McKenzie, L. K. (1998/1999). Using the BASIS-A inventory with adults who are deaf (Doctoral dissertation, Adler School of Professional Psychology, 1998). *Dissertation Abstracts International, 59/12*, B6510.

*McMahan, O. (1997). Programmed distance writing as an intervention for seminary couples (Doctoral dissertation, Georgia State University, 1997). *Dissertation Abstracts International, 51/05*, A3367.

*Meunier, G. F., & Royce, S. (1988). Age and social interest. *The Journal of Individual Psychology, 44*, 50–52.

*Miller, M. J., Denton, G. O., & Tobacyk, J. (1986). Social interests and feelings of hopelessness among elderly persons. *Psychological Reports, 59*, 410.

*Miller, M. J., Smith, T. S., Wilkinson, L., & Tobacyk, J. (1987). Narcissism and social interest among counselors-in-training. *Psychological Reports, 60*, 756–766.

*Miranda, A. O. (1994). Adlerian life styles and acculturation as predictors of the mental health in Hispanic adults (Doctoral dissertation, Georgia State University, 1994). *Dissertation Abstracts International, 55/10*, A3094.

*Miranda, A. O., & Umhoefer, D. (1998). Depression and social interest differences between Latinos in dissimilar acculturation stages. *Journal of Mental Health Counseling, 20*, 150–171.

*Miranda, A. O., & White, P. E. (1993). The relationship between acculturation level and social interest among Hispanic adults. *The Journal of Individual Psychology, 49*, 76–85.

Mosak, H. H. (1991). "I don't have social interest": Social interest as construct. *The Journal of Individual Psychology, 47*, 309–320.

*Mozdzierz, G. J., Greenblatt, R. L., & Murphy, T. J. (1986). Social interest: The validity of two scales. *The Journal of Individual Psychology, 42*, 35–43.

*Mozdzierz, G. J., Greenblatt, R. L., & Murphy, T. J. (1988). Further validation of the Sulliman scale of social interest and the social interest scale. *The Journal of Individual Psychology, 44*, 30–34.

*Mozdzierz, G. J., & Semyck, R. W. (1980). Relationship between alcoholics' social interest and attitude toward success and failure. *The Journal of Individual Psychology, 36*, 61–64.

*Mullis, F. Y., Kern, R. M., & Curlette, W. L. (1987). Life-style themes and social interest: A further factor analytic study. *The Journal of Individual Psychology, 43*, 339–352.

*Murphy, P. L. (1994). Social interest and psychological androgyny: Conceptualized and tested. *The Journal of Individual Psychology, 50*, 18–30.

*Nelson, A. S. (1984). Social interest and job satisfaction among full-time employed nurses (Doctoral dissertation, University of North Texas, 1984). *Dissertation Abstracts International, 45/07*, B2105.

O'Connell, W. E. (1991). Humanistic identification: A new translation for *Gemeinschaftsgefühl*. *The Journal of Individual Psychology, 47*, 26–27.

*Overrocker, J. M. (1991/1992). Identification of items to measure the team player: Relationships between items of the life style personality inventory and observation of behavior during an outdoor ropes experience (Doctoral dissertation, Georgia State University, 1991). *Dissertation Abstracts International, 53/01*, A106.

*Paloutain, R. F., Jackson, S. L., & Crandall, J. E. (1978). Conversion experience, belief system, and personal and ethical attitudes. *Journal of Psychology and Theology, 6,* 266–275.

*Peterson, T. J. (1985). A multitrait-multimethod comparison of two social interest instruments in an alcoholic population (Doctoral dissertation, Iowa State University, 1985). *Dissertation Abstracts International, 46/05,* B1697.

*Peterson, T. J., Epperson, D. L., & Hutzell, R. R. (1985). A comparison of two social interest measures with female convicts. *The Journal of Individual Psychology, 41,* 349–353.

*Pilkington, L. R. (1998/1999). The effects of social context factors on compliance with the treatment of essential hypertension (Doctoral dissertation, Georgia State University, 1998). *Dissertation Abstracts International, 59/10,* B5585.

*Pollock, B. D. (1991). Interpersonal level of functioning in chronic schizophrenics: Its relationship to affective decoding skills and social interest (Doctoral dissertation, University of New Orleans, 1991). *Dissertation Abstracts International, 53/01,* B198.

*Praphruitkit, T. (1987). The relationship among English and oral communication apprehension, social interest, locus of control of Far Eastern students (Doctoral dissertation, North Texas State University, 1987). *Dissertation Abstracts International, 48/03,* A0610.

Rareshide, M., & Kern, R. (1991). Social interest: The haves and the have nots. *The Journal of Individual Psychology, 47,* 464–476.

*Riggins, L. R. (1990). An exploration of Adlerian theory: Social interest and self-esteem of nurses participating in a high social interest treatment program (Doctoral dissertation, Georgia State University, 1990). *Dissertation Abstracts International, 40/02,* A4478.

*Rimi, R. J. (1983/1984). Social interest and threat in interpersonal bargaining: Variables affecting cooperation level (Doctoral dissertation, St. John's University, 1983). *Dissertation Abstracts International, 45/04,* B1323.

*Rodd, J. (1994). Social interest, psychological well-being, and maternal stress. *The Journal of Individual Psychology, 50,* 58–68.

Rosenthal, R. (1994). Parametric measures of effect size. In H. Cooper & L. V. Hedges (Eds.), *The handbook of research synthesis* (pp. 231–244). New York: The Russell Sage Foundation.

Rotter, J. B. (1962). An analysis of Adlerian psychology from a research orientation. *The Journal of Individual Psychology, 18,* 3–11.

*Sanicola, L. C. (1983/1984). The relationship between cooperation and stress-related disorders among organizational personnel (Doctoral dissertation, California School of Professional Psychology, 1983). *Dissertation Abstracts International, 44/11,* B3542.

*Sarowitz, M. (1992/1993). Social interest in alcoholics who are members of Alcoholics Anonymous (Doctoral dissertation, Adler School of Professional Psychology, 1992). *Dissertation Abstracts International, 54/01,* B478.

*Sauls, M. B. (1987). A manager matching strategies model for buyers: A discriminate analysis based on Adlerian and Jungian theory (Doctoral dissertation, Georgia State University, 1987). *Dissertation Abstracts International, 49/03,* B907.

*Schneider, D. L. (1991/1992). Social interest, social concern and possible selves in adolescents: Volunteers vs. non-volunteers (Doctoral dissertation, California School of Professional Psychology, 1991). *Dissertation Abstracts International, 53/02,* A449.

*Schneider, L. J., & Reuterfors, D. L. (1981). The impact of birth order and sex on social interest. *Journal of Individual Psychology, 37,* 102–106.

*Silon, B. (1986). A group therapy treatment model for panic disorder and agoraphobia with an Adlerian emphasis. (Doctoral dissertation, Graduate School of Union of Experimenting Colleges and Universities, 1986). *Dissertation Abstracts International, 47/11,* B4665.

*Smith, J. J. (1994/1995). Early recollections and their use in discriminating the personality characteristics of alcoholics (Doctoral dissertation, Seton Hall University, 1994). *Dissertation Abstracts International, 56/02,* B1122.

*Snyder, M. T. (1997). Differentiating between offenders and non-offenders of child sexual abuse in outpatient treatment settings using the BASIS-A and the functional interview (Doctoral dissertation, Adler School of Professional Psychology, 1997). *Dissertation Abstracts International, 58/10,* B5657.

*Steel, C. A. (1997/1998). The impact of volunteerism on self-efficacy of inner city children (Doctoral dissertation, Adler School of Professional Psychology, 1997). *Dissertation Abstracts International, 59/06,* B3076.

*Stevenson, D. H. (1981). A multidimensional empirical analysis of mature Christian spirituality (Doctoral dissertation, Rosemead School of Psychology, Biola University, 1981). *Dissertation Abstracts International, 42/03*, B1156.

*Stevick, R. A., Dixon, P. N., & Willingham, W. K. (1980). Locus of control and behavioral self-response measures of social interest. *The Journal of Individual Psychology, 36*, 183–190.

*St. John, C. L. (1995/1996). Testing the construct validity of the Sulliman scale of social interest (Doctoral dissertation, University of North Texas, 1995). *Dissertation Abstracts International 56/08*, B4636.

*Suich, P. S. (1991/1992). Social interest: Triangulating the construct with measures of rational attitudes, communal values, and cooperative behavior (Doctoral dissertation, University of Georgia, 1991). *Dissertation Abstracts International, 52/09*, B4988.

Sulliman, J. R. (1973). The development of a scale for the measurement of social interest. *Dissertation Abstracts International, 34/06*, B2914.

*Tavis, T. M. (1990/1991). Social interest: A critique of current models and proposed communitarian interpretation (Doctoral dissertation, University of Texas at Austin, 1990). *Dissertation Abstracts International, 51/11*, A3681.

Thornton, J. M. (1997/1998). A study of relationship among social interest, marital satisfaction, and religious participation (Doctoral dissertation, University of North Texas, 1997). *Dissertation Abstracts International, 58/07*, A2551.

*Tobacyk, J. (1983). Paranormal beliefs, interpersonal trust, and social interest. *Psychological Reports, 53*, 229–230.

*Walsh, S. J. (1997/1998). The interrelationships of Ellis's self interest, Adler's social interests, and dysphoria (Doctoral dissertation, Pacific University, 1997). *Dissertation Abstracts International, 58/12*, B6831.

*Watkins, C. E., Jr. (1983). Some characteristics of research on Adlerian psychological theory, 1970–1981. *The Journal of Individual Psychology, 39*, 99–110.

*Watkins, C. E., Jr. (1984/1985). An examination of the relationship between social interest and self-management effectiveness (Doctoral dissertation, University of Tennessee, 1984). *Dissertation Abstracts International, 45–10*, A3101.

Watkins, C. E., Jr. (1994). Measuring social interest. *The Journal of Individual Psychology, 50*, 69–96.

*Watkins, C. E., Jr., & St. John, C. (1994). Validity of the Sulliman Scale of Social Interest. *The Journal of Individual Psychology, 50*, 166–169.

*Watts, R., & Trusty, J. (1995). Social interest and counselor effectiveness: An exploratory study. *The Journal of Individual Psychology, 51*, 293–298.

*Wheeler, M. S. (1992). Unpublished study of LSPISII and depression.

*Wheeler, M. S., & Acheson, S. K. (1993). Criterion-related validity of the life-style personality inventory. *The Journal of Individual Psychology, 49*, 51–57.

Wheeler, M. S., Kern, R. M., & Curlette, W. L. (1982). *Wheeler-Kern-Curlette Life Style Inventory.* Unpublished manuscript. Georgia State University.

*Wheeler, M. S., & White, P. E. (1991). The relationship between lifestyle personality inventory and external locus of control. *The Journal of Individual Psychology, 47*, 372–379.

*White, M. L. (1990/1991). A study of elite collegiate woman athletes: Psychological characteristics and motivation in sports (Doctoral dissertation, University of Georgia, 1990). *Dissertation Abstracts International, 51/11*, A3683.

*White, P. E. (1989/1990). A multidimensional analysis of the mental health of graduate counselors in training (Doctoral dissertation, Georgia State University, 1989). *Dissertation Abstracts International, 50/11*, 3488.

*Zarski, J. J., Bubenzer, D. L., & West, J. (1986). Social interest, stress, and the prediction of health status. *Journal of Counseling and Development, 64*, 386–389.

*Zauezniewski, J. A. (1992/1993). Health seeking resources and adaptive functioning in depressed and nondepressed adults (Doctoral dissertation, Case Western Reserve University, 1992). *Dissertation Abstracts International, 53/08*, B4038.

CHAPTER 11

Adler's Concept of Social Interest: A Critical Explication

MARK H. BICKHARD[1] and BRIAN LEE FORD

Adler's concept of social interest is not a single concept, but rather a complex of concepts, theoretical propositions, and functional issues whose richness and complexity demand explication. The analysis in this paper proceeds by considering possible explications of social interest that can be derived more or less directly from Adler's writings. Each potential explication is examined in terms of its own internal logic and in terms of its fit with other areas of Adler's theory. Unacceptable explications are dismissed and modified in a process of convergence upon a final valid core concept. The fruits of this process are, hopefully, threefold: (1) a delineation of the boundaries of the core of social interest, (2) an elucidation of a number of apparent interpretations of social interest that are *not* valid, and (3) a clarification of the relationships between social interest and other issues in Adler's theory.

Ontological and Functional Levels of Consideration

An explication of social interest must proceed on two levels: the ontological and the functional. Ontologically, we want to know what social interest *is;* what its nature is and how it differs from other things of the same nature. Functionally, we want to know what the concept *does* in our theory; how it helps to understand and explain reality. As will be seen, aside from the potential for difficulties within each level, there is no a priori guarantee that the two levels are consistent with each other. One of the strongest tools of this explication, in fact, will turn out to be an iteration between what Adler appears to mean by social interest and what he appears to want the concept to do, hopefully coverging on what social interest *must* mean and what it is *possible* for it to do. This iterative dynamic will dominate most of the ensuing analysis.

Initially, we know that "Social feeling means ... a struggle for a communal form" (Adler, 1964, p. 275). "Social interest ... is rooted in the germ cell. But it is rooted as a potentiality, not as an actual ability" (Ansbacher & Ansbacher, 1973, p. 25). Social interest is some relationship to community which must be developed. We also know that "all that constitutes a failure is so because it obstructs social feeling, whether children, neurotics, criminals, or suicides are in question" (Adler, 1964, p. 283). Social interest, then, is in some sense fundamental to mental health.

These general relationships to community and to mental health will form the beginnings of our ontological and functional explorations. What is not so clear is just exactly what social interest is when it is developed and just exactly what relationship it has to mental health.

An Initial Elimination

One potential misunderstanding has been clearly eliminated by Adler himself.

> It is not a question of any present-day community or society, or of political or religious forms. On the contrary, the goal that is best suited for perfection must be a goal that stands for an ideal society amongst all mankind, the ultimate fulfillment of evolution. (Adler, 1964, p. 275)

It is clear that commitment to some particular present-day society is not necessarily associated with mental health. Social interest is a much more abstract concept than that:

> It means particularly the interest in, or feeling with, the community sub specie aeternitatis (under the aspect of eternity). It means the striving for a community which must be thought of as everlasting, as we could think of it if mankind had reached the goal of perfection. (Ansbacher & Ansbacher, 1956, p. 142)

Social Interest as Motive and as Effect

It is here that we begin to encounter difficulties with Adler's lack of preci-sion; when we attempt to discern just what this "interest in" or "feeling with" that constitutes social interest really is, we discover multiple possibil-ities all of which can be supported within Adler's writings. Two possibilities that are particularly troublesome because Adler could be construed as hav-ing contradicted himself concerning them are social interest as *motive* and social interest as *effect*.

Social Interest as Motive

On the one hand, Adler speaks of social interest in terms of a "*striving* [emphasis added] for community" (Ansbacher, 1956, p. 142) or a "*struggle* [emphasis added] for a communal form" (Adler, 1964, p. 275). Social interest "is an innate potentiality which has to be *consciously* [emphasis added] developed" (Ansbacher, 1956, p. 134). Much of the support for social interest as conscious motive is not explicit, but rather implicit in the presuppositions of his discussions of the role of social interest in society, for example: "if the person understood how in evading the demands of evolution he had gone astray, then he would give up his present course and join the general mass of humanity" (Adler, 1964, p. 281). In discussing the possibility of error in social evolution, Adler states, "the only thing that can save us from being crucified on a harmful fiction ... is the guiding star of universal welfare; under its lead we shall be more able to find the path without suffering any setbacks" (Adler, 1964, p. 278). It is easy to derive implications in these and other discussions that social interest is some kind of conscious and preeminent motive structure oriented toward uni-versal welfare.

Social Interest as Effect

On the other hand, Adler is rather explicit in stating that social interest is not a motive, but rather an effect: "We are not speaking here of professed motives. We are closing our ears to professions and looking at achieve-ments" (Ansbacher, 1956, p. 153). We read, for example, that "genius is to be defined as no more than supreme usefulness," "he is useful to culture," "if we apply the social measure to artists and poets, we note that they serve a social function more than anyone else." And, finally, that "this value ... depends upon a high degree of courage and social interest" (all from Ansbacher, 1956, p. 153). Perhaps clearest of all is "the normal man is an individual who lives in society and whose mode of life is so adapted that, *whether he wants it or not* [emphasis added], society derives a certain advantage from his work" (Ansbacher, 1956, p. 154). Motives and intentions are not the point, consequences are.

Analysis of Motive and Effect

It is clear that on internal grounds we would be constrained to accept social interest as effect over social interest as motive if those were the only possibilities available; the evidence for social interest as motive tends to be suggestive and indirect, while that for social interest as effect tends to be straightforward and direct. The apparent support for social interest as motive is possibly a manifestation of Adler's lack of differentiation between goals, assumptions, etc., as actual structures in consciousness, and similar concepts as descriptively useful fictions. In any case, we are not finished with the ontological explication of social interest for two reasons: (1) these are not the only possibilities available, and (2) there are independent reasons not only for rejecting social interest as motive, but for rejecting social interest as effect as well. The basis for rejection is, in both cases, a conflict between these ontological explications and the basic functional role that social interest is to serve in Adler's theory—as a foundation for the concept of mental health.

Analysis of Social Interest as Motive

Social interest as motive would imply that only those individuals were mentally healthy who were explicitly motivated to work toward the general welfare. This eliminates such apparently healthy primary motives as those toward truth, beauty, and so on, except insofar as these motives might be consciously derived from the even more primary motive of the general welfare. Social interest as motive would thus exclude from mental health probably the majority of people that one would reasonably want to consider mentally healthy.

If it is countered that motives directed toward such things as truth or beauty do not need to be explicitly and consciously derived from considerations of the general welfare in the healthy individual, because efforts toward such motives *do* in fact contribute to the general welfare, whether or not that is of consideration to the individual, then we have moved from social interest as motive to social interest as effect: these motives could "count" as social interest only because of their consequences.

Analysis of Social Interest as Effect

Social interest as effect fails as a foundation for mental health in two senses. First, it fails to select some people who would reasonably be considered mentally healthy; it underselects relative to mental health. Specifically, it fails to identify those who on other accounts would be considered healthy and who would have contributed to social evolution if it had not been for some exogenous intervention which destroyed the individual's efforts; e.g., a fire or earthquake that destroys an artist's life work, or a war that eliminates a humanist's reforms, or simply an honest error in what the individual was attempting in the first place. The contributions of an individual's efforts are not entirely of his own making; they depend on extraneous "random" factors as well—the random or probabilistic factors of evolutionary selection.

The counter argument that social interest as effect involves not the actual and ultimate contribution an individual makes, but rather the involvement of the individual in activities that *tend* to make contributions to the general welfare—subject to the normal random selective processes of evolution—might seem to save social interest as effect from the charge of underselection, but it fails to avoid the second problem with respect to mental health; it identifies as healthy some people that could not be reasonably considered mentally healthy (i.e., it overselects relative to mental health). It is easily possible for someone to be highly motivated toward truth or beauty, for example, and even for them to have in fact made significant contributions, and still be quite neurotic; respective examples might be Isaac Newton and Edvard Munch. Social interest as effect thus either underselects or overselects relative to mental health, and thus fails as a critical explication.

Social Interest as Tendency

A possible redemption of the "social-interest-as-tendency-to-contribute" concept would be to argue that social interest is just exactly the biologically innate tendency for individuals to contribute to the evolution of the species' community. A tendency, of course, subject to the natural randomness of evolution. Thus, for example, "we conceive the idea of social interest, social feeling, as the ultimate form of mankind, a condition in which all questions of life, all relationship to the external world are solved. It is a normative ideal, a direction giving goal" (Ansbacher, 1973, p. 35). Social interest, in this passage, is the ultimate perfection of mankind, toward which social evolution is headed, such that "we shall approach a condition of larger contributions, of greater ability to cooperate, where every individual presents himself more fully as part of the whole" (Ansbacher, 1973, p. 35). And, finally, "we are in the midst of the stream of evolution, but we notice this as little as we do the spinning of the earth on its axis" (Adler, 1964, pp. 271–272).

Relating this ontological concept of social interest to mental health, however, turns out to be rather difficult. Clearly it is not desirable to include the tendency of mentally unhealthy individuals to make social contributions in the concept of social interest, for then social interest as a concept would again overaccept relative to mental health. Therefore, it is necessary to describe social interest as the evolutionary tendency of *mentally healthy* individuals to make contributions to the community of mankind. This explication suffers neither from overselection—by definition—nor from underselection. It is consistent with Adler, and, in addition, probably true that all mentally healthy individuals have an innately based tendency to contribute to social evolution. Thus explicated, it is consistent functionally and consistent with Adler, but involves us in a trivial circularity if we attempt to found the concept of mental health upon it: mental health has been used in the explication. It is functionally consistent, but functionally useless—we are forced to some independent basis for explicating mental health. Thus stripped of its primary functional role, as a foundation for mental health, the concept of social interest would become a rather minor appendage to Adler's theory. Such a trivial role is hardly consistent with Adler at all, and in fact, does not do justice to the insights contained in the concept.

At this point in this paper, however, we have not indicated those insights. Three conceivable ontological explications of social interest have been considered, all initially plausible and supportable to varying degrees within Adler's writings, and all have been found upon analysis to be unacceptable.[2]

An Alternative Strategy

In Adler's most concise definition, social interest

> means feeling with the whole, ... under the aspect of eternity. It means striving for a form of community which must be thought of as everlasting, as it could be thought of if mankind had reached the goal of perfection. (Ansbacher, 1973, pp. 34–35)

We have been to this point primarily considering possible interpretations of such words as "feeling" and "striving," without success. That is, we have been exploring what kind of an activity or process social interest might be. An alternative strategy would be to consider such words as "whole" or "community"—to explore the object or goal of the activity— and perhaps to infer the nature of this activity from its object.[3,4] As discussed earlier, one possible object has already been explicitly ruled out by Adler—particular present day societies.

Social and Institutional Structure

Another possible object for social interest (another potential interpretation of "community under the aspect of eternity") might be the perfect society in the sense of the perfect social and institutional structure of a culminated social evolution. Clearly, social evolution is not likely to ever actually culminate, but all Adler needs to successfully provide an object for social interest is a useful fiction, a "normative ideal," and he need not make any particular assumptions about any actual culmination. In accordance with this, we find: "Never can the individual be the goal of the ideal of perfection, but only mankind as a *cooperating community*" (Ansbacher, 1973, p. 40). Adler writes that a real fellow creature must cooperate for the amelioration of the wrongs of the community "and further that he must not expect this amelioration to be brought about by some mythical tendency to evolve, or through the efforts of other people" (Adler, 1964, p. 282). Obviously, no one can expect to know what the ultimate social form might be—"It is obvious that we are concerned not with the possession of truth, but with the struggle for it" (Adler, 1964, p. 279)—but, under the lead of the concept of social interest, "we shall be more able to find the path without suffering any setbacks" (Adler, 1964, p. 278).[5]

The primary difficulty with ideal social and institutional structure as the object of social interest is that it seems impossible to accept this object without also accepting social interest as a motive at the level of individual activity, and we immediately encounter the previously discussed difficulties. Although it is difficult to imagine working toward some ideal institutional structure without some corresponding motive, with some stretching we might coordinate this object with the activity or process of social interest as effect, but again we encounter previously discussed functional problems regarding the identification of mental health. In general, it is difficult to imagine how the concept of ideal social and institutional structures can constitute all or even part of the definition of individual mental health no matter what activity it might be combined with. It is also worth noting that, although Adler wrote a great deal about the elimination of specific social problems such as war, prejudice, etc., he did not himself venture into speculations about ideal social and institutional structures per se. Perfection of social structure, then, is not an acceptable object of social interest.

Man as Socius and Man as Human

It is perhaps of significance that the German word which is translated as social interest is *Gemeinschaftsgefühl* and not *Gesellschaftsgefübl*—that is, feeling for "community" rather than a feeling for "society." Besides giving us further reason to reject ideal institutional structure as the object of social interest, this choice of Adler's (and the fact that it is a choice within the German language) provides an additional suggestion concerning the object or goal of social interest—the ideal community of man in precisely a non-institutional sense of community: the ideal interpersonal fellowship of man, or the ideal man as human being.

Actually, we again have more than one possibility: (1) the ideal of man as interpersonal being, which I will term "man-as-socius,"[6] and (2) the ideal of man as human being, which I will term "man-as-human." Man-as-socius refers to man's capability of relating to and interacting with other human beings, while man-as-human refers to that broader class of particularly human potentialities which would include man-as-socius, but would also include, for example, such potentialities as encountering and transcending one's individual finitude, or deriving meaning from one's own experience. Thus man-as-human is at the same time broader and less specific than man-as-socius.

Man-as-Socius

Again there is support within Adler's writing for alternative interpretations of social interest. Thus, concerning man-as-socius, we find in Adler's strongest comments that social interest "means a striving for a *form* [emphasis added] of community" (Ansbacher, 1973, p. 34), a form of community in which "the individual [can never] be the ideal of perfection, but only mankind as a *cooperating community*" (Ansbacher, 1973, p. 40). In conjunction with such support for man-as-socius as an object of social interest, we also find support for a complementary process or capacity: "We see immediately that this ability coincides in part with what we call identification or empathy" (Ansbacher, 1956, p. 136), and "All of the problems of human life demand, as I have said, capacity for cooperation and preparation for it—the visible sign of social feeling. In this disposition courage and happiness are included" (Adler, 1964, p. 284). Thus social interest appears to be an ability for identification or empathy, which constitutes a capacity for cooperation, which in turn permits a participation in the evolution toward an ideal cooperating community.

Man-as-Human

Concerning man-as-human, the search for textual support must be somewhat more careful than usual; if man-as-socius is included as part of man-as-human, then support for man-as-socius is ipso facto support for man-as-human per se. But we seek support not simply for man-as-human per se, but rather for man-as-human as differentiated from man-as-socius. Thus we must find support for at least some of those characteristics of man-as-human that are not part of man-as-socius; e.g., issues of individual meaningfulness.

Accordingly, we find "what happens to those persons who have contributed nothing? They have disappeared, have become extinct" (Ansbacher, 1973, p. 36) and, even more clearly,

> What has happened to those people who have contributed nothing to the general welfare? ... They have disappeared completely. Nothing remains of them.... It is as though the questioning cosmos had given the command: "Away with you! You have not grasped the meaning of life. You cannot endure into the future!" (Adler, 1964, p. 279)

The intended relevance of social interest to issues of life's meaning, and thus to man-to-human, is apparent. In support of man-as-human as object of social interest, we also find a strong emphasis in Adler's writings on a complementary capacity: the creative power of the individual, the power of individual choice (e.g., Ansbacher, 1973, pp. 86–87, 293–295).

Thus we find support in terms of object and support in terms of capacity for both man-as-socius and man-as-human. We are thus again confronted with two candidates for the ontological explication of social interest. Optimally, we could now, as before, turn to functional considerations to clarify and select between them. This is, in fact, what is intended, but the involvement of functional considerations in the issues of man-as-socius and man-as-human is much broader and more complex than with previous issues, and will require, before we proceed on the ontological level, a further explication of the functional characteristics involved.

Functional Considerations

There are, in fact, three primary functions which Adler attempts to make the concept of social interest serve: (1) as the foundation for morality and moral judgment, (2) as the foundation for human meaningfulness, and (3) as the foundation for mental health. Furthermore, the sense of "foundation" in these functions appears to be the same in all three cases: (1) social interest *is* morality, meaningfulness, and mental health—that is, they are identical kinds of things, and (2) social interest is both necessary and sufficient for morality, meaningfulness, and mental health—that is, social interest is implied by each of the three, and conversely, each is implied by social interest. Taken literally, these functions would together imply that social interest, morality, meaningfulness, and mental health were all different names for the same concept. This is prima facie absurd, and thus there must be an error or errors in the argument; examination will show that there are, in fact, errors regarding all three functions, but that they are not the same in all three cases.

1. Morality

Concerning the identification of social interest with morality, Adler states that "What we call good or bad character can be judged only from the viewpoint of the community" (Ansbacher, 1956, p. 130) and notes that:

> If there exists, at least to some extent, a reliable knowledge of that meaning of life which lies beyond our own experience, then it is clear that this puts those persons in the wrong who flagrantly contradict it. (Adler, 1964, pp. 16–17)

Note that those individuals who contradict the meaning of life are not simply in error, they are wrong. In context, it is clear that the meaning of life referred to is social interest—thus, it is wrong to violate the principles or characteristics of social interest, or, conversely, to develop social interest as a moral imperative. Since social interest is also the criterion for mental health, we also find that to develop mental health is a moral imperative, i.e., psychopathology is by the nature of things always also moral guilt. By thus construing social interest as criterion for both ethical value and mental health, Adler both explains and justifies his pervasive willingness to moralize issues of mental health and mental illness: failures in mental health are always also failures in social interest which, in turn, are always failures in morality.

Objections. There are a number of problems with this. To begin, it is questionable what proper role moral evaluations have in a theory of personality and mental health in the first place. Second, Adler does not develop any arguments for this purported function of social interest; it is rather a claim supported by the unexamined assumptions in Adler's style and usage. Third, the truth of claim is not obvious—it seems easy enough to think of psychopathologies that do not obviously involve ethical failures (e.g., a simple phobia) and thus the claim, even if true, requires argument. Fourth, it is possible to think of examples (e.g., childhood autism) for which the claim seems exceedingly implausible and thus, in the absence of serious counterargument, it must be considered disproven.

Category error. There is a fifth and even more fundamental objection that does not directly involve considerations of mental health, but is rather intrinsic to the identification of morality with social interest. It is a common philosophical claim that issues of ethics cannot proceed solely from issues of fact; you cannot derive "ought" from "is," and to attempt to do so is to confuse completely different kinds or levels of discourse—it is to commit what is called a category error, a confusion of fundamental categories. Adler's claim either violates this philosophical position, and thus requires extensive (and absent) rebuttal of philosophical arguments, or else it makes both social interest and morality not matters of the factual relationship between an individual and his world, but rather pure matters of value judgment. Thus, the conceptual content of social interest would lose contact with the basic factual characteristics of an individual's relationship to the world—it would be impossible to arrive at a value-free understanding of an individual's social interest. This position would seem to be consonant with some of Adler's discussion, such as those in which he moralizes social interest: "and thus each separate individual is not only responsible for every deviation from it [the social ideal] but has also to expiate it" (Adler, 1964, p. 283), but in direct contradiction to others:

> In Individual Psychology all irrefutable facts of experience are looked at and understood from this point of view [that of social feeling], and its scientific system has been developed under the pressure of these experiential facts.... Individual Psychology has done all that is necessary to satisfy the demands of a rigorous scientific doctrine.... If I am venturing now to maintain the right of Individual Psychology to be accepted as a view of the universe, since I use it for the purpose of explaining the meaning of life, I have to exclude all moral and religious conceptions that judge between virtue and vice. (Adler, 1964, pp. 276–277)

Clearly, Adler is involved in internal contradictions concerning social interest and morality.

With regard to the identification of social interest with mental health, this separation from basic facts would imply that it is not possible to make a value free judgment that an individual is in a dysfunctional relationship with his environment; or in other words, that all conceivable judgments of dysfunction are value laden. It is clear that some judgments of dysfunction are value laden, but the implication that all such judgments are necessarily so is highly dubious, and, at a minimum, requires extensive argument in its own right.

In view of these arguments and internal contradictions, and in the absence of any counterarguments, it is necessary to conclude that, at a minimum, Adler did not avoid the objection that there is a category error in his conceptualization of morality. Without a construction that successfully deals with this objection, there can be no satisfactory definition of morality in Adler, for he attempts to define it directly in terms of social interest, which is precisely what must be rejected. This error, incidentally, seems to have definite consequences in Adler's thought; it has the form of a definition of ethical content, but in fact is a definitional tautology without content. Thus, Adler's concepts of both social interest and ethical nature are open to unexamined elements from his own private ethical beliefs, e.g., his characterization of homosexuality and masturbation as perversions (e.g., Ansbacher, 1956, pp. 424–427).

Developmental necessity. Adler's identification of social interest with morality intrinsically involves a claim of the logical necessity and logical sufficiency of each for the other. In the process of rejecting this identification, we have also rejected this claim of necessity and sufficiency.[7] But these are not the only possibilities, and, in particular, we find in Adler's writing the notion that the development of social interest is prerequisite to the development of morality in the individual—a developmental necessity rather than a logical necessity. Thus, we find Furtmüller contending that

> according to this view, ethics and mental hygiene arrive at a particularly close relationship. It is not as if ethics could be a means toward mental health. On the contrary, mental health appears rather to be a prerequisite for genuine ethics. (Ansbacher, 1956, p. 148)

And Adler echoes that "the ethical nature … will always be founded upon the truest social feeling" (Ansbacher, 1956, p. 155). Such a hypothesized relationship between social development and moral development is, as a matter of fact, supported by current research (e.g., Kohlberg, 1969). However, this explanatory function could possibly be of use to us in explicating the concept of social interest only if we had some independent explication of "ethical nature" against which we could test potential versions of social interest. We have just rejected Adler's explication,[8] but research and analysis from other areas could in principle, of course, provide such an independent explication. Suffice it to say that, with respect to its developmental necessity for individual morality, the research mentioned earlier (Kohlberg, 1969), as well as other research in the area, would seem to be interpretable as supporting *either* man-as-socius or man-as-human as explications of social interest.

Developmental Sufficiency. Adler does not seem to have made the claim for the developmental *sufficiency* of social interest for morality. But, if we make it for him by extension from his implicit argument for logical sufficiency, we find, in my opinion, that Kohlberg (1969) and others would provide a stronger foundation for man-as-human as explicating social interest than for man-as-socius. We are by now, however, far afield from the direct contents of Adler's writings, and my above stated opinion would in any case require extensive development of its own. So any such purported support for man-as-human must be considered to be minimal.

Altogether, the ethical function of social interest in Adler's theory would seem not only to be in error, but also not particularly useful in attempting to understand social interest.

2. Meaning

The situation regarding the second theoretical function of the concept of social interest, that is, as a source of human meaningfulness, is complicated in a special way. If we reexamine a critical quote,

> What has happened to those people who have contributed nothing to the general welfare? Nothing remains of them.... It is as though the questioning cosmos had given the command: "Away with you! You have not grasped the meaning of life. You cannot endure into the future!" (Adler, 1964, p. 279),

we find not only a concern with the issue of meaningfulness, the point drawn earlier, but a concern of a very specific form. That is, Adler might seem to imply that the meaning of an individual's life derives from society, that the only source of human meaning is participation in, and thus endurance or continuance through, social evolution. It is as if social evolution is the only access an individual has to eternity, and eternity is the ultimate core of meaning. In support of this view of social evolution as the source of meaning, we find such comments as

> the individual's proper development can only progress if he lives and strives as a part of the whole. The shallow objections of individualistic systems have no meaning as against this view (Adler, 1964, p. 282),

and, "never can the individual be the goal of the ideal of perfection" (Ansbacher, 1973, p. 40).

Relevance to Man-as-Socius and Man-as-Human. The special point to be made regarding this view of meaning is that it contradicts the earlier discussion upon which the distinction between man-as-socius and man-as-human is based. Thus, if those characteristics of man-as-human which I claimed *differentiated* it from man-as-socius are instead in fact *derived* from or identified with man-as-socius, then there is no differentiation, and man-as-human equals man-as-socius. Correspondingly, the two alternative explications of social interest with which we are faced would instead be one, and the task of explication would be much simplified. Thus, it becomes immediately critical to examine this potential construal of Adler's position, to examine this purported function of the concept of social interest.

An initial presupposition of this formulation is that meaning exists independently of and external to any particular individual; meaning is "out there" in some external and eternal, perhaps platonic, form, and the individual may "choose" to draw upon this meaning, to partake of it, and thus to provide meaning for his life. The individual may insert his life in the framework of meaning, or the individual may "choose" to not partake of meaning, and, correspondingly, to live meaninglessly. In fact, Adler implies meaning is "out there" in the specific form of social evolution and the culmination toward which it tends, and to partake of it is identical to participating in this evolution.

There are at least two levels upon which this conceptualization of meaningfulness can be criticized, and it seems fatally flawed on both levels: (1) the assumption of the externality of meaning, and (2) the particular external form that Adler gives it.

Externality of meaning. Concerning the externality of meaning: meaning would seem to be a particularly human property, a property bestowed on various parts and characteristics of an individual's experience by that individual himself. That is, meaning is specific to the individual who provides it. It is derived from the individual, not the other way around; its source is internal, not external. It is not at all clear what the nature of meaning could possibly be that would be consistent with its being derived externally.[9] These sentences, of course, do not really constitute an argument, and even less a definitive argument, but they are rather representative of the conclusions reached by vast literatures of analyses and arguments (e.g., Merleau-Ponty, 1963; Schutz, 1967; Spiegelberg, 1971) with which this interpretation of Adler is in contradiction. As once before, in the absence of meaningful counterargument—and Adler's consists simply of the dismissal of "the shallow objections of individualistic systems" (Adler, 1964, p. 282)—we must consider this assumption disproven.

Social Evolution and Meaning. Concerning social evolution as the particular source of meaning, we may ask why social evolution should be presumed to have any intrinsic meaning at all? Why should it have any more meaning than might be derived from individual human existence? How would or could Adler counter the charge that social evolution, or biological evolution in general, is intrinsically absurd and meaningless? The only hint of an answer that seems extractable from Adler is that social evolution is the individual's only access to the eternal, the only opportunity to "endure"; which raises still further problems. First, why should we presume that the eternal, in the sense of "endurance," has any intrinsic meaning? Secondly, even if we accept that it might, the fact of the matter is that participation in social evolution does not at all insure such endurance. In fact, this argument has the same structure as that for social interest as effect and the same flaw, the randomness of evolution. To assume that meaningfulness depends on continuity through contributions to social evolution is to assume that the meaningfulness of an individual's life is at least in part dependent on factors not of his own making; it is to assume that an individual could be perfect in every other respect, but that accidents of history, geology, or whatever, could render his life meaningless. Such a pessimism of randomness hardly seems consistent with Adler's concept of meaningfulness, and, for that matter, seems inconsistent with the positive spirit of much of the rest of Adler's writings.

Furthermore, the basic argument shares another flaw with that for social interest as effect; it not only fails to include genuinely meaningful lives because of the randomness of evolution, it also includes lives not genuinely meaningful. Contribution to social evolution is no more dependent on living a meaningful life than it is on living a mentally healthy life. Thus, Adler's criterion would have us considering many unactualized, perhaps even evil, people as living meaningful lives by "virtue" of their contributions to social evolution.

A revision. It might be conceded that meaningfulness does not derive per se from any external source, let alone from social evolution; and it might be conceded that meaningfulness derives from the choices of actions and interpretations from which the individual constructs his life, but then countered that, among the possible choices an individual could make, only those which do in some sense involve the individual in the process of social evolution are, in fact, meaningful, and that this constitutes the core of Adler's position. Thus meaningfulness derives from the choice or the choosing, rather than flowing from the chosen, but that some choices are meaningful—those that involve the individual in social evolution—and some are not. This position clearly is not subject to the criticisms of externality, nor is it subject to the simple randomness criticism—it does not depend on endurance, only choice—nor, for the same reason, is it subject to the simple overselection criticism. It is a much more subtle and acceptable position, and probably truer to the basic spirit of Adler, though it contradicts some of his statements.

Though still probably wrong (e.g., it would seem highly desirable to speak of an individual deriving meaning from his confrontation with the fact of his own finitude, and that would not seem to have much to do with choosing to participate in social evolution), the revised position is nevertheless suggestive and stimulating and would be worth pursuing. But it need not be pursued now, for the main point at issue has already been conceded: meaning derives internally, from individual choice, not externally. Individual choice is not a social process, and it is in every sense prior to an individual's participation in that process; thus there is an aspect of man-as-human that is not encompassed within man-as-socius, man-as-human is differentiated from man-as-socius, and we are again faced with two alternative explications of social interest.

Man-as-socius and man-as-human intact. The original "pure" version of Adler's construal of social interest as source of meaning is unacceptable, and thus is not useful to the explication of social interest. The revised version is not so clearly in error, but is not able to help much in the analysis of the man-as-socius and man-as-human alternatives for a different reason; insofar as we focus strictly on the derivation of meaning from the act of choosing, we derive meaning from a specifically man-as-human characteristic, and would seem to lend support primarily to that alternative. But, in fact, even with the revisions suggested, it is clear that Adler's focus regarding the source of meaning is on the chosen, not the choosing. Specifically, it is on the participation in social evolution. It is precisely Adler's interpretation of social evolution that we are trying to explicate, because social interest is the aptitude for or process of participating in that social evolution. Thus meaning is derived from the "choice" to develop social interest, the "choice" to participate in social evolution; that is, to participate either in the evolution as man-as-socius *or* of man-as-human, and still we don't know which.

Necessity and Sufficiency. Regarding the issues of necessity and sufficiency, the identification of the development of social interest with meaningfulness involves an assumption of the logical necessity and sufficiency of social interest to meaningfulness. Although Adler does not seem to have made any explicit claims of necessity or sufficiency in this or any other sense, we could, in principle, make them for him (e.g., in a logical or developmental sense), but to do so we would find ourselves involved again in issues of great complexity far afield from Adler's writings; any implications regarding the explication of social interest would be weak at best.

Thus far we have examined two of the purported theoretical functions of the concept of social interest: as the foundation for morality and as the foundation for human meaningfulness. Neither of these functions has proven useful in explicating social interest. Both, in fact, were found to involve fundamental errors. We turn to the third theoretical function, then, social interest as the foundation for mental health, with man-as-socius and man-as-human both still viable as potential explications of social interest.

3. Mental Health

Adler's position regarding the relationship between social interest and mental health is easily summarized:

> In a neurosis we are always confronted with a highly placed goal of personal superiority .... That such a ... goal of personal superiority betokens a lack of the proper measure of social interest ... is understandable. The striving for personal superiority and the non-development of social interest are both mistakes. However, they are not two mistakes which the individual has made; they are one and the same mistake. (Ansbacher, 1956, pp. 240–241)

> All failures—neurotics, psychotics, criminals, drunkards, problem children, suicides, perverts, and prostitutes—are failures because they are lacking in social interest. (Ansbacher, 1956, p. 156).

> ... all that constitutes a failure is so because it obstructs social feeling. (Adler, 1964, p. 283)

Thus, we clearly see both Adler's basic identification of social interest with mental health, as well as the more specific implications of social interest being both necessary and sufficient for mental health.

No category error. The concepts of mental health and mental illness involve issues of the functionality and dysfunctionality of the psychological processes in the individual. The concept of social interest involves an aptitude for some kind of positive functioning of the individual; man-as-socius and man-as-human specify the current alternatives concerning just what kind of positive functioning. Thus social interest, a positive functioning, would seem compatible with mental health, also a positive functioning, while lack of social interest, a negative functioning, would seem to be compatible with mental illness, also a negative functioning. Thus, there would not seem to be any category error involved.

Accepting that there is no category error, however, is not necessarily accepting a full identification of the terms. A lack of category error implies that the two concepts are of the same kind; it does not necessarily imply that they are identical. In particular, it does not imply either necessity or sufficiency—thus, further analysis is required. In this analysis, we have our last opportunity to select between man-as-socius and man-as-human as explications of social interest.[10]

Necessity. Concerning the issue of necessity, the basic question is whether or not it is conceivable that an individual could be mentally healthy without having a developed social interest. If so, then social interest is not necessary to mental health. With regard to man-as-socius, the answer would seem to be that it is conceivable, but only with rather forced exceptions; e.g., an isolated child raised solely by machines in some science fiction future might be mentally healthy but with no capacity for relatedness. Obviously, even this strained example is contestable. Regarding man-as-human, the answer would seem to be clearly negative. It seems inconceivable that an individual with no sense of meaningfulness of himself or his actions could be regarded as mentally healthy. Thus, both the categorical compatibility of social interest and mental health, and the relationship of necessity between them, seem to be well supported, but supported in ways that do not much differentiate between man-as-socius and man-as-human. Only in a very marginal way would man-as-human seem to be more strongly supported than man-as-socius.

Sufficiency. Concerning the issue of sufficiency, the situation is somewhat different. To argue that the development of man-as-human is sufficient to the development of mental health seems quite easy—to argue otherwise would require the specification of some sense in which being fully human does not imply being mentally healthy, or, conversely, some sense in which it were possible to fail to be mentally healthy that does not also involve a failure to be fully human. The implausibility of this suggests that man-as-human is indeed sufficient to mental health. With regard to man-as-socius, however, we have already seen that a characteristic *not* encompassed by this explication is necessary to mental health—in particular, meaningfulness—but this immediately implies that man-as-socius cannot by itself be sufficient. Thus, for the first time, and with the last possible opportunity, we seem to have a clear functional selection of one possible explication of social interest over the other—of man-as-human over man-as-socius.

Other Considerations

Unfortunately, again the situation is not as simple as would be desired. We have shown that in order to serve the legitimate functions which Adler wants the concept of social interest to serve, it must be explicated as man-as-human. We have also shown that man-as-human is an initially plausible explication of social interest, and, in fact, that Adler explicitly considered a differentiating characteristic of man-as-human—namely, meaningfulness. Functional considerations, however, are not the only ones present. In particular, we have furthermore shown that Adler's introduction of meaningfulness was fundamentally in error: that he introduced it in such a way as to reduce man-as-human, with some capacity to internally derive meaning, to man-as-socius, with no such capacity, thus eliminating man-as-human as a possibility. Also, it is clear in Adler's writing that, although concern for the issue of meaningfulness is often present, it is far overshadowed by Adler's pervasive concern for man-as-socius, that is, for the particular issue of man's capacity for fellowship and cooperation. The extreme generality of the concept of man-as-human would thus blur Adler's primary focus.

Overall, a case can be made for the explication of social interest either as man-as-socius or as man-as-human. Clearly, the concepts are different, though related. Therefore, social interest must be explicated as one and not the other. The case for man-as-socius is noticeably stronger than the case for man-as-human; explicating social interest in terms of man-as-socius does some damage to the theoretical functions that Adler wanted it to serve (in particular, it cannot by itself be considered sufficient to mental health), but explicating it in terms of man-as-human would do extensive damage to Adler's position regarding the nature of meaningfulness and would distort Adler's discussions regarding social interest. In this regard, we note the following comments from Ansbacher:

> The term social interest denotes the innate aptitude through which the individual becomes responsive to reality, which is *primarily* the social situation. In Adler's mature theory, social interest is not a second dynamic force counterbalancing a striving for superiority. Like other psychological processes or traits, it is *a part* of the individual's equipment, although the most important part. It is used by him in his striving for superiority or perfection, which in itself is *socially neutral* [emphasis added]. (Ansbacher, 1956, p. 133)

Clearly, we find here confirmatory recognition that (1) the primary focus of social interest is the social situation—man-as-socius; and (2) there are human characteristics—e.g., the striving for perfection—that are beyond or prior to the characteristics of social interest.

Summary

The discussion has concerned itself with five potential explications of social interest, considered in two primary groups: (1) social interest as motive, (2) social interest as effect, and (3) social interest as tendency to contribute, followed by (4) man-as-socius, and (5) man-as-human. It was argued that the first three candidates involve essential misunderstandings of the functional role that social interest serves in Adler's theory.[11] The latter two possibilities, however, require the involvement of issues at the center of Adler's theory for their resolution. The resolution is not clearcut; what Adler functionally demanded of social interest requires it to be man-as-human; yet what Adler said about the nature of social interest requires it to be man-as-socius. Man-as-socius was chosen as the most appropriate explication.

In the course of the analysis of social interest, a number of important additional issues have been encountered and left for later resolution. First, although the ontological outlines of social interest have been delineated, we are provided at best with a framework for an ultimate understanding of its ontological nature. We know that social interest involves an innate potential for the development of the capacity for cooperative fellowship, but we do not know of what that potential, or that development, or that capacity consists. It was Adler's insight to recognize that social fellowship requires its own cognitive and motivational prerequisites; it remains for others to specify what those prerequisites are.[12] Another issue left unresolved is the relationship of social interest to morality. A human ethic must be grounded on the existence of choice and freedom within the framework of human nature.[13] Adler's recognition of choice is explicit, and his discussions of social interest constitute a primary contribution to the understanding of human nature; the task of deriving an ethic remains.

A connected topic is the relationship of evolution to ethics. Human nature ultimately rests on human evolution; the precise nature of their relationship to ethics, however, is subtle and complex, and is still an issue of disagreement (see, for example, Simpson, 1949). As Adler foresaw, a valid ethic must ultimately fit consistently in an evolutionary framework.

The issue of the relationship of social interest to meaningfulness has also been raised by Adler. It would seem clear that human fellowship can manifest a powerful participation in an individual's construction of a meaningful life, but the opportunities and limitations of that participation have not been as well developed. Schutz (1967) argues that meaning is given in the manner in which we regard our experiences and actions, but there is no argument that such meaning is unboundedly and uniformly arbitrary. The structure of potential meaning must in some sense be framed by the nature of being human, and thus must reflect the existence of social interest, and must, as with ethics, fit consistently in an evolutionary framework.

Finally, the relationship of social interest to mental health provides its own special directions for further exploration. Social interest does not cause mental health, nor does it explain it. Conversely, failures of social interest do not cause or explain failures of mental health; social interest is a (partial) *explication* of mental health, a definition. It describes what mental health *is*, not why it develops nor where it comes from. The theoretical function of explanation, causal or otherwise, must be served by other elements of the theory. For these functions we turn to such concepts as the inferiority (symptom) complex and the striving for personal superiority. The question concerning the precise manner in which these concepts explain failures in the development of social interest, and thus failures in the development of mental health, initiates the explication of other portions of Adler's theory.

References

Adler, A. *Social Interest*. Capricorn Books, 1964.

Ansbacher, H. L. The concept of social interest. *Journal of Individual Psychology*, 1968, 24, 131–149.

Ansbacher, H. L. & Ansbacher, R. R. *The individual psychology of Alfred Adler*. New York: Harper & Row, 1956.

Ansbacher, H. L & Ansbacher, R. R. *Superiority and social interest* (3rd ed.). New York: Viking Press, 1973.

Kohlberg, L. Stage and sequence: The cognitive-developmental approach to socialization. In D. A. Goslin (Ed.), *Handbook of socialization theory and research*. Chicago: Rand McNally, 1969.

Merleau-Ponty, M. *The structure of behavior*. Boston: Beacon Press, 1963.

Schutz, A. *The phenomenology of the social world*. Evanston, 111.: Northwestern University Press, 1967.

Simpson, G. G. *The meaning of evolution*. New Haven, Conn.: Yale University Press, 1949.

Spiegelberg, H. *The phenomenological movement* (2 vols). Martinus Nijhoff, 1971.

Notes

1. My initial contact and interest in Adlerian psychology, including the topic of this paper, is due to discussions with Richard Kopp. Vital encouragement for writing the paper was received from Guy Manaster. Useful comments and criticisms on early drafts were received from Jan Ford, Margaret Iwanaga, and Frank Richardson.

2. Note that it is not crucial to the preceding arguments that Adler actually intended the interpretations presented. It is sufficient that he may be construed as supporting these interpretations to require their consideration and rebuttal.

3. Note that social interest purely as evolutionary tendency has no activity, only an object. It is essentially this lack of an independent conceptualization at the level of activity, process or

capacity, i.e., something resident in the individual, that prevents social interest as tendency from adequately capturing Adler's intentions, either ontological or functional.

4. This distinction between the object and the process of social interest is essentially the same as that in Ansbacher, 1968.

5. Here we find Adler's explicit consideration of the basic randomness of evolutionary selection. The path to truth is not certain or guaranteed; there are, instead, optimal strategies in the face of basic uncertainties.

6. Socius: A companion, an associate, a member.

7. Note that this does not necessarily exclude some such implicational relationship, but that such a relationship would have to derive from a definition of morality beyond that contained in Adler's writings.

8. In any case, Adler's explication of "ethical nature" is not independent of social interest, it is rather defined in terms of it. Note that by thus claiming both the logical and the developmental necessity of social interest for morality, we become involved in still another circularity.

9. Thus the assumption of the externality of meaning is a category error.

10. Recall chat man-as-socius refers to man's capabilities as an interpersonal being, and man-as-human to a being with broader human potentialities, including such differentiating potentialities as those for meaningfulness.

11. Ideal social and institutional structure as a potential object of social interest was found to reduce to either social interest as motive or as effect in terms of process, and thus to be unacceptable for the same reasons.

12. Note that any attempt to assist the development of social interest in children, a vital Adlerian concern, must of necessity be guided by at least implicit hypotheses concerning these ontological questions. The sizeable literature in this area thus already begins such a specification. Kohlberg (1969) presents a highly relevant discussion from outside the Adlerian tradition.

13. It should be noted that such a dual foundation for ethics would be contrary to Sartre, for example, who claims that the realm of human nature is created purely out of man's freedom — in effect, that man has no human nature (Spiegelberg, 1971). Sartre's position does not seem to be tenable, since it would seem to leave no ground upon which one could avoid an ethical nihilism. Adler's concept of social interest could provide an essential correction.

CHAPTER 12

Social Interest as a Distinct Personality Construct: Comparisons with "The Big Five" and Related Prosocial Constructs

MICHAEL J. STASIO and EARL W. CAPRON

Alfred Adler's theory of personality was the first to place importance on responsibility, usefulness, and, above all, social relationships in life. Although often uncredited, Adler's visionary work influenced later schools of neo-Freudian, cognitive, humanist, and existential thought (for reviews see Ansbacher & Ansbacher, 1956; Mozak, 1979). Recently, Mozdzierz and Krauss (1996) argued convincingly that Adler's views on the importance of interpersonal relatedness are supported by emerging research in psychology, anthropology, and evolutionary biology. Given Adler's wide influence, then, one may ask how his personality theory relates to contemporary trait formulations such as "The Big Five." Is the construct of social interest, a theoretical center for Adler, subsumed in current research on empathy, altruism, prosocial behavior, or Machiavellianism? This review argues that social interest as it applies to theories of personality and therapy is meaningfully different from contemporary theories and, therefore, worthy of continued study.

Individual Psychology reflects three basic ideas regarding personality: (1) movement—behavior is motivated throughout life by innate feelings of inferiority and by a subsequent striving to "overcome" them; (2) unity—one's own style of life synchronizes thoughts, feelings, and behaviors to meet life tasks of work, love, and friendship; and (3) value—social interest, or interest in the concerns of humankind, should be adopted and viewed as important to the survival of our species (Ansbacher, 1968). This construct of social interest is therefore a cornerstone for Adler, acting as the valued main personality trait as well as the criterion for mental health.

Defining Social Interest

Precisely defining social interest has proved difficult partly due to the complexities inherent in the construct itself. For example, James Crandall (1981) rightly noted that Adler coupled the term social interest with several main psychological variables, including motivation (urge, striving), cognition (understanding, identification), emotion (empathy, sympathy), and behavior (cooperation, contribution to the common welfare). Adler (1956) extended his mature concept of social interest to include identification with people, things, and even abstractions:

> Social Interest remains throughout life. It becomes differentiated, limited or expanded and, in favorable cases, extends not only to family members but to the larger group, the nation, to all of mankind. It can even go further, extending itself to animals, plants, and even to the cosmos, (p. 138)

In terms of development, Adler's conception of social interest as a biological tendency necessary for the "evolutionary advancement of social feeling … a feeling of belongingness" was refined into a notion of social interest as an "innate potentiality, not an innate ability" (Adler, 1964, p. 34). The idea that social interest can (and should) be developed in one's upbringing remains a core component in Adler's system.

An important aspect of social interest appears to be its predominantly selfless nature. Adler (1964) emphasized social interest as "… a condition in which we imagine all questions of life, all relationships to the external world as solved" (p. 35). Ansbacher & Ansbacher (1956) have noted that the essence of social interest is marked by "an absence of self-centeredness … an ongoing transcendence of the limits of the self and of physical individuality" (p. 137). Crandall (1981) concludes that social interest involves "valuing what's valuable to mankind … usually something outside the self" (p. 14).

Furthermore, as Ansbacher (1968) notes, key aspects of social interest include real concern for the welfare of future societies and the belief that social interest should be cultivated in our daily lives. Of social interest's orientation toward future societies, Adler (1964) writes that:

> ... it is never a present day community or society, nor a political or religious form. Rather the goal which is best suited to perfection would have to be a goal which signifies the ideal community of all mankind, the ultimate fulfillment of evolution. (p. 34)

Therefore, social interest does not refer to feelings of belonging to a certain group or class of people in the present, but rather is concerned with *feeling with the whole, sub specie aeternitatis* (under the aspect of eternity). It means a striving for a form of community "as it could be thought of if mankind had reached the goal of perfection" (Adler, 1964, p. 34).

Recently, Ansbacher (1992) has suggested that social interest may be an inappropriate translation of Adler's *Gemeinschaftsgefühl,* which means literally "community feeling" (p. 402). Although it appears that Adler used the term community feeling much more frequently than social interest, the latter was favored in English translations. Ansbacher (1992) argues that, while related, both terms are distinct "with regard to the processes involved—feeling versus interest." Community feeling suggests an inactive state of mind, whereas social interest signals motivation or movement toward some goal. Furthermore, Ansbacher notes that Adler himself offered a brief clarification of social interest as "the action-line of community feeling," which is an important distinction for researchers (p. 404). For example, in his empirical studies of social interest, Crandall (1981) operationalized social interest as "interest in and concern for others" as a necessity for measurement (p. 24). Ansbacher (1992) agrees that "in trying to decide which term represents the lesser error, social interest is the more practical term" (p. 407). Thus, the term social interest, with its more behavioral emphasis (Ansbacher, 1992), seems preferable for research purposes, and it will be used here with the understanding that it does not capture the depth of Adler's meaning.

Social Interest and Mental Health

Social interest as a criterion for mental health can be understood in relation to Adler's theory of a dynamic, unified, and self-consistent personality. Human motivation exists in the form of a striving for superiority or perfection; this striving is compensatory, originating in infancy from feelings of helplessness and inferiority in relation to the environment. The striving is for "conquest, security, or increase (from minus to plus), either in the right or wrong direction ... the urge from below to above never ceases" (Adler, 1956, p. 103). Thus, normal individuals who strive for "perfection, completion, or overcoming" through social interest are useful to the welfare of others. Therefore, Adler is able to argue that "social interest is the barometer of a child's normality. The criterion which needs to be watched … is the degree of social interest which the child or the individual manifests" (Adler, 1956, p. 154).

Neurotics, conversely, strive for self-centered superiority without regard for social interest or useful behavior. Adler viewed striving in neurotics as directed toward "self-enhancement," "power," "private intelligence," "gaining pleasure," or "personal superiority" in efforts by the individual to safeguard against heightened and intense feelings of inferiority (1956, p. 103). As such, the neurotic person "strives for increased possessions, power, and influence, and for the disparagement and cheating of other persons" (Adler, 1956, p. 112). Alternative dynamic theories, especially those of Freud, which emphasize an "ego-centered basis of social relations" or those which suggest any kind of "private profit," describe neurotic functioning in Adler's system. As Mozdzierz and Krauss (1996) have acknowledged, social interest overlaps with constructs such as altruism, prosocial behavior, and need for interpersonal contact (p. 227). The focus of this paper is to examine whether social interest remains a distinct theoretical and definable construct.

Review of Relevant Personality Research

The Big Five

Recent research suggesting that personality is comprised of five factors (Digman & Inouye, 1986; McCrae & Costa, 1987, 1990; Goldberg, 1990) has received considerable support. In a study by Goldberg (1990), trait adjectives were compared using factor analysis with five varying rotation solutions. Results showed a high intermethod correlation of trait terms ranging from .950 to .996. In a second study, Goldberg found that this five-factor structure generalized across four groups of participants with the mean congruence coefficient across all factors = .91.

McCrae & Costa (1987) have developed a five-factor model of personality known as the NEO-Personality Inventory (NEO-PI). Scores are compared with participant norms on the dimensions of Neuroticism, Extroversion, Agreeableness, Conscientiousness, and Openness to Experience. The NEO-PI model has been supported mainly through analysis of trait terms in the California Q-Sort (CQS) developed by psychodynamically oriented psychologists. Each NEO-PI factor consists of traits at opposite ends of some dimension. Comparison of the NEO-PI factor traits to those of social interest clearly indicate incompatible conceptions of personality.

One major difference between the NEO-PI model and Adler's view involves the conception of neurosis in each system. For example, a participant scoring low on the NEO-PI Neuroticism dimension would necessarily score high on traits such as "calm," "even-tempered," "self-satisfied," "comfortable," "unemotional," and "hardy." In Adler's system, however, the opposite of neuroticism is social interest in all its forms. As previously defined, social interest traits share little overlap with those listed above. Particularly conspicuous is the absence of the terms empathy and identification as opposites to NEO-PI Neuroticism traits. Since Adler contends that empathy and altruism are two central processes in the development of social interest, one may reasonably conclude that each system conceptualizes neuroticism differently.

Similarities between the social interest construct and the NEO-PI center on the items included in the Agreeableness and Conscientiousness dimensions of the five-factor model. For example, Agreeableness scale items include "generosity," "lenient," and "good-natured"; these traits correspond, in our judgment, reasonably well to traits characteristic of social interest. However, other Agreeableness scale items, such as "acquiescent" and "trusting," taken to their extremes, imply a passivity or naive nature that is discordant with Adler's goal-oriented (dynamic) construct of social interest.

While it also appears that social interest and the NEO-PI's Conscientiousness scale may be similar, a closer examination reveals that this relationship is only tangential. For example, the scale name Conscientiousness itself may imply a concern for "justness" or "morality" akin to definitions of social interest, but many items included in the scale, i.e., "achievement," "punctuality," "ambition," do not. Perhaps items included in the Conscientiousness dimension are more related to Adler's theory of motivation—the striving for superiority or perfection—than to social interest. Recall Adler's argument that the striving for superiority can be either self-centered or directed towards the welfare of others. Conscientiousness scale items, such as "achievement," "ambition," and "persistence," therefore, could be used to describe traits characteristic of neurotic individuals striving for selfish personal goals of self-enhancement or self-protection rather than social interest.

The remaining two dimensions of the NEO-PI—Openness to Experience and Extroversion—are comprised of traits that either are not relevant to social interest or are "misplaced." For example, traits related to Openness to Experience include "imaginative" and "original," two items that Crandall (1981) judged to be unrelated to social interest since he included these words only as buffer items in his Social Interest Scale. Furthermore, the Extroversion factor contains a dimension involving "unfeeling–feeling," which should theoretically appear in the Neuroticism factor if indeed the five-factor model were compatible with Adler's view.

McCrae and Costa (1997) have most recently attempted to show that their five-factor model (FFM) is universal and replicable across cultures. In this ambitious study, the NEO–PI-Revised (Costa & McCrae, 1992) was translated into five distinct languages and its factor structure compared across German, Portuguese, Chinese, Korean, and Japanese samples. The authors reported that the FFM showed similar factor structure across samples and argued that this model captures a universal trait structure that obeys "general laws of personality" (p. 514). For example, congruence coefficients comparing Korean and Portuguese samples were .98, .79, .89, .82, and .94 for Neuroticism, Extroversion, Openness to Experience, Agreeableness, and Conscientiousness respectively. Additionally, when sample factors were rotated to converge on the American sample norm, congruence coefficients were reported as .96, .95, .94, .96, and .96 for N, E, O, A, and C respectively. Although these findings are seemingly decisive, the authors themselves allude to important shortcomings with the FFM.

First, the trait facets of the NEO-PI often fail to reach simple structure criteria for their intended factor and are defined by their secondary loadings, thus clouding factor interpretability. Second, the five factors of the NEO-PI have not been replicated across certain samples. For example, only four of five factors were reproduced in a Hungarian sample, and factors not interpretable as the NEO-PI were found in one Chinese sample. Third, participants in this latest study (McCrae & Costa, 1997) were, except for the Portuguese sample, literate college students or their friends and family. Thus, the very lexical nature of trait adjective measures (and their alternative language translations) makes reading ability and comprehension two potential confounds in these results.

Furthermore, Church and Burke (1994) have raised convincing doubts about the FFM structure using confirmatory factor analysis and the NEO-PI. Results indicated that the NEO-PI had weak internal consistency with only 71% of 128 items loading on their intended factor, with Agreeableness being the least interpretable domain. Further criticisms of "The Big Five" factor structure can be found in Eysenck (1992a), Zuckerman et al. (1993), and Block (1995).

The Empathy Construct

Empathy is assumed to be an important trait related to the development of social interest. Davis (1983) asserts that "empathy in the broadest sense refers to the reactions of one individual to the observed experiences of another" (p. 113). In one early validity study concerning the Social Interest Scale, Crandall and Harris (1976) compared the SIS scores of 30 men and 30 women with the empathy scores on the Merabian & Epstein Empathy Scale (1972). Results showed that both measures positively correlated with a "willingness to help others," and overall the SIS positively correlated with empathy scores, $r = .40$, $p < .005$. Such a correlation, however, only shows only that social interest and empathy overlap but not that they are congruent concepts. Although the Merabian & Epstein scale was a popular test in its time, the empathy construct has been further studied and explicated by a number of researchers since then.

The Interpersonal Reactivity Index (IRI; Davis, 1980) is a multidimensional measure of empathy consisting of four independent subscales that include Empathic Concern (EC), Personal Distress (PD), Fantasy (F), and Perspective-Taking (PT). The subscales EC, PD, and F measure emotional empathy, whereas PT intends a cognitive measure of empathy. The three IRI subscales most related to the construct of social interest are EC, PD, and PT, each of which will be briefly considered here.

The Empathic Concern (EC) subscale is characterized by a disposition toward sympathy, warmth, and compassion for other people; it is positively related to shyness, social anxiety, and audience anxiety, and negatively related to loneliness and masculinity. EC subscale traits—sympathy, warmth, and compassion—seem to overlap with Adler's construct of social interest (SI), yet the positive relationship between the EC subscale and anxiety measures is discordant with SI. It would appear that any feeling of anxiety (social or audience) would be inconsistent with social interest because the latter is Adler's conception of mental health. Also, a low EC score is not necessarily comparable to a high social interest score, because high SI represents positive social values reflecting more than simply the opposite of shyness, social anxiety, and audience anxiety.

The Personal Distress (PD) subscale assesses one's own feelings of unease and discomfort in reaction to the negative emotions of others; it has a significant positive correlation with measures of shyness, social anxiety, extroversion, and fearfulness. The PD subscale was also found to have a negative correlation with self-esteem. In considering the relationship between PD and social interest, it may be reasonable to assume that a person with high social interest could also experience personal distress in reaction to others' negative emotions. However, one could also reasonably assume that high social interest is associated with positive experiences in relation to others' positive emotions, too. For example, a person with high social interest may experience happiness in the presence of another happy individual, or even upon hearing good news about a stranger in another country. Thus, the very trans-situational nature of social interest differentiates it from the more limited personal distress component of empathy. Furthermore, the self-focused discomfort that may be experienced by persons in emergency situations is discordant with the expression of social interest in everyday life; in other words, social interest is not self-focused, and it is demonstrated mostly in the nonemergency situations of day-to-day living. Additionally, low levels of personal distress and low social interest are not synonymous; a low level of personal distress is simply one facet of low social interest.

Perspective-Taking (PT) is of particular interest because of its nonemotional and cognitive nature, seemingly reflecting Adler's belief that we all must choose social interest as a major value in life. The PT subscale is positively related to self-esteem and other-oriented sensitivity, and negatively related to boastfulness, arrogance, and self-oriented sensitivity. Davis (1983) describes Perspective-Taking as "the tendency to spontaneously adopt the psychological perspective of other people in everyday life—to entertain the point of view of others" (p. 117). Therefore, it would seem that the PT dimension of the IRI comes close to approximating Adler's idea of empathy in relation to social interest.

While clear similarities appear between social interest and some current views of empathy, there are also important differences. Although Davis's Perspective-Taking subscale seems to describe an important aspect of social interest—adopting another's point of view—it relegates itself to a narrow and incomplete form of social interest. Neither the PT subscale, nor the four IRI subscales taken together, account for important meanings of social interest concerning identification with humanity and the universe as a whole (i.e., "community feeling"). More importantly, current empathy scales measure present-day empathic feelings and cognitions; they are not intended as measures of empathy toward a future ideal society. Also, while Davis's empathy subscales partially predict some measures of social adjustment—social anxiety, shyness, self-esteem, other-orientation—the IRI is not conceptualized as a criterion for mental health.

Altruistic and Prosocial Personalities

Is there an altruistic personality? This question has received considerable attention lately (e.g., Batson, 1991; Carlo et al., 1991; Oliner & Oliner, 1988; Rushton & Sorrentino, 1981). Researchers have studied the altruistic disposition as a cluster of personality variables such as other-oriented empathy, sympathy, social responsibility, ascription of responsibility, and perspective taking (Carlo et al., 1991). In addition, Mozdzierz and Krauss (1996) note that recent research, specifically by Guisinger and Blatt (1994), has shown support for the notion that humans have an "innate capacity and need for relatedness to others even if labeled according to overlapping constructs such as altruism, prosocial behavior, or social interest" (p. 227). Since social interest is seen as a stable personality characteristic consisting of many traits, the relationship of Adler's construct to the altruistic personality is of particular interest.

Batson and his colleagues have studied the question of dispositional altruism using the methodology designed for their empathy-altruism paradigm and have found little evidence for it. In one study, Batson (1987) proposed that individuals with altruistic personality traits such as social responsibility, ascription of responsibility, dispositional empathy, and positive self-esteem may actually be motivated by egoism to help to avoid shame and guilt associated with not living up to their self image. Their predictions were supported: there was no evidence that any of the "altruistic" personality variables led to non-egoistic helping. Undaunted, researchers have continued to study constellations of stable traits indicative of altruistic personalties.

In 1991 Carlo et al. developed the Prosocial Composite Index (PCI), which contains many items relevant to the construct of social interest. The PCI subscales include ascription of responsibility (Schwartz, 1968), social responsibility (Berkowitz & Lutterman, 1968), social desirability (Crowne & Marlowe, 1964), affective intensity (Larsen & Diener, 1987), and empathy (Davis, 1980). While specific PCI items overlap with many social interest items, other SI items are omitted (e.g., morality) or are unclear (e.g., social responsibility). For example, social responsibility as described by the PCI most likely does not reflect the importance that social interest places on that aspect of social responsibility that involves concern for future generations of people and for all things on the earth. Furthermore, the reliability of the social responsibility subscale was very low (alpha = .55), so it is unclear what this subscale actually measures.

Lou Penner and his colleagues recently developed a measure called the Prosocial Personality Battery (PSB); Penner, Craiger, Fritzsche, & Freifeld (1995), which merits further discussion here in relation to social interest. The final version of the PSB contains 54 items from the following scales: ascription of responsibility (Schwartz & Howard, 1981); Interpersonal Reactivity Index (Davis, 1980, excluding the fantasy scale); helpfulness (Rushton & Sorrentino, 1981); and moral reasoning (Kolhberg, 1984; Gilligan, 1982). Factor loadings reveal a two-factor solution, each of which is sufficiently reliable. The first factor, Other-Oriented Empathy, involves "both affective and cognitive empathy ... to feel responsibility for and concern about the welfare of others" (p. 150). Helpfulness, the second factor, is a self-reported history of being helpful and describes people who are "unlikely to experience self-oriented discomfort when another person is in extreme distress" (pp. 150–151). The Other-Oriented Empathy factor, however, was significantly correlated with social desirability, and this raises important questions concerning this factor.

Penner's group offers two explanations for this positive correlation with social desirability. First, the authors suggest that individuals scoring high on the Other-Oriented Empathy factor may desire the approval of others; and second, that they may have a "positivistic bias" regarding themselves as good people who engage in positive actions. Further, the authors report that the social desirability was partialled out of subsequent analyses without a significant decrease in the zero-order correlation. In response, one may argue that if participants do indeed endorse PSB items to win approval of others or to unconsciously show positive biases about themselves, that suggests an egoistic, self-enhancement tendency on the part of the participants. As previously discussed, egoistic motivations are not compatible with Adler's concept of social interest; therefore, the PSB must be measuring another motivational construct.

In PSB validity studies, the Other-Oriented Empathy factor appears to perform slightly better than the Helpfulness factor. Penner & Fritzsche (1993) administered the PSB to 68 volunteers who worked for a charity within the last month and those who did not; the charity volunteers scored significantly higher on both factors of the PSB. Another finding showed that Other-Oriented Empathy was positively correlated with Agreeableness in the NEO-PI; however, the Helpfulness factor was not. Additionally, the authors compared both factors to the Nurturance and Dominance scales on the Interpersonal Adjective Scale-Revised (IAS-R, Trapnell & Wiggins, 1990), an eight-dimension measure of personality. Other-Oriented Empathy was found to correlate with Nurturance; however, the Helpfulness factor was found to correlate with the Dominance scale on the IAS-R, which measures "mastery and power which enhance and protect the individual" (p. 89). High dominance is not characteristic of high social interest.

One major difference between the construct of social interest and the PSB involves the fact that the PSB was not designed as a measure of adjustment and mental health. Some initial evidence suggesting that the PSB is not conceptualized as a measure of adjustment is the fact that Spielberger, Kling, and O'Hagen's Sociopathy Scale (1978), originally included as a PSB subscale, was dropped during the process of scale refinement. Furthermore, a recent personal communication with Dr. Penner indicates that the PSB does not correlate with neuroticism and correlates negatively, but not significantly, with anxiety.

Machiavellianism

The term "Machiavellianism" refers to a descriptive set of personality traits based on the political and social ideas in Machiavelli's *The Prince* (1532), which were developed and refined into a test by Christie and Geis (1970). Machiavellianism has come to be associated with one who is selfish, cynical, deceitful, and manipulative of others. The Mach IV scale version is relevant to this paper because its items deal with beliefs about the nature of humankind, values, and behaviors that may be opposed to those of social interest—for example, "a white lie is often a good thing," and "it's wise to flatter important people."

The Mach IV has been shown to be positively related to personality traits such as external locus of control (Solar & Bruehl, 1971), competitiveness (Hunter, Gerbing, & Boster, 1982), narcissism (Biscardi & Schill, 1985), and neuroticism (Ramanaiah, Byravan, and Detwiler, 1994), but the psychometric properties of the test are still at issue. The reliability of the Mach IV has been reported to be .71 (Christie & Geis, 1970), but Ray (1983) reported a lower alpha (.63) for a group of 128 Australian participants using the Mach IV, and an even lower alpha (.43) for the latest version, Mach V. In a study of construction workers, Panitz (1989) found two factors comprising the Mach IV; he argues that Machiavellianism may be a multidimensional construct.

Although Machiavellianism and social interest may represent opposite ends of some spectrum of personality, their exact relationship remains unclear. Both scales seem related, as evidenced by comparative measures of neuroticism: theoretically, social interest is associated with low neuroticism scores and Machiavellianism with high neuroticism scores. However, the numerous studies that question the reliability and factorial validity of the Mach IV and Mach V make conclusions regarding the relationship between the two scales premature. Even if it were demonstrated that social interest and Machiavellianism are diametrically opposed constructs, it would be unwise to simply assume that a low score on the Machiavellianism scale automatically means a high score on social interest. A low Machiavellianism score could be due to a variety of factors, such as high agreeableness or conscientiousness, neither of which is synonymous with social interest.

Conclusion

The foregoing review suggests that Adler's construct of social interest as it relates to mental health is distinct from contemporary trait theories of personality as well as similar constructs such as empathy, altruism, and prosocial behavior. If, as Mozdzierz and Krauss (1996) cogently argue, the social interest construct embodies important guiding principles for social policy-making decisions, efforts to distinguish and measure what is unique to social interest become increasingly important. Thus, efforts to study the social interest construct as a core component of Adler's system of personality and therapy should be continued.

References

Adler, A. (1956). The Individual Psychology of Alfred Adler: A systematic presentation in selections from his writings. H. L. Ansbacher & R. R. Ansbacher (Eds.). New York: Basic Books.

Adler, A. (1964). Superiority and social interest: A collection of later writings. H. L. Ansbacher & R. R. Ansbacher (Eds.). New York: W. W. Norton & Company.

Ansbacher, H. L. (1968). The concept of social interest. Journal of Individual Psychology, 24, 131–149.

Ansbacher, H. L. (1992). Alfred Adler's concepts of community feeling and of social interest and the relevance of community feeling for old age. Journal of Individual Psychology, 48(4), 402–412.

Ansbacher, H. L., & Ansbacher, R. R. (1956). The Individual Psychology of Alfred Adler; A systematic presentation in selections from his writings. New York: Basic Books.

Batson, C. D. (1987). Prosocial motivation: Is it ever truly altruistic? In L. Berkowitz (Ed.), Advances in experimental social psychology (vol. 20, pp. 65–122). New York: Academic Press.

Batson, C. D. (1991). The altruism question: Towards a social psychological answer. Hillsdale, NJ: Lawrence Erlbaum Associates.

Berkowitz, L., & Lutterman, K. C. (1968). The traditional socially responsible personality. Public Opinion Quarterly, 32, 169–185.

Biscardi, D., & Schill, T. (1985). Correlations of narcissistic traits with defensive style, Machiavellianism, and empathy. Psychological Reports, 57, 354.

Block, J. (1995). A contrarian view of the five-factor approach to personality description. Psychological Bulletin, 117, 187–215.

Carlo, G., Eisenberg, N., Troyer, D., Switzer, G., & Speer, A. L. (1991). The altruistic personality: In what context is it apparent? Journal of Personality and Social Psychology, 61, 450–458.

Christie, R., & Geis, R. L. (1970). Studies in Machiavellianism. New York: Academic Press.

Church, A. T., & Burke, P. J. (1994). Exploratory and confirmatory tests of the big five and Tellegen's three- and four-dimensional models. Journal of Personality and Social Psychology, 66, 93–114.

Costa, P. T., Jr., & McCrae, R. R. (1992). Revised NEO Personality Inventory and Five Factor Inventory Professional Manual. Odessa, FL: Psychological Assessment Resources.

Crandall, J. E. (1981). Theory and measurement of social interest: Empirical tests of Alfred Adler's concept. New York: Columbia University Press.

Crandall, J. E., & Harris, M. D., (1976). Social interest, cooperation, and altruism. Journal of Individual Psychology, 32, 50–54.

Crowne, D. P., & Marlowe, D. (1964). The approval motive. New York: Wiley.

Davis, M. H. (1980). A multidimensional approach to individual differences in empathy. JSAS Catalog of Selected Documents in Psychology, 10, 85.

Davis, M. H. (1983). Measuring individual differences in empathy: Evidence for a multi-dimensional approach. Journal of Personality and Social Psychology, 44, 113–126.

Digman, J. M., & Inouye, J. (1986). Further specification of the five robust factors of personality. Journal of Personality and Social Psychology, 50, 116–123.

Eysenck, H. J. (1992). Four ways five factors are not basic. Personality and Individual Differences, 13, 667–673.

Gilligan, C. (1982). In a different voice: Psychological theory and women's development. Cambridge, MA: Harvard University Press.

Goldberg, L. R. (1990). An alternative "description of personality": The big-five factor structure. Journal of Personality and Social Psychology, 59, 1216–1229.

Guisinger, S., & Blatt, S. J. (1994). Individuality and relatedness: Evolution of a fundamental dialectic. American Psychologist, 49, 104–111.

Hunter, J. E., Gerbing, D. W., & Boster, F.J. (1982). Machiavellian beliefs and personality: Construct invalidity of the Machiavellian dimension. Journal of Personality and Social Psychology, 43, 1293–1305.

Kohlberg, L. (1984). Essays on moral development: Vol II. The psychology of moral development. San Francisco: Harper & Row.

Larsen, R.J., & Diener, E. (1987). Affect intensity as an individual difference characteristic: A review. Journal of Research in Personality, 21, 1–39.

Machiavelli, N. (1981). The Prince. Translated by George Bull. New York: Penguin Books.

McCrae, R. R., & Costa, P. T., Jr. (1987). Validation of the five-factor model of personality across instruments and observers. Journal of Personality and Social Psychology, 52, 81–90.

McCrae, R. R., & Costa, P. T., Jr. (1990). Personality in adulthood. New York: Guilford Press.

McCrae, R. R., & Costa, P. T., Jr. (1997). Personality trait structure as a human universal. American Psychologist, 52(5), 509–516.

Merabian, A., & Epstein, N. (1972). A measure of emotional empathy. Journal of Personality, 40, 525–543.

Mozak, H. H. (1979). Adlerian psychotherapy. In R. Corsini (Ed.), Current psychotherapies (2nd ed., pp. 46–63) Itasca, IL: Peacock Publishers.

Mozdzierz, G. J., & Krauss, H. H. (1996). The embeddedness of Alfred Adler in modern psychology: Social policy and planning implications. Individual Psychology, 52(3), 224–236.

Oliner, S. P., & Oliner, P. M. (1988). The altruistic personality: Rescuers of Jews in Nazi Europe. New York: Free Press.

Panitz, E. (1989). Psychometric investigation of the Mach IV scale measuring Machiavellianism. Psychological Reports, 64, 963–968.

Penner, L. A., & Fritzsche, B. A. (1993, August). Measuring the prosocial personality: Four construct validity studies. Paper presented at the annual meeting of the American Psychological Association, Toronto, Canada.

Penner, L. A., Craiger, J. P., Fritzsche, B. A., & Freifeld, T. S. (1995). Measuring the prosocial personality. In J. N. Butcher & C. D. Spielberger (Eds.), Advances in personality assessment, (vol. 10, pp. 147–163). Hillsdale, NJ: Lawrence Erlbaum Associates.

Ramanaiah, N. V., Byravan, A., & Detwiler, F. R. J. (1994). Revised NEO Personality Inventory profiles of Machiavellian and non-Machiavellian people. Psychological Reports, 75, 937–938.

Ray, J. J. (1983). Defective validity of the Machiavellianism scale. The Journal of Social Psychology, 119, 291–292.

Rushton, J. P., & Sorrentino, R. M. (1981). Altruism and helping behavior: Social, personality, and developmental perspectives. Hillsdale, NJ: Lawrence Erlbaum Associates.

Schwartz, S. H. (1968). Words, deeds, and the perception of consequences and responsibility in social situations. Journal of Personality & Social Psychology, 10, 232–242.

Schwartz, S. H., & Howard, J. A. (1981). A normative decision-making model of helping behavior. In J. P. Rushton & R. M. Sorrentino (Eds.), Altruism and helping behavior (pp. 251–266). Hillsdale, NJ: Lawrence Erlbaum Associates.

Solar, D., & Bruehl, D. (1971). Machiavellianism and locus of control: Two conceptions of interpersonal power. Psychological Reports, 29, 1079–1082.

Spielberger, C. D., Kling, J. K., & O'Hagen, S. E. J. (1978). Dimensions of psychopathic personality, antisocial personality, and anxiety. In R. D. Hare & A. Schalling (Eds.), Psychopathic behavior: Approaches to research (pp. 23–46). New York: Wiley.

Trapnell, P. D., & Wiggins, J. S. (1990). Extension of the Interpersonal Adjectives Scales to include the Big Five dimensions of personality. Journal of Personality and Social Psychology, 59, 781–790.

Zuckerman, M., Kuhlman, D. M., Joireman, J., Teta, P., and Kraft, M. (1993). A comparison of three structural models for personality: The Big Three, the Big Five, and the Alternative Five. Journal of Personality and Social Psychology, 65(4), 757–768.

V
Lifestyle

CHAPTER 13

Style of Life

PAUL R. PELUSO

Open up any introductory psychology textbook, and you will find it. Following a long description of all of Freud's theories and their historical impact, and just before a long description of Jung's theories and their historical impact, there will be a tiny entry for Alfred Adler, which will look something like this:

> Alfred Adler, an early follower of Freud, broke with him over the centrality of the sex drive in the formation of the personality. Created the term *life style*,[1] though it was not used the way it is today. Instead, it was more akin to personality.

And that's it. Maybe, there will be some mention of birth order, or social influences on personality, or the democratic ideals, but the one central concept that stands out in the evaluation of the overall field of psychology is life style or style of life.[2] And yet, there is so much more. There is so much more to Adler's theory, and there is so much more to the style of life. The former will arguably be demonstrated by the other sections contained in this work. The latter will be addressed in this introduction, as well as in the articles contained in this section.

Definition and Development of the Style of Life

Again, another problem is confronted here. "Defining" the style of life is difficult to do, and somewhat artificial in this particular context. Adler called his theory "Individual Psychology" not because it was focused on "the individual" or the "self" as some people believe, but rather from the Latin word individuum meaning undivided or whole (Adler, 1964; Dreikurs, 1989). Yet to define something means that we must be able to break it down, divide and conquer it, and dissect it in order to understand its functioning. This may be the very reason that the style of life is so difficult to grasp for many people (Allen, 2003). It defies a simple definition. It is much like the argument in physics over the definition of light in the early 20th century. There were those scientists who believed that light was a wave, because it behaved with all of the properties of waves. However, there were also those physicists who demonstrated that light is made of discrete particles, since it could be harnessed and controlled much like a stream of particles. Today, thanks to quantum mechanics, we understand light to be both. Photons, the elements of quantum theory, are discrete emanations of radiation (e.g., light) that have the properties of both waves and particles. I think the same may be true with the style of life. It is a unique property of the individual, but has common elements with all humans. It develops in a predictable manner, but is idiographic in its actual development. It is whole, yet can be studied from a variety of points of view, or by looking at discrete phenomenon (i.e., behaviors).

In this text, like many others on Individual Psychology, there are discrete sections on so many different aspects of Adler's theory that are related to the style of life. It is impossible to discuss the style of life without taking into consideration the creative self, social interest, encouragement, the family constellation, inferiority, compensation, and phenomenology (in other words, the other sections of this entire book). While these phenomena are important by themselves as a part of the human experience, at the same time, they create something that is "greater than the sum of its parts" as the individual makes sense of the world. As a result, there will, by necessity, be some redundancy in this discussion in order to begin to describe the style of life in a coherent fashion.

So what is the *style of life*? Adler (1964) believed that the individual was an active participant in the creation of the style of life. This subjective creation is shaped at a very early age, as a result of interactions within the family unit. According to Adler, it is from this subjective view of life (which he called the "schema of apperception") that the individual constructs a "private logic"; that is, the collection of attitudes and reactions the individual has about life, and his or her place in it. Adler stated that:

> In considering the structure of a personality, the chief difficulty is that its unity, its particular style of life and goal, is not built upon objective reality, but upon the subjective view that the individual takes of the facts of life. (1964, p. 183)

This process takes place by about the age of 6 (with some variability due to individual or cultural differences). At this stage of development, individuals make decisions about their place in the world, what behaviors or strategies they will need to employ in order to belong in a social group, and how this belonging to a social group will help them get basic physical and emotional needs met. The social feeling (*Gemeinschaftsgefühl*) that the individual innately has, and the extent to which it gets expressed, is tied into the overall family atmosphere and the conclusions that the individual draws from it. Hence, the family, as the prototypical social group for the child, plays a crucial role related to the development of this private logic and eventual lifestyle. According to Adler (1964), this life style becomes the response set for life, and is the common thread that weaves together an individual's thoughts, feelings, and actions into a coherent pattern. Dreikurs (1989), also employs an artful metaphor to describe the style of life:

> Out of the individual's specific life plan develops the life style which characterizes him and every thing he does. His thoughts, action and wishes seize upon definite symbols and conform to definite patterns. The life style is comparable to a characteristic theme in a piece of music. It brings out the rhythm of recurrence into our lives. (pp. 43–44)

In addition, once it is set in place, the style of life remains relatively stable through adulthood (Peluso et al., 2004). As Lombardi, Melchior and Murphy (1996) describe in their article:

> Life-style is a blueprint for the way in which we live our lives. It determines how one perceives and interprets information as well as one's reaction to that information. Life-style is a pervasive and encompassing concept whose theme is found in all a person is or does, and is consistent over time. It affects the way one lives, wears old age, and dies. Nothing is foreign to, or divorced from, life style. Its echo is found everywhere. (p. 39)

This is not to say that the style of life is static and unchanging, but that it comprises the stable and predictable aspects of the person throughout their life. In fact, Adlerians believe that individuals can learn how to make their particular style of life work better for them either through life experiences or psychotherapy (Adler, 1964).

Clinical Importance of the Style of Life

Of course, the purpose of Individual Psychology is to provide a system of understanding human behavior and development in order to help those individuals who are either suffering from serious mental illnesses or having difficulty mastering the basic tasks of life. As such, the style of life is probably the most crucial element in Adlerian psychotherapy. It is central to the origin and maintenance of the problem as well as to the development and implementation of the solution. The style of life flows from the client's perceptions and experiences of the world (especially in the family of origin) and is manifest in client behavior, or movement in the world. It is also evidenced in the client's relations with others in terms of the quality and quantity of relationships. In fact, according to Lombardi et al. (1996) for the clinician:

> Understanding life-style as the forerunner to distorted personality development is important in understanding personality disorders and other clinical disorders. Life-style is formed in early childhood and manifested in all aspects of one's life. Personality disorders are not usually evidenced until adolescence stemming from the established life-style. (p. 35)

In other words, personality disorders, mental illness, and other problematic symptoms or behavior *cannot* be separated from the style of life. Therefore, the therapist, for his or her part, must be able to grasp the construction of the style of life, and its utilization by the client to create the present problem situation. Moreover, the clinician must recognize that the style of life is neither all good nor all bad, but rather the result of the individual being placed (or placing him- or herself) in difficult, overwhelming situations, and having a creative solution (usually in the form of some psychological "symptom" or problem) to deal with it. This creative solution takes on a *paradoxical* nature when the client comes to therapy to have the problem "fixed" (when, ironically, it was the client's present application of their unique style of life that has created the problem in the first place).

The challenge for most therapists (both Adlerian and non-Adlerian) is to recognize how the individual is applying a particular style of life to his or circumstances. This is not as easy as it seems; as Adler (1929) wrote, there are times when it is more apparent than others:

> We see the style of life under conditions of environment and it is our task to analyze its exact relation to the existing circumstances, inasmuch as mind changes with alteration of the environment. As long as a person is in a favorable situation, we cannot see his style of life clearly. In new situations, however, where he is confronted with difficulties, the style of life appears clearly and distinctly. A trained psychologist could perhaps understand a style of life of a human being even in a favorable situation, but it becomes apparent to everybody when the human subject is put into unfavorable or difficult situations. (1964, p. 173)[3]

Since crisis is the point where the person usually comes into therapy, the analysis of the life style is usually relatively simple to the trained professional. However, it is either when the crisis passes, or when the client is in therapy unwillingly, that Adler's idea becomes most prescient. These circumstances create the atmosphere where most therapists label the client as "difficult" because the therapist is stymied. Yet, for Adlerians, understanding the style of life and the purposefulness of the behavior (i.e., safeguarding tendencies, private logic, etc.), as well as the differential impact of stress on the expression of the style of life, generally allows them to work with these clients more effectively.

Yet, despite the power of this clinically, there is still the problem of the introductory psychology textbook mentioned at the beginning. Indeed, while Individual Psychology is credited by their founders with substantially influencing neo-analytical, humanistic, existential, transactional analysis, and cognitive-behavioral theories, many other theorists are unaware of Adler's theory, or are unwilling to acknowledge it, even though they may be directly utilizing it (Eckstein & Kern, 2002; May, 1989; Watts, 2003). This has become affectionately known as the "lack of recognition" problem by many Adlerians. It begs the question, if the construct of the style of life (to say nothing of Adlerian psychotherapy, as a whole) is so good, why is it not better known? Many reasons have been posited (e.g., Adler wasn't really much of a scholar; the training psychoanalysts in medical schools shut out him and his followers; the behaviorists in the universities dismissed his approach as not rigorous enough), but perhaps the most salient in today's world is the lack of empirical research validating the core constructs, or establishing the effectiveness of the approach. Nevertheless, despite the lack of research and wider recognition, the approach has continued to stand the test of time, and reads fresh to new practitioners almost 70 years after Adler's death. The challenge for Adlerians today is to decide whether more rigorous research is a goal worth striving for. Given the tenor of this volume—as well as my own personal viewpoint—it is not only worthy, but also necessary if Individual Psychology is to continue into the 21st century as anything but a historical footnote.

Research on Constructs Related to the Style of Life

We claim to have one of the oldest systems of psychotherapy around, beginning formally in 1911, long before the cognitive approaches and even predating behaviorism (if one follows the conventional wisdom that J. B. Watson founded behaviorism in 1913 with his address to Columbia University), yet we are still relative newcomers in the realm of research. As mentioned above, one of the major venues for gaining recognition and acceptance in the scientific community, and now the psychotherapeutic community, is through empirical validation. One powerful source of support for the validity of Adler's theory and constructs is through independent research on related constructs performed by investigators who are not Adlerian. This may be where the lack of recognition problem may actually benefit Adlerians, because it virtually eliminates any experimenter bias or confirmation bias (the idea that the experimenter might unwittingly influence the results to confirm his or her hypotheses) since the investigator(s) are unaware of Individual Psychology. In fact, Allen (2003) has presented some interesting findings from psychophysiology and social psychology related to the style of life. In this section, two additional areas of research on related constructs that seem to provide additional empirical support for the style of life will be discussed. They are the need to belong, and attachment theory.

The Need to Belong

Both Adler and Dreikurs (along with several modern Adlerians) have discussed how important the need to belong is to understanding the individual's development of his or her style of life, but also how it explains the purposefulness of the individual's behavior (Adler, 1937; Dreikurs, 1989). In an article wholly unrelated to Individual Psychology, Baumeister and Leary (1995) conducted an exhaustive review of the literature on research findings in social and developmental psychology on the need to belong. They concluded that the need to belong is crucial for personal well-being (i.e., survival). Interestingly, they found that personal perceptions of self-esteem differentially impacted individual behaviors in social groups. It seems that individuals who have a high level of self-esteem do not join social groups just to meet the need to belong, but rather deliberately and willingly join out of a desire to contribute; whereas individuals with low self-esteem seem to join groups primarily to meet the need to belong (Sperry & Peluso, 2004). These findings are tantalizing for Adlerians as they seem to confirm the connection between the style of life and *Gemeinschaftsgefühl*. Baumeister and Leary (1995) subsequently found that the need to belong alone is sufficient for individuals to both *form* social bonds, as well as *avoid rupturing* existing bonds without additional, ulterior motives (e.g., personal gain). These social bonds shape the way a person thinks about situations, and are crucial for the experience of positive emotions (by meeting the need to belong) as well as the opposite case. The authors found that the need to belong can be satisfied by maintaining a certain number of close relationships, and that when individuals are deprived of relationships or when the quality of relationships is poor they report diminished satisfaction. They concluded that the preponderance of the evidence points to the fact that a need to belong is a fundamental, pervasive and powerful motivator for humans. This seems to follow Adler's prediction that the style of life is a created plan for the individual to meet the need to belong, and that an individual's personal view of themselves and their social feeling (*Gemeinschaftsgefühl*) impact their style of life and, consequently, their emotions, cognitions, and behavior in the world (Sperry & Peluso, 2004).

In fact, Baumeister and Leary (1995) grasp the effect on the self of the psychological implications of failing to meet the need to belong from a decidedly Adlerian perspective:

> [A] great deal of people's psychological difficulties reflect emotional and behavioral reactions to perceived threats to social bonds ... many of the emotional problems for which people seek professional help (anxiety, depression, grief, loneliness, relationship problems and the like) result from people's failure to meet their belongingness needs. Furthermore, a great deal of neurotic, maladaptive and destructive behavior seems to reflect either desperate attempts to establish or maintain relationships with other people or sheer frustration and purposelessness when one's own need to belong goes unmet. (p. 521)

Remarkably, this sounds as if it could have been written by an Adlerian! Nonetheless, the striking point to all of this is that research was conducted by social psychologists, independent and unaware of Individual Psychology. Their work seems to have validated a crucial element of Adler's concept of the style of life, namely that the need to belong is a primary motivator for the individual's development of personality and coping strategies (hence, the style of life), within a social context (Sperry & Peluso, 2004).

Attachment Theory

Arguably, the most dynamic, modern theoretical approaches to have emerged since the mid-1990s are those that have utilized John Bowlby's attachment theory. Emotion-focused therapy (EFT), which is based in part on attachment theory, has proven that these constructs can be applied in a coherent therapeutic context and that they can empirically be shown to have a positive effect (Johnson, 2002, 2003). Constructivists and cognitive therapies who have begun to look for a theoretical grounding for these approaches have also embraced attachment theory as a major underpinning to explain their impact on clients (Watts, 2003). Perhaps because it is a psychodynamic approach that has not been stigmatized by that label in the eyes of the cognitive-behavioral therapists, or because of the impressive body of research that has been conducted primarily by developmental and social psychologists, attachment theory has emerged as a major force in the psychotherapeutic literature. A cursory overview of the basic tenets of the theory reveals some striking similarities to Individual Psychology (Peluso, Peluso, White, & Kern, 2004; Weber, 2003). Two major areas of convergence between the two theories are that each includes a coherent and stable view of the self and the world, and both acknowledge the importance of social interaction for the expression of these patterns.

The two main theoretical constructs in attachment theory are the attachment style and the internal working model of self and others. They are intertwined, as one influences the development of the other. The attachment style refers to the relational behaviors that occur between the individual and the primary caregiver in order to get basic needs met (initially), and then to develop a schema (or response set) for interacting with the world (and others) around them (Peluso et al., 2004) The development of the attachment style has been described as a "womb" for the "psychological birth" of the infant, and necessary for the health of a child (Hughes, 1997). Greenberg and Speltz (1988) described the mechanisms for developing attachment style as follows:

> [D]evelopmental changes involve progression through hierarchically-organized levels from: (a) behavioral interaction (attachment behaviors); to (b) the organization of behavior systems; to (c) the development of representation models of both self and other and

the manner in which such models both influence and are influenced by observable behavior. (p. 179)

Hence, it is reasonable to think of the development of style of life and the development of attachment as similar. Initially, just as the development of attachment is thought to begin with the primary behavioral interactions between the child and parent, Adlerian theorists believe that the style of life originates in the behavioral combinations that a child tries in order to find a place in the family to get his or her needs met. In the next phase of development, attachment behaviors become more organized into a working model of self and others, just as the private logic of the child—the methods for solving problems and confronting the tasks of life—is organized into a schema of apperception and eventually the style of life. From this working model, the individual defines the quality and nature of his or her affective, behavioral, cognitive, and physical development (Greenberg & Speltz, 1988; Hughes, 1997). Finally, as the individual matures, an internal working model of the world is developed from the attachment style, just as the style of life is set and employed with friends, school, work, family, and other social settings (Adler, 1964; Bowlby, 1988; Greenberg & Speltz, 1988). Hence, it is reasonable to conclude that there are many overlaps between Individual Psychology and attachment theory. This linkage can mutually benefit both approaches, but for the purposes of this discussion, it seems to provide (as does the work of Baumeister) some independent validation for the style of life (Peluso et al., 2004).

Research on Style of Life

The title of Wheeler, Kern, and Curlette's 1991 article triumphantly states: "Lifestyle can be measured." It was forward looking in its recognition of the dawning era of empirically validated treatments and of the need for Adlerians to move away from reliance on the strength of their convictions about the efficacy of Individual Psychology and toward well-developed, empirical research. However, in the early 21st century, it remains to be seen if this was a statement of fact, an exhortation to other Adlerians, or perhaps a little bit of both. There are still relatively few empirical studies being generated, or published, by Adlerians. In fact, one of the major critiques of Adlerians related to the "lack of recognition" problem is that there is too little research conducted and, when it is done, it is generally published in strictly Adlerian journals[4] (Carlson, 2000).

The first step in accomplishing the task of empirical validation is establishing whether the theoretical constructs put forth by Adler and his followers in fact exist and can be measured. Indeed, the two aspects of a sound theory are its predictive quality and the ability to falsify its basic structures (that is, empirically validate or disprove them). While there are many constructs in the common parlance and vernacular of counseling and psychotherapy today (e.g., "the unconscious," archetypes, the id, etc.) that do not meet these criteria of validation, many aspects of Individual Psychology—the style of life being among them—have qualities that are amenable to measurement (Wheeler et al., 1991). Though Adler was not systematic in his writings, and despite the fact that he was not an active researcher, Adler did provide extensive definitions of the elements of this theory. As a result, his definition of Individual Psychology coupled with advances in research methodology that were not available in Adler's time, give researchers the ability to test the validity of some aspects of his theory (including the style of life) (Hoffman, 1994). Hence, given some of the findings from research on similar constructs (as well as some here), it is possible to assert that researchers in Adlerian psychology have begun to develop a body of evidence for validation, but have much more to work to do (Sperry & Peluso, 2004).

This is where an assessment instrument like the Basic Adlerian Scales for Interpersonal Success-Adult Form (BASIS-A) (Wheeler, Kern & Curlette, 1993) have given researchers a tool with which to begin to answer some of the questions relating to the attributes of the style of life. The BASIS-A was the refinement of the Lifestyle Personality Indicator (LSPI) described by Wheeler et al. in 1991. It was designed for both research and clinical purposes. Specifically, it measures individual responses along dimensional themes that indicate an individual's style of life in its expression in the present.[5] According to Eckstein (2003) the BASIS-A is "the most empirically validated lifestyle questionnaire" (p. 420) developed to date. As a testament to this, the BASIS-A was reviewed in the *Mental Measures Yearbook,* which gave a favorable review (Choca, 1998; Gallagher, 1998). Additional validation research with diverse groups was conducted with positive results (Miranda, Frevert, & Kern, 1998; Peluso et al., 2004). In addition, research that has been conducted looking at aspects of the style of life (as measured by the BASIS-A) includes using for subjects perpetrators of domestic violence, inmates, and aggressive adolescents; it has also been used to assess self-efficacy, attachment style, stress, eating disorders, and substance abuse (Belangee, Sherman, & Kern, 2003; Dinter, 2000; Kern, Gfroerer, Summers, Curlette, & Matheny, 1996; Peluso, 2001; Peluso & Kern, 2002; Slaton, Kern, & Curlette, 2000; Smith, Kern, Curlette, & Mulis, 2001), to name a few.

However, just as defining the style of life is difficult, so is accurately measuring it. As with all things in Individual Psychology (and in most of the field, interestingly, these days), the *individual* should not be overlooked in the zeal to produce research. Writing in 1933, Adler provides both caution and encouragement to researchers in Individual Psychology:

> Types, similarities, and approximate likenesses are often either entities that owe their existence merely to the poverty of our language, which is incapable of giving simple expression to the nuances that are always present, or they are results of a statistical probability. The evidence of their existence should never be allowed to degenerate into the setting up of a fixed rule. Such evidence cannot bring us any nearer to the understanding of the individual case. It can only be used to throw light on a field of vision in which the individual case in its uniqueness must be found. The observation of an increased inferiority, for instance, tells us nothing as yet of the nature and characteristics of the individual case .... The uniqueness of the individual cannot be expressed in a short formula, and general rules—even those laid down by Individual Psychology, of my own creation—should be regarded as nothing more than an aid to a preliminary illumination of the field of view in which the single individual can be found—or missed. (1964, pp. 193–194)

Indeed, Adler cautions the clinician who would rely solely on "general rules" to dictate his or her treatment of the individual. At the same time, he acknowledges the value of uncovering these basic formulas in "shedding light" on the client's basic guiding line, and providing some external (at least to the clinician) method for making these predictions. Likewise, for the researcher, this illumination of the general rules is valuable for evaluating the predictive ability of Adlerian theory. According to Kern et al. (1993) the sum total of any assessment and measurement is to provide "the starting point for an individual's understanding of his or her purposes, strivings and private logic" (pp. 2–3, italics added). It is in that spirit that such instruments as the BASIS-A should be developed and demonstrate their usefulness. Perhaps others may then be encouraged to follow suit with other research agendas.

New Areas of Research Methodology and the Style of Life

To be sure, instruments such as the BASIS-A have made quantitative research into style of life themes possible, as well as helping to produce research into aspects of the style of life. However, since the mid-1990s there has been a revolution in research methodology (efficacy studies, quantitative methodology, structural equation modeling), which is making the analysis of narratives (such as the type that would be contained in traditional style of life analysis) possible.

Efficacy and Effectiveness Studies

In general, most researchers agree that *some* treatment is better than *no treatment at all*. However, this does not mean that all therapeutic approaches are equally efficacious. As a result, some standard for evaluating the practical use of each theoretical approach must be employed. Pinsof and Wynne (1995) have described six primary characteristics of well-conducted efficacy studies: (1) the research occurs within a controlled laboratory clinical setting; (2) it is focused on a specific and definable psychiatric disorder or problem; (3) it involves at least two groups of conditions—an experimental condition and a control condition; (4) clients are randomly assigned to the experimental or control condition; (5) the experimental and control treatments are specified and directed by manuals and the therapist's application of these treatments is monitored during the study by adherence ratings; and (6) all clients are measured at least pre- and posttherapy on standardized outcome measures. In addition, Pinsof and Wynne (2000) recommend that follow-up data be collected at some point following the end of treatment as part of any "gold standard" clinical efficacy research design.

However, to those clinicians who may be reading this and either thinking that this is just one more call for laboratory research with no clinical application, or beginning to nod off to sleep, or turning to another chapter, don't go just yet! Just because a theory or approach is shown to be *efficacious* in a well-controlled research study does not necessarily mean that it will be *effective* (i.e., that its findings will be reproduced in clinic settings). That is the role of the *effectiveness* study (Sperry, Carlson, & Peluso, 2005). In fact, Pinsof and Wynne (2000) have suggested that efficacy research in itself will not be enough. Instead, they foresee that in the near future, researchers will need to focus beyond either outcome or process research, and toward client-focused progress (i.e., effectiveness) research. Until now, most process research has not provided any data about differential interventions by therapists or client processes with the particular outcome. Client-focused progress research uses information about a client's systemic change processes (i.e., style of life data) during therapy so that therapists can "make decisions about what to do with particular clients at particular points in time over the course of therapy" (Pinsof & Wynne, 2000, p. 5). They argue that this type of research would be more palatable to practitioners because it would apply more naturally in the clinical setting and be idiographically related to their practice. Hence, client-focused progress research would seem to be tailor-made for clinical research on the style of life by Adlerians, and worth investigation.

Qualitative Research

Quantitative research (data using numerical representations of phenomena that produce descriptive or inferential statistics) was once considered the sine qua non of empirical research. These designs often (but not always) require large sample sizes and some experimental control. As a result, some critiques of quantitative research findings see it as artificial or laboratory-oriented with little practical application. Since the mid-1990s, qualitative research has made strong inroads into many therapy journals as an alternative path to create knowledge and evaluate observed phenomena in therapy. Its methods are often open-ended, emphasize context or client perspective over "objectivity," and usually incorporate the coding of audio- or videotaped behavior (i.e., narratives). Analysis is usually in a descriptive format and may include the frequency or percentage of an observed behavior. This allows for more naturalistic research to be conducted, more relevant to practitioners (Sperry et al., 2005). Qualitative research is seen as an effective method for observing naturalistic phenomenon and generating hypotheses (exploratory research). Among its drawbacks are that the coding is often time-consuming and labor-intensive. However, breakthroughs with computer coding and analysis software packages have made it easier to conduct this type of research. Thus, analyses of narratives, such as a traditional "life style interview," are becoming more feasible and could yield good qualitative data for validation research (both efficacy and effectiveness research studies).

Structural Equation Modeling

Structural equation modeling (SEM) is a way of measuring the relative influence of theoretical constructs, or directly unobservable phenomenon called latent variables. The model allows for causal relationships to be identified and measured, as well as for identification of mediating variables which indirectly impact other observable or latent variables (Pedhazur, 1997). In terms of the style of life, SEM offers researchers the ability to look at the impact of social interest, birth order, family atmosphere, need to belong, and other latent (theoretical) elements in the development of the style of life, and to gauge the relative impact (statistically through regression coefficients) of each on a given set of behaviors or attitudes. A conceptualization of the relationships between these elements are graphically depicted in a path diagram. Figure 13.1 presents an approximation of

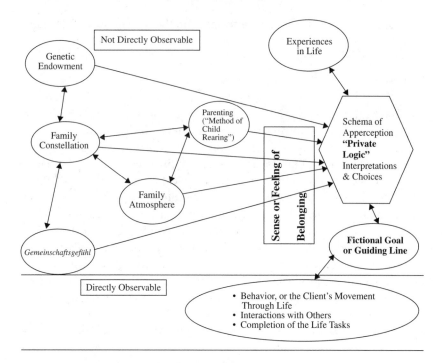

Fig. 13.1 Structural equation model of the style of life.

what a path diagram, or structural equation model, of the elements of the style of life might look like.[6]

Again, Adler, and many other Individual Psychology theorists have left an enduring legacy in the form of rich descriptions and definitions of the style of life and other constructs from which to be able to create a viable and (most importantly) testable model. SEM provides the statistical and methodological tools to be able to do just that.

Conclusion and Suggested Directions for Research into Style of Life and Adlerian Theory

Just as it was valuable to look at theoretical constructs similar to those espoused by Adler and other Individual Psychology theorists for empirical validation, it may well be valuable to look at other approaches and branches of psychology for methodological guidance. Clearly, researchers in attachment theory have conducted extensive research within the developmental and social psychology literature, which have validated many of the underlying theoretical constructs. In addition, Emotion-Focused Therapy (EFT), a derivative of attachment theory, has been subjected to validation with randomized trials on a number of occasions, to investigate its effectiveness (Greenberg & Speltz, 1988; Johnson, 2003). It has been found to be effective with couples relative to other treatment approaches. In head-to-head studies with Traditional Behavioral Couples Therapy (TBCT), EFT was found to be more effective in reducing marital distress. While EFT is but one example of empirically validated approaches, several factors warrant its singling out for discussion here: first, the theoretical overlaps between attachment theory and Individual Psychology (Peluso, 2001; Peluso et al., 2004; Weber, 2003); and, second, is the systematic fashion that Johnson and her colleagues have gone about creating a research paradigm that systematically established the effectiveness of EFT. All of this may serve as guide (dare I say guiding line?) for possible research of Individual Psychology constructs, particularly the style of life, as well as studies of clinical usefulness.

Clearly, this essay is not an exhaustive review of either the definition of the style of life and its components, or of the research that has been conducted on the style of life. The focus of this chapter has been to provide some additional context to the articles that are reprinted in this section, as well as to provide some suggestions for future "illuminations" (to borrow from Adler). Therefore, if the style of life is as ubiquitous as Lombardi and associates (1996) report, and if it can be measured as Wheeler and others (1991) have asserted, then it should not be hard to take the next step and validate the underlying predictions of the theory, and then to generalize to other schools/ approaches of psychology. The challenge for modern-day Adlerians is to have the "courage to be imperfect," make an effort at starting to conduct research, and begin a process that has been long called for by many (as outlined in the Introduction to this volume). This could be accomplished by the following:

1. Perform basic validation research on the theoretical constructs, as well as their effects on the style of life.
2. Use *all* of the research tools that are now available: qualitative analyses, quantitative analyses, and structural equation modeling analyses to validate the theoretical constructs of Individual Psychology.
3. In addition, conduct clinical efficacy and effectiveness studies comparing clients in treatment against wait-listed clients, and perhaps even head-to-head with other psychotherapeutic approaches.
4. Conduct clinical effectiveness studies in individual, couple, and family therapy, which would have the benefit of showing the relative strength of Individual Psychology across treatment domains (individual, couples, and family therapy).

In conclusion, while Individual Psychology has a long and proud history of good clinical work, grounded on solid principles, only by submitting it to the forge of research will proponents of Individual Psychology be provided with the evidence of scientific rigor that is needed to earn a larger place in the introduction to psychology textbooks (to say nothing of the field as a whole), to the betterment of all.

References

Adler, A. (1937). Mass psychology. *International Journal of Individual Psychology, 2*(2), 111–120.

Adler, A. (1964). *The individual psychology of Alfred Adler: A systematic presentation in selections from his writings* (H. L. Ansbacher & R. R. Ansbacher, Eds.). New York: Harper & Row.

Allen, T. W. (2003). The lifestyle interview: Notes from the golden age and current possibilities for "the rest of us." *Journal of Individual Psychology, 59*(4), 366–375.

Baumeister, R. F., & Leary, M. F. (1995). The need to belong: Desire for interpersonal attachment as a fundamental human motivation. *Psychological Bulletin, 117* (3), 497–529.

Belangee, S. E., Sherman, M. E. & Kern, R. M. (2003). Exploring the relationships between lifestyle personality attributes and eating disorder symptoms and behaviors in a non-clinical population. *Journal of Individual Psychology, 59*(4), 461–474.

Bowlby, J. (1988). *A secure base.* New York: Basic Books.

Carlson, J. (2000). Individual Psychology in the year 2000 and beyond: Astronaut or dinosaur? Headline or footnote? *Journal of Individual Psychology, 56*(1), 3–13.

Choca, J. P. (1998). Review of the BASIS-A Inventory (Basic Adlerian Scales for Interpersonal Success-Adult Form). In J. C. Impara & L. L. Murphy (Eds.), *The thirteenth mental measures yearbook* (pp. 80–81). Lincoln, NE: Buros Institute.

Dinter, L. D. (2000). The relationship between self-efficacy and lifestyle patterns. *The Journal of Individual Psychology, 56*(4), 462–473.

Dreikurs, R. (1989). *Fundamentals of Adlerian psychology.* Chicago, IL: Adler School of Professional Psychology.

Eckstein, D. (2003). Footprints and fingerprints of my 30 year journey in lifestyle assessment. *The Journal of Individual Psychology, 59*(4), 410–436.

Eckstein, D., & Kern, R. M. (2002). *Psychological fingerprints: Lifestyle assessment and interventions.* Dubuque, IA: Kendall/Hunt.

Gallagher, P. E. (1998). Review of the BASIS-A Inventory (Basic Adlerian Scales for Interpersonal Success-Adult Form). In J. C. Impara & L. L. Murphy (Eds.), *The thirteenth mental measures yearbook* (pp. 81–82). Lincoln, NE: Buros Institute.

Greenberg, M. T., & Speltz, M. L. (1988). Attachment and the ontogeny of conduct problems. In J. Belsky & T. Nezworski (Eds.), *Clinical implications of attachment* (pp. 177–218). Hillsdale, NJ: Erlbaum.

Hoffman, E. (1994). *The drive for self: Alfred Adler and the founding of individual psychology.* New York: Addison-Wesley.

Hughes, D. A. (1997). *Facilitating developmental attachment.* Northvale, NJ: Jason Aronson.

Johnson, S. M. (2002). *Emotionally focused couples therapy with trauma survivors: Strengthening attachment bonds.* New York: Guilford Press.

Johnson, S. M. (2003). Couples therapy research: Status and directions. In G. P. Sholevar (Ed.), *Textbook of family and couples therapy* (pp. 797–814). Alexandria, VA: American Psychiatric Publishing.

Kern, R. M., Gfroerer, K., Summers, Y., Curlette, W., & Matheny, K. (1996). Lifestyle, personality and stress-coping. *Journal of Individual Psychology, 52*(1), 42–53.

Kern, R. M., Wheeler, M. S., & Curlette, W. L. (1993). *Basic Adlerian Scales for Interpersonal Success-Adult Form (BASIS-A) Interpretive Manual.* Highlands, NC: TRT Associates.

Lombardi, D. N., Melchior, E. J., & Murphy, J. G. (1996). The ubiquity of life-style. *Individual Psychology, 52*(1), 31–41.

May, R. (1989). *The art of counseling.* New York: Basic Books.

Miranda, A. O., Frevert, V. S., & Kern, R. M. (1998). Lifestyle differences between bicultural and low- and high-acculturation-level Latino adults. *Journal of Individual Psychology, 54*(1), 119–134.

Pedhazur, E. J. (1997). *Multiple regression in behavioral research: Explanation and prediction.* Ft. Worth, TX: Harcourt Brace.

Peluso, P. R. (2001). Measuring lifestyle and attachment: An empirical investigation linking Individual Psychology and attachment theory. *Dissertation Abstracts International: Section B: The Sciences & Engineering, 62*(8-B), 3789.

Peluso, P. R., & Kern, R. M. (2002). An Adlerian model for assessing and treating the perpetrators of domestic violence. *Journal of Individual Psychology, 58*(1), 87–103.

Peluso, P. R., Peluso, J. P., Buckner, J. P., Kern, R. M., & Curlette, W. L. (2004). An analysis of the reliability of the BASIS-A inventory using a northeastern and southeastern sample. *Journal of Individual Psychology, 60*(3), 294–307.

Peluso, P. R., Peluso, J. P., White, J. F., & Kern, R. M. (2004). A comparison of attachment theory and Individual Psychology: A review of the literature. *Journal of Counseling and Development, 82*(2), 139–145.

Pinsof, W. M., & Wynne, L. C. (2000). Toward progress research: Closing the gap between family therapy practice and research. *Journal of Marital and Family Therapy, 26*(1), 1–8.

Slaton, B. J., Kern, R. M., & Curlette, W. L. (2000). Personality profiles of inmates. *The Journal of Individual Psychology, 56*(1), 88–109.

Smith, S., Kern, R. M., Curlette, W. L., & Mulis, F. (2001). Lifestyle profiles and interventions for aggressive adolescents. *The Journal of Individual Psychology, 57*(3), 224–245.

Sperry, L., Carlson, J., & Peluso, P. R. (2005). *Couples therapy: Integrating theory, research, and practice.* Denver, CO: Love Publishers.

Sperry, L., & Peluso, P. R. (2004, May/June). The need to belong: An unexpected validation and a serious challenge to Adlerian psychology. *The NASAP Newsletter, 37*(3), 1.

Watts, R. E. (Ed.). (2003). *Adlerian, cognitive, and constructivist therapies: An interactive dialogue.* New York: Springer.

Weber, D. (2003). A comparison of Individual Psychology with Attachment Theory. *The Journal of Individual Psychology, 59*(3), 246–262.

Wheeler, M. S., Kern, R. M., & Curlette, W. L. (1991). Life-style can be measured. *Individual Psychology, 47*(2), 229–240.

Wheeler, M. S., Kern, R. M., & Curlette, W. L. (1993). *Basic Adlerian Scales for Interpersonal Success-Adult Form (BASIS-A) Inventory.* Highlands, NC: TRT Associates.

Notes

1. Of course, in today's nomenclature, "lifestyle" also means something different (e.g., "alternative lifestyle"). It is an interesting irony that if Adler had been talking about homosexuality, his theory would probably be tremendously popular today! Moreover, like others of his time, his view of homosexuality is bound up in the cultural context of the day and seems out of step to us today. This is a topic that has been discussed by modern-day Adlerians, and will not be addressed here other than as a point of irony.

2. While some translations of Adler's work have used the term *life style*, many Individual Psychology writers have reverted to using the term *style of life*, which is closer to Adler's original conceptualization. This term will also be used here, though life style will be used in the articles presented in this section.

3. Interestingly, Adler was one of the first clinicians to acknowledge the mediating effects of the personality (style of life) on the interaction between stress and behavior, which would not be fully appreciated in the field until the last decades of the 20th century.

4. Technology, particularly the use of the Internet to access journal articles may actually begin to lessen the problem of *access* to Adlerian-based research (either through interlibrary loan, or especially with the recent full-text posting online of such journals as *The Journal of Individual Psychology*), but not the *perception* that Adlerian researchers either *cannot* get their articles published in a broader range of journals, or are unwilling to do so. However, there is evidence that this is beginning to change for the better.

5. It should be noted that although the BASIS-A items are all worded as reflections on childhood, the interpretation of the results are in terms of *present-day* functioning, in keeping with Adlerian theory.

6. I am *indebted* to Gerry Mozdzierz and Richard Watts for their comments on this figure. It is my hope that this may inspire additional response and refinement as well as research!

CHAPTER 14

The Ubiquity of Life-Style

DONALD N. LOMBARDI, ERIK J. MELCHIOR,
JAMES G. MURPHY, and AMY L. BRINKERHOFF

The concept of life-style is one of paramount importance in Individual Psychology. The holistic approach espoused by Alfred Adler views the person as an integrated whole whose thoughts, emotions, and behavior are consistent rather than contradictory (Adler, 1929). Every individual from earliest childhood develops his or her own unique law of movement. The direction of this movement aims always at overcoming the difficulties of one's life (Ansbacher & Ansbacher, 1964). The individual's consistent movement toward a personal goal of security and significance is his or her life-style. Adler (Ansbacher & Ansbacher, 1956) summarized lifestyle as a "general concept composing, in addition to the goal, the individuals' opinion of himself and the world and his unique way of striving for this goal in his particular situation" (p. 172). Adler (1933/1938) viewed life-style as "command[ing] all forms of expression," including "instincts, impulses, feeling, thinking, acting, attitude to pleasure and displeasure, and finally self-love and social interest" (p. 8).

Adler (Ansbacher & Ansbacher, 1956) described Individual Psychology as a centralist philosophy in that it is essential to examine the nucleus of the personality before peripheral expressions can be understood and assessed. All aspects of a person can be seen as unified in striving for a goal or purpose. One's unique life-style is a bridge toward achieving a personal goal (Ansbacher & Ansbacher, 1956). Ansbacher (1978) further states, "man is increasingly understood as a self-consistent and self-directed unity whose central theme is reflected in all his actions, as forward oriented, purposive, determined by his own values rather than physiological factors, and in interaction with his environment" (p. 9).

Complete understanding of a person can only occur through a clear grasp of his or her life-style. Organic and environmental concerns, while contributing to the development of life-style, are of secondary importance. The genetics or environment of an individual fail to explain his or her behavior; it is the person's unique interpretation or response that is of primary importance (Ansbacher, 1977).

Lombardi (1975) also stresses the pervasiveness of life-style throughout all aspects of the unified self. He describes life-style as both offensive and defensive. Outward manifestations of life-style are evident in personality traits, which direct our consistent patterns of acting toward others. We also express life-style through defensive reactions, our psychic defenses. Life-style is the strategy people use to achieve a sense of significance, or a place in this world (Lombardi, 1975). It is an organized and consistent manner of viewing oneself, others, and adapting to life in one's own personal manner. Life-style can also be distinguished from personality. One's personality is a compilation of all that an individual possesses and is a descriptive term. Life-style, on the other hand, is the expression of what one has. It is an active term. Life-style is personality in action.

The notion of parsimony is an increasingly important consideration in psychology. As the number of diagnostic labels continues to expand, a frugality or economy of disorders is desirable. Adler's concept of life-style is a useful term that retains its breadth despite the division of diagnostic categories. Life-style is a ubiquitous concept that subsumes many expressions of psychopathology, including symptomless disorders. These disorders, generally characterized by a tendency toward maladjustment rather than observable symptoms, are actually faulty life-styles.

The purpose of this article is to illustrate that many abnormal behavior patterns are nothing more than expressions of faulty life-styles. These behavior patterns include personality styles, neurotic styles, personality disorders, and academic styles. Berne's (1972) transactional analysis concept of scripts, cognitive maps, premorbid personality, and transference and countertransference will also be shown to be related to life-style. Since life-style is an important and ubiquitous concept, it is not surprising that it is inherent in all behavior patterns as well as some theoretical constructs.

Personality Styles

Horowitz, Marmor, Krupnick, Wilner, and Kaltreider (1984), in a Freudian vein and within a context of brief psychotherapy, put forth the concept of personality styles. This refers to "a repertoire of states of mind, self-concepts and patterns of relationships, and ways of coping with stress and defending against threat. This includes characteristic patterns of regulating perceptions, thoughts, feelings, decisions, plans and actions" (Horowitz et al., 1984, p. 68). Personality style is a broad term. On the one hand, it may refer to distinct patterns of behavior evident in many aspects of one's life. However, it may also refer to personality traits triggered by stressful occasions. It has been offered as a replacement for *Diagnostic and Statistical Manual (DSM)* Axis II personality disorders. Personality disorders are limited since they fail to include the organizational level of the self-concept and object conceptualization (Horowitz et al., 1984).

Often peculiar defensive patterns and personality traits appear in the process of treating an Axis I disorder such as posttraumatic stress disorder or adjustment disorder. These more general personality styles may not meet the criteria for personality disorders. However, proper recognition of this style is necessary to facilitate treatment of the Axis I disorder (Horowitz et al., 1984). In a similar manner, life-style transcends DSM axis classification. Life-style is evident in Axis I and II disorders, and must be understood for effective treatment.

Neurotic Styles

Neurotic styles can be defined by dissecting the term itself. Style refers to the characteristic manner of individual functioning observable through specific acts or behaviors. By neurotic style, it is meant that this manner of functioning is idiosyncratic of neurotic conditions, particularly subjective experiences, modes of thinking and experiencing emotions (Shapiro, 1965). Angyal (1965) described neurosis as comprehensive. It is the general way a person lives his or her life, not a specific deficit in an otherwise healthy personality. If the latter were true, a neurosis would be easy to overcome without the strong resistance manifested within the individual that is generally a part of neurosis. The strength of the neurosis lies not in its characteristic twists on a personality, but in the neurotic organization of that personality. There is a certain personality organization conducive to neurosis, with its own goals, attitudes, and motives (Angyal, 1965). This predisposition, of itself, can be considered a neurosis, with the neurotic "symptoms" appearing as a manifestation of the underlying faulty personality (Adler, 1913/1963).

Accordingly, life-style encompasses all aspects of one's unique life, including personality. Neurosis, as a materialization of a faulty personality organization, is also a materialization of life-style. Shapiro (1965), in describing obsessive-compulsive neurosis, uses "rigidity," a style of categorical, inflexible thinking, to illustrate a faulty personality trait, or component of an obsessive-compulsive neurotic style. These symptoms, or traits, are consistent with one's attitudes, modes of thinking, and subjective experiences. They are not something cognizantly planned or created, nor are they contradictory to the general striving of the whole person. All symptoms tend to make sense when considering the neurotic perspective of those attitudes, modes of thinking, or subjective experiences (Shapiro, 1989). The neurotic style is a direct derivative of the formulation of one's life-style that is faulty in its expression or movement toward a goal.

The concept of neurosis is no longer included as a diagnostic category in the DSM-IV classification system (American Psychiatric Association [APA], 1994). This absence suggests it is less of a discrete disorder, and more a general pattern of behavior. Carson and Butcher (1992) conceptualize neurotic styles as being symptomless tendencies toward maladjustment, but not evidenced by concrete, observable symptoms.

Personality Disorders

Allport (1937) defines personality as "the dynamic organization within the individual of those psychophysical systems that determine his characteristic behavior and thought" (p. 28). Most individuals are able to function and thrive in their environments. However, the development of some individuals may be blocked or distorted. When problematic personality traits develop as the result of a faulty life-style, personality disorders are likely to arise.

According to DSM-IV, "a personality disorder is an enduring pattern of inner experience and behavior" (APA, 1994, p. 629). These disorders are divided into three clusters: Cluster A includes paranoid, schizoid, and schizotypal disorders; Cluster B is comprised of antisocial, borderline, histrionic, and narcissistic disorders; and Cluster C contains the avoidant, dependent, and obsessive-compulsive disorders. When diagnosing a disorder, one must evaluate the individual's inflexible, maladaptive personality traits, specifically those which have developed by early adulthood and have occurred consistently over time. Personality disorders are primarily revealed through behavioral deviations (APA, 1994; Carson & Butcher, 1992).

Understanding life-style as the forerunner to distorted personality development is important in understanding personality disorders and other clinical disorders. Life-style is formed in early childhood and is manifested in all aspects of one's life. Personality disorders are not usually evidenced until adolescence, stemming from the established life-style. However, these disorders are only manifested in limited aspects of one's life. No life-style can be expected to be free of faulty assumptions. Personality disorders can be viewed as the diagnostic classifications of those life-styles that tend toward a particular pattern of maladjustment.

The classification of personality disorders on Axis II of DSM-IV separates them from Axis I clinical disorders. The purpose of this is to ensure that "consideration will be given to the possible presence of Personality Disorders ... that might otherwise be overlooked when attention is directed to the usually more florid Axis I disorders" (APA, 1994, p. 26). Certain Axis I disorders are closely related to personality disorders. In some cases, an individual may be diagnosed as having a disorder on both axes, with personality disorder as an underlying factor in some Axis I clinical disorders (Carson & Butcher, 1992). The starting point for understanding personality disorders and certain Axis I classifications begins with grasping the dynamics of lifestyle.

Academic Styles

Learning disabilities represent a topic currently an enigma in terms of etiology, dynamics, and treatment (Carson & Butcher, 1992; Barlow & Durand, 1995). Although there are some structural and functional differences in the brains of people with learning disabilities, these differences are not consistent across individuals (Hynd & Semrud-Clikeman, 1989). Reading problems, such as dyslexia, and difficulties in spelling and math are considered by some to be due to subtle organic factors (Pennington & Smith, 1988; Reeve & Kauffman, 1988). This is especially true when these children are found to be average and above average in intelligence. In a school setting, many such children are classified as minimal brain dysfunction (MBD), neurologically impaired (NI), and perceptually impaired (PI). However, there is no conclusive evidence for genetic, physical, or neurological causes for learning disabilities (Hynd & Semrud-Clikeman, 1989). Laterality and mixed dominance have also been considered as a cause, but again there is a lack of evidence (Kessler, 1988).

McGuinness (1985) believes that when children have difficulty learning, it may simply be due to individual differences in abilities. Some children are slower to learn than others. Taylor (1988) indicates that psychological and motivational factors tend to have a more significant impact on the eventual outcome of learning disabled individuals. Dunn and Dunn (1978) advocate a practical approach that involves teaching students through their individual learning styles. Perhaps learning disabilities and the peaks and valleys in the academic profile can be viewed in light of the life-style. Learning and academic styles are shaped by the individual's life-style. For example, difficulty in reading may reflect a fear of making mistakes, or difficulty in arithmetic could be related to dependency on a parent or teacher.

Transactional Analysis and the Concept of Scripts

Transactional analysis is a psychological perspective that emphasizes the study of ego status. Ego status is defined as "a coherent system of thoughts and feelings manifested by corresponding patterns of behavior" (Berne, 1972, p. 11). Berne (1972), the originator of transactional analysis, speaks of "script" and "script analysis." He states that one decides early in childhood how he or she will live and die. All important behaviors and life decisions are dictated by one's script or life plan. Scripts are also methods of structuring time and attaining the greatest satisfaction from a given situation. Periods of one's life, or even an entire lifetime, are organized to accommodate one's unique script. Every person is the personal architect of his or her script and, with the appropriate freedom, has the power to carry out that unique script. Script analysis is a focal point of transactional analysis. An understanding of a client's script is expected to shed light on current behaviors, behavioral antecedents, as well as future goals (Berne, 1972).

The concept of script is remarkably similar to Adler's life-style concept. In fact, Berne credits Adler with coming the closest to "speaking like a script analyst" (Berne, 1972, p. 58). Like life-styles, scripts are personal life plans which shape all attitudes, beliefs and behaviors. They are formed early in life with parental influence, yet also contain an element of conscious choice. Both scripts and life-styles involve the striving for a particular goal. The primary difference is that scripts involve specific and even short-term goals. Life-style entails a more general striving for personal significance. The life-style concept is thus further illustrated as a ubiquitous concept evident in the theoretical constructs of transactional analysis.

Cognitive Maps

All individuals have a unique perception and interpretation of the world based on distinctive life experiences. Each person formulates a representation of his or her world that serves to guide one's behavior. These maps or schemas are based on subjective perception rather than objective reality (Bandler & Grinder, 1975). Cognitive maps serve as a frame of reference to determine an individual's reaction to future situations. However, a misinterpreted event or poor self-image can leave a false impression on one's cognitive map and possibly result in a predisposition to maladaptive behavior.

Cognitive maps may take on several different functions. For example, Money (1986) first identified a love map in the early 1980s, that he defined as "a developmental representation or template in the mind and in the brain depicting the idealized lover and the idealized program of sexuoerotic activity projected in imagery or actually engaged in with that lover" (Money, 1986, p. 290). A lovemap is generally formed by puberty and thereafter difficult to influence or change.

When the development of the lovemap is distorted as a result of sexual abuse or other traumatic experiences, a sexual dysfunction may arise. Money (1986) stated, "as in the case of any wound, a vandalized lovemap tries to heal itself. In the process it gets scarred, skewed and misshapen. Some of its features get omitted, some get displaced, and some get replaced by substitutes that would not otherwise be included" (p. 19). Life-style and social supports may be key elements in maintaining the wholeness of the affected individual.

Whatever the function of the cognitive map may be, its skewed development is instrumental in an individual behaving in accordance with erroneous ideas. This relates to the concept of life-style; it is more practical to use this term as opposed to cognitive map because of its ubiquitous nature. Life-style is an all-encompassing notion relating to an individual's consistent pattern of behavior. Just as a distorted lovemap leads to a problematic expression of sexual behavior, so does a faulty life-style lead to deviations in all realms of behavior.

Premorbid Personality

Premorbid personality is defined as the personality as it was before the onset of psychopathology. It is the personality prior to the traumatic event that precipitated the abnormal symptoms and behavior. When an accident, illness, natural disaster, or some other severe stressor is experienced, the response of the individual depends on previous experience and enduring life-style. This was a topic that was referred to by the Greeks and Romans in the history of abnormal psychology. For example, the Roman physician Arateus believed that emotional disorders were merely an extension or exaggeration of normal personality traits (Zax & Cowen, 1976).

There has been research and theorizing about how normal individuals versus those previously maladapted react to stressful events. On the one hand, there is the professional opinion that a psychological disorder can result in a normal and healthy individual (Dohrenwend & Egri, 1981). The other viewpoint is that problems are likely to occur in those vulnerable and at risk on the basis of their premorbid personalities (Depue & Monroe, 1986; McFarlane, 1986). For example, the most pronounced effects of rape on its victim are in those persons with prior difficulties (Atkeson, Calhoun, Resick, & Ellis, 1982; Koss, 1983). In other words, the premorbid personality is a factor that can facilitate the emergence of problems.

It is unlikely that one's personality and level of adjustment would not affect how that individual will interpret and respond to a given stressor. It is not just a question of having earlier psychopathology, but concerns the type of personality and traits that the individual has, as well as his or her expectations. In other words, premorbid personality is a variant of the life-style. Not only is life-style consistent throughout the entire personality, but there is also a temporal consistency. Premorbid personality determines one's interpretation and reaction to a stressor, as well as subsequent responses, including relapse and recovery. Because of life-style consistency, it is not suprising that people with healthy life-styles are better able to cope with traumatic experiences. Conversely, people with unhealthy life-styles are likely to experience continuing problems. Knowing about one's life-style reaps many benefits. Understanding life-style is like deciphering a code that unlocks the mystery of one's personality and behaviors.

Transference and Counter-Transference

Since Freud (1901) introduced the concepts of transference and counter-transference, many psychotherapists are aware of their effects in a counseling/therapy relationship. Transference is a person's reacting to people in the present on the basis of similar encounters he or she has had with others at an earlier time. Ingrained learning patterns continue to exist with different people and in different places. Transference in the counselor, a reaction to the patient or client, is referred to as counter-transference (Wicks, 1993). Analysis of transference and counter-transference reactions in the therapeutic relationship and their resolution become important issues. Adler (Ansbacher & Ansbacher, 1956) described transference as merely nothing more than social interest; in this case, the social situation is the therapeutic relationship. One way of viewing these reactions is to know and explain them as the result of two interacting life-styles. Thus, another evidence for the ubiquity of life-style is the way one's life-style dictates the manner in which he or she perceives and interacts with others. This is true of all social encounters, including the therapeutic relationship.

Conclusion

More than 50 years after his death, Alfred Adler's influence on psychology remains pronounced. Life-style is one of his most significant contributions, as it is a forerunner of many ideas and concepts in psychology. Some of them have been treated in this article. Regardless of one's theoretical orientation, the therapeutic search is for consistent patterns of behavior. Although theorists and therapists may refer to it by different names, they are essentially looking for an individual's life-style.

Life-style is a blueprint for the way in which we live our lives. It determines how one perceives and interprets information, as well as one's reaction to that information. Life-style is a pervasive and encompassing concept whose theme is found in all a person is or does, and is consistent over time. It affects the way one lives, wears old age, and dies. Nothing is foreign to, or divorced from, life-style. Its echo is found everywhere. Thus, life-style is truly a ubiquitous concept.

Reference Note

Appreciation is expressed to Gerald Mozdzierz for calling our attention to Eric Berne's recognition of the importance of Adler's life-style.

References

Adler, A. (1929). *The science of living*. New York: Greenburg.

Adler, A. (1938). *Social interest: A challenge to mankind*. (J. Linton & R. Vaughn, Trans.) London: Faber & Faber. (Original work published 1933.)

Adler, A. (1963). Individual-psychological treatment of neuroses. (P. Radin, Trans.). In C. K. Ogden (ed.) *Individual Psychology*. Paterson, NJ: Littlefield, Adams. (Original work published 1913.)

Allport, G. W. (1937). *Pattern and growth in personality*. New York: Holt, Rinehart, and Winston.

American Psychiatric Association. (1994). *Diagnostic and statistic manual of mental disorders* (4th ed.). Washington, DC: Author.

Angyal, A. (1965). *Neurosis and treatment: A holistic theory*. New York: Viking.

Ansbacher, H. L. (1977). Individual psychology. In R. J. Corsini (Ed.), *Current personality theories*. Itasca, IL: F. E. Peacock.

Ansbacher, H. L. (1978). Life style: A historical systematic review. In L. G. Baruth and D. G. Eckstein (Eds.), *Life style: Theory practice and research*. Debuque, IA: Kendall/Hunt.

Ansbacher, H. L., & Ansbacher, R. R. (Eds.). (1956). *The individual psychology of Alfred Adler: A systematic presentation from his writings*. New York: Basic.

Ansbacher, H. L., & Ansbacher, R. R. (Eds.). (1964). *Superiority and social interest: A collection of later writings*. Evanston: Northwestern University Press.

Atkeson, B. M., Calhoun, K. S., Resick, P. A., & Ellis, E.M. (1982). Victims of rape: Repeated assessment of depressive symptoms. *Journal of Clinical and Consulting Psychology, 50*, 96–102.

Bandler, R., & Grinder, J. (1975). *The structure of magic* (Vol. 1). Palo Alto, CA: Science and Behavior Books.

Barlow, D. H., & Durand, V. M. (1995). *Abnormal psychology: An integrative approach*. New York: Brooks/Cole.

Berne, E. (1972). *What do you say after you say hello?* New York: Grove.

Carson, R. C, & Butcher, J. N. (1992). *Abnormal psychology and modern life*. (9th ed.). New York: HarperCollins.

Depue, R. A., & Monroe, S. M. (1986). Conceptualization and measurement of human disorder in life stress research: The problem of chronic disturbance. *Psychological Bulletin, 99*, 36– 51.

Dohrenwend, B. P., & Egri, G. (1981). Recent stressful life events and episodes of schizophrenia. *Schizophrenia Bulletin, 7*, 12–23.

Dunn, R., & Dunn, K. (1978). *Teaching students through their individual learning styles*: A practical approach. New York: Reston.

Freud, S. (1901). Fragment of an analysis of a case of hysteria. In J. Strachey (Ed.) *Complete psychological works of Sigmund Freud*. London: Hogarth.

Horowitz, M., Marmor, C., Krupnick, J., Wilner, N., & Kaltreider, N. (1984). *Personality styles and brief psychotherapy*. New York: Basic.

Hynd, G. W., & Semrud-Clikeman, M. (1989). Dyslexia and brain morphology. *Psychological Bulletin 106*, 447–482.

Kessler, J. W. (1988). *Psychopathology of childhood*. (2nd. ed). Englewood Cliffs NJ: Prentice Hall.

Koss, M. P. (1983). The scope of rape: Implications for the clinical treatment of victims. *Clinical Psychology, 36*, 88–91.

Lombardi, D. N. (1975). *Search for significance*. Chicago: Nelson Hall.

McFarlane, A. C. (1986). Post traumatic morbidity of a disaster: A study of cases presenting for psychiatric treatment. *Journal of Nervous and Mental Disorders, 174*, 4–14.

McGuiness, D. (1985). *When children don't learn*. New York: Basic.

Money, J. (1986). *Lovemaps: Clinical concepts of sexual/erotic health and pathology, paraphilia and gender transposition*. New York: Irvington.

Pennington, B. F., & Smith, S. D. (1988). Genetic influences on learning disabilities: An update. *Journal of Clinical and Consulting Psychology, 56*, 817– 823.

Reeve, R. E., & Kauffman, J. M. (1988). Learning disabilities. In V. B. Van Hasselt, P. S. Strain, & M. Hersen (Eds.) *Handbook of developmental and physical disabilities*. New York: Pergamon.

Shapiro, D. (1965). *Neurotic styles*. New York: Basic.

Shapiro, D. (1989). *Psychotherapy of neurotic character*. New York: Basic.

Taylor, H. G. (1988). Learning disabilities. In E. G. Mash & C. G. Terdal (Eds.), *Behavioral assessment of childhood disorders* (2nd. ed.). New York: Guilford.

Wicks, R. J. (1993). Countertransference and burnout in pastoral counseling. In R. J. Wicks, R. D. Parsons, & P. Capps (Eds.), *Clinical handbook of pastoral counseling, 1*, 76–96. Mahwah, NJ: Paulist.

Zax, M., & Cowen, E. L. (1976). *Abnormal Psychology—Changing conceptions*. (2nd ed.). New York: Holt. Rinehart, and Winston.

CHAPTER 15

Life-Style Can Be Measured

MARY STREPPA WHEELER, ROY M. KERN,
and WILLIAM L. CURLETTE

Adlerian theory proposes that individuals are characterized by certain "life-style" themes which organize their perceptions about themselves and their world (Ansbacher & Ansbacher, 1956; Dinkmeyer, Pew, & Dinkmeyer, 1979). Although life-style analysis is a major construct in Adlerian psychology, little research has been done in this area. One reason for the lack of research on life-style is that the life-style interview requires one to two hours to complete. Another is that the subjective nature of the life-style analysis adds uncontrolled variables to the process. The idiosyncratic nature of life-styles and confusion as to whether typologies should be identified have contributed to the unfortunate belief that life-style cannot be measured. The authors think it can be measured in a reliable and valid manner using a paper and pencil test.

Research has supported the presence of basic similarities among Adlerian life-styles (Davis, 1979; Kaiser, 1979; Langenfeld & Main, 1983; Mullis, Kern, & Curlette, 1987; O'Phelan, 1977; Thorne, 1975; Thorne & Pishkin, 1975; West & Bubenzer, 1978; Wheeler, 1980; Wheeler, Kern, & Curlette, 1986). The Life Style Personality Inventory (LSPI) (Wheeler, Kern, & Curlette, 1982) is an empirically derived measure of life-style themes that is based on the assumption that although individual differences exist among life-styles, similarities can still be measured and be helpful in understanding the individual, as well as the relationship Adlerian life-styles have to each other and various other variables.

Personality tests may be developed from several different methods, consisting of rational and theoretical on the one hand and empirical methods such as group difference and factor analysis on the other.

The Minnesota Multiphasic Personality Inventory, for example, is empirically derived. Items were chosen on the basis of their ability to distinguish between groups of patients and their relatives and visitors. Thus what an item appears to measure (face validity) may not agree with the actual keying of the item for an MMPI subscale because the keying is based on the ability of the item to distinguish groups. The 16PF is also empirically derived, although that test is based on the statistical procedure of factor analysis. The Thematic Apperception Test, on the other hand, is derived from Murray's theory rather than from an empirical base. Modern test developers believe in using as many of these methods as possible. Lanyon and Goodstein (1982) state that "a balanced and sophisticated method might involve the initial selection of test stimuli based upon theoretical or rational consideration, with factor analysis for the attainment of internal consistency and final refinement based upon clear-cut empirical findings. Although this type of test derivation is both time consuming and costly, it is generally regarded as a model for future efforts in test construction" (p. 93). Millon's Clinical Multiaxial Inventory is one example of a test which combines the theoretical and empirical approaches. The LSPI is another.

The Life-Style Personality Inventory

Adler theorized that personality is fairly well developed by an early age (Ansbacher & Ansbacher, 1956). Thus the LSPI uses questions which reflect perceptions about childhood events. All the statements begin with the phrase, "When I was a child, I … The person is asked to rate various phrases ending this sentence on a continuum of "strongly disagree" to "strongly agree." Because these items relate to events in one's childhood, they should reduce defensiveness which might arise from having to admit to negative behaviors at the present time. Thus the social desirability factor is somewhat mitigated. Providing a range of alternatives allows individuals to project their own interpretation of the degree to which the statement applies to them. According to Adlerian theory, it is not one's situation that is of utmost importance but how one interprets that situation. This allows for differences in perceptions over time.

The purpose of this paper is to describe the development of the LSPI and to report on the research evidence gathered to date. Both reliability and validity results will be presented.

Development of the LSPI

Instrument development began with an attempt to conceptualize the constructs of Adlerian life-styles according to Adlerian theory. Originally, items were chosen based on Mosak's (1959, 1968, 1971, 1977, 1979) typologies and Adlerian thinking on life-styles.

Exploratory factor analysis. First, an exploratory factor analysis was conducted on an item pool of the 48 childhood items from Wheeler's (1980) questionnaire. These items had been administered to 715 subjects. Iterated principal factor analysis was used with an oblique rotation (direct quartimin) on the factors with eigenvalues greater than one. This analysis produced four factors, similar to Dreikurs' four goals of misbehavior (Wheeler, Kern, & Curlette, 1986). The authors had not intended to validate Dreikurs' theory; however, the results did provide empirical support for the four goals of children's misbehavior.

Inter-judge study. The next step in the process was to write more items related to the four themes produced in the initial factor analysis. Five judges, who are all acknowledged experts in Adlerian psychology, were asked to participate in this part of the study to demonstrate construct validity of the inventory items for the four life-style themes (Mullis, 1984). The judges were asked to categorize each of the 163 items into one of the four themes. The percentage of agreement on items for each theme ranged from 50% better than chance to 82% better than chance, which tends to validate the constructs of the LSPI.

Confirmatory factor analysis. Mullis (1984), using confirmatory factor analysis, identified nine factors that were related to the previously defined life-style themes and the Social Interest Index. Items that had a factor coefficient of .25 or greater were considered significant for the interpretation of a factor. Two factors which represented different aspects of the "Exploiting" theme were collapsed into one factor because of their similar emphasis. This resulted in eight scales (a Social Interest Index and seven life-style themes) on the LSPI. On each of these scales a respondent receives his/her average score ranging from one to five on a Likert scale.

The items were further analyzed to make sure that none of them contained statements that were racially biased. In addition, a reading expert reviewed the items and suggested changes to bring the reading level of the instrument to the sixth grade level. These changes were made in the items.

Normative sample. A total of 1,010 subjects participated in the second factor analysis (Mullis, 1984), the current normative group for the LSPI. In this sample, 65% were female and 34% male, with a median age of 30 years. The sample was 83.3% white, 13.5% black, and 2.7% of other races. Approximately 55% of the respondents were high school, undergraduate, or graduate students, and the majority (70.4%) of the nonstudents were employed in white-collar occupations. The median number of years of school completed was 15, and the median income was $21,100. Most of the respondents (88.9%) resided in the Southern region of the United States.

Reliability Data

Coefficient alpha calculated on each subscale of the LSPI using the norm sample resulted in excellent reliabilities, ranging from .82 to .93. Reliabilities and other descriptive statistics are provided in Table 1.

Test-retest reliability coefficients (product-moment correlations) are presented in Table 2. The relatively lower reliability of Theme 1 (Conforming/Active) may reflect a treatment effect of taking the test. In other words, having taken the test and formulated thoughts as to how they should respond, in future administrations of the test, subjects may have changed their responses to these items, which reflect feelings of being successful. This scale also has a greater restriction of range than some of the other scales, which would produce lower correlations. Thus the lower reliabilities for Theme 1 may be a result of characteristics of the population or of scale construction. This needs further research.

TABLE 15.1 Reliability and Normative Data for the LSPI

Themes	Alpha	No. of Items	Mean	S.D.
1. (Conforming/Active)	.860	21	3.718	.44366
2. (Conforming/Passive)	.825	13	3.656	.5444
3. (Controlling/Active)	.882	14	2.709	.6512
4. (Controlling/Passive)	.821	12	2.542	.5878
5. (Exploiting/Active)	.890	25	2.311	.5058
6. (Exploiting/Passive)	.930	25	2.249	.6384
7. (Displaying Inadequacy)	.863	13	2.355	.6050
Social Interest Index	.926	23	3.680	.6106

TABLE 15.2 Summary of LSPI Test-Retest Reliability Using Pearson Correlation

LSPI Scale	One Week	One Month	Ten Weeks
1. (Conforming/Active)	.78	.64	.49
2. (Conforming/Passive)	.83	.83	.77
3. (Controlling/Active)	.91	.81	.81
4. (Controlling/Passive)	.92	.88	.85
5. (Exploiting/Active)	.89	.90	.79
6. (Exploiting/Passive	.92	.82	.91
7. (Displaying Inadequacy)	.85	.77	.84
Social Interest Index	.92	.82	.82

In general, the test-retest results support the reliability and stability of the LSPI over periods of up to ten weeks. Reliabilities over a one-month period range from .64 to .90.

Validity

Establishing validity is a matter of accumulating evidence for the meaningfulness, usefulness, and appropriateness of the test scores for making inferences. For convenience, validity of an instrument is often grouped into the categories of content validity, construct validity, and criterion-related validity. Content validation assesses whether or not the content of the instrument is representative of some universe of content. In Wheeler's 1980 study, the content domain was defined and expert judgment was used to determine the representativeness of the items. Items were selected based on Mosak's typologies and current thinking on Adlerian life-styles. In addition, expert judges were used in the study by Mullis (1984) to determine if the items reflected the constructs theorized. Furthermore, the judges had the option of not assigning the item to any of the themes specified. This study provided evidence for both the content and construct validity of the LSPI.

Additional information for item selection was obtained from a group difference study to help establish discriminant validity. The item means from a junior college sample were compared to item means from a sample of mothers of moderately to severely troubled children using independent *t*-tests. Most items showed evidence that they discriminated between the two groups in accordance with Adlerian theory (Curlette, Kern, & Mullis, 1984).

Several methods were used in relation to construct validation. After the first factor analysis by Wheeler (1980), the constructs were refined, new items were written, and a second factor analysis was performed (Mullis, 1984). The nature of the factors was anticipated in the definition of the constructs, and the clustering of items by the factor analysis generally confirmed our expectations, contributing to the construct validity of the LSPI.

Many criterion-related and construct validity studies have been conducted on the LSPI. Their results will be included in the description of the individual scales which follows.

Scale Descriptions

The Social Interest Index. This index measures social interest and is conceptualized as a measure of one's sense of belonging in the world and ability to face the life tasks cooperatively. It is presumed to be a measure of mental health according to Adler's concept of social interest.

There is significant research to validate the Social Interest Index. Wheeler (1990) found positive correlations with assertiveness in college students ($r = .38$, $p < .001$), and Johnston (1988) found positive correlations with the Fundamental Interpersonal Relations Orientation-Behavior (FIRO-B) Expressed Inclusion Scale ($r = .253$, $p < .01$) and the Millon Behavioral Health Inventory Sociable Style Scale ($r = .389$, $p < .001$). The former measures comfortableness in social settings and tending to move toward people. The latter reflects those who are talkative, charming, and outgoing.

In addition, negative correlations have been found with external locus of control ($r = -.26$, $p < .001$) (Wheeler & White, 1989), two measures of depression ($rs = -.276, -.267$, $ps = .014, .006$) (Johnston, 1988), the Schizophrenia, Psychopathic Deviate, and Social Introversion scales of the Minnesota Multiphasic Personality Inventory ($rs = -.242, -.284, -.363$, $ps = .012, .003, .001$) (Johnston, 1988), and with child abuse potential ($rs = -.36$ to $-.40$, $ps < .01$) (Wheeler, Braswell, & Milner, 1990). Johnston (1988) also found negative correlations with two scales of the Millon Behavioral Health Inventory, Social Alienation and Inhibited Style ($rs = -.503, -.496$, $ps < .001$). The Social Alienation Scale purports to assess the level of familial and friendship support, with high scorers prone to physical and psychological ailments. High scores on the Inhibited Style scale are purported to be hesitant with others and shy. Boynton (1988) also found low scores on the Social Interest Index in a drug dependent group and correlation ($r = -.40$, $p < .001$) between the Social Interest Index and Global Severity Index of the Symptom Checklist-90-Revised (SCL-90-R).

On an earlier version of the instrument, the mothers of troubled children also responded to the Depression Adjective Checklist, an established instrument to measure depression. A correlation of $r = -.31$ $(p < .03)$ between the Depression Adjective Checklist and the social interest subscale provided some evidence of construct validity (Curlette, Kern, & Mullis, 1984).

Although the Social Interest Index appears to be the most clearly defined of the LSPI scales, it should be noted that no correlation has been found between the Social Interest Index and Crandall's Social Interest Scale (SIS) (Highlander, 1984). Crandall's SIS was found to be indirectly related to Theme 3 (Controlling/Active) and Theme 5 (Exploiting/Active), suggesting again that the two scales are measuring different constructs.

Theme 1 (Conforming/Active). This theme relates to seeking approval from others by active efforts to succeed. Evaluation of the self is derived from external sources, and there is a fear of making a mistake and being rejected by others. Sauls (1987) found the Myers-Briggs unable to discriminate between high performing and low performing buyers of a major retail chain, whereas the Conforming/Active Theme of the LSPI and age were able to discriminate between the groups.

Theme 2 (Conforming/Passive). Theme 2 relates to going along with others and being passively obedient. This theme appears similar to Mosak's Person Who Needs to Be Good. Low scores for the Conforming/Passive Theme have been found in a drug dependent group (Boynton, 1988). He also found a negative correlation with the Global Severity Index of the (SCL-90-R) $(r = -.21, p < .01)$. Wheeler (1990) found this theme to be negatively correlated with chronic self destructiveness $(r = -.29, p < .01)$.

Theme 3 (Controlling/Active). Theme 3 reflects a need to actively control others. Items relate to being bossy and taking charge of group activities. Mosak's Controller appears to be related to this theme. The Controlling/ Active Theme has been supported by a relationship between the FIRO-B Expressed Control Scale $(r = .258, p = .007)$, which measures taking on responsibility involved in a leadership role (Johnston, 1988), and by a positive correlation with a measure of assertiveness in college students $(r = .27, p < .01)$ (Wheeler, 1990). Boynton (1988) found a small positive correlation between this scale and the Global Severity Index of the SCL-90-R $(r = .20, p < .05)$.

Theme 4 (Controlling/Passive). Theme 4 relates to being dependent on others and reflects the use of passive forms of manipulation. This theme seems to reflect a person who is spoiled and expects to get his or her way. The only research available to date on this theme reflects a small positive correlation with assertiveness in college students ($r = .19$, $p < .05$) (Wheeler, 1990). Although the Controlling/Passive Theme has a theoretical basis in Adlerian theory and an empirical basis in factor analysis, it may not prove to be very useful in application.

Theme 5 (Exploiting/Active). Theme 5 is associated with behavior intended to hurt others. This theme seems related to Dreikurs' goal of revenge. The Exploiting/Active Theme is supported by correlations with an instrument which purports to measure child abuse potential ($rs = .20s$, $ps < .05$) (Wheeler, Braswell, & Milner, 1990). It has been found to be one of the elevated scales in a drug dependent group and to be related to the Global Severity Index of the SCL-90-R ($r = .41$, $p < .001$) (Boynton, 1988). Wheeler (1990) also found a positive correlation with chronic self-destructiveness ($r = .24$, $p < .01$).

Theme 6 (Exploiting/Passive). Theme 6 describes the extent a person feels hurt by others. The items reflect a negative relationship with parents. This theme may be similar to Mosak's Victim. The Exploiting/Passive Theme is supported by correlations with child abuse potential ($rs = .38, .40, .50$, $ps < .05, .001$) (Wheeler, Braswell, & Milner, 1990). Boynton (1988) also found Theme 6 to be elevated in a drug dependent group and a positive relationship to the Global Severity Index of the SCL-90-R ($r = .43$, $p = .001$). A positive relationship has been found with external locus of control ($rs = .20$, $.41$, $ps < .05, .001$) (Wheeler & White, 1989), and the Psychopathic Deviate Scale of the MMPI ($r = .321$, $p < .01$) (Johnston, 1988). The latter scale appears to measure many things, including social maladjustment, complaints about family and authority figures, and social alienation. The Exploiting/Passive Theme is further supported by negative correlations with social interest (see Table 3) (Johnston, 1988; Mullis, 1984; Sauls, 1987).

Theme 7 (Displaying Inadequacy). Theme 7 reflects feelings of worthlessness and the inability to successfully compete with others. This theme appears to reflect the most discouragement, and appears similar to Mosak's inadequate person. Boynton (1988) found the Displaying Inadequacy Theme to be elevated in a combined drug dependent group and found it to be related to the Global Severity Index of the SCL-90-R ($r = .41$, $p < .001$), to the SCL-90-R Depression scale ($r = .39$, $p < .001$), and to the SCL-90-R Interpersonal Sensitivity scale ($r = .40$, $p < .001$).

Theme 7 has been found to be positively correlated with external locus of control ($rs = .22, .30$, $ps < .05, .001$) (Wheeler & White, 1989). Wheeler

(1990) found it to be positively correlated with chronic self-destructiveness ($r = .44$, $p < .001$) and manifest anxiety ($r = .43$, $p < .001$); and it has also been found to be correlated with two other depression scales ($rs = .258$, 223, $ps = .007$, .050) (Johnston, 1988) and with child abuse potential ($rs = .25 - .40$, $ps < .05$) (Wheeler, Braswell, & Milner, 1990).

Correlations with the Millon Behavioral Health Inventory also support the Displaying Inadequacy Theme. The Future Despair Scale, which measures the lack of willingness to plan and look forward to the future, the Inhibited Style Scale, and the Premorbid Pessimism Scale which measures the dispositional attitude of helplessness and hopelessness, were all found to positively correlate with Theme 7 ($rs = .246$, .432, .282, $ps = .016$, .001, .006) (Johnston, 1988). In addition, negative correlations have been found with the social interest index (see Table 3) (Johnston, 1988; Mullis, 1987; Sauls, 1987).

Relation to the Social Interest Index. Several studies have explored the relationship of the seven themes to the Social Interest Index. As Table 15.3 illustrates, Themes 6 (Exploiting/Passive) and 7 (Displaying Inadequacy) appear to have a moderately strong negative relationship to social interest. In other words, if these themes are present, social interest is likely to be low.

Conclusion

It is comforting that the empirical results using the LSPI have generally followed predictions from Adlerian theory. Certainly, additional research is needed to further the ongoing process of validation of this instrument.[1]

TABLE 15.3 LSPI Scales and Social Interest Index Correlations

Theme	Normative Sample Mullis, 1984	Department Store Buyers Sauls, 1987	Chronic Back Pain Patients Johnston, 1988
1. (Conforming/Active)	.000	−.0506	.0356
2. (Conforming/Passive)	.073	−.1428	.1677
3. (Controlling/Active)	.116	−.1859	.1081
4. (Controlling/Passive)	.018	−.0427	−.1163
5. (Exploiting/Active)	−.158, −.168*	−.1174	−.1494
6. (Exploiting/Passive	−.416	−.3514	−.5763
7. (Displaying Inadequacy)	−.441	−.4722	−.7728

*The Mullis (1984) sample indicates correlations prior to the combination of the two Exploiting/Active scales.

Theme 4 (Controlling/Active) is lacking in corroborating evidence, although it is supported by Adlerian theory and has an empirical basis in factor analysis. Further studies could be directed at this construct in particular. Theme 1 (Conforming/Active) is not as reliable over time as the other themes. The only test-retest reliability study was done on a student population, which limits generalizability of implications of stability to other populations. An additional scale may need to be added to the LSPI to detect faking good. In addition, more data are needed to further elaborate on the interpretation of the conforming and controlling themes. The scales may prove to be more useful when interpreted as bipolar scales. Predictive validity studies and studies using behavioral correlates as opposed to self-report inventories are needed.

Nevertheless, the amount of research evidence accumulated to date is impressive. The Social Interest Index appears to be a strong measure of mental health. Although it appears to be measuring something other than the construct measured by Crandall's Social Interest Scale, it instead reflects an outgoing personal style, comfortableness in social settings, and the tendency to move toward people. The consistent negative correlations with measures of psychopathology suggest that when Social Interest is high, a healthy interpersonal style exists.

Theme 6 (Exploiting/Passive), which describes the extent a person felt hurt by others, appears to be strongly related to psychopathology and adds validation to the theory that childhood factors contribute to adult psychopathology. Theme 7 (Displaying Inadequacy) appears to reflect the most discouragement, and is well supported by research evidence correlating it with measures of chronic self-destructiveness, manifest anxiety, depression, and an attitude of helplessness.

The Life Style Personality Inventory has so far been used mainly for research purposes; nevertheless, its potential contribution to understanding Adlerian life-styles and in counseling and therapy appears to be considerable. As a supplement to the life-style interview and early recollections, which provide valuable information about a person's uniqueness, the LSPI can provide easily gathered information about how a person's life-style compares with others. As research accumulates and the constructs become more clearly defined, the LSPI can make important contributions to understanding life-styles.

This article summarizes over ten years of research devoted to developing the LSPI and establishing its reliability and validity as an objective measure of social interest and Adlerian life-style themes. The authors feel they have presented a strong case for the idea that life-style can be measured in a reliable and valid manner.

References

Ansbacher, H. L., & Ansbacher, R. R. (Eds.). (1956). *The individual psychology of Alfred Adler*. New York: Basic Books.

Boynton, R. D. (1988). *Drug addiction, life style personality factors and psychopathology*. Unpublished doctoral dissertation, Georgia State University.

Curlette, W. L, Kern, R. M., & Mullis, F. Y. (1984). *An overview of the development of a personality instrument to measure Adlerian life styles*. Paper presented to the National Council on Measurement in Education, New Orleans.

Davis, J. B., Jr. (1979). Reliability and validity issues of Adlerian life style analysis. (Doctoral dissertation, Georgia State University, 1978). *Dissertation Abstracts International, 39*, 5060B.

Dinkmeyer, D. C., Pew, W. L., & Dinkmeyer, D. C., Jr. (1979). *Adlerian counseling and psychotherapy*. Monterey, CA: Brooks/Cole.

Highlander, D. H., Jr. (1984). Adlerian life style, social interest, and depression in parents. *Dissertation Abstracts International, 45*, 12516A.

Johnston, T. B. (1988). Validation of the life style personality inventory and the prediction of success in treating pain. (Doctoral dissertation, Georgia State University, 1988). *Dissertation Abstracts International, 49*, 2406B.

Kaiser, L. L. (1979). A study of the Adlerian life style in relation to psychiatric diagnosis. (Doctoral dissertation, Georgia State University, 1978). *Dissertation Abstracts International, 39*, 5563B.

Langenfeld, S., & Main, F. (1983). Personality priorities: A factor analytic study. *Individual Psychology, 39*, 40–51.

Lanyon, R. I., & Goodstein, L. D. (1982). *Personality assessment: Second edition*. New York: Wiley.

Mosak, H. H. (1959). The getting type: A parsimonious social interpretation of the oral character. *Individual Psychology, 15*, 193–198.

Mosak, H. H. (1968). The interrelatedness of the neuroses through central themes. *Individual Psychology, 24*, 67–70.

Mosak, H. H. (1971). Life Style. In A. G. Nikelly (Ed.), *Techniques for behavior change: Applications of Adlerian theory*. Springfield, IL: Charles C. Thomas.

Mosak, H. H. (1977). The controller—a social interpretation of the anal character. In *On purpose: Collected papers of Harold H. Mosak, Ph.D*. Chicago, IL: Alfred Adler Institute.

Mosak, H. H. (1979). Mosak's typology: An update. *Individual Psychology, 35*, 192–195.

Mullis, F. Y. (1984). *Factor analysis of the Wheeler-Kern-Curlette life style personality inventory*. (Doctoral dissertation, Georgia State University, 1984). *Dissertation Abstracts International, 45*, 682B.

Mullis, F. Y., Kern, R. M., & Curlette, W. L. (1987). Life-style themes and social interest: A further factor analytic study. *Individual Psychology, 43*, 339–352.

O'Phelan, M. L. (1977). Statistical evaluation of attributes in Adlerian life style forms. *Individual Psychology, 33*, 203–212.

Sauls, M. B. (1987). A manager matching strategies model for buyers: A discriminant analysis based on Adlerian and Jungian theory. (Doctoral dissertation, Georgia State University, 1987). *Dissertation Abstracts International, 49*, 906B.

Thorne, F. C. (1975). The life style analysis. *Journal of Clinical Psychology, 31*, 236–240.

Thorne, F. C., & Pishkin, V. (1975). A factorial study of needs in relation to life styles., *Journal of Clinical Psychology, 31*, 240–248.

West, J. D., & Bubenzer, D. L. (1978). A factor analytic consideration of life style data. *Journal of Individual Psychology, 34*, 48–54.

Wheeler, M. S. (1980). Factor analysis of an instrument developed to measure Adlerian life styles. (Doctoral dissertation, Georgia State University, 1979). *Dissertation Abstracts International, 40*, 5032B.

Wheeler, M. S. (1990). Validity of the life style personality inventory. Presentation at the Southeastern Psychological Association, Atlanta, GA.

Wheeler, M. S., Braswell, G. R., & Milner, J. S. (1990). Relationship of the life style personality inventory to child abuse potential. Presentation at the Southeastern Psychological Association, Atlanta, GA.

Wheeler, M. S., Kern, R. M. & Curlette, W. L. (1982). Wheeler-Kern-Curlette life style personality inventory. Unpublished inventory.

Wheeler, M. S., Kern, R. M., & Curlette, W. L. (1986). Factor analytic scales designed to measure Adlerian life style themes. *Individual Psychology, 42,* 1–16.

Wheeler, M. S., & White, P. E. (1989). The relationship between the life style personality inventory and external locus of control. Presented at the Southeastern Psychological Association, Washington, DC.

VI
Children

CHAPTER 16

The Four Goals of Misbehavior: Clarification of Concepts and Suggestions for Future Research

THOR M. JOHANSEN

The counseling of children and families is an important part of Adlerian psychology. Adlerians have always considered the education of children and the prevention of psychological problems through democratic child rearing to be of high importance. Attempting to understand the behaviors of children, Rudolf Dreikurs developed a typology based on Adler's assumption that behavior is purposeful and that all people, including children, strive to belong. Dreikurs called his typology the *four goals of children's disturbing behavior* (Dreikurs, 1948), but it was later referred to as the four goals of misbehavior. Dreikurs stated that the four goals of misbehavior could be found in Adler's writings and that he simply identified and developed them into a categorical system (Terner & Pew, 1978).

Dreikurs' four goals of misbehavior has been considered one of his "major and finest contributions to Adlerian Psychology" (Mosak & Mosak, 1975, p. 14). His contribution remains a cornerstone of Individual Psychology's approach to counseling children and families. However, the technique was not put to use without problems. In 1975, Mosak and Mosak published an article clarifying several misconceptions that had come to light. Belt and Johansen (2004) also pointed to some common problems with the application of the technique.

In an attempt to encourage research in all areas of Individual Psychology, this section focuses on Dreikurs' four goals of misbehavior. The strategy is unique to Adlerian psychology and plays a major role in Adlerian counseling and psychotherapy. The technique is also based on fundamental Adlerian concepts. Consequently, the technique is deserving of empirical examination. Findings may lead to a confirmation of the technique's effectiveness, to knowledge about appropriate applications and uses, and perhaps to a reconsideration of the concept and even the theory behind it.

However, for any theoretical concept to be studied it needs to be evaluated and clarified to provide a consistent basis for research. The purpose of this chapter is to explore the original concept of the four goals of misbehavior and attempt to provide a clear definition or explanation of the technique. The author hopes to clarify the concept by examining misconceptions and other problems with the technique. The author also aims at providing suggestions and ideas for future research.

The Four Goals of Misbehavior

In his paper, "How the Child Selects His Symptoms," Adler (1946) examined various contributing factors that lead a child to choose a particular symptom. He discussed organ inferiority, the child's family situation, and, perhaps most important, parenting. In his paper, Adler discussed how these factors might influence a child's choice of symptoms. He stated that "no two symptoms have ever exactly the same significance" (p. 67). However, he also stated that a child's symptoms or misbehavior are always directed toward some chosen goal. He believed that one needed to identify and understand what goal the child had chosen in order to be able to help him or her. This is where Dreikurs' four-goal technique becomes useful.

Children are social beings, thus their strongest motivation is the desire to belong socially (Dreikurs & Soltz, 1990). Dreikurs stated that everything a child does is aimed at finding his or her place and gaining a feeling of belonging within the family group. Though the desire to belong is the basic goal, the method used to attain this basic goal becomes the child's immediate goal. As the child does what is required of him or her in various situations and gains a sense of belonging through constructive and useful participation, the child will not misbehave. Misbehavior, according to Dreikurs (1948) comes about only when a child becomes discouraged and has a feeling of not belonging to the social group. Dreikurs defined misbehavior as any behavior that is not in accord with the needs of the situation

(Dreikurs & Soltz, 1990). Thus, misbehavior can be thought of as being contrary to, or the opposite of, cooperation.

Dreikurs (1971) stated that children directed their misbehavior toward one of four possible goals.

> We have observed four goals in child misbehavior. They express the child's mistaken assumption about being significant and having a place ... it is enough to say that the child is not aware of his intentions. (p. 84)

Dreikurs (1948) identified the four mistaken goals children pursue in order to reach their basic goal of belonging as the desire for undue attention, power, revenge, and display of complete inadequacy. Regardless of which of these four goals the discouraged child adopts, he or she believes that this approach is the most effective way to find a place within the family group. The child chooses this without being aware of the direction of his or her behavior.

The first goal of misbehavior is the desire for undue attention (Dreikurs, 1948). The child has the belief that he or she is only significant when the center of attention. A child who misbehaves in order to get attention may do something that is annoying to his or her parents, such as whining or teasing other children. Once a parent naively intervenes, the child has gotten attention and thus reached his or her goal. The parents of a child who is misbehaving in order to get attention are likely to find themselves feeling annoyed.

The second goal of misbehavior is the struggle for power (Dreikurs, 1948). Here, the child believes that it is only possible to belong by being "in charge" or by being "the boss." The child may refuse to do what the parents request, fight with the parent, or may do things extremely slowly or poorly. If the child complies with the parents' demands, he or she is likely to lose a sense of personal value. The parents of a child who is misbehaving in order to be powerful may find themselves feeling angry.

Dreikurs (1948) suggested that revenge is the third goal of misbehavior. If a child cannot be in charge, he or she may decide that the way to belong is to get even. The child feels significant only when hurting other people as the child feels he or she has been hurt. The child may do or say things that are mean to the parents, thus leaving them feeling hurt.

Discouraged children who believe they can gain a sense of belonging only by demonstrating their complete inadequacy use the fourth and final goal of misbehavior that Dreikurs (1948) identified. Using this tactic, the child gives up completely and becomes helpless and incompetent. The child will avoid any challenges in which he or she expects failure. This behavior is likely to leave the child's parents feeling discouraged and helpless.

The four-goal technique involves behaving in a manner so that the child does not reach his or her goal through misbehaving. In order for an adult to correct a child's misbehavior, the particular goal must be identified. This will allow the adult to understand the movement of the child and intervene accordingly. For example, if the adult learns that the child is attempting to get them involved in a power struggle, the parent may work toward avoiding the power struggle. If a child is attempting to gain attention, the adult may choose to avoid attending to the child because of the misbehavior. The adult may also be more conscious about giving the child attention at times when he or she is cooperating.

Recognizing the Four Goals of Misbehavior

Mosak and Maniacci (1999) outlined three approaches to identifying the child's goal of misbehavior. First, the response a child receives when misbehaving might be what he or she is looking for. By observing what happens when a child misbehaves, the adult can get an understanding of what the child is attempting to achieve. Second, by paying attention to how one feels when a child misbehaves, the adult can also get a sense of what the child is trying to achieve through the misbehavior. The reaction of the adult at the time of the misbehavior will indicate to them the child's goal. For example, as mentioned above, parents might find themselves feeling annoyed when a child is seeking undue attention or they may find themselves feeling angry when the child is inviting a power struggle. When a child seeks revenge, the parent often experiences feeling hurt and saddened. Finally, when a child displays his or her inadequacy the parent is likely to feel discouraged. The third approach involves observing the child's response when he or she is naively corrected. For example, when a child is seeking undue attention and is asked to stop whatever he or she is doing, the child may stop for a while, but will soon resume the same behavior. In similar situations, a child who is attempting to gain a sense of power is likely to intensify the misbehavior when naively corrected by an adult.

The misbehavior of children can take two main forms. Dreikurs believed that misbehavior could be either passive or active and may use constructive or destructive methods. In his article "Why Children Misbehave," Pepper (1980) outlined four types of behavior patterns often observed in children. These behavior patterns include active-constructive, active-destructive, passive-constructive, and passive-destructive. The active-constructive type is often very cooperative and conforming. The child may be very ambitious and strive for success. The active-destructive type may be defiant, clownish, or disrespectful. The child may attempt to show off or create mischief in order to gain attention. The passive-constructive type includes children who are more passive in their actions, but who operate on the useful side of life. They may often be admired for who they are, and they may be very flattering and sensitive. Finally, the passive-destructive type includes children characterized as lazy, dependent, or fearful. They may also be forgetful, hopeless, and sometimes malicious. Pepper (1980) outlined the characteristic behaviors these various types may adopt in order to get attention: power, revenge, or inadequacy.

Clarifying the Concept

The application of the four-goal technique has resulted in numerous misunderstandings. In an attempt to clarify the concept of the four goals of misbehavior, it is important to examine the misconceptions and frequent problems with the technique. Such misunderstandings are important to amend in order to provide a consistent and accurate approach for research.

Mosak and Mosak (1975) clarified several misconceptions regarding the four-goal technique. First, the four goals do not include all of children's *behaviors*. The four goals in question concern themselves only with the *misbehavior* of children. Second, the four-goal technique should only be applied to children. Dreikurs and Grey (1968) stated that "these four goals can also be observed in teenagers and even in adults; but there they are not all-inclusive" (p. 28). As a result, applying the technique to anyone other than children would constitute a simplistic way of trying to understand an individual's behavior. Dreikurs stated that the four-goal technique should only be applied to children about 10 years or younger (Mosak & Mosak, 1975).

A third clarification made by Mosak and Mosak (1975) emphasized the difference between long-range and immediate goals. The four goals are the immediate goals of misbehavior as opposed to the long-range goals found in the individual's life style. Thus, one cannot determine the life style based on a child's goal of misbehavior. The goal of any child may vary depending on the circumstance. For example, a child may attract attention at one moment, and soon decide to assert his or her power at another. Consequently, the four goals are situational and not indicative of the life style.

Fourth, the four-goal technique is intended to explain the goals of the misbehavior of children, or in other words, *disturbing behavior*. It is not intended to explain the goals of a disturbed or maladjusted child. Finally, another important point outlined by Mosak and Mosak (1975) involves the term *attention getting mechanism* (AGM). Mosak and Mosak (1975) felt that Dreikurs made an error when he named the first goal of attention getting as AGM. The term *mechanism* may be thought of as an automatic function, whereas Adlerian theory would suggest that attention getting is a free choice the child makes. Thus, the term is inconsistent with Adlerian theory and incorrectly implies that the goals of misbehavior are not purposeful.

Belt and Johansen (2004) also pointed to some problems with the four-goal technique and outlined three common mistakes in its application. First, many clinicians and parents mechanistically place given behaviors in certain categories because they often believe that a child can only maintain one goal at a time. For example, if a child's misbehavior is believed to be directed toward gaining attention, adults often believe that the child cannot also be attempting to gain a sense of power at the same time. Dreikurs (1948) alluded to this idea when he suggested that parents should look for the *predominant* goal of misbehavior. In so doing, he suggested that a child's misbehavior can be directed toward two or more goals simultaneously. Hence, when two or more goals are identified, the adult needs to address both in order to correct the child's misbehavior.

A second problem involves using one's emotions to determine the child's goal of misbehavior. Relying only on one's feelings to identify the child's goal of misbehavior may be ineffective. Adults can experience emotions that are unrelated to the particular behavior of the child, and so incorrectly assess the child's goal. For example, an adult may feel angry and frustrated because of an argument at work. Coming home to the family that feeling may intensify as one of the children misbehaves in order to get attention. Noticing the feelings of anger, the adult may mistakenly attribute the child's misbehavior to a power struggle, rather than to attention seeking.

Finally, parents are often taught that certain behaviors can be attributed to specific goals. Many Adlerian parenting books use specific behavioral examples of things children do to reach the various goals. This has led some to believe mistakenly that certain behaviors are directly attributable to a specific goal. For example, interrupting is often believed to be a way of attaining attention, whereas being stubborn is often thought to be a way of exerting power. No specific behaviors can be associated with a specific goal in any situation.

Operational Definitions

Considering the numerous misunderstandings and misconceptions regarding the four goals of misbehavior and lack of research involving the concepts, functional operational definitions are needed.

In his doctoral dissertation, Seymour Schneider (1974) studied the ability of untrained lay and professional personnel to recognize the four goals of misbehavior and redirect the child in question. In doing so, he provided operational definitions for the actual goals of misbehavior; that is, he outlined a definition of attention, power, revenge, and display of inadequacy. His definitions are both appropriate and consistent with the definitions provided by Dreikurs and may be useful for future research. He defines the four goals as:

1. *Undue Attention*: [The child] feels that he only counts or is worthwhile when he is being noticed, serviced or catered to.
2. *Power*: [The child] wants to demonstrate to others that he can do what he wants to do and they cannot do anything to stop him].
3. *Revenge*: [The child] has given up hope of being accepted via constructive activities and feels that the only way to get recognition is to retaliate against others for the way he feels he has been treated.
4. *Display of inadequacy*: [The child] does nothing required or expected of him as protection against certain failure if he tries.

Schneider (1974) also provided behavioral definitions of what constitutes misbehavior. He listed several behaviors including being fearful, running away, fighting, annoying, and damaging property. He provided these behaviors in short vignettes in order to describe the child's family/social situation in which the misbehavior was depicted as not being in accord with the needs of the various situations. In this manner, his definition was consistent with that of Dreikurs and Soltz (1990). The following vignette is an example of misbehavior according to Schneider (1974).

> Marge, 13, is an only child. She is continually getting into a great deal of fights with her friends and hassles with her teachers. She refuses to do assignments. She has seen counselors and has been given specific things she can do to stop the fights, but she has never followed through on them. She does average work in school and has never failed a subject. (p. 84)

In an attempt to encourage consistent research on the outcome effectiveness of the four goals of misbehavior, a definition of the technique is needed. A definition that is consistent with the original concept would provide a useful starting point for research in this area. The following factors may serve as hypotheses to be evaluated and may be used collectively to provide a definition for the four-goal technique.

1. The so-called four goals of misbehavior is a technique or strategy applied by adults to correct the misbehavior of children 10 years or younger.
2. The actual four goals include attention, power, revenge, and display of inadequacy.
3. The misbehavior can be active or passive.
4. The adult attempts to identify the goal of the child's misbehavior. He or she then uses that information/knowledge to develop a plan of how to intervene.
5. Intervention involves behaving in such a manner that the child fails at reaching the goal through misbehavior, and encourages constructive behaviors when they occur.
6. The four goals of misbehavior include only the goals of children's *misbehavior*, not all of their behavior.
7. These goals apply to all children when they misbehave.
8. The goals of misbehavior can change from situation to situation.
9. The goals of misbehavior are the immediate (or situational) goals of the child.
10. A child can seek more than one goal at a time.

These factors, coupled with the operational definitions provided by Schneider (1974), enable future research in this area. These definitions are useful and clearly defined, yet other areas within the four-goal technique need to be addressed. For example, how do we reliably identify the goals? How do we measure whether a child is actually attempting to get attention? How do we operationalize the concept of passive and active misbehavior? What are some other ways of defining or operationalizing misbehavior?

Research on the Four Goals of Misbehavior

A literature search resulted in no effectiveness studies conducted in the use of the four-goal technique. In addition, little research has been conducted directly involving the four goals of misbehavior. Research in Adlerian parent education effectiveness (Berrett, 1975; Burnett, 1988; Croake & Burness, 1976; Croake & Glover, 1977; Frazier & Mathes, 1975; Freeman, 1975; Gordon-Rosen & Rosen, 1984; Mullis, 1999; Todres & Bunston, 1993; Wiese, 1989) has often included the four-goal technique. However, the four-goal technique has not been studied separately from other parenting strategies, such as the use of natural and logical consequences, encouragement, and the family council. One question that arises is whether parents can use the four-goal technique effectively without learning and understanding these related strategies. Although many of the studies in parent education have included the four-goal technique, they do not provide adequate results or information specific to the technique itself. Thus, a clear need exists for research that specifically examines the effectiveness and usefulness of this technique.

Future research should aim to answer four main questions in regard to the four-goal technique. First, how can we reliably verify or identify the goals of misbehavior? Second, the effectiveness of the technique as a method of discouraging or reducing misbehavior in children should be studied. Third, for whom is this technique useful? What groups can effectively use the technique? For example, are parents, clinicians, or day care providers able to use it effectively? Does it apply to the developmentally delayed? Does effectiveness depend on level of psychological training? Fourth, is the technique itself effective, or is it effective only in conjunction with other strategies? The technique should be studied separately from other parenting strategies often taught in Adlerian parenting classes such as natural and logical consequences and use of the family council.

How do we attempt to verify or identify the goals of misbehavior? Another way to pose this question is by asking, "How do we know that children actually are seeking the various goals through their misbehavior?" How do we know that these goals actually exist? This is a difficult area to study and attempting to measure such an abstract idea presents several challenges. However, Dreikurs theorized that children would respond with a recognition reflex when their goal was revealed to them (Dreikurs, 1948). The presence of this reflex is believed to confirm the adult's accurate interpretation of the child's goal. If this is true, it leads us one step closer to verifying the goals of misbehavior. Dreikurs defined the recognition reflex in the following ways:

> This reaction is immediate and automatic, a "recognition reflex," and indicates the correctness of the interpretation. It consists of a roguish smile and a peculiar twinkle of the eyes, characteristic of the cat who swallowed the canary. (Dreikurs, 1948, p. 89)

> [Children] give themselves away through some facial or bodily mannerism that we term the recognition reflex. This recognition reflex usually expresses itself through a smile, a grin, an embarrassed laughter or a twinkle in the eye. (Dreikurs, Grunwald, & Pepper, 1982, p. 28)

In order to measure the recognition reflex, an operational definition of what physical reactions constitute the reflex would have to be determined. Dreikurs provides actual behaviors to look for in future studies. Such a study would probably seek to answer whether or not the recognition reflex can actually be identified. In addition, does the reaction occur every time a child's goal of misbehavior is revealed? Does the reaction occur if an inaccurate goal is revealed? Are there other parental behaviors that cause a recognition reflex? One could hypothesize that the recognition reflex would occur every time a goal is revealed, and only occurs if and when the correct goal has been identified. Observational studies in which children are videotaped as their goal is being revealed to them could be a useful method in studying this concept.

In studying the recognition reflex of children, it is important to consider the manner in which the adult reveals the goal of misbehavior to the child. Mosak and Mosak (1975) stated that "to merely label his [or her] goal as attention-getting is to lose sight of the child's uniqueness" (p. 15). Hence, when revealing a child's goal it is important to comment on the child's movement instead of simply naming the goal. For example, "instead of saying that a child is attempting to get attention, the adult could comment on the child's behavior as a way of keeping his or her parents engaged with him or her all day long" (p. 15).

In an attempt to study the effectiveness of the four-goal technique, both short- and long-term outcome studies would be necessary. Outcome studies in parent education effectiveness have successfully used various parent symptom checklists as one way of measuring outcome effectiveness. Others have also used various parent satisfaction questionnaires to determine the parents' sense of success. Both of these strategies could effectively be used in measuring effectiveness of the four-goal technique. As well, observational studies in which adults attempt to correct children's misbehavior would serve as a useful tool in determining effectiveness and the competent use of the technique. For example, is the technique immediately effective? Does misbehavior resume shortly after correction has occurred or does the child engage in more constructive behaviors? How does the adult's attitude play a part in successfully redirecting the child? Exactly what parental responses assist in changing or correcting the child's misbehavior?

Could the four-goal technique be effectively applied in various settings outside the home? The technique has been used in classroom settings to discourage misbehavior in schools. The effectiveness of the technique should be studied in these and other settings. For example, is the four-goal technique more useful than other techniques in classroom settings? How effective is it? Are children whose teachers use this technique in the classroom more cooperative at home? Studies on the four-goal technique should also include settings such as inpatient psychiatric hospitals as well as day care settings. Can the technique be taught to staff in such settings and effectively used in these settings?

In terms of studying the usefulness of the technique, it would be helpful to determine if certain children are more receptive or responsive to the use of the technique. For example, are there differences in outcome among girls and boys? Does outcome depend on the age of the child? For example, are younger children more responsive than older ones? A very important question discussed in the literature is whether the technique is applicable to adolescents (Dreikurs & Grey, 1968). Dreikurs suggested the technique could only be used for children 10 years and younger. Thus, studying the effectiveness of the technique with children older than 10 years of age would be useful. Any positive findings in such studies would possibly prompt a reconsideration of the concept of the four goals of misbehavior.

As parent education groups that have included the four goals of misbehavior have been successful, it would be useful to isolate the technique from other parenting strategies to determine its effectiveness. For example, examining outcome studies in which parents have only been taught the four-goal technique would help answer whether the technique itself is useful, or if it needs to be used in conjunction with other strategies. Finally, other important questions need consideration. For example, does the use of the technique lead to other changes in overall parenting styles? Are parents likely to use the technique long term? How do children experience being subjected to the strategy? If the technique is applied in the home environment, what are the effects on the child's behavior in school?

Summary

Research examining the four goals of misbehavior is gravely needed and the opportunities for research are enormous. However, in encouraging future research in this area the importance of remaining consistent with the original concepts cannot be emphasized enough. Research that is consistent with the original Adlerian concepts helps advance our knowledge and understanding of Individual Psychology. It also provides for a consistent body of research that can contribute to the advancement of Adlerian psychology and possible changes in its theory. Definitions and misconceptions of the four goals of misbehavior have been discussed in an attempt to clarify the concept. Finally, suggestions for future research were presented. It is to be hoped that this discussion and the papers that follow will provide clarity and encourage research in this area.

References

Adler, A. (1946). How the child selects his symptoms. *Individual Psychology Bulletin, 5*(3), 67–78.

Belt, J. L., & Johansen, T. M. (2004). Four goals of misbehavior: Problems with the application of the four-goal technique. *The Canadian Journal of Adlerian Psychology, 34*(1), 27–32.

Berrett, R. D. (1975). Adlerian mother study groups: An evaluation. *Journal of Individual Psychology, 31*(2), 179–182.

Burnett, P. C. (1988). Evaluation of Adlerian parenting programs. *Individual Psychology, 44*(1), 63–76.

Croake, J. W., & Burness, M. R. (1976). Parent study group effectiveness after 4 and after 6 weeks. *Journal of Individual Psychology, 32*(1), 108–111.

Croake, J. W., & Glover, K. E. (1977). A history and evaluation of parent education. *Family Coordinator, 26*, 151–158.

Dreikurs, R. (1948). *The challenge of parenthood.* New York: Duell, Sloan & Pearce.

Dreikurs, R. (1971). *Social equality: The challenge of today.* Chicago: Regnery.

Dreikurs, R., & Grey, L. (1968). *Logical consequences: A new approach to discipline.* New York: Hawthorn.

Dreikurs, R., Grunwald, B. B., & Pepper, F. C. (1982). *Maintaining sanity in the classroom: Illustrated teaching techniques* (2nd ed.). New York: Harper & Row.

Dreikurs, R., & Soltz, V. (1990). *Children: The challenge.* New York: Plume.

Frazier, F., & Mathes, W. A. (1975). Parent education: A comparison of Adlerian and behavioral approaches. *Elementary School Guidance and Counseling, 10*, 31–38.

Freeman, C. W. (1975). Adlerian mother study groups: Effects on attitudes and behavior. *Journal of Individual Psychology, 31*(1), 37–50.

Gordon-Rosen, M., & Rosen, A. (1984). Adlerian parent study groups and inner-city children. *Individual Psychology, 40* (3), 309–316.

Mosak, B., & Mosak, H. H. (1975). Dreikurs' four goals: The clarification of some misconceptions. *The Individual Psychologist, 12* (2), 14–16.

Mosak, H. H., & Maniacci, M. P. (1999). *A primer of Adlerian psychology: The analytical-behavioral-cognitive psychology of Alfred Adler.* Philadelphia: Brunner/Mazel.

Mullis, F. (1999). Active parenting: An evaluation of two Adlerian parent education programs. *Journal of Individual Psychology, 55*(2), 225–232.

Pepper, F. C. (1980). Why children misbehave. *The Individual Psychologist, 17* (1–2), 19–37.

Schneider, S. (1974). An Adlerian approach to the study of both trained and untrained lay and professional personnel in the recognition and redirection of children's mistaken goals. *Dissertation Abstracts International, 35*(4–A).

Terner, J., & Pew, W. L. (1978). *The courage to be imperfect: The life and work of Rudolf Dreikurs.* New York: Hawthorn.

Todres, R., & Bunston, T. (1993). Parent education program evaluation: A review of the literature. *Canadian Journal of Community Mental Health, 12*(1), 225–257.

Wiese, M. J. (1989). Evaluation of an Adlerian parent training program with multiple outcome measures. *Dissertation Abstracts International, 50*, A3538.

CHAPTER 17

How the Child Selects His Symptoms

ALFRED ADLER

In my opinion the problem of symptom-selection is the most difficult of all subjects in neurosis-psychology and psychology in general, and I believe that it should not be approached before the psychologist has mastered the numerous complexities that neurosis-psychology and psychiatry are forever presenting to us. In addition he must begin by discarding all vague prejudices and personal biases, for symptom-selection is a problem that demands absolutely water-tight conclusions, and not one of the links in the chain can afford to be a weak one. In fact the psychologist must go so far as to be able to say: "Were I in the same position as this child, had I the same misinterpretation of the meaning of life and had I been trained as he has been trained, then I, too, would have suffered from approximately the same symptoms." Only then, after identifying himself wholly with the child, can he conclude that he has really understood the case and discovered the reason for the child's selection of certain symptoms.

We can understand symptom-selection only if we look upon symptoms as creations, as works of art. We must forget our self-imposed judgements and accept with admiration the fact that every individual is an artist in his mode of life, even in his very errors. Behind his mistakes lie influences that could not have been good ones and to which he reacted with an erroneous response.

Thus when we try to prove something from any particular symptom we can do so only if we look upon the symptom as a single part of a complete whole, i.e., we must find in every symptom something that lies deeper than the outward and visible signs, something that underlies the actual manifestation and the form of suffering itself. We must look *behind* the headache, the anxiety-symptom, the obsession-idea, *behind* the fact of an individual being a thief, or a loafer in school. For behind lies something more, something personal and entirely individual. Phrases and formulae will not help us, as the more clearly we observe symptoms and the more we understand of the structure of the psyche, so the more will we realize that no two symptoms have ever exactly the same significance. There are always distinctions, some of which are very obvious indeed. But there is one assumption we can make in all cases; we can always say: "In this symptom, in this creative accomplishment—whose creator and master is always the patient himself—*there is inevitably a movement heading toward some kind of successful achievement.*" There is always an "*I will,*" never an "*I am*"; a will-to-become that cannot fail to be visible to the student of symptom-selection. Whether we realize it or not this student cannot help but connect the selection of a symptom with the individual's struggle to reach a chosen goal, but he will never grasp and understand this struggle if his point of view is at fault.

First we must stop to consider the question of heredity and see if it plays any part in symptom-selection, for often when we examine a patient's family-tree, we find a certain similarity of symptoms existing. Well, I have already said that we can never draw conclusions from external similarities of symptomatic resemblances, and here we can well say that when two individuals—even if related to one another—tackle the same job the result is *not* the same. In Individual Psychology we try to discover *all* the factors that have caused the individual to take the wrong path and the first of these factors is the child's opinion of his own physical self, his attitude towards the body that is to accompany him through life and withstand the demands of the outer world. It does not take us long to see just where the child feels he "stands" and how he feels he should behave in life; it is not hard to see that one child is self-confident, another less so, one very active, another less active; one apprehensive and thinking always of himself, another ready to mix with others, do things with them, help and play cooperatively and not always ready to put the whole burden on someone else's shoulders, etc. Of course, in these examples, I have only picked out certain general types, and this will not be enough for our solving of the individual problems, as there are invariably thousands of variations to be considered in the various individual cases. Still, we can observe very quickly the influence that the child's physical constitution has had upon him and the extent to which he is organically sound; also how he has reacted to his body and organs and how he adapts and employs them. It is very easy for the child to go wrong. No matter what his environment may be he finds himself confronted by the demands of life, and no matter how slight these demands may be, still they have their effect upon the child's respiration, movements, assimilation of food, cleanliness, etc. Naturally all these everyday functions have a relationship with the child's organic soundness. Individual Psychology can state with a greater degree of certainty than existed hitherto, that children who are born with defective organs are in one way or another impressed by the fact; they are given an impression of personal weakness, insecurity and inferiority, which becomes particularly strong when they find themselves in a difficult situation.

Here I must mention an important point that will bring us nearer to an understanding of symptom-selection. If such a condition of insecurity, of inferiority feeling, persists over a long period, it is clear that the child will plan its life and life-style accordingly. So we can conclude that physical defects act as a *training* for the child, a training that teaches it to form a certain attitude toward the tasks of life, a training that is chiefly characterized by the fact that the child becomes abnormally self-centered and develops certain character-tendencies that the outside will condemn as improper and unjustified. But, from the child's point of view, these tendencies are both necessary and sensible. You will find, for instance, that such a child displays exaggerated caution, and that is a trait that tells us he has very little self-confidence and suspects the world of being full of dangers. You will find traits of hyper-sensitivity; a sign that the child has a great fear of being the loser in the event of attack. You will find traits of impatience, and these, too, are the stamp of an individual who is lacking in self-certainty, who cannot wait, but believes his desires must be fulfilled immediately as otherwise he will feel he has suffered a defeat.

As you know, there exist symptoms of a physical nature which constantly recur or even become chronic although no organic cause is behind them. Often, however, they divulge the individual's "place of least resistance" (locus minoris resistantiae). While in later years distinct manifestations of organic injury may come to light, in childhood we find that the child, not feeling in the least that he is acting at all oddly, will take a particular interest in tending and developing the creative ability of his "place of least resistance." Children who suffer in some way from weakness of vision take a particular interest in observing perspective, colour, line, shadow and levels, in order to grasp them more completely. There is no doubt that they suffer from an unusually strong tension, which sometimes can be put to great advantages; a tension that they may direct later into channels that will give them a better grasp of visible things (painting, etc.). Sometimes, however, they give up very soon and do not bother anymore with visual matters, because they have tried and met with no success. The same applies to other defective organs, to inferiority of nutritive organs, for instance. Children with defects of the nutritive tract often suffer for a long time and have to go hungry in order to be healthy or even in order to live; they have to gulp down unpleasant forms of food and watch over their nutrition in every way, with the result that their interest becomes linked up artificially with the problem of food. (This Czerny pointed out many years ago.) Frequently one finds that not only is their nutritive apparatus susceptible and subject to illness, but sometimes the same susceptibility will be found in their family-tree. Often such individuals develop a great interest in food, love to talk about food, and can even turn their interest to a certain advantage. But in actuality they impose a burden upon life and behave in a way that is not conducive to harmonious living. For we must realize something that is emphasized in every sphere of existence, namely, that if anything in our composition, in the structure of our psychic existence, is subject to over-emphasis, the harmony of communal life is upset.

Cleanliness for example. Say a child decides to over-emphasize cleanliness and to regard it as the most important thing in life. When he grows up, if this thought is still paramount in his mind and he feels that everything else must take second place to washing, he is but a short step from a wash-compulsion neurosis. Such an individual will present himself to the world (not in words, but letting his cleanliness speak for him) in all his immaculateness, much to the detriment of others, and the fact that he will never consider other people to be properly clean will not help him toward cooperative work. So far as I can see, there is perhaps one function that cannot be made personally and socially harmful by being over-stressed, and that is the function of social interest. I believe that recognition of the vital part played by over-emphasis can help us greatly in understanding a vast number of symptoms both within and without the sphere of neurosis.

For example, let us take again the child who has experienced nutritive difficulties. As he is deeply concerned with all problems of food, is avidly voracious and desires food above all, it is not long before he sees a connection between the problem of food and the problem of money and stretches his interest to include the latter. We often find this double-avidity in a type which I described a long time ago as the "pocket Napoleon." There are many examples of this kind and sometimes they open up vistas of so interesting a nature that I can warmly commend you to bear this aspect well in mind. A long time ago Czerny pointed out the importance of the nutritive system in regard to the individual's psychic development and also in relation to problems of neurosis. In each individual case there are other noteworthy points I cannot go into now and can only indicate to the psychologist the line he should follow. Of course, sometimes the line is clearly visible, and sometimes very tortuous to follow and is not found solely in cases of organ inferiorities which have influenced the life-style, but in all cases of children who have in some way or other placed themselves artificially in sharp opposition to the problems of life and are thus unprepared to meet the demands of civilization.

We must also consider the influences connected with the child's upbringing, which come to bear upon the child at an early age. Not simply the economic conditions in the family, the attitude of the child's teachers, and the skill and experience of the mother, but also the *entire* family situation. For the waves of social life lap into the nursery itself and are forever at work influencing the growing child.

To protect his personality, the child is obliged to adopt some attitude toward his family; he must find a "direction" in which to move, and this direction will be one that aims, by this or that route, at having done with the problems of life. He will take a direction which promises to lead him to an ideal state, in which all his problems are resolved. But at the same time, the family situation will be a strongly stimulating and motivating factor, one that can easily influence the child's choice of symptoms, and we must never neglect to consider how the child's psyche has been affected by it. The child has to prepare to meet a constant stream of demands from life, demands which are fairly uniform for every person. His preparation for this battle is one with which his mother must help him to the best of her ability, for the attitude he forms can only be a man-made creation and thus will always fall short of an *ideal* solution to his problems. Hence we can see, too, that all manner of results will obtain from the rearing of the child, from the attempt to bring his primitive capabilities into harmony with civilized life. We can see that innumerable false moves will be made, mistakes that will sway the child's attitude and make him lean in a certain direction, so that the inevitable arrival of the problems and tasks of life will find him in a state of inadequate preparation. We can consider these problems of life (not absolutely literally, of course) in the light of mathematical problems. A correct solution will be found only by the individual who has had mathematical training. So we must train the child in such a way that he will become a cooperating individual, as our culture demands he should be; train him to be prepared to solve the many problems that cannot be overcome without social interest; problems of "I" and "Thou," problems of occupation, problems of love; in all of which it is essential for the individual to have a sufficiency of interest in his partner, and in other people generally.

As we know, the life-style is fixed by the fifth year of life at most and does not undergo any change unless the child understands the flaws in the faulty construction and corrects them. This life-style has a form and breadth that corresponds with the stage of progress reached in the child's life at the time the style becomes fixed. So the question arises; how will this specially constructed life-style—with its ingrained influence of mother, environment, and, also, the child's *own* creative abilities—respond when the child is confronted by a problem for which his life-style is not prepared? The response tells us immediately to what extent misconceptions of the outside world have crept into the construction of his life-style and left their mark within it. Sometimes a child will respond by depending entirely upon another person, thereby binding that person to him, and this is the case with the pampered child. In actual fact there are only very few children who are *not* pampered and possibly every child, at the beginning of its life, is bound to experience a certain degree of pampering. Thus the proper mode of training is one that teaches the child to become an independent cooperator as soon as possible and it is to this end, of course, that our educational efforts are devoted. We certainly would not even mention symptoms, failures and the family paths followed by the psyche, if we were able to believe that those at fault were co-operators, and that they lived, worked and loved in a cooperative way. But that is just what they do not do, and thus mankind is forever occupied with creating laws, and with instituting corrective improvements, etc. Since the perfect method of conducting a child's upbringing is only very rarely employed, there will always be many weak spots in the development of every child. But this is where really the most vitally important function of upbringing comes in, namely the discovering and improving of these weak spots at an early stage in the child's life. People often come to me and protest: "I have done absolutely everything I could; I have tried to make the child independent and there just hasn't been any success. For instance, he makes trouble about eating, won't go to bed, won't evacuate his bowels easily, is jealous of his younger sister, wets the bed, calls out at night, etc." We can only reply, "Your method was not a successful one." Today probably we have not yet reached the stage of being able to educate a child to such a degree that he will, as a matter of course, move in a cooperative direction. Society could certainly do better than it is doing today in this respect and if it would only do more we would certainly not have to put up with children who refused to carry out the daily functions of civilized life. For a child rejects such civilized functions only when the mother is unable to succeed in handing them on to him. Though there may be difficulties to be met with in training the child, there is no doubt at all they may be successfully overcome and if anyone doubts this, I would like to say: "If you don't believe that one can train a child in such a way he will come into line with civilized demands, won't you at least believe that it is possible to train any child to be just the contrary; to mess its bed, be difficult over eating, not go to sleep, and hate its father or mother?" It would certainly not be difficult to do this. Thus we can see that the whole problem of symptoms is a matter of upbringing, and it is mainly pampered children—who have not reached the point of being able to meet the problems of life and who are accustomed to see their every wish fulfilled—who hate anyone who tries to stand in the way of their desires. They are the children who bind themselves tightly to one person and try to eliminate all others from their lives. They are the children who, later, (and even at quite an early stage) can in extreme cases be described as having an Oedipus Complex. They are children who have rejected culture, who are opposed to culture because no one has succeeded in imbuing them with it. They have an intense love for themselves, and boast "I come first; I do what I want and don't bother myself about other people." We see their rejection of cooperation at an early age: their training for maladjustment begins on the first day of life. I cannot stress enough how important it is not only that the child should not be pampered in its early years but also that a definite method be introduced into its life from the very beginning, so that the danger of a future clash with the demands of civilized life be avoided. As a rule we can be successful. But it is no use to look upon the situation simply as though unclean children were "naturally" inclined to be nuisances.

Let us now discuss the problem of the pampered child. Pampered children live in a situation in which their inferiority feeling is outstandingly intensified; and we all know today that this condition exists because the pampered child regards any alternative situation as a danger, as a limiting of his sphere of power, so that he lives in a world in which he is forever suspecting dangers, insecurity, and defeat. Within the pampering circle at least he is determined to be a king, and we know that pampered children are better trained to become home-tyrants than to become anything else. The mother is the first person to become subject to this tyranny because she is the first person to offer herself to the child, so that actually pampering on the part of the mother is the principal cause of a child taking to erroneous paths. Now there are innumerable parents who have no proper grasp of the facts of life; sometimes they have a pampered childhood of their own behind them and are encircled by fallacious traditions. They make the mistake of passing on their false notions to the child. For instance, they lay exaggerated emphasis on the question of eating, thereby giving the child the opportunity of rebelling against eating. If a pampered child notices that by rebelling in such a way he gets a lot of attention and pampering, he rebels all the more. There can be no question that a child who rejects food has a far greater sense of superiority and a far greater satisfaction of his striving for superiority than is felt by other children. These pampered ones, after a few preliminary trials, hit on just the right point from which to carry on the battle. Like practised strategists they attack where the resistance is most vulnerable. Thus, if the family lays great stress upon the necessity for cleanliness in bed, and the child has reason to suppose that he will be able to get his mother's attention by night as well as by day, we can well expect him to become a bed-wetter. In saying this I am not neglecting the fact that defective organic functions, physical anomalies, etc., can also play a part in the game. But if a pampered child who suffers from any minor physical trouble (and also a pampered child who does *not* have these troubles) is constantly being lectured to on a certain subject—say on the proper way to speak, eat, sleep, evacuate the bowels, urinate, etc.—and lectured to in such a manner that he is quickly able to notice a way in which to get a hold on others, then he will almost certainly become a stutterer, make difficulties over eating and sleeping, and a bed-wetter. The same applies to difficulties over bowel-evacuation. There are many parents who regard the evacuation of the bowels as a matter of vital importance. A pampered child will spot this fact at once and force the family to spend a vast amount of time in attending to his bowel-evacuation. He moves quite instinctively, striving frantically to gain his own ends, and automatically places his own satisfaction on an elevated plane so that somehow or other he may force his way into the center of the pampering circle.

There are other aspects to be considered, of course, but my chief intention is to show how the selection of certain symptoms is occasioned by defective upbringing. If symptoms disappear later on it is always because the individual is in a situation in which they are no longer of any benefit to him. When an individual grows up and enters a situation in which he does not find himself prepared, the reason is always to be found in his defective ability to be a social member, a cooperator. In such a situation a *physical tension* arises, a tension which, through the vegetative system, grips the inferior organs or, to say the least, the organic-inferiority manifests itself. When a certain method is tried out and found to be successful, the pampered individual will use it again and again. As in neurosis, his aim is always to enlist the support of others; to exploit the social services of other people.

I have deliberately chosen to cite simple cases in this chapter, for my aim primarily has been to show how one can learn to understand the child's selection of a certain symptom. In continuing I want to say that there are children who, owing to a lack of social interest are found also to lack a more important ability, an ability that really determines the value of an individual, namely active *performances*. Now in modern life, even in childhood, it is very hard to avoid all active performance, but one can go a long way toward doing so, as we see in cases of neurosis. The dues of life are demanded of all of us because we live in a community-world, but they can be cut down to the minimum through neurosis. The neurotic attaches himself to someone who shoulders his dues for him; he insists upon the cooperation of others, but at the same time contributes practically nothing himself. Such a situation can arise only if an individual feels himself threatened by a defeat: when he has to a greater or lesser degree the vague impression that he is too weak, that he has no real value. Such people are individuals who think only of themselves and of their vanity: they cannot ever forget themselves, can never concentrate their whole strength on a bit of work and can only think: "How do I look? What impression am I making? What do people think about me? What do I get?" It is among such people that we find strong antagonistic feelings, jealousy, spite, obstinancy, etc.—always signs that their attitude toward society has become a hostile one. This is a trend that may be traced back to the beginning of the individual's life and shows that his education was not successful in moulding the prototype into a cooperative individual. In every case you will find corroboration of this fact if the line of life is examined from childhood onwards.

There still remains for us to discuss the question of how the individual's creative powers are displayed in the forming of his symptoms. Let me give an example: If I have in my mind's eye a goal that means the avoidance of performance, and on account of my anxiety feelings I have been trained since childhood to let another person work for me, look after me, support me, sacrifice personal freedom for me, and become my very slave, I must, so long as I follow such a path, make it as foot-worthy a path as possible so that I will reach my goal safely. Now how am I to *fashion* my anxiety, the anxiety which absolves me from taking part in any social cooperation and forces another person to relieve me of my anxiety-burden?

Patients give us a very clear answer to this question. They do not understand what they are telling us and they have no idea that they are opening the windows of their mental-factories and allowing us to look in and observe what is going on when they say, for instance: "I feel the ground is unsteady," or "I think of my husband's death," or "I am afraid that I will become unconscious, that I will have a heart-attack," etc. Particularly with the pampered individual, thoughts of death of others play an unbelievably large role, because death might rob him of his supports, might take away one of his tyrannized subjects. The patient is forever preoccupied with thoughts of how awful it would be to him if his supports were to fall away from him, but by means of these thoughts, which are questions of life and death to him, he is enabled to create a strong anxiety-state, to feel as if the person concerned were *really* dead. That is to say, he identifies himself with a situation which might possibly exist in the future. We see this with melancholies who live as though disaster had already occurred.

In other studies, the reader will have ample opportunity to examine the problem of symptom-selection in nervous adults. So for the moment I will only say that if a certain symptom is selected in childhood and found workable, the neurotic adult will often employ it in his later life as a means of furthering his asocial ends. This cannot be described as "repression"; it is a definite employment of past experiences for present and future use.

In closing the present study, I would like to cite two simple case histories which will help the reader to see the whole problem of symptom-selection in a clearer light.

Case 1. A boy, 13, was in his fifth year at public school, which meant that he had "repeated" twice already. He was considered the worst pupil in the school, and apart from that he had committed thefts on various occasions and several times had run away from home and disappeared for some days until found and brought back by the police. The teacher had tried to improve the boy by punishing and reprimanding him, but neither punishment nor kindness had done the boy any good. So eventually he was sent to a reformatory and arrived there with a certificate stating that he was feeble-minded.

One of the teachers in the reformatory was a pupil of mine, and this man did not merely consider the *symptoms* of the case, but also studied the boy's life-style and, thereby, his *choice* of symptoms, being convinced that no two thieves are exactly similar to one another. Because he realized that the boy's mistakes were manifestations of his whole personality, he strove to probe to the kernel of the personality in order to find the "psychic constitution."

He realized too that he could approach the examination from any angle he chose, because (to revert to our musical simile) in every symptom will be found the individual's complete, basic Leitmotiv. So he began by collecting the boy's school reports. There he found that the boy had had good reports for the first three grades and had only got a bad one when he reached the fourth grade. From this he concluded that the boy must, for some reason or other, have been unprepared to face the fourth grade. He decided that the boy had had a new teacher in the fourth grade, which proved to be correct. He was able to find out that for the first three years the boy had had a friendly teacher, and an unfriendly one in the fourth year, so that his life-style had not been prepared for an unfriendly master. He could conclude that the boy was a pampered child who only progressed *conditionally* (as his life-style demanded), i.e., only when he was treated pleasantly. As a result of such a psychic constitution, it was obvious that if the child had to face some test of his functional ability—as, in this case, the test of a strict teacher—he was bound to respond with a symptom that expressed refusal. The teacher was able to conclude this much simply by examining the child's school reports, and the child himself confirmed the teacher's guesses. The teacher asked him: "What did you do with the things and the money you stole?" The boy replied: "I gave them to the other boys so that they'd be my friends, because I haven't got any friends; because I'm poor and the worst in the class, the others always avoid me."

Here again we see the strong basic Leitmotiv at work; one that leads to thieving being selected as a symptom. We can see the desires of this boy, his craving for affection and his readiness to obtain the affection of others by bribery. We can guess that his mother pampered him, but we will have to corroborate this guess. "What was your purpose in running away from home?" he was asked next. He said: "I hid myself in the woods, or in a barn. But at night I always went to the woods and collected fire-wood and put it in front of the kitchen door so that my mother would have fuel for her cooking." Again he steals, this time in order to bribe his mother, to get her affection, just as he did with his companions. This is the only way he knows of getting enough of the pampering attention which to him is the whole object in life.

Can anyone suggest a better way? He is a bad pupil, knocked about by his teacher, unprepared to make his way in the world—how is he to make friends? Under such circumstances I can think of no more efficient means of doing so than the means he chose. We can say that despite his school record this boy is intelligent. He has done his job as thoroughly as any other intelligent person!

Here you can see the selection of a symptom; the way he attacks at the vulnerable point in order to reach his goal. At school he only expected to be reprimanded. If I expected such treatment I should certainly not go to school either. This choice of a symptom is intelligent, apt and forceful. He ran away from home because his father was strict and because if he brought home bad reports his father beat him, his mother cried and became unfriendly. He ran away to touch his mother's heart. So you see how in each of his symptoms there is more than meets the eye; there is always the one Leitmotiv. He thieves to bribe others, he runs away to frighten his mother and win her affection, and he rejects school work as a protest against his teacher's lack of affection. These symptoms are all part of a striving to get warmth, to be pampered. In this case I also want to show you how the psychic constitution stretches far back into this boy's childhood. I will do this by giving two of his earliest recollections because, as I explained on other occasions, his recollections will tell us just which of the many incidents in his life have made an impression upon his memory:

"When I was four years old my father sent me to get a paper, but—".

Already we can comment on this. The word "but" is enough to tell us that this child is about to try and circumvent the demands made upon him by his strict father. He is not interested in his father's wants, just as later he was not interested in the strict teacher. The recollection ended as follows:

"But I went to my uncle who gave me some cakes which I took home to my mother."

When we follow this plan of procedure we are able to see that the child is only interested in his mother and will only be partial to another person—be it man or woman—if that person coddles him "like his mother." Without coddling he never goes ahead.

In regard to treatment for this child we can see that he cannot be influenced *unless he is pampered first;* and this fact can only be comprehended if one has really grasped his whole life-style. We certainly won't achieve anything only by pampering him; it is the same treatment as he has had before. But unless we pamper and "warm" him at the *beginning* he will not become receptive. This fact was realized by the teacher in the reformatory who began by handling the child along these lines.

Another of this child's recollections was:

"I was at a railway station and a freight-car caught fire. In the car there were a lot of children's toy balls. The workmen tried to save these balls from being burnt and threw them out in the open. A whole crowd of children and grown-ups were standing around and took the balls when they were thrown out."

We see that when he was only three years old thieving had become something that could be done easily and presented real possibilities. It is easy for a child to conclude from such an event that things may be come by lightly, without difficulty, without cooperation, without personal accomplishment—simply by letting others do all the work. One is assured of the help of others and may partake of the fruit of their labors.

I want to give another example, not a complicated one, but one that expresses very clearly the process of symptom-selection. In reading it I will ask you to remember something I mentioned before; that pampered children are cowardly and anxious, because they are always accustomed to being supported, and thus when they find themselves in a threatening situation they always exhibit anxiety-symptoms.

Case 2. A boy who, at the age of five, was one of the most refractory children imaginable. He demanded so much of his mother that she was always in a state of exhaustion. He would climb onto the table, with his shoes on, put his hands into the soup-tureen, take a screw-driver and remove all the screws from the bed-frame, smash all his toys, etc. If his mother wanted to read he would put all the lights out, if she played the piano he shut his ears and began to scream at the top of his voice. Obviously he was a terrible burden and the parents did everything they could to reform him. We can tell already that this naughtiness is obviously the result of the child having been put to the test in some way or other; he has come up against something he cannot face. The parents were given any amount of advice and were told to send him out with other boys. When they did so the boy got hold of innumerable smutty expressions and always came home filthy.

His father took him to the Zoo to divert his mind. For a long time the boy had gained the attention of his parents by sleeping troublesomely, screaming out at night (as pampered children often do) and even walking in his sleep sometimes. After he had been to the Zoo he screamed still more at night and made a lot of bother about going to bed; he couldn't shut his eyes because as soon as he did he saw the snakes his father had shown him at the Zoo. So you see, one can take this child to the Zoo—and he will simply utilize that institution according to the dictates of his life-style. He had been put to the test when his younger brother was born; as a result of this birth his sphere of power was narrowed, and he tried by every possible means to extend it again so as to be the central figure once more.

We see that this child selected *anxiety* as a symptom. Why did he not choose to wet his bed? Why did he not choose to make trouble over defecation? Has he perhaps a different inherited disposition? Has he other "erogenous zones"? I reply that should you wish I could *make* this child a bed-wetter and cultivate in him a tendency to make trouble over evacuating his bowels. No, we must conclude that his mother gave little attention to questions of urination and bowel-evacuation, so that the child never had occasion to realize that they too would be good weapons to employ.

The problem of symptom-selection cannot be understood if it is treated like a problem in mathematics which demands no more than a formula for its solution. We must reject all formulae. We must realize that:— To understand is to find proof of what you are able to guess at by virtue of far-reaching experience.

One must, of course, employ the general diagnosis of Individual Psychology, but that in itself is not nearly enough and must be followed up with a special diagnosis until the totality, the personality, of the individual has been revealed.

Hence the name: "Individual Psychology."

CHAPTER 18

The Relationship of Dreikurs's Four Goals of Children's Disturbing Behavior to Adler's Social Interest—Activity Typology

HEINZ L. ANSBACHER

Rudolf Dreikurs (1948, p. 190) formulated four goals of children's disturbing behavior, or as later also worded, misbehavior. This is considered one of his "best known contributions to understanding the behavior of children" (Shulman & S. G. Dreikurs, 1978, pp. 156–157), one of his "major and finest contributions to Adlerian psychology" (Mosak & Mosak, 1975, p. 14). Dreikurs repeatedly commented on this contribution "that these four goals could be found in Adler's writings ... and ... he simply identified and developed them into a systematic conceptual scheme" (Terner & Pew, 1978, p. 157). Yet this relationship to Alfred Adler's writings was never explicated.

The present paper will show that regardless of what may be interspersed in Adler's writings pertaining to these four goals, there is an indirect relationship to Adler. Dreikurs (1948, p. 193) presented a typology of behavior patterns to which he related the four goals, and this typology is essentially identical with a typology by Adler.

It is to be noted that when Adler (1935/1979) introduced his typology he warned: "A human being cannot be typified or classified.... [Classification] is a temptation to which, in practical work, we must never yield. It is for teaching purposes only—to illuminate the broad field—that I designate here four different types in order, temporarily, to classify the attitude and behavior of individuals toward outside problems" (p. 68).

Dreikurs's Four Goals and Typology

Dreikurs's four goals of children's misbehavior are: (1) attention getting (designated at first as AGM, for attention-getting mechanism), (2) power, (3) revenge, and (4) demonstration of inadequacy, assumed disability, arranged by him in order of increasing "social discouragement." He related these goals to four types of behavior pattern, formed by the two important dimensions of active-passive and constructive-destructive. The resulting four types are: (1) active-constructive, (2) passive-constructive, (3) active-destructive, and (4) passive-destructive, arranged by him in order of "diminished social interest." The relationship of the goals to the types of behavior pattern, and the specific behaviors from which the goals may be assumed for each type was presented by Dreikurs (1957/1968, p. 30) in a chart which is reproduced here (Figure 18.1).

The dotted lines in the chart refer to frequent deteriorating sequences. Line a, "the most frequent deteriorating sequence," runs "from active-constructive attention to active-destructive attention to active-destructive power to active-destructive revenge" (p. 31). Line b, next in frequency, goes from passive-constructive attention to passive-destructive attention, power, revenge, assumed disability. Line c goes directly from passive-constructive attention to passive-destructive assumed disability.

With the active-passive dimension Dreikurs associated self-confidence, courage, and self-esteem, respectively their opposites, when he wrote: "Whether the child responds actively or passively depends on his self-confidence and courage. This basic pattern ... reflects the infant's evaluation of himself" (p. 29).

The constructive-destructive dimension also includes further characteristics, as can be seen from Figure 18.1, where constructive is combined with useful and more social interest; destructive, with useless and less social interest.

In terms of Dreikurs's fourfold typology, Figure 18.1 lends itself readily to rearrangement into a 2 x 2, or fourfold table, as in Figure 18.2.

The new chart offers several advantages. While it includes all the information of the original, and additional relevant terms exclusively from Dreikurs, it would seem to be clearer than the original. The significance

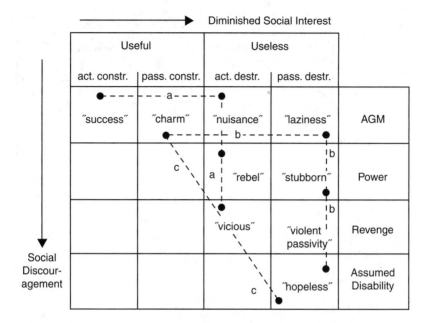

Fig. 18.1 The four goals of children's disturbing behavior as related to four types of behavior pattern (From Dreikurs, 1957/1968, p. 30).

of the dotted lines a, b, and c is more easily recognized as the lines no longer overlap and are shorter. The chart also demonstrates that there is no one-to-one relationship between the goals and the types of behavior pattern, as one might easily assume, because both are four in number, which, however, is sheer coincidence; there might have been more or less than four goals. Goal 1 is represented in all four behavior patterns, Goals 2 and 3 are presented in two patterns, while only Goal 4 is related to only one pattern. Finally, and with regard to this study most importantly, the new chart provides the bridge to Adler's typology.

Adler's Typology

When Adler (1933/1979) introduced the concept of activity as a personality variable, he stated that in conjunction with social interest this "opens an entirely new and valuable perspective for psychiatric treatment, education, and prophylaxis" (p. 61). The "style of life … carries within itself as most important structures a specific degree of activity and a specific degree of the direction-giving social interest" (p. 63).

Adler thus posited in fact a two-dimensional personality theory that specified four types: (1) high-activity—high social interest, (2) low activ-

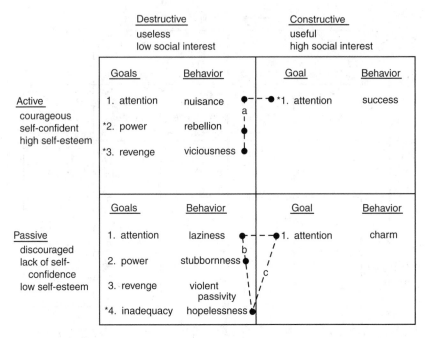

Fig. 18.2 Revised presentation of the four goals of children's disturbing behavior as related to four types of behavior pattern. *Outstanding goals for the respective types.

ity—high social interest, (3) high activity—low social interest, and (4) low activity—low social interest. Adler (1935/1979) described these types as follows: (1) "The socially useful type [is] prepared for cooperation and contribution. We can always find a certain amount of activity which ... is in agreement with the needs of others; it is useful, normal, rightly embedded in the stream of evolution of humanity" (p. 69). (2) "A second type— surely the most frequent one—expects everything from others and leans on others. I might call it the 'getting' type" (p. 68). (3) Such people "from early childhood through their entire lives [show] a more or less dominant or 'ruling' attitude ... in all their relationships" (p. 68), the "ruling" type. If confronted by a difficult situation "a person of this type acts in an unsocial way. The more active ... become delinquents, tyrants, sadists" (p. 69). (4) "A person of this type merely tries to 'side-step' a problem, in an effort thereby to avoid defeat" (p. 68), the "avoiding" type. Neuroses and psychoses belong here (p. 70).

This typology was presented in a fourfold table by Ansbacher (1977, p. 63). Several years prior to his typology, Adler (1927/1969, pp. 147–148) had discussed the four temperaments of the ancients as formulated by Hippocrates. He described these temperaments very similarly to the four types: the sanguine matching the socially useful type; the phlegmatic, the getting or leaning type; the choleric, the ruling type; the melancholic, the avoiding type. Thus we added the temperaments to the table.

This earlier table, merged with Figure 18.2 in a less elaborate form, is reproduced here as Figure 18.3. The contents of Figure 18.2 are identified by italics.

Only Adler's second type, the getting or leaning type, does not quite fit this fourfold arrangement. Adler had described this type as low in social interest, whereas it is now placed on the relatively high social interest side. But as Adler (1935/1977) called it "surely the most frequent" (p. 68), we feel justified in stressing its inactivity and de-emphasizing lack of social interest. Otherwise this type also would be too similar to the avoiding type.

Dreikurs-Adler Synthesis

It can readily be seen that Dreikurs assumed the same two basic behavioral variables or dimensions as Adler had done, except for some differences in naming. Under the name "constructive-destructive" Dreikurs included useful-useless and degree of social interest. Adler's name for this dimension was "degree of social interest" under which he included usefulness, contribution, and cooperation. The second dimension, called "active-passive" by Dreikurs, was called "degree of activity" by Adler. But whereas Adler included nothing further, Dreikurs included self-confidence, courage, and self-esteem, and their respective opposites, as mentioned earlier. Because Dreikurs assumed the same basic behavioral variables as Adler, it was possible to merge the revised presentation of Dreikurs's types and four goals of Figure 18.2 with Adler's typology, which we did in Figure 18.3.

Yet there are important differences between Adler's and Dreikurs's parts of Figure 18.3. Adler was concerned with enduring life-style behavior of adults and thus by implication with long-term goals, whereas Dreikurs was concerned with immediate goals of children's disturbing behavior. "Life-style goals and the four goals are not synonymous" (Mosak & Mosak, 1975, p. 14). According to Dreikurs (1968, p. 28), however, immediate goals similar to the four goals, "can be also observed in teenagers and even in adults; but there they are not all-inclusive."

A second difference between Dreikurs and Adler refers to self-confidence and courage. Dreikurs in this context did not distinguish between constructive and destructive activity, making the general statement that a child's activity "depends on his self-confidence and courage," as mentioned earlier. Adler (1933/1979) speaking of the adult, holds, "activity should not be confused with courage.... Only the activity of an individual

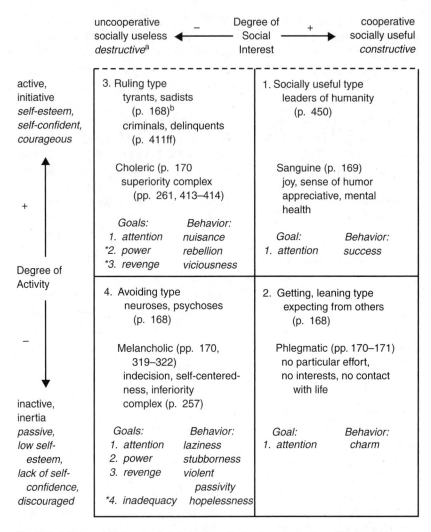

Fig. 18.3 Adler's social interest—Activity typology, the four temperaments and Dreikurs' four goals of children's disturbing behavior. [a]Italics refer to terms taken over from Dreikurs (Figure 18.2). [b]Page numbers refer for simplicity's sake to Adler (1964). [*]Outstanding goal(s) of types 3 and 4.

who plays the game, cooperates, and shares in life can be designated as courage" (p. 60). Crime, although requiring activity, "is a coward's imitation of heroism" (Adler, 1964, p. 414). The criminal's apparent self-confidence is deceptive. "He hides his feeling of inadequacy by developing a cheap superiority complex" (p. 414).

The gains from recognizing the essential identity of Adler's and Dreikurs's basic behavioral variables, in spite of some differences, are twofold. First, Dreikurs's four goals and respective disturbing behaviors can be seen as an extension of Adler's typology into childhood, even if these childhood goals must be understood as immediate rather than life-style goals.

Second, to the extent that a child comes to rely on a constant type of behavior pattern, one may anticipate the corresponding adult type. The harmless kind of attention seeking of Type 1 points toward ideal normality. Children who regularly use charm as a means of keeping adults involved with them, Type 2, never have to initiate anything to get what they want. This would perhaps lead to the adult getting, leaning, or expecting type; among the temperaments, the phlegmatic. The goals of power and revenge of Type 3, and respective behaviors, if firmly established, would point toward the later ruling type or the criminal, the choleric. A constant demonstration of inadequacy in childhood, Type 4, would be found in the later avoiding type, the neurotic, psychotic, melancholic.

Summary

It has been shown that Dreikurs's types of behavior pattern and related four goals of children's misbehavior fit within Adler's social interest-activity typology. The synthesized typologies indicate the adult type toward which a child's misbehavior may develop if it should change from short-term immediate goal-seeking into constant, life-style goal-seeking.

Reference Note

The author wants to express his gratitude to Dr. James R. Bitter for his part in this paper. The paper originated and developed in discussions with him, and many of his thoughts are reflected in it. But the author takes the sole responsibility.

References

Adler, A. (1964). *The Individual Psychology of Alfred Adler*. H. L. Ansbacher and R. R. Ansbacher (Eds.). New York: Harper & Row.
Adler, A. (1969). *Understanding human nature* (1927). New York: Fawcett Publications.
Adler, A. (1979). The forms of psychological activity (1933). In H. L. Ansbacher and R. R. Ansbacher (Eds.), *Superiority and social interest* (pp. 59–65). New York: W. W. Norton.
Adler, A. (1979). Typology of meeting life problems (1935). In H. L. Ansbacher and R. R. Ansbacher (Eds.), *Superiority and social interest* (pp. 66–70). New York: W. W. Norton.
Ansbacher, H. L. (1977). Individual Psychology. In R. J. Corsini (Ed.), *Current personality theories*. Itasca, IL: Peacock Publishers.

Dreikurs, R. (1948). *The challenge of parenthood.* New York: Duell, Sloan, & Pearce.

Dreikurs, R. (1968). *Psychology in the classroom* (1957). New York: Harper & Row.

Mosak, B., & Mosak, H. H. (1975). Dreikurs's four goals: The clarification of some misconceptions. *The Individual Psychologist, 12*(2), 14–16.

Shulman, B. H., & Dreikurs, S. G. (1978). The contribution of Rudolf Dreikurs to the theory and practice of Individual Psychology. *Journal of Individual Psychology, 34,* 153–169.

Terner, J., & Pew, W. L. (1978). *The courage to be imperfect: The life and work of Rudolf Dreikurs.* New York: Hawthorn Books.

VII
Encouragement

CHAPTER 19

An Overview of the Current Status of Adlerian Encouragement

MICHAEL R. CARNS and ANN W. CARNS

Adlerian encouragement is based on fundamental principles of attachment. Adler, in consultation with the social investigators of his day, concluded that there is an inborn connection between humans that functions to ensure the survival of the species. He concluded that the desire to belong to a group, while primary, can be shaped toward positive prosocial behavior or toward negative and discouraged behavior through interaction with significant others in their primary social group (the family). Thus, he provided a philosophical construct of human behavior that bridges the instinctual and the learned. In addition, he bypassed the idea of behavior as good or evil. Instead, through his basic principles of human nature, he suggested that psychological development is an adaptation to the environment. The aim of this development is to achieve a fit into the social group, and thus the physical and psychological survival of the individual.

Here, we explore the evolution of Adlerian encouragement from its beginnings to its current fit into the postmodern era of counseling. Suggestions for future research are made based on a search of the current literature on Adlerian encouragement. These suggestions emphasize the investigation of Adlerian encouragement in interaction with tenets and techniques from human developmental theory and techniques designed for behavioral and psychological remediation.

The Importance of Encouragement

Adler believed that people are oriented toward positive self-development from birth and that people engage in negative, self-destructive, and antisocial behaviors because their natural drives have become discouraged through maladaptive interpersonal interactions originating in the family of origin. Adler thought that the desire for prosocial behavior was embedded in the nature of human beings. A need to belong and contribute to the group, he said, is inborn (Adler, 1958). This striving or need for belonging may, in fact, be instinctual. Borrowing from Darwinian and Lamarckian theories of evolution, Adler made the point that a deeply engrained mechanism ensures the survival of the species. Commitment to the group and finding one's place of importance in the group (Adlerian tenets) are behaviors that, in the history of mankind, were crucial to the survival and adequate function of early man.

In his earliest writings, Adler emphasized the individual as socially embedded in a predestined evolutionary imperative based on survival needs of the species. He later modified his thinking to include this "social evolution" as subject to conscious control and learned behaviors. So, while he initially joined with the deterministic views of the day, he never lost sight of social influences and eventually modified his thinking to include those environmental influences. His entire theoretical position became a response to the popular theoretical positions of the day that excluded an individual's ability to make choices regarding his or her own destiny, and which denied a relationship between internal processes and external social/emotional factors in making those choices (Peluso, Peluso, White, & Kern, 2004).

Adler's belief was that one is born with social interest—defined as a need to contribute to the family and, eventually, to the society in which one finds oneself. He further stated that when an individual loses that social interest or engages in antisocial behavior, that such an individual is a victim of a discouraging social structure, specifically the family. He also stated, and observed, that the trend of discouragement was reversible. Significant others, both within the family and within the larger society of the individual, can, through direct, intimate psychological bonding and by providing prosocial modeling, recreate the initial social interest of the discouraged individual (Adler, 1958; Dinkmeyer, 1972; Dinkmeyer, Dinkmeyer, & Sperry, 1987; Dinkmeyer & Losoncy, 1980; Dreikurs, 1967; Mosak, 1979; Mosak & Maniacci, 1998; Neuer, 1936; Peluso et al., 2004; Sweeney, 1998; Watts & Pietrzak, 2000).

This would make encouragement an important element in the development of adaptive, prosocial individuals as well as fundamental in remediation in the counseling process. This view is supported by current research in parenting, information-processing theory, ecological developmental theory, and research on the remediation of attachment disorder and anti-social/oppositional defiant children and adolescents (Eisenberg, et al., 1995; Klahr & MacWhinney, 1998; Repacholi, 1998; Spinrad, et al., 1999).

Adlerian Therapy in the Postmodern, Constructivist Era

As noted in our earlier publication (Carns & Carns, 1998), encouragement means different things to different people. Most often, "praise" and "reward" are interchangeable with encouragement. A major reason for this is that everyday society does not view behavior change as a co-created situation. Society teaches that parents control the learning process of their children and instill values, attitudes, beliefs, and behaviors (extrinsic learning). Such Adlerian ideals of self-evaluation and cooperative input into the learning process (intrinsic learning) have little credence. Even in the professional literature, current definitions of encouragement do not distinguish behavioral terms such as praise and reward and punishment as distinct from Adlerian encouragement application, but rather focus on emotional and psychological intent in applying these constructs. Adlerians believe that the source of instilling prosocial behavior is not the technique but, rather, the process. The parent or significant other is experiencing and expressing neutral to positive emotional affect as well as thoughts focusing on acceptance of the individual and instilling prosocial behavior. Encouragement is holistic, attending to both the behavior and external factors of behavior while equally attending to internal factors of perception, effort, and improvement. The intended result is self-assessment and the maximum interactional functioning of external behavior and internal cognitive processes (Cheston, 2000, p. 298). In summary, "the holistic nature of Adler's concept of encouragement emphasizes the act of supporting and respecting the whole client" (Cheston, 2000, p. 303).

Although much Adlerian literature has stated the fundamental difference between praise and encouragement, intrinsic motivation must, at times and in many cases, coexist with extrinsic motivation. Azoulay (1999) stated:

> The Individual Psychology outlook emphasizes not only behavior but also cognition. The concern is for how a child perceives, interprets, and assigns meaning to events in the environment. We are trying to affect the child's view of self and the world. Thus the

reward in encouragement is used to reinforce a specific belief system in children.…. Also, Adlerians attempt to convey with their encouragement their own beliefs in the strength of the child. The child must view the encouragement as showing respect and acceptance of him or her as a person equal to worth to the adult. (p. 94)

In a 2000 article, Watts and Pietrzak compare the similarities between solution-focused brief therapy (SFBT) and Adlerian therapy. They state, "the therapeutic process of SFBT remarkably parallels the Adlerian process of encouragement in at least three areas: perspective on maladjustment, counselor-client relationship, and facilitating change" (p. 444). Solution-focused brief therapy and Adlerian therapy both take a nonpathological approach, choosing to focus on the client as discouraged or demoralized. Regardless of one's theoretical orientation, however, the encouragement process may be usefully integrated in a counselor's approach to counseling. The assumptions, characteristics, and methods of encouragement help to create an optimistic, empowering, and growth-enhancing environment for clients; a place where they feel "en-abled" rather than "dis-abled" (Watts & Pietrzak, 2000).

While there are many commonalities between Adlerian therapy and current constructivist approaches, Adlerians still maintain that they are unique in approaching therapy from the holistic approach. Adler's definition of the individual is that he or she is a unit in which many elements of the psyche need to be addressed. Operationally, this means that encouragement attends to effort as well as to outcome. Encouragement is unique in that it often precludes the client's attempts at cognitive or behavioral change. Encouragement lies in neither the intrinsic nor the extrinsic domain, but is a bridge or connection between the two (Azoulay, 1999; Dinkmeyer & Losoncy, 1980; McKay, 1992).

The Adlerian approach, more than other approaches, seeks to consider the future outcome of therapeutic intervention and resulting behavioral and cognitive changes. In stressing the individual as socially defined, Adlerians are concerned with an ultimate goal in therapy of aiding clients to construct a template that allows the client to problem solve effectively in society at large. In accomplishing this goal, encouragement, when internalized, facilitates a cognitive process that enables the individual, in an often-discouraging world, to assess progress and process rather than focusing on product and outcome. The end result is an individual who trusts his or her own internal processes, who understands imperfection as courageous, and who focuses on his or her positive attributes and those of others (Azoulay, 1999; Dinkmeyer & Losoncy, 1980; Evans, 1995; McKay, 1992).

Current Research

In our original article on encouragement, most of the studies discussed were descriptive. However, empirical data tended to support the Adlerian definition of encouragement as effective in motivating positive counseling and therapy outcomes. We found that because the authors defined the construct of encouragement in varied ways, any attempt to draw general conclusions about encouragement as any one set of ideas or a unified definition was frustrated (Carns & Carns, 1998). Our conclusion in 1998 was that "[t]he greatest challenge to research appears to be operationally defining encouragement" (p. 83).

An attempt has been made to construct a standard instrument to measure Adlerian encouragement. A 1997 article discusses initial attempts to validate an encouragement scale (Evans, Dedrick, & Epstein, 1997). In three preliminary studies, the authors found statistically significant measures of reliability and validity that provided the foundation from which an instrument might be constructed. Yet, the authors cautioned that both the limited size and randomization of the samples created limits on the generalizability of the findings. In addition, this first set of studies provided an incomplete analysis of the instrument. The initial analysis of the encouragement instrument investigated the relationships between what the authors described as "first order factors." These, they indicated, were self, others, openness, and belonging. They suggested further investigation of a "second order" construct of Adlerian encouragement using confirmatory factor analysis, larger samples and a variety of statistical analyses (Evans et al., 1997). In conclusion, the authors suggested the following uses for this measure of Adlerian encouragement:

> As a research tool, this instrument could be used to evaluate the effectiveness of encouragement training and other interventions designed to enhance the attitudes of teachers and school staff. This instrument could also be used as a measure of school climate and as a way to investigate the relationships among school characteristics (e.g., size), school personnel attitudes (e.g., encouragement), and student outcomes (e.g., achievement, engagement in school, self-esteem, and self-confidence). Information from these studies should help advance our understanding of encouragement and its role in improving human relations. (p. 168)

In a study using the encouragement scale, Phelps, Tranakos-Howe, Dagley, and Lyn (2001) compared ethnic pride with encouragement, using minority college students as subjects. The results of this study indicated a positive relationship between ethnic pride and encouragement. This, the authors indicated, demonstrated a positive relationship between Adlerian constructs of high intrinsic locus of control and high individual capacity to face daily tasks and challenges by ethnic minorities in a white dominated environment. The authors state that Adlerian encouragement used with ethnic minorities helps individuals process and consider their adequacy and worth in a more empowered way. The result is an enhancement of individual self-worth and an ability to perceive oneself as valid within the larger social context.

In an observational study, Spinrad et al. (1999) examined the effect of parental affect and encouragement on children's moral emotions. Children in the study completed a questionnaire designed to evaluate their level of empathy (the ability of the child to understand another's perspective) and sympathy (the ability of the child to experience another person's emotions). Two different procedures were used. Children were instructed not to play with a group of attractive toys. All adults left the room and the children were observed to see if they violated the rule. The researcher then reentered the room and asked if the children had played with the toys while no adult was present. A majority of the children who played with the toys denied that they had (significantly more boys than girls). A major question that appears to emerge from this study concerns the distinctive results concerning honesty. In a separate part of the study, parents were then observed on two occasions interacting with their children. Results indicated that positive affect and encouragement were positively related to children's sympathy but not empathy. This would seem to indicate that either there are subtle differences over time in terms of parent–child messages on morality delivered to boys and girls, or there are significant societal messages already impacting the subjects in this study, either from the parent or society, to the effect that "boys will be boys."

In a study by Kelly (2002), 177 students in grades 4, 6, and 8 were given a paper and pencil test to examine their preference for adult verbal statements reflecting either encouragement (intrinsic self-evaluation) or praise (extrinsic other evaluation). A sample item from the scale is:

> Susan wrote an essay on the American Civil War for a social studies project. She asked her mother to read it. Afterward her mother responded:
>
> A. It looks like you put a lot of effort and thought into preparing this essay, Susan. I found it very interesting.
> B. This essay is excellent, Susan. I didn't notice any mistakes in it. You're such a good writer. (Pety, Kelly, & Kafafy, 1984, p. 95)

The results indicated a preference by elementary age children for encouragement, while junior high students showed the opposite. The authors indicated that early adolescent preference for praise might be due to developmental challenges of that age group that would enhance the student need for adult affirmation. Another possibility is that the adolescents have become accustomed to "praise" responses. Of course, as the authors note, this study indicates preference by children, but not necessarily the most effective form of adult–child communication to achieve an internal locus of control.

While Adler included the idea of culture as impacting prosocial development, he did not seem to include culture as a separate issue from the family. That is, while the family is a powerful transmitter of social mores, values, and adaptive prosocial skills, later researchers such as Bronfenbrenner include society as a separate and powerful developmental influence as the child individuates from the family and enters society through school, peer groups, and career choices (Bronfenbrenner, 1998). Studies investigating children's prosocial moral behavior across cultures appear to indicate that cultures through school, peer groups, and career expectations provide important messages about how to behave in that culture. These messages seem to provide the same messages as defined by Adlerian encouragement. They aid children to self-evaluate and to learn through observation and interaction with significant others, and provide internalized means of self-evaluation and adaptive skills to deal with the continual stresses of living in society at large. Differences in processing the same moral dilemmas across cultures indicate that messages from each society, comparable to Adlerian encouragement, shape the child's adaptive moral decision-making process in accordance with the expectations of that society. Therefore, the results of Adlerian encouragement, prosocial behavior, and internal self-processing may behaviorally look very different from culture to culture (Baek, 2002).

The study by Spinrad and associates (1999) appears to be investigating Adlerian encouragement from the most recent holistic definition, embracing both extrinsic and intrinsic means of encouragement. As noted earlier, the holistic concept, including the typical definition of Adlerian encouragement, emphasizes internal or self-evaluation as well as external motivation including praise, reward, and modeling. In addition, this study discusses Adlerian encouragement from a developmental perspective; that is, it discusses the role of Adlerian encouragement in the age-related developmental tasks of perspective taking and cognitive and emotional self-regulation that result in the Adlerian "encouraged individual." While the study specifically notes that verbal messages from parents to children were coded in accordance with Adlerian expectations (messages that emphasized child self-assessment vs. messages that focused on pleasing or meeting the expectations of the parent), the discussion of the results indicated a need to look at a much broader context of what produces moral behavior (empathy and sympathy) in children. Developmental and socialization messages include the differences in messages from mothers vs. fathers, the identification of children with one parent's values over the other, nonverbal affective messages emphasizing reasoned emotional moderation, and the basic temperament of the child, which may elicit more negative or positive responses from parents. In addition, the authors wondered about overall societal messages that emphasized different gender-role expectations when considering both understanding and feeling for others and the impact of those messages on young children.

In place of Adlerian encouragement, some developmental researchers use the term *social referencing*. Social referencing occurs when the child actively seeks emotional and relational information from a significant other in an uncertain situation. Social referencing is a powerful learning process that shapes emotional self-regulation, self-conscious emotions, and perspective taking (empathy) (Eisenberg et al., 1995; Repacholi, 1998). Braumrind (1971) emphasizes the authoritative parenting style as the most powerful approach in contributing to these important human traits and behaviors, which produce either encouraged or discouraged people (Fletcher, 1999; Isabella, 1993; Pederson & Moran, 1996). We believe that Adlerians would agree that the principles of Adlerian encouragement might be seen in authoritative parenting: nonjudgmental sharing of parental observations and emotions, an emphasis on effort rather than on outcome in children's behavior, an appreciation for thoughtful acts and thoughtful verbal expressions, and a basic parental belief in the capabilities of the child. Thus, the authoritative parenting style contributes to an encouraged child.

Future Research Considerations

The relationship between Adlerian encouragement and the complex interactions both within the family and between family and society at large is unclear as to their interactive contribution in producing prosocial human traits. Our current review of the literature leads us to conclude that Adlerian encouragement requires more investigation concerning its power and function in the interactive context of skill-development techniques, for instilling prosocial traits and remediating discouraged individuals.

Adlerian encouragement is a holistic concept (Cheston, 2000). The concept is about the process between significant others and the individual. It is also about providing a process in which an individual begins to understand the connections between internal events (cognition and affect) and external events (observable behavior).

Research in infant, child, and adolescent development has identified a parenting and significant other interpersonal style (authoritative) that produces prosocial behavior in affective, cognitive, and problem-solving behaviors (Braumrind, 1971; Spinrad et al., 1999). What seems to be missing is an understanding and definition of the extent to which the process of promoting the link between internal processing and external behavior is critical in instilling emotional and cognitive self-regulation, perspective-taking, and adaptive problem-solving processes.

Adlerian encouragement is delivered as a construct of positive emotion and reflective verbal statements. We suggest that a hierarchy of verbal messages (external to internal referencing) may be necessary in constructing and promoting an internal locus of control. This seems a reasonable question when considering the level of independent cognitive ability of early to late child development. When involved in remediation, we also suggest that a hierarchy (external to internal referencing) be investigated in terms of constructing and promoting an internal locus of control. Such an investigation would involve severe to moderately impaired cognitive ability, dependent to independent problem-solving abilities, and severe to moderate emotional and psychological impairment.

It would be helpful to study the above in the context of a variety of cultural settings and cultural norms. Certainly, in today's world it would prove valuable to determine if there is a common threat among diverse cultures concerning Adlerian encouragement, prosocial individuals, and the remediation of discouraged individuals.

References

Adler, A. (1958). *The practice and theory of Individual Psychology*. Paterson, NJ: Littlefield, Adams.

Azoulay, D. (1999). Encouragement and logical consequences versus rewards and punishment: A re-examination. *The Journal of Individual Psychology, 55*, 91–99.

Baek, H. J. (2002). A comparative study of moral development of Korean and British children. *Journal of Moral Education, 31*, 373–392.

Braumrind, D. (1971). Current patterns of parental authority. *Developmental Psychology Monograph* 4 (1, Pt.2).

Bronfenbrenner, U. (1998). Ecological systems theory. In R. Vasta (Ed.), *Annals of child development* (pp. 187–251). Greenwich, CT: JAI.

Carns, M., & Carns, A. (1998). A review of the professional literature concerning the consistency of the definition and application of Adlerian encouragement. *The Journal of Individual Psychology, 54*, 72–84.

Cheston, S. (2000). Spirituality of encouragement. *The Journal of Individual Psychology, 56*, 296–303.

Dinkmeyer, D. (1972). Use of the encouragement process in Adlerian counseling. *The Personnel and Guidance Journal, 51*, 177–181.

Dinkmeyer, D., Dinkmeyer, D. C., Jr., & Sperry, L. (1987). *Adlerian counseling and psychotherapy*. Columbus, OH: Merrill.

Dinkmeyer, D., & Losoncy, L. (1980). *The encouragement book: Becoming a positive person.* Englewood Cliffs, NJ: Prentice-Hall.

Dreikurs, R. (1967). *Psychodynamics, psychotherapy, and counseling.* Chicago: Alfred Adler Institute of Chicago.

Eisenberg, N., Fabes, R., Murphy, B., Maszk, P., Smith, M., & Karbon, M. (1995). The role of emotionality and regulation in children's social functioning: A longitudinal study. *Child Development, 66,* 1360–1384.

Evans, T. (1995). The encouraging teacher. In G. M. Gazda, F. Asbury, M. Blazer, W. Childers, & R. Walters (Eds.), *Human relations development* (pp. 261–269). Boston: Allyn & Bacon.

Evans, T., Dedrick, R., & Epstein, M. (1997). Development and initial validation of the encouragement scale. *Journal of Humanistic Education and Development, 35,* 163–175.

Fletcher, A. (1999). Well-being as a function of perceived interparental consistency. *Journal of Marriage and Family, 61,* 599–611.

Isabella, R. (1993). Origins of attachment: Maternal interactive behavior across the first year. *Child Development, 64,* 605–621.

Kelly, D. (2002). The effects of locus of control, gender, and grade upon children's preference for praise and encouragement. *The Journal of Individual Psychology, 58,* 197–207.

Klahr, D., & MacWhinney, B. (1998). Information processing. In D. Kuhn & R. S. Siegler (Eds.), *Handbook of child psychology: Cognition, perception, and language* (pp. 631–678). New York: Wiley.

McKay, G. (1992). *The basics of encouragement.* Coral Springs, FL: CMTI.

Mosak, H. H. (1979). Adlerian psychotherapy. In R. J. Corsini (Ed.), *Current psychotherapies* (pp. 44–94). Itasca, IL: Peacock.

Mosak, H. H., & Maniacci, M. P. (1998). *Tactics in counseling and psychotherapy.* Itasca, IL: Peacock.

Neuer, A. (1936). Courage and discouragement. *International Journal of Individual Psychology, 2,* 30–50.

Pederson, D., & Moran, G. (1996). A categorical description of infant–mother relationships in the home and its relation to Q-sort measures of infant-mother interactions. In E. Waters, B.Vaughn, G. Posada, & K. Kondo-Ikemura (Eds.), Care-giving, cultural, and cognitive perspectives on secure-base behavior and working models: New growing points of attachment theory and research. *Monographs of the Society for Research in Child Development, 60* (23–30).

Peluso, R., Peluso, J., White, J., & Kern, R. (2004). A comparison of attachment theory and Individual Psychology: A review of the literature. *Journal of Counseling and Development, 82,* 139–151.

Pety, J., Kelly, F., & Kafafy, A. (1984). The praise-encouragement preference scale for children. *Individual Psychology, 40,* 92–101.

Phelps, R., Tranakos-Howe, S., Dagley, J., & Lyn, M. (2001). Encouragement and ethnicity in African-American college students. *Journal of Counseling and Development, 79,* 90–97.

Repacholi, B. (1998). Infants' use of attentional cues to identify the referent of another person's emotional expression. *Developmental Psychology, 33,* 12–21.

Spinrad, T., Losoya, S., Eisenberg, N., Fabes, R., Sheppard, S., Cumberland, H., Guthrie, I., & Murphy, B. (1999). The relations of parental affect and encouragement to children's moral emotions and behavior. *Journal of Moral Education, 28,* 323–337.

Sweeney, T. J. (1998). *Adlerian counseling: A practitioner's approach.* Muncie, IN: Accelerated Development.

Watts, R., & Pietrzak, D. (2000). Adlerian "encouragement" and the therapeutic process of solution-focused brief therapy. *Journal of Counseling and Development, 78*(4), 442–445.

CHAPTER 20

A Review of the Professional Literature Concerning the Consistency of the Definition and Application of Adlerian Encouragement

MICHAEL R. CARNS and ANN W. CARNS

Introduction

Encouragement is one of the essential constructs of Adlerian Psychology (Adler, 1946). Adlerian advocates such as Sherman and Dinkmeyer (1987) view encouragement as the most important technique in behavior change. They state: "Encouragement is considered by Adlerian therapists as perhaps the most important technique available for the promotion of change. Most interpersonal problems are the result of discouragement" (Sherman & Dinkmeyer, p. 50). They define encouragement in the following way: "Encouragement, then, is a set of specific skills: faith and belief in the clients, acceptance of them as they are, validating the goal and intention of their behavior, and reframing their behavior in a positive framework" (Sherman & Dinkmeyer, p. 51). Kelly and Chick (1982) offer an Adlerian definition of encouragement in their presentation of basic parental counseling skills. They state: "What is encouragement? It is both a condition and a process, and it applies both to the child who becomes courageous and to the process that facilitates that outcome" (p. 24). They state that the elements of encouragement are to: (1) value children as they are; (2) use words that build the child's self-esteem; (3) plan for experiences that create success; (4) demonstrate genuineness to children; (5) demonstrate nonverbal acceptance through touch; (6) use humor; (7) spend regular time with children; (8) recognize effort; (9) avoid emphasis on liabilities; (10) show appreciation for children's cooperation; and (11) avoid comparing children. Their manual emphasizes the use of Adlerian parenting constructs to help children explore themselves occupationally.

A 1988 study of encouragement versus praise in improving the productivity of the mentally retarded defined encouragement in both a broader context and a specific Adlerian one. Pitsounis and Dixon (1988) in their investigation state that

> encouragement is used to inspire with spirit, to foster hope, to stimulate, to support, or to instill courage and confidence. Encouragement was simply a statement such as "you can do it" or "keep on" delivered to an individual while attempting or completing a task. (p. 509)

In the same section of the article they cite a strictly Adlerian definition from McKay (1976): "In Adlerian terms, encouragement is a comment which shows acceptance, emphasizes effort and improvement, appreciates contributions, gets one to evaluate his/her own performance, and instills faith and confidence" (p. 509). Pitsounis and Dixon's findings suggest that when social praise is not given, the production rates of mentally retarded workers reach baseline levels. In contrast, when mentally retarded workers were allowed to reinforce themselves for their work, they became more productive and less dependent on external stimulation, such as verbal praise. Such a conclusion clearly indicates the power of intrinsic motivation.

A 1993 survey was conducted by Evans, Dedrick, and Dinkmeyer to inquire among Adlerian therapists as to their usage of Adlerian constructs in their everyday practices and the relevance of Adlerian Therapy in the field of marriage and family today. They sent questionnaires to 328 members of the North American Society of Adlerian Psychology. The authors reported that respondents see Adlerian therapy as very functional in the current field of marriage and family therapy and that almost all of them report using encouragement (Evans, Dedrick, & Dinkmeyer, 1993). Adlerians view encouragement as essential in reducing negativism among family members, promoting prosocial behavior change, and overcoming illogical and maladaptive thought patterns (Sherman, Oresky, & Rountree, 1991). When encouragement is used in counseling, a variety of socially appropriate behaviors and attitudes and an enhancement of the client's self-worth emerge (Sherman & Dinkmeyer, 1987). It was Adler's conclusion (1946) that when extrinsic praise and reinforcement are replaced by encouragement, one would gain the ability to look at one's own mistaken beliefs and a process of self-evaluation would result. This self-evaluation in turn is to lead to a valuing of self rather than being overly concerned with being valued by others, especially authority figures (Sherman, Oresky, & Rountree, 1991).

The Use of Encouragement in Classroom Management

Modern-day Adlerians steadfastly endorse Adler's notion that encouragement, rather than extrinsic reinforcement and punishment, promotes the most healthy self-concepts and behavior patterns in children (Thompson & Rudolf, 1992; Dinkmeyer & McKay, 1990). Two of the articles on the use of encouragement discussed the use of Adlerian-defined encouragement to develop positive self-concepts in educational settings (Gilbert, 1989; Kyle, 1991). These articles were not investigative studies but rather descriptions of programs and suggestions for behavioral management interventions in the classroom. Several articles in this area investigate the use of encouragement as it affects academic performance. An article entitled "The Rewards of Learning" (Chance, 1992) states that encouragement and intrinsic reinforcements are important but not sufficient for learning to occur. Intrinsic motivation must be combined with such extrinsic rewards as praise and compliments in the weakest reinforcement possible to strengthen a behavior. This observation is not, however, empirically based.

In a study using encouragement to increase academic performance in the early elementary grades, Rathvon (1990) asked a teacher to deliver encouragement to reduce off-task behavior in 5 first graders. The conclusion is that encouragement succeeds in reducing off-task behavior but is not successful in increasing academic productivity. Contrary to these findings, Van Hecke and Tracy (1987) examined the effectiveness of adult encouragement on 80 eighth-grade students on two easy and two difficult computer learning tasks in a one-to-one adult-to-child learning situation. Their findings are that this increases student motivation. The students' achievement motivation may be due to the encouragement or the individual attention received from adults.

Would the same encouragement process succeed with groups of students? An article by Huhnke (1984) indicates that the answer to this question might be yes. She reviews research articles covering teacher behaviors, classroom climate, and factors to consider in giving rewards. She concludes that the teacher should provide an atmosphere conducive to learning:

that external reinforcement systems be kept to a minimum; that students participate in determining their own educational goals; and that all students be given opportunities to succeed. An article by Hitz and Driscoll (1989) supports Huhnke's findings about involving children as active participants in the learning process. The authors investigate six articles that assess the relative merits of praise versus encouragement in the classroom. Their summary concludes that praise lowers student confidence in themselves, is a weak reinforcer, and is an impractical tool in the classroom. It concludes that teachers who use encouragement create a classroom environment where students accept evaluation and make mistakes and learn from their mistakes without undue anxiety. Superstein (1994) supports this conclusion through a study in which 380 high school students were polled. The purpose of the survey was to investigate the underlying causes for the educational crisis in North America. The investigator asked the students what are encouraging and discouraging factors about their educational process. The article concludes: "The educational system would benefit greatly by having teachers treating students with respect, by being able to relate to the students as individuals and to the class as a whole in an encouraging manner" (p. 189).

The Use of Encouragement in Parent Education and Parent Counseling

A traditional area of the use of Adlerian encouragement is in parent counseling and parent education (Dinkmeyer & McKay, 1990). Carmack and Carmack (1994) describe the presentation of parental education programs based on Adlerian parental education in Russia. Constructs taught in these parenting workshops include the goals of misbehavior, the use of encouragement to build self-esteem, and natural and logical consequences for discipline. The parental education approach is based on the Adler/Dreikurs model. The researchers taught the participants to provide encouragement through requesting children to self-evaluate. No statistical data were offered. The authors make a strong theoretical argument for an Adlerian parenting program citing the arguments of Dreikurs and Soltz (1964) that a movement from autocratic parenting to democratic parenting without the knowledge of how to instill such family practices were a major contribution to delinquency. Carmack and Carmack felt that it was essential that the children of modem-day Russia be reared in households practicing Adlerian parenting principles.

Another article on the international use of Adlerian parenting constructs is that of Ogden (1990) comparing an American and British parenting group. Ogden uses the same reference by Dreikurs and Soltz

(1964) to build a case for autocratic societies moving toward democratic principles to use democratic parenting practices. A significant difference is found between the two groups in their attitudes toward the Adlerian principles taught. The American group rated success based on how well the principles taught helped change the children's behavior. The British, on the other hand, related the teaching to themselves and considered it a novel idea to apply such principles directly to their child-rearing practices. Ogden concludes: "The Adlerian concepts translated well, although certain cultural considerations need to be taken into consideration" (p. 165).

Moore and Dean-Zubrisky in a 1979 study collected statistical data on an Adlerian parent-study group. They found that the experimental-group parents demonstrated a significant increase over the control-group parents in democratic child-rearing practices, including the use of Adlerian encouragement. The generalizability of the results would be in question, however, as the experimental group consisted of only eight parents.

In another parental study, a group of parents were seen in a parenting group for 8 months in a university practicum (Riley, 1995). The parents were provided with lectures on parenting skills, homework assignments to carry out concerning lecture material, role-play to enhance the success of homework assignments, and videotape presentations on parenting skills. The parents were then asked to observe behind a one-way mirror while their children engaged in group activities. Parents were then asked to enter the room and provide encouraging and positive comments to their children. The Piers Harris Children's Self Concept Scale was administered before and after the practicum, along with observational checklists measuring increased eye contact between children in the group and increased eye contact with parents.

A statistically significant difference on pre- and post-measures on children's self-concept was found as measured by the Piers Harris Children's Self Concept Scale. This positive change in self-concept in the children in this study was accomplished in two ways. The researchers conducted a well-structured parenting group emphasizing positive parenting skills along with the opportunity to practice those skills. The specific reason for the change in behavior was not ascertained, however, since encouragement was not operationally defined and thus the intervention might really have been praise. The children and adults knew they were being observed, so it may have been a Hawthorne Effect. In one section Riley stated that "the parents observed their children participating in group interaction as well as an opportunity to practice giving their children positive feedback, encouragement, and support when they joined the children's group immediately after observing them through the mirror" (p. 48). Later Riley stated: "The results of this practicum also indicated that training parents to use positive communication skills, praise and encouragement, and authoritative discipline in dealing with their child significantly impacts on that child's self esteem" (p. 51).

The main question from an Adlerian perspective left unanswered by this study is the impact of extrinsic versus intrinsic motivation on the outcome of the study. It would have been beneficial to divide the parents in two groups, one providing intrinsic and the other extrinsic motivation and compare the effect on children's self-concept.

A study by Steinberg, Lamborn, Dornbusch, and Darling (1992) investigated the impact on adolescent school achievement of authoritative parenting practices. They defined authoritative parents as individuals who give children high acceptance and psychological autonomy, provide freedom within reasonable limits, engage in verbal give-and-take with their children, and respond to children's needs and wishes. Their findings support the Adlerian posture on encouragement. They state that authoritative parenting leads to better school performance and stronger concentration on studies than other styles of parenting. This study is based on a report of 6,400 students comparing their parents' child-rearing practices with these students' academic achievement over a two-year period.

Maniacci and Maniacci (1989) discusses Adlerian encouragement and its importance with parents as well as their children. They indicate that parents in their investigation are discouraged because they lacked confidence in their own parental judgment, their view is that parents need reassurance, support and encouragement to self-evaluate their parental role and function. They state a well-defined use of Adlerian encouragement in parental education:

> Part of the encouragement process involves accepting others as they are, and when parental values are in line with social interest, then accepting and supporting the parent taking a more active, assertive role in rearing their children is a crucial part of working with families. (p. 511)

Echoing the need to empower adults as well as children in the parenting process, Turnbull and Turnbull (1983) offer guidelines for stepparents and suggest that stepparents must be encouraged through the emphasis on understanding their problems. They state:

> There is a need for more understanding of the problems faced by those families and perhaps more importantly, for the provision of support and encouragement for the stepparenting as he or she faces the difficult task of developing a role for which few realistic guidelines exist. (p. 228)

The authors did not define the form that the encouragement should take. It is clear in this article however, as well as the articles reviewed on parenting, that these authors consider attention to adult emotional and self-concept needs as important as attending to those of their children.

A 1977 study by Kern and Wheeler contrasts Watzlawick's paradoxical principles of change with Adlerian childrearing practices. The article possesses some interesting comparisons and discussions on the two schools of counseling, however, no statistical data is offered to support the power of either intervention. The authors provide explanations as to why parents tend to favor extrinsic over intrinsic motivation. The first idea was the "Utopian Syndrome" which the article described as a desire on the part of parents to pursue unattainable goals in their children. Kern and Wheeler (1977) state: "As they push for the unattainable, their children become discouraged and misbehave. This may make it totally impossible for parents to see functional behavior in their children, 'the realizable'" (p. 224). Kern and Wheeler (1977) discuss a second construct that leads parents toward extrinsic and autocratic parenting styles: "the principle that adults are superior and children are inferior" (p. 224). The article concludes by drawing significant parallels between Adlerian and Strategic Family therapy interventions in parenting:

> More specifically, the principles of second-order change were similar to democratic techniques as they were applied to such problem as dealing with attention getting, power struggles, and feelings of discouragement. In addition, the principle of change through paradox was applied to the actual teaching of democratic principles of childrearing. (p. 231)

This concluding statement by Kern and Wheeler (1977) recognizes the need to deal with fundamental parent-child relational issues. It also expands the idea of encouragement into paradoxical counseling techniques. The authors suggested that it would provide encouragement if the counselor appears accepting of the dysfunctionality. The intervention is to encourage self-examination on the part of the parent through the principle of therapeutic double binding or paradox. Encouraging all things to remain the same encourages self-exploration of more adaptive alternatives.

The Use of Encouragement in Teacher Education

The authors' review in the literature indicates those value sets of the participants toward discipline practices become an intervening variable in delivering Adlerian encouragement. Bain, Houghton, and Williams (1991) concludes that teacher encouragement of students' on-task behavior increased during the intervention period of a study. When the program was terminated, teacher encouragement decreased. Teachers gave "lip service" to the project and quickly returned to other more familiar and comfortable forms of student motivation. The authors state "This may indicate the need for an ongoing feedback or self-monitoring procedure for teachers participating in the program in order to maintain appropriate levels of encouragement" (p. 258). Teachers need to be encouraged so they can in turn be encouraging to students.

Kowalski, Stipek, and Daniels (1987) add to this concern over the ability of teachers to deliver sustained encouragement. Their study attempted to have teachers rate the different motivational levels on students and student level of academic achievement. The participating teachers rate students as either motivated or unmotivated and were unable to differentiate among motivational levels of students. In these two studies teachers were very extrinsically oriented in their approach to teaching and motivating students to learn. Reeve (1989) in a study of factors contributing to intrinsic motivation determine that it appears much easier to turn off than to turn it on. Pallak, Costomiris, Sroka, and Pittman (1982) determine that intrinsic motivation is negatively affected when the participants had had a significant amount of prior experience with extrinsic reward.

The Use of Encouragement in Enhancing Self-Esteem and Academic Performance

Accomplishment was the aspect of encouragement most documented when investigating in the school setting. It is, however, quite possible to have highly discouraged children with low self-concept engaging in high productivity. The problem is that their drives for achievement may have come from the anxiety, fear, and mistrust associated with low self-esteem. Their productivity could have been security and safety driven. Their self-esteem was not enhanced. The importance of self-esteem or the affective domain of self-concept in children cannot be overemphasized. For example, Clemens and Dean (1981) find that children with high self-concept act positively, assume responsibility, tolerate frustration well, feel able to influence their environments, and are proud of their accomplishments. Children with a low self-concept are easily manipulated by others, easily frustrated, blame others for their failures, and avoid difficult situations. Meredith & Evans (1990) note that Adlerian encouragement has been practiced for more than half a century. They emphasize, however, that few parents use it or even know about it. They state: "One possible explanation is that few parents have gone beyond first force psychology (Behaviorism) in their thinking about human relationships and have never experienced encouragement" (p. 188). The authors discuss both second force psychology (Freudian) and third force psychology (Phenomenological). It was in the third force psychology that Meredith and Evans view Adlerian encouragement. They conclude with this very powerful statement on encouragement: "Encouragement is a key concept in helping parents improve relationships in their families. Parents can learn to be more hopeful and encouraging. To do this they must go beyond behavioristic psychology and obedience training. Adlerian and Third Force Psychology offers a chance for a real breakthrough" (p. 192).

Encouragement as an Extrinsic Directive in Education

This group of studies like previous studies discussed in this article use encouragement as a secondary means to change behavior; encouragement is used as an extrinsic directive and advice-giving means of changing behavior, rather than an intrinsic self-evaluative concept. Studies surveyed indicate encouragement used in intervening with at-risk black males, preventing female dropouts, aiding transition from high school to college, encouraging high school girls to take more nontraditional electives, providing support to students dealing with death and dying in an educational environment, helping teachers to build students' self-esteem in the classroom, helping faculty acquire more positive attitudes toward bilingual minority students in high school, aiding postsecondary minority students to transcend from two-year to four-year colleges, helping students and faculty face alcohol addiction in their families, and providing an intervention to treat childhood obesity in the public schools (Cobbs & McCallum, 1992; Earle & Roach, 1989; Esperon, 1986; Faddis & Hutchison, 1980; Floerchinger, 1989; Gilbert, 1989; Goldsmith, 1987; Keenan & Braxton-Brown, 1991; Kyle, 1991; Lucas, 1993; Mendel & Lincoln, 1991; Pitman, 1990; Strauss, 1981; Turk, 1990; Walz, 1987).

Encouragement is noted as a means to promote attendance and completion in a literacy program (Anderson & Helmick, 1988); to improve student motivation to attend a math lab (Capps, 1984); to promote interest in new "older-than-average" college students to seek out information (Chickering, 1987); to reduce math anxiety by promoting parental involvement in student learning (DeBronac-Meade & Brown, 1982); to promote female involvement in the sciences (Grew, 1986); to improve attendance of migrant children in schools (Mangan, 1989); and as a factor in developing mature college students. None of these studies specifically define encouragement. The context in which encouragement was used in these studies would lead the reader to assume a primarily extrinsic usage.

Examples of statements authors considered encouraging are: "to show an interest in someone"; or "to provide motivational talks with someone"; or "give a pep talk to someone"; or "participate with someone"; or "to provide immediate feedback"; or "provide resources that make it possible for a goal to be obtained."

Anderson and Helmick (1988) note that "to minimize dropout and poor attendance, it is important to determine the recruitment methods, selection criteria, program configuration, and types of encouragement that best predict program completion and attendance" (pp. 6, 7). None of the studies cited above determine which experimental variables were most powerful, or how each variable contributes to the outcome of the study.

The Use of Encouragement in Individual and Marriage and Family Therapy

Articles in the areas of individual therapy, and marital and family therapy, are more specific in their definition of encouragement than are articles focused outside of a traditional therapeutic milieu. While better defined, there is still the element of extrinsic encouragement. Minuchin (1974), for instance, in his study of low socioeconomic chaotic families found that a therapist who operates in a permissive and reflective manner will end up with greater chaos. He finds success in therapy as an authority figure, setting tight limits and expectations on the family. He believes that to succeed in encouraging clients one must assess the capability of the client for self-direction, and the client's motivation to take risks and self-evaluate. Mimesis, an adoption of the clients' style of communication and metaphorical style, creates the conditions for the broadest enactment of encouragement (Minuchin, 1974). For instance, if the family is slow paced and focused on athletics as a value in the family, the therapist becomes slow paced and uses baseball analogies to make therapeutic points. Minuchin indicates an authoritarian approach initially with families and individuals with very limited impulse control, need for immediate gratification, and volatile acting-out behavior. He proposes that a developmental progress moving from extrinsic to intrinsic is necessary with low-functioning clients. Through mimesis, however, he is attempting to contact the world of the clients so that they can engage in self-evaluation. This self-evaluation is certainly a goal of encouragement.

Another example of extrinsic encouragement seems to be the use of paradox. This intervention is discussed by a number of authors (Baideme, Kern & Taffel-Cohen, 1979; Kern & Wheeler, 1977; Dinkmeyer, 1991; Dinkmeyer & Eckstein, 1993). Dinkmeyer and Eckstein state:

One specific technique psychologists employ to help individuals change from a fearful to a courageous approach is the use of paradox. Positive growth often occurs when a person can be encouraged to do the very thing he or she fears. Acting "as if" one has the courage to confront one's concerns is a paradoxical power strategy which often improves self-confidence. (p. 15)

The use of paradox as a means of encouragement fits with the view of Minuchin earlier cited, that clients must first be helped to experience success and to feel understood before they can assume the responsibility of self-motivation and self-assessment. The Adlerian concept of acting "as if" also fits this view.

Dinkmeyer (1993) writes of the absolute importance of Adlerian encouragement in couples therapy. He then defines four specific characteristics of "the encouraged marital system." He states that the encouraged couple possesses social interest, recognizes their assets to build a relationship, knows alternatives to overcoming problems, and possesses a sense of humor. Again, Adlerian encouragement is seen as beneficial in a wide variety of presenting concerns (McBrien, 1993; Fisher, 1993; Carlson & Sperry, 1993; Powell & Gazda, 1979; Baideme, Kern & Taffel-Cohen, 1979).

The Use of Encouragement in Career Counseling

Career counseling uses encouragement extensively. Encouragement is used as a tangential construct to the main intervention strategies being investigated such as academic tutoring, behavior modification techniques, and structured workshops (Bloomfield, 1989; Hanks, 1982; Herr, 1989; Kerr, 1990; Kistler, 1982; & Schulz, 1986). Two of the studies, however, take a more direct look at encouragement. Dorn, in a 1987 study, investigates the effect that a career counseling program using specific concepts from social influence theory have on career decisiveness of students. The social constructs investigated are perceived need, counselor interpretation, and encouragement for reattribution. This study attempts to isolate social influence as a means for behavioral change, though encouragement was still not defined or a clear statement made of how it was employed.

A study by Lauria, Williams, Waldo, and Waldo (1983) focuses specifically on the construct of encouragement and its influence on traditional and nontraditional career choices of a group of college freshmen men and women. Encouragement is being used in this study as a separate entity from counseling to provide more information, and to provide more specific programming such as a training program for this group. Again encouragement is not clearly defined. The contextual usage indicates that the investigators attempt to discern an interest expressed by significant others toward these students to pursue non-traditional career choices. Recommendations following the study are: "… the expending of more resources to identify and encourage nontraditional women and more specific counseling programs for traditional women" (p. 4).

Encouragement and Its Use in the Health Profession

Britzman and Henkin (1992) comment on the use of Adlerian encouragement in the pursuit of holistic wellness. Holistic wellness is defined as the merging of emotional, physical, and intellectual growth. They state this very powerful thought on the use of Adlerian encouragement in the area of holistic wellness: "The Adlerian philosophy of altering perception and supporting efforts to expand behavior repertoires can awaken inner resources, lead to feelings of significance and well-being, and facilitate one's wellness process" (p. 201).

McClam (1988) conducted a study to determine means to retain hospice volunteers and reduce volunteer turnover. He concludes: "It is also probable that supervision as needed over and above the supervision regularly supplied provides the support, encouragement and rewards most valued by these volunteers" (p. 10). The author promotes support, encouragement, and reward as separate constructs, or as interchangeable, when she further states: "It would appear, then, that the rewards most appropriate and effective for this group were intrinsic, i.e., rewards and relationships that come from work itself" (p. 10).

Conclusion

The articles reviewed contain a wide variety of definitions of encouragement. However, with very few exceptions, regardless of definition, encouragement is perceived as helpful in promoting behavior change. The most consistently defined categories of studies reflecting an Adlerian definition of encouragement are parent education, parent counseling, teacher education, classroom management, and individual and marriage and family counseling. Encouragement has the widest variety of definitions in the areas of academic performance, career counseling, and in the health professions. Most of the studies are descriptive with little empirical data offered. Empirical data, when collected, is often supportive of Adlerian encouragement (Pitsounis & Dixon, 1988; Rathvon, 1990; Van Hecke & Tracy, 1987; Ogden, 1990; Moore & Dean, 1979; Riley, 1995; Steinberg, Lamborn, Dornbusch & Darling, 1992; Bain, Houghton & Williams, 1991; Clemens & Dean, 1981). Results which appear to refute or greatly question the power of encouragement in changing behavior are studies defining encouragement extrinsically (Anderson & Helmick, 1988; Capps, 1984; Chickering, 1987; DeBronac, Meade & Brown, 1982; Crew, 1986; Mangan, 1989; Anderson & Helmick, 1988). Comparison of data is hampered because studies had different and therefore noncomparable definitions of encouragement.

The greatest challenge to research appears to be operationally defining encouragement. The literature in several instances uses encouragement, praise, and reward interchangeably. This was most probably due to the socially ingrained valuing of praise and reward. Praise and reward are widely used in business, in schools, and in families, to attempt to promote high performance and adaptive social behavior. They are widely viewed as synonymous with encouragement. Encouragement is widely viewed outside of the Adlerian community as an extrinsic concept.

Future studies need to define more clearly both the construct of encouragement and how it is being carried out in the study. A hierarchy of interventions based on the capacity of the client to self-assess and self-motivate would enhance successful delivery of the encouragement process. It may not initially be defined by the client or recipient as encouraging, but as threatening or fear producing. Encouragement may be delivered with the cooperation of the client or recipient or, as with paradoxical intervention, may be applied strictly from the analysis of whoever is delivering such an intervention. The ultimate goal is self-analysis and self-monitoring by the client or recipient. Through the intent of encouragement to enhance self-esteem, increase moral reasoning and cooperation, the client or recipient learns to appreciate the encouragement process.

Studies should use for their definition and basis of investigation the full range of Adlerian encouragement as reflected in this article. Encouragement and praise should be compared in parenting groups and family therapy. There are parenting programs being used in both large and small school districts that follow both behavioral and Adlerian guidelines. Therapists could deliver counseling services to a set of families using encouragement and Adlerian parenting principles as the focus, and conduct therapy with a set of families in which praise and behavior modification was the focus of treatment. Pre-post measures of parent and child self-concept could be applied in both types of investigations.

Classroom management interventions based on Adlerian encouragement could be designed and investigated. The Adolescent Discouragement Indicator (ADI) (Lingg & Wilborn, 1992) could be used to construct hierarchial Adlerian encouragement interventions for adolescent school children. Elementary children could be observed using the Four Goals of Misbehavior (Dinkmeyer & McKay, 1990) as a guideline to construct hierarchial Adlerian encouragement interventions. Outcome variables of self-concept, school grades, and student behavior rating scales taken pre-post could then be used to measure the success of these interventions. The studies should last ten weeks to correspond with the length of most parenting groups and with the average length of stay in family therapy.

There has been very little done empirically to document the effectiveness of Adlerian Encouragement. Encouragement is well recognized as a positive concept, and its usage is widespread and widely defined. A construct so basic to a school of thought as encouragement is to Adlerian Psychology, left with such varied definitions in the eyes of the general public and viewed by the general public as a distant second to reward and punishment and defined synonymously with reward and punishment, will probably be used with minimum effectiveness or forgotten. We need to demonstrate that Adler's constructs, which Adlerians understand as fundamental to the successful teaching of democratic principles and the enhancement of personal psychological growth, are highly effective in enhancing emotional and psychological quality of life.

References

Adler, A. (1946). *Understanding human nature.* New York: Greenburg.

Anderson, S. B., & Helmick, J. S. (1988, August). *Literacy in the United States: How?* Paper presented at the Annual Meeting of the International Council of Psychologists, 46th, Singapore. (ERIC Document Reproduction Service No. ED 308 491).

Baideme, S. M., Kern, R. M., & Taffel-Cohen, S. (1979). The use of Adlerian family therapy in a case of school phobia. *Journal of Individual Psychology, 35,* 58–69.

Bain, A., Houghton, S., & Williams, S. (1991). The effects of a school-wide behaviour management programme on teachers' use of encouragement in the classroom. *Educational Studies, 17,* 249–260.

Bloomfield, W. (1989). *Career beginnings: Helping disadvantaged youth achieve their potential.* Bloomington, IN: Phi Delta Kappa Educational Foundation (ERIC Document Reproduction Service No. ED 316 618).

Britzman, M. J., & Henkin, A. L. (1992). Wellness and personality priorities: The utilization of Adlerian encouragement strategies. *Individual Psychology, 48,* 194–202.

Capps, J. P. (1984). *Mathematics laboratory and personalized system of instruction: A workshop presentation.* Somerville, NJ: Somerset County College (ERIC Document Reproduction Service No. 246 969).

Carlson, J., & Sperry, L. (1993). Extending treatment results in couples therapy. Special issue: Marriage and couples counseling. *Individual Psychology, 49,* 450–455.

Carmack, C., & Carmack, E. (1994). Children and change: The challenge of parent education in the new Russian federation. *Individual Psychology, 50,* 321–328.

Chance, P. (1992). The rewards of learning. *Phi Delta Kappan, 74,* 200–207.

Chickering, J. N. (1987). *Warmline training manual: Peer counseling returning adult students.* Memphis, TN: Memphis State University, Center for Student Development (ERIC Document Reproduction Service No. ED 289 125).

Clemens, H., & Dean, R. (1981). *Self-Esteem, the key to your child's well-being.* New York: Putnam.

Cobbs, C., & McCallum, O. (1992, November). *Positive Impact Program (PIP) for at-risk black males.* Paper presented at the annual meeting of the Mid-South Educational Research Association, Knoxville, TN (ERIC Document Reproduction Service No. ED 354 437).

DeBronac-Meade, M. L., & Brown, R. (1982, March). Reduction of mathematics anxiety: *A cognitive behavior modification approach.* Paper presented at the Annual Meeting of the American Educational Research Association, New York, NY (ERIC Document Reproduction Service No. ED 218 553).

Dinkmeyer, D. C. (1991). Encouragement: Basis for leader training and participative management. Special issues: On beyond Adler. *Individual Psychology, 47,* 504–508.

Dinkmeyer, D. C., & Eckstein, D. G. (1993). *Leadership by Encouragement.* Dubuque, IA: Kendall/ Hunt Publishing.

Dinkmeyer, D., & McKay, G. D. (1990). *Systematic training for effective parenting.* Circle Pines, MN: American Guidance Service.

Dreikurs, R., & Soltz, V. (1964). *Children: The challenge.* New York: Hawthorn & Dutton.

Earle J., & Roach, V. (1989). Female dropouts: A new perspective. National Association of State Boards of Education, Alexandria, VA. Washington, D.C.: Women's Educational Equity Act Program (ERIC Document Reproduction Service No. ED 320 970).

Esperon, J. P. (1986, April). *Social support over a life transition:* College graduation. Paper presented at the Annual Convention of the American Association for Counseling and Development, Los Angeles, CA (ERIC Document Reproduction Service No. ED 270 686).

Evans, T. D., Dedrick, R. F., & Dinkmeyer, D. (1993). A survey of Adlerian marital therapy. Special issue: Marriage and couples counseling. *Individual Psychology, 49,* 468–474.

Faddis, B. J., & Hutchison, B. (1980). Sex equity in Lincoln County Schools: A report of a needs assessment. National Demonstration of Educational Equity for Women: Design Phase. Washington, D.C.: Women's Educational Equity Act Program (ERIC Document Reproduction Service No. ED 212 695).

Fisher, S. K. (1993). A proposed Adlerian theoretical framework and intervention techniques for gay and lesbian couples. Special issue: Marriage and couples counseling. *Individual Psychology, 49,* 438–449.

Floerchinger, D. S. (1989). Bereavement: Applying Erikson's theory of psychosocial development to college students (ERIC Document Reproduction Service No. ED 312 577).

Gilbert, J. I. (1989). Logical consequences: A new classification for the classroom. *Individual Psychology, 45,* 425–432.

Goldsmith, R. G. (1987). Students concerned about tomorrow: A dropout intervention program. Final report. Virginia State Dept. of Education, Richmond. Div. of Vocational Education. Arlington, VA: People, Inc. (ERIC Document Reproduction Service No. ED 288 103).

Grew, P. C. (1986, April). *New directions for intervention: Report from the National Science Foundation Committee on Equal Opportunities in Science and Technology.* Paper presented at the Annual Meeting of the American Educational Research Association, San Francisco, CA (ERIC Document Reproduction Service No. ED 269 256).

Hanks, M. (1982). Careers for homemakers (a displaced homemakers program). St. Louis: St. Louis Community College (ERIC Document Reproduction Service No. ED 222 225).

Herr, E. L. (1989). Career Development and Mental Health. *Journal of Career Development, 16,* 5–18.

Hitz, R., & Driscoll, A. (1989). *Praise in the classroom.* Urbana, IL: ERIC Clearinghouse on Elementary and Early Childhood Education (ERIC Document Reproduction Service No. ED 313 108).

Huhnke, C. (1984). *An annotated bibliography of the literature dealing with enhancing student motivation in the elementary school* (ERIC Document Reproduction Service No. ED 252 310).

Kelly, F. D., & Chick, J. M. (1982). *Basic parent counseling skills for the occupational specialist.* Tallahassee: Florida State University. Center for Studies in Vocational Education (ERIC Document Reproduction Service No. ED 236 455).

Keenan, T. P., & Braxton-Brown, G. (1991, Spring). Techniques: Coach, consultant, critic, counselor: The multiple roles of the responsive facilitator. *Journal of Adult Education, 19,* insert (ERIC Document Reproduction Service No. ED 336 562).

Kern, R. M., & Wheeler, M. S. (1977). Autocratic vs. democratic childrearing practices: An example of second-order change. *Journal of Individual Psychology, 33,* 223–232.

Kerr, B. (1990). *Career planning for gifted and talented youth.* Reston, VA: Council for Exceptional Children (ERIC Document Reproduction Service No. ED 321 497).

Kistler, K. (1982). REPP: *A case study in federal financing—long term fiscal and instructional implications.* A Project Report. Eureka, CA: College of the Redwoods (ERIC Document Reproduction Service No. ED 266 809).

Kowalski, P., Stipek, R., & Daniels, D. (1987). *The relationship between teacher's ratings and students' self-reported motivation.* Paper presented at the Annual Meeting of the American Educational Research Association.

Kyle, P. B. (1991). Developing cooperative interaction in schools for teachers and administrators. *Individual Psychology, 47*, 261–265.

Lauria, E. B., Williams, E., Waldo, S., & Waldo, M. (1983). *A Longitudinal Comparison of Traditional and Nontraditional Career Choices by Sex.* College Park: University of Maryland. Counseling Center (ERIC Document Reproduction Service No. ED 248 366).

Lingg, M., and Wilborn, B. (1992). Adolescent discouragement: Development of an assessment instrument. *Individual Psychology, 48*, 65–75.

Lucas, T. (1993). Applying elements of effective secondary schooling for language minority students. East Lansing, Ml: National Center for Research on Teacher Learning (ERIC Document Reproduction Service No. ED 364 105).

Maniacci, M. P., & Maniacci, S. V. (1989). Parental values as parameters for limit setting in a democratic atmosphere. *Individual Psychology, 45*, 509–512.

Mangan, K. S. (1989). Defying odds, children of migrant workers attend college with help from federal program offered on 5 campuses. *Chronicle of Higher Education, 36*, 39–43.

McBrien, R. (1993). Laughing together: Humor as encouragement in couples counseling. *Individual Psychology, 49*, 419–427.

McClam, T. (1985, April). Volunteer motivations and rewards: shaping future programs. Paper presented at the Annual Conference of the American Association for Counseling and Development, New York, NY (ERIC Document Reproduction Service No. ED 265 481).

Mendel, R. A., & Lincoln, C. A. (1991). *Guiding children to success: What schools and communities can do, realizing America's hope.* Chapel Hill, NC: MDC, Inc., South Carolina Educational Television Network (ERIC Document Reproduction Service No. ED 338 982).

Meredith, C. W., & Evans, T. D. (1990). Encouragement in the family. *Individual Psychology, 46*, 187–192.

Minuchin, S. (1974). *Families and family therapy.* Cambridge, MA: Harvard University Press.

Moore, M. H., & Dean-Zubrisky, C. (1979). Adlerian parent study groups: An assessment of attitude and behavior change. *Journal of Individual Psychology, 35*, 225–234.

Ogden, P. (1990). Cultural considerations at work in an Adlerian parent study group in Great Britain. *Individual Psychology, 46*, 157–165.

Pallack, S. R., Costomiris, S., Sroka, S., & Pittman, T. S. (1982). School experiences, reward characteristics, and intrinsic motivation. *Child Development, 53*, 1382–1391.

Pitman, R. (1990). *Children of alcoholics in schools: A call to compassion.* CRIS perspectives on the school. Washington, DC.: Council for Religion in Independent Schools (ERIC Document Reproduction Service No. ED 344 180).

Pitsounis, N. D., & Dixon, P. N. (1988). Encouragement versus praise: Improving productivity of the mentally retarded. *Individual Psychology, 44*, 507–512.

Powell, G. S., & Gazda, G. M. (1979). Cleaning out the trash: A case study in Adlerian family counseling. *Journal of Individual Psychology, 35*, 45–57.

Rathvon, N. W. (1990). The effects of encouragement on off-task behavior and academic productivity. *Elementary School Guidance and Counseling, 24*, 189–199.

Reeve, J. (1989). Intrinsic motivation and the acquisition and maintenance of four experiential states. *Journal of Social Psychology, 129*, 841–854.

Riley, G. M. (1995). *Increasing self-esteem in children 8–12 years old from dysfunctional families: A twofold solution to a twofold problem.* ED.D. Practicum, Nova Southeastern University (ERIC Document Reproduction Service No. ED 387 729).

Schulz, W. E. (1986, April). *Structured group counseling for employment counselors.* Paper presented at the Annual Convention of the American Association for Counseling and Development, Los Angeles, CA (ERIC Document Reproduction Service No. ED 268 418).

Sherman, R., & Dinkmeyer, D. C. (1987). *Systems of family therapy.* New York: Brunner/Mazel.

Sherman, R., Oresky, P., & Rountree, Y. (1991). *Solving problems in couples and family therapy: Techniques and tactics.* New York: Brunner/Mazel.

Steinberg, L., Lamborn, S., Dornbusch, S., & Darling, N. (1992). Impact of parenting practices on adolescent achievement: Authoritative parenting, school involvement, and encouragement to succeed. *Child Development, 63,* 1266–1281.

Strauss, C. (1981, April). *Childhood obesity: A school-based program.* Paper presented at the Annual Convention of the American Personnel and Guidance Association, St. Louis (ERIC Document Reproduction Service No. ED 208 325).

Superstein, D. (1994). Adolescents' attitudes toward their schooling: The influence of encouragement and discouragement. *Individual Psychology, 50,* 183–191.

Thompson, C. L., & Rudolph, L. B. (1992). *Counseling Children* (3rd ed.). Pacific Grove, CA: Brooks/Cole.

Turk, B. (1990). Kids with courage. *Individual Psychology, 46,* 178–183.

Turnbull, S. K., & Turnbull, J. M. (1983). To dream the impossible dream: An agenda for discussion with stepparents. *Family Relations, 32,* 227–230.

Van Hecke, M., & Tracy, R. J. (1987). The influence of adult encouragement on children's persistence. *Child Study Journal, 17,* 251–268.

Walz, C. R. (1987). *Combating the school dropout problem: proactive strategies for school counselors.* East Lansing, Ml: National Center for Research on Teacher Learning (ERIC Document Reproduction Service No. ED 287 112).

VIII
The Family Constellation

CHAPTER 21

Family Constellation: Meaning, Research, and Future Research

GUY J. MANASTER

This essay on family constellation research began as a standard literature review and critique. After 40 years of reading books and articles on the subject, mostly on birth order, and carrying out and publishing some research in the field, I felt fairly confident with this topic. After two months of collecting new material, appraising current literature, and considering the whole issue, I had to throw out the standard format. The term *family constellation*, as commonly understood, draws many thousands of matches on a Google search and almost 5,000 citations on PsychINFO. Some of these refer to research articles.

Birth order research and literature ranges from serious scientific studies relating to intelligence, sexual preferences, differences in animal growth and health, and, of course, personality characteristics, to some that are on a par with astrology and party games. With over 7 million Google matches, the relatively small number of PsychINFO citations, 2,500, indicates the degree of regard for this area in the field. Ninety citations match birth order with Individual Psychology. Most of the literature that hypothesizes about differences in intelligence and achievement is not Adlerian and suggests that family size diminishes resources for "later borns." The animal growth and health literature and the sexual preference studies suggest biological differences between early and late borns. Although the suggested differences are not based on Adlerian theory, the areas and notions should be of interest to Adlerians.

The sheer number of citations, with so few serious research studies of family constellation and birth order and personality, make a literature review and analysis arduous and perhaps not even productive or worthwhile.

Thus, this essay describes the meaning of family constellation, and especially birth order, its most frequently mentioned aspect, critiques usual research strategies for the study of family constellation, and suggests issues and approaches that might be useful to investigate its idiographic nature as well as its universality. The complexity and variety in family constellations allow us to understand their uniqueness, creativity, and purpose in the development of individual life styles and personalities. Measurement and quantification, as well as categorization and generalization of facets of family constellation such as birth order, decrease the uniqueness and specificity of our understanding of the personality, life style, of an individual. This constitutes an unavoidable dilemma in the use of quantitative empirical, nomothetic, methods to explain a psychological theory that is generally considered universally applicable to individuals, that is, idiographic.

Family Constellation Definition

Family constellation is a concept used to describe the child's perception of his or her most central and important environment, the family, and thereby, the most important and central influence(s) on the child's personality development. Family constellation should be thought of holistically; it includes all familial aspects that might affect the child's view of self and the world, and therefore the ways the child feels or unknowingly conceives what he or she has to be or what has to be done in order to belong, to have a place in the world, and to feel significant.

The problem here, as with all holistic notions, is a lack of specificity, which results in our inability to make anything of a holistic effect on something else, in this case the particulars of an individual's life style. We can complacently accept that the nature and entirety of the family concerns the child's personality development, but this leaves us with little specific, practical, and particular understanding of development.

In order to get to the child's phenomenological view, on which the child relies for information and feeling of who he or she is and will be, we need to analyze the components of the family from the child's viewpoint. This demands unraveling the components and dynamics of the family from the child's perspective.

The portions of family constellation that Adlerians generally look at to determine the dynamic perspectives that constitute the child's personality are most often gathered (or inferred from comments and behavior) from all family members in a family counseling setting, or from an adult remembering how he or she saw, felt, and understood the various aspects of the family when young. In essence, the important information about the family constellation has to do with the attitudes, values, behavior, and personality of each individual, as well as the central dyads, such as parents, as well as the groupings of siblings, usually those siblings closest in age.

Very briefly, we look at the attitudes, values, behaviors, and personality of each parent, with emphasis on attitudes toward sex roles, strongly held attitudes and values, and which of these the parents have in common or in conflict. The same type of data is gathered for each child while comparing the data across sibling groups and each parent. From these data, an overall picture can be drawn of the mood and atmosphere of the family, of alliances, overriding values, and particular value and behavior tensions—concluding with a panoramic view of the setting in which the child sees him- or herself having to fit. Adlerians insist that from this picture, in developing a life style, the child determines, by choosing from the options he or she sees and imagines, those ways of being and operating that the child believes will provide a place of belonging and significance in the family.

Clinical life style interpretations are formal diagnostic procedures intended to determine the way in which the patients see themselves, the world, and the ways they concluded, when young, that they must be or operate in order to have a place in the world. In the abstract, the child could make these judgments from all combinations of values, attitudes, behaviors, and personalities imaginable. In reality, the child is limited to what he or she thinks, knows, and encounters.

Nonetheless, the potential combinations and conclusions are immense. Yet, by signifying the important values, attitudes, behaviors, and personalities the child recognizes in the family, and their combinations within the family, the observant interpreter can pinpoint those central to the child's view which, in turn, constitute the child's, and eventually the adult's, specific, unique creation—his or her life style.

Research on Family Constellation

Thus, again, we confront the dilemma of research into *family constellation* (as the term is understood by Adlerians)—how to study a theory and procedure intended to ascertain a particular and unique personality and personality development with methods that compare and contrast categorized and quantified group data. No easy or obvious way presents itself to resolve this dilemma fully. The special and the unique will always be lost in this quest for the general. The enormous number of variables possible in family constellation research magnifies the dilemma, resulting in very little such research.

Birth order is a component of family constellation, the portion that has to do with sibling influence on personality development. Briefly, the notion is that with or without siblings with whom to interact, compete, or cooperate, the individual child figures out a way to garner a sense of significance within the perceived tangible and emotional resources of a family. If a first child tries one way, the second child may battle the older sibling over that way or try another way. The third child, and so on, will make a similar endeavor, albeit within the perceived available resources. An only child has no sibling competitors. A last child has only older competitors or cohabitors. Sex of the child and the meaning and value of each sex in a family affects choices and availability of means to achieve belonging. Spacing, the age between siblings, affects the child's view of which sibling or which group of siblings are relevant to belonging and fitting in to the family.

No matter how the child construes the family and his or her place within it, an emerging private logic undergirds the construal. Thus, within the child's family, the child perceives things idiosyncratically, drawing a personal, unique conclusion by weighing the values, attitudes, and behaviors of all the members. How can it be, then, that particular attributes and characteristics have been associated with birth order positions, as seen in the article by Adler in this section? If one considers all of the possible views, construals, decisions, and conclusions each child can come to in all the possible family constellations, how can a similarity arise among children of each birth order position, as Adler seems to suggest?

Adler does not describe characteristics of children of a birth order position unequivocally. He speaks of generalities, relative frequencies, and probabilities. The process is unequivocal—"a child imitates only that kind of behavior which he finds to be a successful way of asserting an equality which is denied to him on other grounds" *as the child sees it*. The specifics, the characteristics a child develops, are most likely to be evident in the family constellation, in parental and sibling values, attitudes, behaviors, and personalities. These values, attitudes, and behaviors, to some considerable degree, likely express the values, attitudes, and norms of the family's culture and society and time in history.

To my mind, significant historical, societal, and cultural factors have great bearing on the resultant similar characteristics Adler observed among individuals of each birth order position. Two themes seem to recur most frequently as the basis for the characteristics: to be good (or not) and to be successful and to achieve (or not). Were these not the two primary themes of the Judeo-Christian tradition as exemplified in European and American society in the 20th century? Are these not the simple basis of the Protestant Ethic?

Knowing that this brief, simple observation deserves a full treatise, let me proceed as if it were completely valid. In concordance with this view, then, families generally will emphasize goodness and success with nuances and definitions acceptable within the specifics of their situation. For each child, the tasks of finding one's place and of finding a sense of significance probably involves accepting, rejecting, or finding relevant alternatives to these themes as communicated in the family. The struggles and conflicts within sibling groupings frequently revolve around appreciation for being good or bad, being good or bad as a boy or as a girl, achieving success or failure, and the means for being these ways, such as being noticed or liked or controlling or number 1.

It follows, I think, that common characteristics will tend to occur in children of each birth order position as siblings jockey for position within similar value and attitude, and similar cultural and social environments. The article by Campbell, White, and Stewart (chapter 23 of this volume) may be interpreted along the lines I have been describing. They took the usual descriptors of characteristics presumed for birth order positions and then related these to the actual birth order positions. They found a *tendency* for those in specific birth order positions, though not a *majority* of those in specific birth order positions, to hold the psychological characteristics associated with that position. Their article reinforces the notion that persons of a particular birth order position may be similar in some ways. That notion has now been presented in many studies, resulting in some support for the commonly hypothesized characteristics for birth order positions and, as well, resulting in considerable lack of support in those and other studies. The strength of the Campbell et al. study is that the characteristics explored were directly based on Adlerian theory and experience.

Unlike the study by Campbell et al., Watkins' article (chapter 24 of this volume) and a review of numerous other birth order studies show that very few submit hypotheses about psychological birth order, about characteristics of persons of each birth order position, as does the Campbell et al. study. Moreover, with regard to the cultural–societal value thesis presented here, one finds very few cross-cultural studies, even fewer comparative cross-cultural studies, and a serious lacuna of birth order studies in which the authors have bothered to state the racial, ethnic, religious, class, or regional characteristics of their sample. If, as I am suggesting, some or much of the commonality of birth order positions emanates from the l–societal values and attitudes of the subjects and their families, the absence of this information may weaken the findings. For example, where multiple subgroups exist but are not separately analyzed within a sample, their value and attitude differences may lower the commonality within birth order positions for the whole sample, while commonalities among birth order positions within subgroups are overlooked.

Many researchers choose to look for differences between birth order positions with regard to whatever variable is otherwise of interest to them or available to their study. It is easy to measure and identify differences in birth order position or ordinal position according to some specific definition. Yet, many birth order studies appear to be afterthoughts, the last publications drawn from larger studies that happened to have birth order information. Hence, in birth order research one finds a large number of contradictory, unexplainable and, forgive me, trivial findings.

New Approaches to Family Constellation Research

As has been noted, Adlerians have designated particular aspects of the family useful to consider in analyzing and interpreting family constellation. Interpreters, and especially researchers, neglect some aspects that I think may be important.

Relevant birth order studies will sometimes show some of the hypothesized characteristics for birth order positions associated with the correct birth order position but, as often as not, with some of the characteristics correctly associated in one study and not in another. In the birth order literature, greater achievement motivation or achievement is the characteristic most frequently associated and found with the first-born position. Nonetheless, although it is the most consistent, it is by no means found invariably.

Adlerians are convinced that family constellation dynamics involve and explain much in the development of personality. Conveying the veracity of that conviction to others would be facilitated greatly by research studies validating this conviction. This is also the case for the dynamics of birth order. The heuristic value of generalization and characterization of birth order positions remains, but using the generalized characterizations as *descriptors* is not appropriate or correct, and obscures important basic dynamics.

The definition of psychological birth order may be one factor in obscuring the dynamics. Campbell et al. defined psychological birth order as the behavioral and personality characteristics mentioned by Adlerians as common to each birth order position. Concerning process rather than content, psychological birth order can be defined as the sense a child has of being an oldest, middle, youngest, or only child with whatever that means to the child. In this view, a child has a sense of the group of siblings of which he or she is or is not a part, and has a sense of position in relation to these others. Because of other aspects of the family constellation, such as age, spacing, and gender, a middle child can feel like an oldest of a grouping, or a youngest of a grouping, or an only between two other groupings. The child's strivings and decisions will relate to his or her feelings about options in that position. Research that accounts for this definition of psychological birth order could increase understanding of the process of personality development as influenced by birth order.

It seems to me that the aim of research in this area should be to illustrate the dynamics of the process and interpretations, and to maximize recognition of the relevant aspects of family considered in the quest to fulfill the demand for holistic understanding. Two major analyses naturally emanate from this line of research. The first would identify the major components of the family constellation, such as parental values, attitudes, behavior and personality, gender roles, family atmosphere, and mood. The second would identify these characteristics in each of the children, essentially the way in which characteristics are distributed across the siblings. Built on the two analyses, research could delineate family types and predictions could be made about birth order position characteristics in the family types.

By briefly describing and juxtaposing examples of individuals of different birth order positions in different families from different cultures and different times, I hope to illustrate the value of the research design approach I am suggesting.

- In a family with a brilliant and dominant father, the oldest girl of five sisters became a world-renowned scientist and a member of the National Academy. On the other hand, the oldest child and only daughter with three younger brothers was weary as she raised her own three children after helping raise her siblings in her traditional family of origin.
- Consider the only daughter in the midst of three brothers luxuriating as the princess. Alternatively, the only boy, fourth child among four sisters, feeling he must succeed wildly to be the man both in his family of origin and the family he creates. Or, again, the youngest of three brothers of an industrialist's family who waits contentedly in pleasure and luxury as the little prince until he must assume his rightful place in the family business.
- You may recognize this one—the rebel middle child in a preacher's family, who puzzles the family and the congregation by being so bad

when the others are so good. In contrast, look at the youngest boy of three whose father has been in and out of jail throughout the boy's life, whose older brothers had pulled off major crimes and been jailed, and who felt a failure for not having the courage or desire to be a criminal.

- Two only-child Asian women come to mind—one an aggressive and ambitious graduate student, the other a shy and submissive wife in an arranged marriage to a graduate student.

This list could be extended endlessly. Of course, we agree it could, because each individual is unique, the creator of his or her life style. Yet, we maintain that people come to their unique personality through the same processes. I am suggesting that the process is what we have to validate. Further, I am suggesting that any similarities among people of the same place in the process, of the same birth order, are based on the similarities among their families—that, in turn, have to do with the societal and cultural similarities of the families.

To my view, the most provocative aspect of the family that has not been prominently considered in Adlerian family constellation diagnosis and research is *culture, including ethnicity and religion, as well as subculture, such as social class and region.* These factors may be contained in the information gathered from a client in data collection but may not be recognized for their potential usefulness. As individuals and families identify with them, culture and subculture provide a background of assumptions, values, attitudes, and preferred behaviors. These may have a stronger impact on individuals within the family context than individually derived preferences. This is an issue for Adlerian psychology as it assumes universality and is especially crucial when it assumes that particular behaviors or goals result from particular placement in families. The values and attitudes of the family, of the parents, may be set in those of their particular cultures, religions, classes, and regions.

Another frequently overlooked influence on the views of family members is cohort. When *was* the child a child, and when *were* the parents both parents and children themselves? The time and place in which people are raised influence their values, attitudes, and behaviors. Cultural and cohort affects on values and behaviors of families should not be overlooked or underestimated and should, I think, be included in family constellation research.

The effects of culture and cohort rightly imply that changes over historical time might alter the nature both of families and of birth order positions. Among the notable changes since Adler's hypothesized birth order characteristics are actual changes in families themselves. His proposed characteristics are generalizations for all children of a birth order position. Should we not also question whether we might find differences in characteristics for birth order positions in differing kinds of families? Not only should we investigate the universality of the dynamics in different types of families, but, as well, the characteristics. If there are such differences, their strength and significance is currently being obscured. It might well be worthwhile to investigate birth order characteristics in traditional families and divorced families, single-parent families of each sex, blended families, and other less so-called traditional arrangements.

Summary and Conclusion

In this essay I have tried to speak to Adlerian understandings of family constellation and birth order and digest and critique the relevant research ending with some suggestions for future research approaches. Very little Adlerian family constellation research exists per se. Nevertheless, the bulk of the enormous family research literature investigates systems, approaches, and variables that might be of interest to Adlerians. To be useful to Adlerians, these results need translation or contortion to fit Adlerian premises. The challenge to Adlerian researchers is to accommodate as many of the significant aspects of family constellation as possible to approach a holistic family view. I suggest that research to determine the relative importance of the elements of family constellation focusing on personality development and characteristics be carried out so that subsequent research can construct predictive models. This would be no easy task, but might constitute a useful long-term research agenda.

Numerous birth order studies have produced contradictory and meaningless findings. Adlerians continue to contend that much of personality development occurs within the sibship, within the family constellation. That assertion, I maintain, demands the thrust of research efforts. Investigative designs that take into account other aspects of the family and explore their distribution and affects across sibling sets would be appropriate.

The continuing effort to match personality characteristics with birth order positions, particularly trying to support characteristic matches that were proposed decades ago, has had moderate success at best. Overall, the results of this type of research have merely *suggested* that there is something to the notion. No hard and fast associations representing large percentages of persons in a birth order position have been found.

Herein, I have hypothesized that the similarities Adler observed and proposed for persons in each birth order position, and that so many researchers since have tried to find, may be related to the similarities among families of a certain type at a certain time and place. The population available for study now is far more heterogeneous than the population with which Adler was in contact. Cultural differences—racial, ethnic, and religious—social differences, socioeconomic status and region, cohort and age, and family organization may all affect the nature of families. Research that analyzes these differences may well find that contemporary value and attitude priorities in families influence children's views and siblings' choices and struggles. If there is potential for strong relationships between personality characteristics and birth order positions it will be found, I suggest, through studying and analyzing both within subgroup similarities and between subgroup differences.

CHAPTER 22

Position in Family Constellation Influences Life-Style

ALFRED ADLER

It is a common fallacy to imagine that children of the same family are formed in the same environment. Of course there is much which is the same for all children in the same home, but the psychic situation of each child is individual and differs from that of others, because of the order of their succession.

There has been some misunderstanding of my custom of classification according to position in the family. It is not, of course, the child's number in the order of successive births which influences his character, but the *situation* into which he is born and the way in which he *interprets* it. Thus, if the eldest child is feeble-minded or suppressed, the second child may acquire a style of life similar to that of an eldest child; and in a large family, if two are born much later than the rest, and grow up together separated from the older children, the elder of these may develop like a first child. This also happens sometimes in the case of twins.

Position of the First Child

The first child has the unique position of having been the only one at the beginning of his life. Being thus the central interest he is generally spoiled.

In this he resembles the only child, and spoiling is almost inevitable in both cases. The first child, however, usually suffers an important change of situation, being dethroned when the second baby is born. The child is generally quite unprepared for this change, and feels that he has lost his position as the center of love and attention. He then comes into great tension for he is far from his goal and there begins a striving to regain favor. He uses all the means by which he has hitherto attracted notice. Of course he would like to go the best way about it, to be beloved for his goodness; but good behavior is apt to pass unnoticed when everyone is busied with the new-comer. He is then likely to change his tactics and to resort to old activities which have previously attracted attention—even if it was unfavorable attention.

If intelligent, he acts intelligently, but not necessarily in harmony with the family's demands. Antagonism, disobedience, attacks on the baby, or even attempts to play the part of a baby, compel the parents to give renewed attention to his existence. A spoiled child must have the spotlight upon himself, even at the cost of expressing weakness or imitating a return to babyhood. Thus, under the influence of the past, he attains his goal in the present by unsuitable means; suddenly showing inability to function alone, needing assistance in eating and excretion and requiring constant watching, or compelling solicitude by getting into danger and terrifying the parents. The appearance of such characteristics as jealousy, envy, or egotism has an obvious relation to the outside circumstances, but he may also indulge in—or prolong—illnesses such as asthma and whooping cough. The tension in certain types (depending upon the bodily organization) may produce headache, migraine, stomach trouble, petit mal, or hysterical chorea. Slighter symptoms are evinced in a tired appearance and a general change of behavior for the worse, with which the child impresses his parents. Naturally, the later the rival baby is born, the more intelligible and understandable will the methods appear which the first child uses in his change of behavior. If dethroned very early, the eldest child's efforts are largely "instinctive" in character. The style of his striving will in any case be conditioned by the reaction of others in the environment and his evaluation of it. If, for instance, the dethroned child finds that fighting does not pay, he may lose hope, become depressed, and score a success by worrying and frightening the parents. After learning that such ways are successful for him he will resort to ever more subtle uses of misfortune to gain his end.

The type of activity which in later life will be based on the prototype was shown in the case of a man who became afraid to swallow for fear of choking. Why did he select this symptom instead of another? The patient had an immediate social difficulty in the behavior of an intimate friend, who attacked him violently. Both the patient and his wife had come to the conclusion that he must put up with it no longer, but he did not feel strong enough to face the struggle. Upon inquiry into his childhood, it appeared that he had had such a difficulty in connection with swallowing before. He was the eldest child, and had been surpassed by his younger brother, but he had at that time been able, by means of difficulty in eating, to make his father and mother watch over him. Now faced with a personal defeat in later life, and not knowing what to do about it, he fell back upon this old line of defense, as though it might make someone watch over him and help him.

Effects of Dethronement

The dethronement of the first child by another may make it turn away from the mother towards the father, and a very critical attitude towards the mother will then persist ever after. A person of this type is always afraid of being "pushed back" all through life; and we notice that in all his affairs he likes to make one step forward and then one backward, so that nothing decisive can happen. He always feels justified in fearing that a favorable situation will change. Towards all the three life-questions he will take up a hesitative attitude, with certain problem behavior and neurotic tendencies. Problem behavior and symptoms will be felt by him to be a help and a security. He will approach society, for example, with a hostile attitude; he may constantly be changing his occupation; and in his erotic life he may experience failure in functioning, and may show polygamous tendencies —if he falls in love with one person he very quickly falls in love with another. Dubious and unwilling to decide anything, he becomes a great procrastinator. I met a very perfect example of this type once, and his earliest remembrance was this: "At three years of age I caught scarlet fever. By mistake my mother gave me carbolic acid for a gargle, and I nearly died."

He had a younger sister who was the favorite of his mother. Later in life this patient developed a curious fantasy of a young girl ruling and bullying an older one. Sometimes he imagined her riding the old woman like a horse.

First Child May Keep Position

The eldest child may, however, be so firmly fixed in the parents' favor that he cannot be supplanted. This may be either by virtue of his own good native endowment and development, or because of the second child's inferiority, if the latter is ugly, organically handicapped, or badly brought up. In such a case it is the second child who becomes the problem, and the eldest may have a very satisfactory development, as in the following case:

Of two brothers, differing four years in age, the elder had been much attached to the mother, and when the younger was born the father had been ill for some time. Caring for the father took the entire time and most of the attention of the mother. The elder boy, trained in friendship and obedience to her, tried to help and relieve her, and the younger boy was put into the care of a nurse, who spoiled him. This situation lasted for some years, so that the younger child had no reasonable chance to compete with the elder for the love of the mother; and he soon abandoned the useful side of life, and became wild and disobedient. His behavior became still worse four years later, when a little sister was born, to whom the mother was able to devote herself owing to the death of the father. Thus twice excluded from the mother's attention and spoiled by the nurse, this second child turned out to be the worst pupil in his class, while the elder boy was always the best. Feeling hopelessly handicapped in competition with his brother, unloved at home, and reproached at the school (from which he was finally expelled), this second son could find no goal in life but to dominate his mother by worrying her. Being physically stronger than either the brother or sister, he took to tyrannizing over them. He trifled away his time, and at puberty he began to waste money and to incur debts. His honest and well-meaning parent provided a very strict tutor for him who did not, of course, grasp the situation, and dealt with it superficially by punishments. The boy grew into a man who strove to get rich quickly and easily. He fell an easy prey to unscrupulous advisers, followed them into fruitless enterprises, and not only lost his money but involved his mother in his dishonorable debts.

The facts of the case clearly showed that all the courage this man ever displayed resulted from his unsatisfied desire to conquer. He played a queer game from time to time, especially when things went against him. His nurse was now an old woman, earning her living in the family as a superior servant; she still worshipped the second boy and always interceded for him in his numerous scrapes. The odd sport in which he indulged was to lock her in a room with him and make her play at soldiers with him, commanding her to march, to fall and to jump up again at his orders; and sometimes he quickened her obedience by beating her wth a stick. She always obeyed although she screamed and resisted.

This singular sport revealed what he really wanted, the completest domination in the easiest way. Some writers would describe this as sadistic conduct, but I demur at the use of a word which implies a sexual interest, for I could discover nothing of the kind in it. In sexual matters the man was practically normal, except that he changed his mates too frequently and always chose inferiors. Genuine sadism itself is a domineering tendency availing itself of the sexual urge for its expression, owing to the discouragement of the individual in other spheres.

In the end this man brought himself into very bad circumstances, while the elder brother became very successful and highly respected.

Attitude of Eldest Toward Authority

The eldest child, partly because he often finds himself acting as representative of the parental authority, is usually a great believer in power and the laws. The intuitive perception of this fact is shown in the ancient and persistent custom of primogeniture. It is often observable in literature. Thus Theodore Fontane wrote of his perplexity at his father's pleasure in hearing that ten thousand Poles had defeated twenty thousand Russians. His father was a French emigrant who had sided with the Poles, but to the writer it was an inconceivable idea that the stronger could be beaten; he felt that the status quo should be preserved and that might must, and ought to, succeed. This was because Theodore Fontane was a first child. In any case the eldest child is readier than others to recognize power, and likes to support it. This is shown in the lives of scientists, politicians, and artists, as well as in those of simpler people. Even if the person is a revolutionary we find him harboring a conservative tendency, as in the case of Robespierre.

Position of Second Child

The second child is in a very different situation, never having had the experience of being the only one. Though he is also petted at first, he is never the sole center of attention. From the first, life is for him more or less of a race; the first child sets the pace, and the second tries to surpass him. What results from competition between two such children depends on their courage and self-confidence. If the elder becomes discouraged he will be in a serious situation, especially if the younger is really strong and outstrips him.

If the second child loses hope of equality he will try to *shine* more rather than to *be* more. That is, if the elder is too strong for him, the younger will tend to escape to the useless side of life. This is shown in many cases of problem behavior in children where laziness, lying or stealing begins to pave the way towards neurosis, crime, and self-destruction.

As a rule, however, the second child is in a better position than the first. His pacemaker stimulates him to effort. Also, it is a common thing for the first child to hasten his own dethronement by fighting against it with envy, jealousy and truculence, which lower him in the parental favor. It is when the first child is brilliant that the second child is in the worst situation.

But the elder child is not always the worst sufferer, even when dethroned. I saw this in the case of a girl who had been the center of attention and extremely spoiled until she reached the age of three, when a sister was born.

After the birth of her sister she became very jealous and developed into a problem-child. The younger sister grew up with sweet and charming manners, and was much the more beloved of the two. But when this younger sister came to school the situation was not to her taste; she was no longer spoiled and, being unprepared to encounter difficulties, was frightened and tried to withdraw. To escape defeat both in fact and in appearance, she adopted a device very common among the discouraged—she never finished anything she was doing, so that it always escaped final judgment, and she wasted as much time as possible. We find that time is the great enemy of such discouraged people for, under the pressure of the requirements made on them by social living, they feel as if time were persecuting them continually with the question, "How will you use me?" Hence their strange efforts to "kill time" with silly activities. This girl always came late and postponed every action. She did not antagonize anyone, even if reproved, but her charm and sweetness, which were maintained as before, did not prevent her from being a greater worry and burden than her fighting sister.

When the elder sister became engaged to be married the younger sister was desperately unhappy. Though she had won the first stage of the race with her rival by gentleness and obedience, she had given up in the later stages of school and social life. She felt her sister's marriage as a defeat, and that her ony hope of regaining ground would be to marry also. However, she had not courage enough to choose a suitable partner, and automatically sought a second-best. First she fell in love with a man suffering seriously from tuberculosis. Can we regard this as a step forward ? Does it contradict her preestablished custom of leaving every task unfinished? Not at all. The poor health of her lover and her parents' natural resistance to the match were sure causes of delay and frustration. She preferred an element of impossibility in her choice. Another scarcely eligible partner appeared later in her life, in a man thirty years older than herself. He was senile, but did not die as the previous one had done, and the marriage took place. However, it was not a great success for her, as the attitude of hopelessness in which she had trained herself did not allow her to undertake any useful activity. It also inhibited her sexual life, which she considered disgusting, feeling humiliated and soiled by it. She used her usual methods to evade love and postpone relations at the appropriate times. She did not quite succeed in this, however, and became pregnant, which she regarded as another hopeless state, and from that time onward not only rejected caresses but complained that she felt soiled, and began to wash and clean all day long. She not only washed herself, but cleaned everything that had been touched by her husband, by the maid servant or the visitors, including furniture, linen, and shoes. Soon she allowed no one to touch any of the objects in her room, and lived under the stress of a neurosis—in this case, a washing-compulsion. Thus she was excused from the solution of her problems, and attained a very lofty goal of superiority—she felt more fastidiously clean than anyone else.

Exaggerated striving for a lofty goal of high distinctiveness is well expressed in the neurosis of "washing-compulsion." As far as I have been able to ascertain, this illness is always used as a means of avoiding sexual relations by a person who feels that sex is "dirty." Invariably it gives the fantastic compensation of feeling cleaner than everybody else.

However, due to his feeling life to be a race, the second child usually trains himself more stiffly and, if his courage holds, is well on the way to overcome the eldest on his own ground. If he has a little less courage he will choose to surpass the eldest in another field, and if still less, he will become more critical and antagonistic than usual, not in an objective but in a personal manner. In childhood this attitude appears in relation to trifles: he will want the window shut when the elder opens it, turn on the light when the other wants it extinguished, and be consistently contrary and opposite.

This situation is well described in the Bible story of Esau and Jacob, where Jacob succeeds in usurping the privileges of the eldest. The second child lives in a condition like that of an engine under a constantly excessive head of steam. It was well expressed by a little boy of four, who cried out, weeping, "I am so unhappy because I can *never* be as old as my brother."

The fact that children repeat the psychic behavior of older brothers and sisters and of parents is, by some writers, attributed to an "instinct" of imitation or to "identification" of the self with another; but it is explained better when we see that a child imitates only that kind of behavior which he finds to be a successful way of asserting an equality which is denied to him on other grounds. Psychic resemblances to the conduct of ancestors or even of savages do not signify that the pattern of psychic reaction is hereditary, but that many individuals use the same means of offense and defense in similar situations. When we find so much resemblance between all first children, all second, and all youngest children, we may well ask what part is left for heredity to play in determining those resemblances. Thus, as psychologists we have also not sufficient evidence to accept the theory that the mental development of the individual ought to repeat the development of the race of mankind in successive stages.

In his later life, the second child is rarely able to endure the strict leadership of others or to accept the idea of "eternal laws." He will be much more inclined to believe, rightly or wrongly, that there is no power in the world which cannot be overthrown. Beware of his revolutionary subtleties! I have known quite a few cases in which the second child has availed himself of the strangest means to undermine the power of ruling persons or traditions. Not everybody, certainly not these rebels themselves, would easily agree with my view of their behavior. For though it is possible to endanger a ruling power with slander, there are more insidious ways. For example, by means of excessive praise one may idealize and glorify a man or a method until the reality cannot stand up to it. Both methods are employed in Mark Antony's oration in "Julius Caesar." I have shown elsewhere how Dostoievsky made masterly use of the latter means, perhaps unconsciously, to undermine the pillars of old Russia. Those who remember his representation of Father Zosima in "The Brothers Karamazov," and who also recall the fact that he was a second son, will have little difficulty agreeing with my suggestion regarding the influence played by position in the family.

I need hardly say that the style of life of a second child, like that of the first, may also appear in another child—one in a different chronological position in the family—if the *situation* is of a similar pattern.

Situation of Youngest Child

The youngest child is also a distinct type, exhibiting certain characteristics of style which we seldom fail to find. He has always been the baby of the family, and has never known the tragedy of being dispossessed by a younger, which is more or less the fate of all other children. In this respect his situation is a favored one, and his education is often relatively better, as the economic position of the family is likely to be more secure in its later years. The grown-up children not infrequently join with the parents in spoiling the youngest child, who is thus likely to be too much indulged. On the other hand, the youngest may also be too much stimulated by elders—both mistakes are well known to our educationists. In the former case (of over-indulgence) the child will strive throughout life to be supported by others. In the latter case the child will rather resemble a second child, proceeding competitively, striving to overtake all those who set the pace for him, and in many cases failing to do so. Often, therefore, he looks for a field of activity remote from that of the other members of the family—in which case, I believe, he gives a sign of hidden cowardice. If the family is commercial, for instance, the youngest often inclines to art or poetry; if scientific, he wants to be a salesman. I have remarked elsewhere that many of the most successful men of our time were youngest children, and I am convinced this is also the case in any other age. In biblical history we find a remarkable number of youngest children among the leading characters, such as David, Saul, and Joseph. The story of Joseph is a particularly good example, and illustrates many of the views we have advanced. His younger brother Benjamin was seventeen years his junior and, therefore, played little part in Joseph's development. Joseph's psychological position, therefore, was that of a youngest child.

It is interesting to note how well Joseph's brethren understood his dreams. More precisely, I should say that they understood the feeling and emotion of the dreamer, a point to which I shall return later. The purpose of a dream is not to be understood but to create a mood and a tension of feeling.

In the fairy tales of all ages and peoples the youngest child plays the role of a conqueror. I infer that in earlier times, when both circumstances and men's apprehension of them were simpler, it was easier to collect experiences and to understand the coherent current of the life of the latest-born. This traditional grasp of character survives in folk-lore when the actual experiences are forgotten.

A strange case of the type of youngest child who is spoiled, which I have already given elsewhere, is that of a man with a "begging" style of life. I found another such case in that of a physician who was having difficulties with his mouth and was fearful of cancer. For twenty years he had been unable to swallow normally and could take only liquid food. He had recently had a dental plate made for him, which he was continually pushing up and down with his tongue, a habit which caused pain and soreness of the tongue, so that he feared he was developing cancer.

He was the youngest of a family of three, with two older sisters, and had been weakly and much indulged. At the age of forty he could eat only alone or with his sisters. This is a clear indication that he was comfortable only in his favorite situation—of being spoiled by the sisters. Every approach to society had been difficult for him. He had no friends, and only a few associates whom he met weekly in a restaurant. His attitude towards the three questions of life being one of fear and trembling, we can understand that his tension when with other people made him unable to swallow food. He lived in a kind of stage fright, fearful that he was not making a sufficiently good impression.

This man answered the second life-question (that of occupation) with tolerable competence, because his parents had been poor and he could not live without earning, but he suffered exceedingly in his profession, and nearly fainted when he had to take his examinations. His ambition, as a general practitioner, was to obtain a position with a fixed salary, and, later on, a pension. This great attraction to a safe official position is a sign of a feeling of insecurity. People with a deep sense of inadequacy commonly aspire to the "safe job." For years he gave himself up to his symptoms. When he became older he lost some of his teeth, and decided to have a plate made, which became the occasion of the development of his latest symptom.

When he came to me, the patient was sixty years of age, and was still living in the care of his two sisters. Both were suffering from their age, and it was clear to me that this man, aging, and spoiled by two unmarried and much older women, was facing a new situation. He was very much afraid his sisters would die. What should he do in that case—he who needed to be continually noticed and watched over? He had never been in love, for he could never find a woman whom he could trust with his fragile happiness! How could he believe that anyone would spoil him as his mother and older sisters had done. It was easy to guess the form of his sexuality—masturbation, and some petting affairs with girls. But recently an older woman had wanted to marry him; and he wished to appear more pleasant and attractive in behavior. The beginning of a struggle seemed imminent, but his new dental plate came to the rescue. In the nick of time he became anxious about contracting cancer of the tongue.

He himself, as a doctor, was very much in doubt about the reality of this cancer. The many surgeons and physicians he consulted all tried to dissuade him from belief in it; but he persisted in his uncertainty, continued to press his tongue against the plate until it hurt; then he consulted another doctor.

Such preoccupations—"overvalued ideas," as Wernicke calls them—are carefully cherished in the arrangement of a neurosis. The patient shies away from the right objective by fixing his glances more and more firmly upon a point somewhere off a good, productive course. He does this in order to swerve out of a direction which is beginning to be indicated by logical necessity. The logical solution of his problem would be antagonistic to his style of life, and as the style of life rules (since it is the only way of approach to life the individual has learned), he has to establish emotions and feelings which will support his life-style and will insure his escape.

In spite of the fact that this man was sixty years old, the only logical solution was to find a trustworthy substitute for his spoiling sisters before their departure. His distrustful mind could not rise to the hope of achieving this possibility; nor could his doubts be dissipated by logic, because he had built up throughout his life a definite resistance to marriage. Because it improved his appearance, the dental plate should have been a help towards marriage but he made it into an insuperable impediment.

In the treatment of this case it was useless to attack-the belief in the cancer. When he understood the coherence of his behavior the patient's symptoms were very much alleviated. The next day he told me of a dream: "I was sitting in the house of a third sister at a birthday celebration of her thirteen-year-old son. I was entirely healthy, felt no pain, and could swallow anything." But this dream was related to an episode in his life which took place fifteen years before. Its meaning is very obvious: "If only I were fifteen years younger." Thus is the style maintained.

Difficulties of Only Child

The only child also has his typical difficulties. Retaining the center of the stage without effort, and generally pampered, he forms a style of life that calls for his being supported by others and at the same time ruling them. Very often he grows up in an intimate environment. The parents may be fearful people and afraid to have more children. Sometimes the mother, neurotic before this advent, does not feel equal to rearing more children, and develops such behavior that everyone must feel, "It is a blessing that this woman has no more children." Birth control may absorb much of the attention of the family, in which case we may infer tension, and that the two parents are united to carry on their life in anxiety. The care then devoted to the only child never ceases by day or night, and often impresses the child with a belief that it is an almost mortal danger not to be watched and guarded. Such children often grow up cautious, and sooner or later they may often become successful and gain the esteem and attention they desire. But if they come into wholly different conditions where life is difficult for them, they may show striking insufficiency.

Only children are often sweet and affectionate, and later in life they may develop charming manners in order to appeal to others, because they have trained themselves this way both in early life and later. They are usually closer to the more indulgent parent, which is generally the mother; and in some cases develop a hostile attitude towards the other parent.

The proper upbringing of an only child is not easy, but it is possible for parents to understand the problem and to solve it correctly. We do not regard the only child's situation as dangerous, but we find that, in the absence of the best educational methods, very bad results frequently occur which would have been avoided if there had been brothers and sisters.

Case of Homosexual Development

I will give a case of the development of an only child, a boy whose attachment was entirely to the mother. The father was of no importance in the family; he contributed materially but was obviously without interest in the child. The mother was a dressmaker who worked at home, and the little boy spent all his time with her, sitting or playing beside her. He played at sewing, imitating his mother's activity, and ultimately became very very proficient in it, but he never took any part in boys' games. The mother left the house each day at five P.M. to deliver her work, and returned punctually at six. During that time the boy was left alone with an older girl cousin, and played with sewing materials. He became interested in timepieces, because he was always looking for his mother's return. He could tell the time when he was only three years old.

The cousin played games with him in which she was the bridegroom and he was the bride, and it is noteworthy that he looked more like a girl than she did. When he came to school he was quite unprepared to associate with boys, but he was able to establish himself as a favored exception, for others liked his mild and courteous disposition. He began to approach his goal of superiority by being attractive, especially so to boys and men. At fourteen years of age he acted the part of a girl in a school play. The audience had not the slightest doubt that he was a girl; a young fellow began to flirt with him and he was much pleased to have excited such admiration.

He had worn girlish dress during his first four years, and until the age of ten he did not know whether he was a boy or a girl. When his sex was explained to him he began to masturbate, and in his fantasy he soon connected sexual desire with what he had felt when boys touched him or kissed him. To be admired and wooed was his goal in life; to this end he accommodated all his characteristics in such a way that he might be admired especially by boys. His older cousin was the only girl he had known, and she was gentle and sweet, but she had played the man's role in their games and otherwise she had ruled him like his mother. A great feeling of inferiority was his legacy from his mother's overindulgent and excessive care. She had married late, at the age of thirty-eight, and she did not wish to have more children by the husband she disliked. Her anxiety, then was doubtless of earlier origin, and her late marriage indicative of a hesitant attitude to life. Very strict in sexual matters, she wanted her child to be educated in ignorance of sex.

At the age of sixteen this patient looked and walked like a flirtatious girl, and he soon fell into the snare of homosexuality. In order to comprehend this development we must remember that he had had, in a psychological sense, the education of a girl, and that the difference between the sexes had been made clear to him much too late in his development. Also he had experienced his triumphs in the feminine role, and had no certainty of gaining as much by playing the man. In the imitation of girlish behavior he could not but see an open road to his goal of superiority.

It is my experience that boys who have this type of upbringing always look like girls. The growth of the organs and probably also of the glands is partially ruled by the environment and the child's attitude toward it; and they are adapted to them. Thus if such an early environmental training towards femininity is succeeded by a personal goal of the same tendency, the wish to be a favored girl will influence not only the mind, but also the carriage and even the body.

This case illustrates very clearly how a pervert trains himself mentally into his abnormal attitude towards sex. There is no necessity to postulate an inborn or hereditary organic deviation.

When the boy in question came to me he was involved in a relationship with another boy who was the neglected second child of a very domineering mother; this boy's striving was to overcome men by his personal charm. It was by his charm that he had succeeded early in ruling his weak father. When he reached the age of sexual expression he was shocked. His notion of women was founded upon experience of his dominering mother, who had neglected him. He felt the need to dominate but he entertained no hope of dominating women for, in accordance with the generalization he had made of his early experiences connected with a strong and ruling mother, he had come to feel that a woman was too powerful to control. His only chance to be the victor, he felt, was in relationship with men; so he turned homosexual. Consider then the hopeless situation of my patient! He wanted to conquer by female means—by having the charm of a girl—but his friend wanted to be a conqueror of men.

I was able to make my patient realize that, whatever he himself thought or felt in this liaison, his friend felt himself to be a conquering man-charmer. My patient, therefore, could not be sure that his was the real conquest, and his homosexuality was accordingly checked. By this means I was able to break off the relationship, for he saw that it was stupid to enter into such a fruitless competition. This also made it easier for him to understand that his abnormality was due to a lack of interest in others, and that his feeling of inadequacy, as the result of being pampered, had led him to measure everything in terms of personal triumph. He then left me for some months; when he visited me again he had had sexual relations with a girl, but had tried to play a masochistic part towards her. He obviously wished, in order to prove to himself that his original view of the world was correct, to experience with her the same inferiority that he had felt with his mother and cousin. This macochistic attitude was shown in the fact that his goal of superiority required that the girl should do to him what he commanded, and he wished to complete the act at this point, without achieving sexual intercourse, so that the normal was still excluded.

The great difficulty of changing a homosexual lies not only in his lack of general social adjustment, but also in the invariable absence of right training toward the sexual role, which ought to begin in early childhood. The attitude towards the other sex is strained in a mistaken direction almost from the beginning of life. In order to realize this fact one must note the kind of intelligence, of behavior, and of expectations which such a case exhibits. Compare normal persons walking in the street or mixing in society with a homosexual in the same situations! Those who are normal are chiefly interested in the opposite sex, the homosexuals only in their own. The latter evade normal sexuality not only in behavior but even in dreams. The patient I have just described used frequently to dream that he was climbing a mountain, and ascending it by a serpentine road. The dream expresses his discouraged and circuitous approach to life. He moved rather like a snake, bending his head and shoulders at every step.

In conclusion I will recall some of the most disastrous cases I have known among only children. A woman asked me to help her and her husband in the case of their only boy, who tyrannized over them terribly. He was then sixteen, a very good pupil at school, but quarrelsome and insulting in behavior. He was specially combative toward his father, who had been stricter with him than had the mother. He antagonized both parents continually, and if he could not get what he wanted he made open attack, sometimes wrestling with his father, spitting at him, and using bad language. Such a development is possible in the case of a pampered and only child who is trained to give nothing but to expect everything—and gets it, until the time comes when indulgence can go on no longer. In such cases it is difficult to treat the patient in his old environment, because too many old recollections are revived, which disturb the harmony of the family.

Another case was brought to me, a boy of eighteen, who had been accused of murdering his father. He was an only child, and a spoiled one, who had stopped his education and was wasting, in bad company, all the money he could extort from his parents. One day when his father refused to give him money, the boy killed him by hitting him on the head with a hammer. No one but the lawyer who was defending him knew that he had killed another person several months before. It was obvious that he felt perfectly sure of escaping discovery this second time.

In yet another case of criminal development, an only boy was brought up by a very well-educated woman who wanted him to be a genius. At her death another experienced woman continued his nurture in the same way, until she became aware of his tyrannical tendencies. She believed it to be due to sexual repression, and had him analyzed. His tyrannical attitude did not cease, however, and she then wished to be rid of him. But he broke into her house one night intending to rob her, and strangled her.

All the characteristics which I have described as typical of certain positions in the family can, of course, be modified by other circumstances. With all their possibilities of variation, however, the outlines of these patterns of behavior will be found to be substantially correct. Among other possibilities, one may mention the position of a boy growing up among girls. If he is older than they are he develops very much the same as an elder brother close to a younger sister. Differences in age, in the affection of the parents, and in the preparation for life, are all reflected in the individual pattern of behavior.

Where a female majority and feminine influence dominates the whole environment, a single boy is likely to have a goal of superiority and a style of life which are directed towards femininity. This occurs in various degrees and various ways: in a humble devotion to women and worship of them, in an imitative attitude, tending towards homosexuality, or in a tyrannical attitude towards women. People usually avoid educating boys in a too feminine environment; for it seems to be a matter of general experience that such children develop towards one of two extremes—either exaggerated vanity or audacity. In the story of Achilles there are many points from which we may assume that the latter case was well understood in antiquity.

Importance of Evaluation of Women and Men

We find the same contradictory possibilities in the cases of only girls who grow up among boys or in a wholly masculine environment. In such circumstances a girl may, of course, be spoiled with too much attention and affection; but she may also adopt boys' attitudes and wish to avoid looking like a girl. In any case, what happens is largely dependent upon how men and women are *valued* in the environment. In every environment there is always a prevailing attitude of mind in regard to this question; and it is largely in accordance with the relative value given to men and women in that attitude that the child will wish to assume the role of a man or of a woman.

Other views of life which prevail in the family may also influence the pattern of a child's behavior, or bring it into difficulties, as for example the superstition about character being inherited, and the belief in fancy methods of education. Any exaggerated method of education is likely to cause injury to the child, a fact we can often trace in the children of teachers, psychologists, doctors, and people engaged in the administration of laws—policemen, lawyers, officers, and clergymen. Such educational exaggerations often come to light in the life-histories of problem-children, delinquents, and neurotics. The influence of both factors—the superstition regarding heredity and a fanatical mode of training—appear in the following case:

A woman came to me with a daughter of nine, both of them in tears and desperation. The mother told me that the girl had only recently come to live with her, after having spent years under the care of foster parents in the country. There she had completed the third grade of her schooling, and she had entered the fourth grade in the city school, but her work became so bad that her teacher had her put back into the third grade. Soon afterwards her work had become still worse, and she was graded still lower and put in the second. The mother was thoroughly upset at this and obsessed with the idea that her daughter's deficiency was inherited from the father.

At first sight it was evident to me that the mother was treating the child with exaggerated educational insistence, which in this case was particularly unfortunate, because the girl had been brought up in a congenial, easy environment and expected still greater kindness from the mother. But in her eagerness that her child should not be a failure the mother was over-strict, and this gave the child the keenest disappointment. She developed a great emotional tension which effectually blocked her progress both at school and at home. Exhortation, reproaches, criticism, and spanking only intensified the emotion, with consequent hopelessness on both sides. To confirm my impression, I spoke with the girl alone about her foster parents. She told me how happy her life with them had been; and then, bursting into tears, told me also how she had at first enjoyed being with her mother.

I had to make the mother understand the mistakes in which she had become involved. The girl could not be expected to put up with such a hard training. Putting myself in her place I could perfectly understand her conduct as an intelligent reaction—that is, as a form of accusation and revenge. In a situation of this type, but where there is less social feeling, it is perfectly possible for a child to turn delinquent, neurotic, or even to attempt suicide. But in this case I was sure it would not be difficult for the girl to improve if the mother could be convinced of the truth, and could impress the child with a sufficiently definite change of attitude. I therefore took the mother in hand, and explained to her that the belief in inheritance was nothing but a nuisance, after which I helped her to realize what her daughter had not unreasonably expected when she came to live with her, and how she must have been disappointed and shaken by such disciplinary treatment, to the point of utter inability to do what was expected of her. I wanted the mother to confess to the child that she had been mistaken and would like to reform her method, so I told her I did not really believe she could bring herself to do it, but that it was what I would do in the circumstances. She answered decidedly, "I will do it." In my presence and with my help, she explained her mistake to the child, and they kissed and embraced and cried together. Two weeks later they both visited me, gay and smiling and very well satisfied. The mother brought me a message from the third-grade teacher: "a miracle must have happened. The girl is the best pupil in the class."

CHAPTER 23

The Relationship of Psychological Birth Order to Actual Birth Order

LINDA CAMPBELL, JOANNA WHITE, and ALAN STEWART

The importance of birth order was first identified and described by Alfred Adler in 1918 (Ansbacher & Ansbacher, 1956). In developing his perception of the importance of birth order, Adler emphasized, "It is not the child's number in the order of successive births which influences his character, but the situation into which he is born and the way in which he interprets it" (Adler, 1956, p. 377). Birth order is a location in a social structure (family) and the psychological position of children is the way they locate or perceive themselves in the family structure (Shulman & Mosak, 1977). Individuals do not, by virtue of birth-order position, necessarily exhibit any traits or patterns common to persons of that birth-order position. The psychological position of the person is of greater importance (Manaster & Corsini, 1982).

Every person has a self-perceived place in his or her family. This perceived position may or may not be the person's chronological place in the ordinal birth order of the family. This perceived position is the psychological birth order of an individual.

Adler (1928) described common characteristics of particular birth-order positions and these descriptions have been supported in the literature over time (Dreikurs & Soltz, 1964; Pepper, 1964; Sweeney, 1981). Adler (1928) identified oldest children as often feeling powerful and influential. Because they are only children for some time, they enjoy being the center of attention; however, when the second child is born, they often feel dethroned. Second children always follow in the footsteps of an older child, seeing life as a race against the older sibling.

When the third child is born, the second child becomes "squeezed" (Pepper, 1964) and often competes with the youngest. Last or youngest children work to find significance in light of the siblings preceding them. They may become discouraged and lazy. Pepper (1964) described only children as typically pampered, enjoying the center of attention, and often feeling insecure due to the parents' anxiety.

As Adler cautioned (1928), each preceding author cautions that children make early decisions related to their place in the family based upon their individual creative perceptions. Therefore, it is more important to understand a person's psychological birth order. Also, variables such as gender, spacing, and family atmosphere must be taken into account.

Psychological birth order is recognized as a critically important variable in birth-order research (Jordan, Whiteside, & Manaster, 1982); however, few studies have attempted to classify individuals by psychological rather than ordinal birth order (Lohman, Lohman, & Christensen, 1985). More frequently, researchers have used the ordinal position as an independent variable with implications for psychological birth order.

Lohman et al. (1985), in distinguishing between psychological and birth-order positions, found that in assessing differential trait identification (a) 80% of the firstborn children identified with the psychological position of the oldest and, therefore, may be a more homogeneous group, (b) psychologically first children rate themselves higher on socially desirable traits than others rate themselves, and (c) birth-order and psychological position are different especially for middle and youngest children.

Criticisms of birth-order studies have most frequently identified the need to include gender of subject and siblings (Jordan, Whiteside, & Manaster, 1982), family size and density (Fraser & Nystul, 1983; Gallagher & Cowen, 1977), birth spacing (Schooler, 1972), and psychological birth order (Melillo, 1983; Shulman & Mosak, 1977).

The purpose of this study is to (a) present evidence supportive of the existence of the psychological birth-order construct, (b) introduce an instrument, the psychological birth-order inventory (PBOI), that measures psychological birth order, and (c) examine the patterns of relationships that exist among PBOI scores and other relevant variables such as age and gender of the respondents and their siblings (Jordan, Whiteside, & Manaster, 1982).

Method

Subjects

There were 561 persons in the study (390 females and 171 males) from graduate and undergraduate classes in southeast urban universities. The ages of subjects ranged from 16 to 65 years; the mean age of males was 23.82 years whereas the mean age of females was 28.70 years. There were 208 subjects who had 1 sibling, 156 who had 2 siblings, 78 had 3 siblings, 52 had 4 siblings, 29 had 6 or more siblings, and 39 were only children; the median number of siblings was 3.

Instrument

The White-Campbell Birth Order Inventory (PBOI) was developed by the authors for this study. Ten statements (answered in a "yes" or "no" format) for each of four birth-order positions were developed from the literature on differential characteristics of birth order; the four birth-order categories were oldest, middle, youngest, and only.

The statements related to oldest children were an attempt to include the descriptions shared by Adler (1928) such as feeling powerful, important, achieving, and subsequently dethroned. For example, one statement is, "It was important to me to advise my brothers and sisters about right and wrong."

The middle-child statements were designed to address those issues of competition with the oldest and youngest, feeling squeezed, and feeling less important than the others. For example, "It seemed like I was less important than other members of my family" was one such statement on the inventory descriptive of this position.

Adler (1928) described youngest children as typically being the boss and having others do for them. "I was pampered by my family members" is one youngest child statement on the questionnaire.

Lastly, only children are described in the literature as being the center of attention and anxious about the pressure on them. "I felt like I lived in a fishbowl" is an only-child statement on the inventory. The PBOI was comprised of 40 statements in all. The statements were constructed under the primary criterion that each be highly descriptive of at least one birth-order position.

Validity of the PBOI was assessed in two ways. First, content validity was examined by submitting the 40 statements to four Ph.D.-level counselor educators with several years of training in Adlerian psychology and clinical work. They were asked to evaluate each statement for its ability to discriminate one psychological birth category from another. This first-round approach resulted in an edited set of 10 statements of each of the four birth-order positions.

The construct validity of the PBOI was investigated through a factor analysis of the 40 items. The PBOI was administered to 600 graduate and undergraduate students, 461 of whom participated in the present study. Each of the 40 items were intercorrelated with each other using the phi coefficient as the appropriate measure of association. The resulting correlation matrix was factor analyzed, using principal components as the factor extraction method. Although several different rotation techniques were tried, including an oblique solution, the best and most interpretable solution was an orthogonal rotation.

Four factors, accounting for 30.7% of the total variance, were extracted and corresponded to the four psychological birth-order positions. Examination of individual item loadings on each factor revealed that a majority of items from each psychological birth order were most highly correlated with the factor representing that birth order. There were a number of items, however, that loaded on factors not representing the birth order for which the items were originally created. Five "only" and four "youngest" items loaded onto other factors; all items for first and middle loaded onto their respective factors as expected. Examination of the realigned only and youngest items revealed aspects about the way in which they could be interpreted by subjects that could account for their loadings on other factors; in such cases the item realignments were allowed to stand.

After the realignment of items, the firstborn scale contained 12 items, the middle contained 14, the youngest contained 9, and the only contained 7. The distributions of each of these scales were approximately normal and the standard errors were all approximately equal. Since the scales contained different numbers of items following the realignment of some items from the factor analysis, the scales were linearly transformed to z scores; the z scores were further transformed by adding 5 and multiplying by 10, creating standard scores for the birth-order scales ranging from approximately 20 to 82.

Reliabilities of each birth-order scale were assessed through a test-retest correlation with a five-week interval; 31 subjects participated in the reliability study. Reliabilities were generally high, with the exception of the only-child scale. The reliabilities were as follows: first $(r = 0.828)$, middle $(r = 0.866)$, youngest $(r = 0.824)$, and only $(r = 0.700)$. The lower reliability for the only scale was probably an artifact of the fewer number of items comprising this scale; subsequent revisions of the PBOI will attempt to develop additional items for the only scale.

Design

The statistical design of this investigation was constructed so that the relationships between psychological birth order (PBO), as assessed by the PBOI, and other theoretically relevant variables such as actual birth order (ABO), gender and age of respondents, gender and age of siblings, and number of siblings in the family could be assessed. Since the actual birth order of an individual may contribute to one's psychological birth order in a more fundamental way than the other variables, contingency tables were constructed with actual birth order comprising one axis and psychological birth order the other. Analyses were performed on contingency tables for: (a) all people, (b) males, and (c) females. The effects of other variables such as age, sibling gender, and spacing data were assessed within each of the 16 cells created by the contingency table for all persons; the relationships among variables in each cell were examined using Pearson correlation coefficients.

Results

The results of this study indicate a significant relationship between the 556 respondents' actual birth order and psychological birth order. The chi-square analysis conducted on frequency of cases by actual birth category and psychological birth category reveal a significant relationship between the two variables, ^{2} $(9, N = 556) = 68.68567$, $p < .00001$. The asymmetric lambda tells us more about prediction than the chi-square. For all people, for instance, knowing one's actual birth order results in a 12% reduction in error in predicting psychological birth order; for women the reduction in error is 18%, while for men the lambda is 1%. Clearly, actual and psychological positions are related, albeit imperfectly.

As shown in Table 23.1, all four birth-order categories evidence a higher than expected number of persons reporting the same actual and psychological birth order (main diagonal). The responses for the oldest child category exceed the expected frequency by 52%, the middle born by 49%, the youngest by 44%, and the only category by 34%.

The distribution of actual first, middle, and youngest born across psychological birth orders reflect the highest frequency of response occurring in the respondents' actual birth-order category. That is, 40.2% of all oldest children correspond to the psychologically oldest category. Within the middle-child group, 28.4% correspond to the psychologically middle category items, and 45.7% of the actual youngest born correspond to the psychologically youngest child category. The actual birth-order category for only children who responded psychologically as only children ($n = 12$)

TABLE 23.1 Observed and Expected Frequencies of Psychological and Actual Birth-Order Identification—For All Respondents

Psychological Birth Order	Actual Birth Order				Row Total
	Oldest	Middle	Youngest	Only	
Oldest	74	35	32	6	147
	(48.6)	(35.4)	(52.6)	(10.3)	26.4%
Middle	22	38	42	4	106
	(35.1)	(25.5)	(37.9)	(7.4)	19.1%
Youngest	35	33	91	17	176
	(58.2)	(42.4)	(63.0)	(12.3)	31.7%
Only	53	28	34	12	127
	(42.0)	(30.6)	(45.5)	(8.9)	22.8%
Column	184	134	199	39	556
Total	33.1%	24.1%	35.8%	7.0%	100.0%

Note: The numbers in parentheses denote the expected values.

was superseded by responses of actual only children to the youngest birth-order category $(n = 17)$.

Within the total group of respondents, 215 (39%) shared the same psychological and actual birth order, and 341 (61%) reported different psychological and actual birth order. The majority of the respondents, therefore, reflect different actual and psychological birth orders.

The contingency table contains 12 off-diagonal cells which reflect a difference for the respondents between actual and psychological birth order. Three of these cells record a higher frequency of cases than was expected. Within these off-diagonal cells, PBOI scales were intercorrelated with age differences of siblings and gender of siblings yielding these results.

1. The number of actual oldest whose highest response rate was for the only category items is 26% greater than expected. Scores on psychologically only are significantly correlated with scores on actual first, $r = .4946$, $p < .001$. It was suspected that the wider the age gaps between the first and the subsequent siblings, the higher the only scale score; this result, however, was not obtained. In fact, the only score is negatively correlated with age gaps for all other siblings, which means that close spacing of children in time results in higher only scores.

2. The number of actual youngest whose highest response rate was in the middle-child category is 10% greater than expected and occurs when the youngest child is male (see Tables 23.2 and 23.3). Although the psychological birth order here is for the middle, the higher the age of the second oldest

TABLE 23.2 Observed and Expected Frequencies of Psychological and Actual Birth-Order Identification—For Male Respondents

Psychological Birth Order	Actual Birth Order				Row Total
	Oldest	Middle	Youngest	Only	
Oldest	18	7	10	2	37
	(11.6)	(8.1)	(15.3)	(2.0)	21.9%
Middle	5	6	15	0	26
	(8.2)	(5.7)	(10.8)	(1.4)	15.4%
Youngest	17	12	32	4	65
	(20.4)	(14.2)	(26.9)	(3.5)	38.5%
Only	13	12	13	3	41
	(12.9)	(9.0)	(17.0)	(2.2)	24.3%
Column	53	37	70	9	169
Total	31.4%	21.9%	41.4%	5.3%	100.0%

Note: The numbers in parentheses denote the expected values.

sibling, the higher the youngest child's score on the middle scale, $r = .4603$, $p < .01$. Additional examination revealed that the youngest of two children ($n = 14$) had a higher mean score on the middle scale ($M = 65.29$) than the youngest of three children ($n = 18$, $M = 58.94$).

3. The number of only children whose highest response rate was for the youngest category items is 38% higher than expected and occurs primarily when the gender of the only child is female (see Tables 23.2 and 23.3).

The intercorrelations of variables on gender and age yield interesting results in two categories. First, the scores of youngest who responded to the psychologically only category ($n = 34$) are correlated with the age of the oldest sibling. Generally the higher the age of the oldest, the more likely it is that the youngest child will have a higher only-child score, $r = .4167$, $p < .01$.

Secondly, even though the category of youngest who identify with youngest ($n = 91$) is one in which the actual and psychological birth orders concur, spacing and gender results seem pertinent. The higher the score on youngest, the higher the age of the second oldest sibling, $r = .3716$, $p < .01$. The mean of youngest children in the cell is 24.85 years, whereas, the mean of the second oldest sibling is 30.1163. In families having four or more siblings, the youngest score is significantly correlated with the gender of the third oldest sibling, $r = .6743$, $p < .001$; specifically, the higher the youngest score, the more likely it is that the third oldest sibling is a female.

TABLE 23.3 Observed and Expected Frequencies of Psychological and Actual Birth-Order Identification—Female Respondents

Psychological Birth Order	Actual Birth Order				
	Oldest	Middle	Youngest	Only	Row Total
Oldest	56	28	22	4	110
	(37.2)	(27.6)	(36.7)	(8.5)	28.4%
Middle	17	32	27	4	80
	(27.1)	(20.1)	(26.7)	(6.2)	20.7%
Youngest	18	21	59	13	111
	(37.6)	(27.8)	(37.0)	(8.6)	28.7%.
Only	40	16	21	9	86
	(29.1)	(21.6)	(28.7)	(6.7)	22.2%
Column	131	97	29	30	387
Total	33.9%	25.1%	33.3%	7.8%	100.0%

Note: The numbers in parentheses denote the expected values.

Discussion

This study was conducted in an attempt to investigate the construct of psychological birth order through the development of an instrument capable of such assessment and to utilize the instrument in examining the relationship of psychological and actual birth order.

The results suggest a significant relationship between psychological and actual birth order. A pattern has emerged, however, which also suggests the presence of factors that influence the variance of psychological birth order from actual birth order. All four birth orders evidenced a high frequency of individuals who, in fact, are psychologically congruent with their actual birth order. This is not to say that other variables have not influenced the degree of identification these individuals have with their actual birth order.

The scope of the present study was limited to examination of those variables which appear to be most influential in explaining the variance or incongruence between psychological and actual birth order. Findings in birth-order research have suggested several factors that may affect how and where individuals perceive themselves in their families. Age, gender, blended nature of family, number of parents, death, divorce, step-parenting are but a few factors which have been identified that significantly affect the family. Clearly, the complexity of combinations of factors contribute to the difficulty in accounting for variance in birth-order identification. The present study identified variance and then analyzed the factors of age and gender only as a starting point in what must be continued research in understanding the interactive relationship of all birth-order variables.

Categories of Significant Incongruence

Three psychological birth-order categories were found to occur more frequently than expected by chance.

1. Firstborn evidenced a high relationship psychologically with the only child. This result is not particularly surprising in that all first children were once only children. The finding that was surprising, however, was the lack of evidence for a spacing relationship between those who remain psychologically only children and those who make the conversion to first. In fact, according to the results, close spacing among all siblings is often the case when firstborn remain onlys.

2. The youngest identification with the middle child seems to occur primarily if there are two children in the family. The younger may tend to reject the baby role in favor of following in the footsteps of the oldest and in trying to compete, specifically if the youngest is a male. If the youngest is the only male, and thereby the only son, he may be encouraged to be more responsible and mature than is typically expected of the youngest. If the older sibling is also male, the desire to compete and overcome the older brother could be even greater.

3. The occurrence of only children, primarily females, who identify psychologically with the youngest may stem from the belief that only and youngest children share a specialness in their roles in the family that other children don't enjoy. The roles of the two positions are typically very clear in the family. They both receive a unique form of attention and focus by parents, other members of the family, or both. The identification with the youngest experienced by the only male may be tempered by the expectations for an "only son" which could include responsibilities and behavioral, specifically achievement, expectations imposed by the parents. An only daughter may receive the pampering and protection of a youngest child in an even more pronounced form.

The Influence of Age and Gender Factors

An interesting finding is that the actual birth-order position of the youngest is the only position in which spacing and/or gender data consistently appear to be related to psychological birth order. Perhaps this result has occurred because youngest children have had older brothers and sisters to develop relationships with from birth, whereas first and middle children have no, or fewer, such siblings.

1. The youngest tend to score higher on the only psychological birth-order category as the oldest sibling's age increases. The widening of the age interval between the oldest and youngest may well result in the youngest being treated as an only child.

2. The youngest children score increasingly higher on the youngest scale psychologically as the age of the second oldest sibling increases. In families of three, an average of six years between the middle and youngest was found. This spacing interval could contribute to an increasingly higher youngest score for the youngest by virtue of the middle child's likelihood of joining the family in pampering and focusing on the youngest. If the middle child and youngest were close in age, it may be more likely that the middle child would compete with the youngest and possibly have jealousy toward the youngest. Further examination of this particular family pattern is warranted given these preliminary results.

In families of four in which the third child is a female, the youngest scores higher on the youngest psychological birth-order category. If the female child is encouraged to mother the baby or take on some form of a parental role, the youngest could be highly rewarded for exhibiting heightened characteristics of the youngest. The youngest may then receive special attention from the family as a whole, even if the third sibling is close in age, as contrasted with a youngest who received special attention from parents and older siblings but was resented or competed against for attention by the next older sibling.

The need is great for further research in psychological birth order. The construct has been a popular and stable one in conventional birth-order theory, yet the difficulty of identification and measurement has proven a formidable obstacle in research efforts. Further investigation must be made in identifying the role of spacing and gender in psychological birth order followed by research which examines the complexity of combinations of factors which influence birth-order perception. The overarching goal of identification and explanation of causes of variance in psychological birth order is a challenging, yet important goal in this field of research. The present investigators will continue validation studies in furthering efforts to increase the accuracy of their instrument.

References

Adams, B. N. (1976). Early recollection changes after counseling: A case study. *Individual Psychology,* *32*(2), 212–223.

Adler, A. (1927). *The practice and theory of Individual Psychology.* New York: Harcourt Brace.

Adler, A. (1928). Characteristics of the first, second, third child. *Children: The Magazine for Parents,* *3*(5), 14–52.

Adler, A. (1956). The origin of the neurotic disposition. In H. L. Ansbacher & R. R. Ansbacher (Eds.), *The individual psychology of Alfred Adler.* New York: Basic Books.

Ansbacher, H. L, and Ansbacher, R. R. (1956). *The individual psychology of Alfred Adler.* New York: Harper Torchbooks.

Dreikurs, R., & Soltz, V. (1964). *Children: The challenge.* New York: Hawthorn.

Eckstein, D. G. (1976). Early recollection changes after counseling: A case study. *Journal of Individual Psychology, 32*(3), 411–439.

Forer, L. (1977). Bibliography of birth order literature in the '70's. *Journal of Individual Psychology, 33*(1), 122–141.

Frank, R., Reinhart, M. A., & Fitzgerald, H. E. (1987). Birth order reconceptualized and the second youngest child. *Individual Psychology, 43*(3), 360–363.

Fraser, R., & Nystul, M. S. (1983). The effects of birth order and sex on locus of control. *Individual Psychology, 39*(1), 63–65.

Gallagher, R., & Cowen, E. L. (1977). Birth order and school adjustment problems. *Journal of Individual Psychology, 33,* 70–77.

Jordan, E. W., Whiteside, M. M., & Manaster, G. J. (1982). A practical and effective research measure of birth order. *Individual Psychology, 38*(3), 253–260.

Lohman, J. F., Lohman, T. G., & Christensen, O. (1985). Psychological position and perceived sibling differences. *Individual Psychology, 41*(3), 313–327.

Manaster, G. J. (1977). Birth order: An overview, *Journal of Individual Psychology, 33*(1), 3–8.

Manaster, G. J., & Corsini, R. J. (1982). *The development of personality.* Itasca, IL: Peacock Publishing.

Melillo, D. (1983). Birth order, perceived birth order, and family position of academic women. *Individual Psychology, 39*(1), 57–62.

Pepper, F. (1964, January). *The characteristics of the family constellation.* Paper presented at the meeting of the Oregon Society of Individual Psychology, Portland.

Perlin, M., & Grater, H. (1984). The relationship between birth order and reported interpersonal behavior. *Individual Psychology, 40*(1), 22–28.

Pulakos, J. (1987). The effects of birth order on perceived family roles. *Individual Psychology, 43*(3), 319–328.

Rosenberg, M. (1965). *Society and the adolescent self-image.* Princeton, NJ: Princeton University Press.

Schooler, C. (1972). Birth order effects: Not here, not now! *Psychological Bulletin, 78*(3), 161–175.

Shulman, B. H., & Mosak, H. H. (1977). Birth order and ordinal position: Two Adlerian views. *Journal of Individual Psychology, 33*(1), 114–121.

Sweeney, T. J. (1981). *Adlerian counseling: Proven concepts and strategies.* Muncie, IN: Accelerated Development.

CHAPTER **24**

Birth-Order Research and Adler's Theory: A Critical Review

C. EDWARD WATKINS, JR.

Birth-order research, when it has been critically reviewed, has been criticized for its failure to adequately control for intervening variables (Ernst & Angst, 1983) or take the "psychological position" of the child into account (Shulman & Mosak, 1988). Such inadequate control has been thought to lead to the mixed, sometimes inconsistent research results that we see in this body of literature. But how has more recent Adlerian-oriented birth-order research controlled for intervening variables (e.g., sex)? and what can we learn from this research that might guide our future research efforts in this area? This brief review addresses these two questions.

Because some of the strongest arguments for "variable control" in birth-order research have been made in the last 10 years (Ernst & Angst, 1983), birth-order studies appearing in *Individual Psychology (IP)* from 1981 through mid 1991 were reviewed. A total of 25 articles were identified for analysis. Table 1 indicates the sample characteristics, assessment methods used, variables controlled for, and primary results of each study. Variables controlled for, which seem to be among the most important to take into account (see Ernst & Angst, 1983; Steelman & Powell, 1985; Shulman & Mosak, 1977, 1988), included: "Psychological position," subject

TABLE 24.1 Characteristics of Birth-Order Research Studies

Authors	Sample Characteristics	Age (Years)	Assessment Methods Used	Variables Controlled For	Primary Results	Comments
Allred & Poduska (1988)	88 married subjects from two Utah cities (44m, 44f)	Most between 25 and 45	Comparative "Happiness" questions	Sex, sibship size; stratified random sampling method used	Male and female last-borns generally scored lower on happiness items than subjects from any other same-sex birth orders	Only five male and eight female last-borns in sample variable income levels
Brink & Matlock (1982)	76 undergraduate students (sex NS)	Range = 15 to 50	50-item author-designed questionnaire	None	Oldest sibling least likely to report having nightmares in adulthood; youngest sibling most likely	Frequency of nightmares among groups not reported (see McCann & Stewin, 1987)
Bryant (1987)	65 firstborns, 98 last-borns, all female, from private sex-segregated Catholic high school	16 or 17	Strong-Campbell Interest Inventory	Sex	Firstborns scored higher comparatively on academic comfort, social and conventional themes, and teaching, merchandising, business management, and office practice interests	Highly select sample

Eckstein & Driscoll (1983)	215 females from 16 different groups, ranging from day-care workers to prison inmates	Range = 18 to 58	Sociometric nominations	Sex	Trend for firstborns to be over-represented in leadership and popularity roles but results were not statistically significant	Middleborns actually appeared to be represented more so than firstborns
Fraser & Nystul (1983)	Undergraduate psychology students from Australia	Range = 18 to 30	Locus of Control Scale	Sex, sibship size, & SES	Birth order in conjunction with sex predicted locus of control	Cross-cultural study
Gold & Dobson (1988)	150 married couples, members of a Reformed, Catholic, or Baptist Church	Most 30 to 40	Brothers and Sisters Form Dyadic Adjustment Scale Marital Stability Scale	Sex	No statistically significant relationships found between birth-order complementarity and marital stability or marital quality	Most subjects well-educated, Caucasian, had incomes greater than $25,000 per year, and were active church goers
Ivancevich, Matteson & Gamble (1987)	363m, 422f undergraduate students in upper-level business administration courses (about half Caucasian, other)	NS	Thurstone Temperament Activity Schedule Subscale Jenkins Activity Survey—Student Form	Sex	Firstborn/only children had more Type A characteristics than youngest/other children	Birth-order positions combined (first/only and youngest/other)

(Continued)

TABLE 24.1 Characteristics of Birth-Order Research Studies (*Continued*)

Authors	Sample Characteristics	Age (Years)	Assessment Methods Used	Variables Controlled For	Primary Results	Comments
Kiracofe & Kiracofe (1990)	282f, 213m counseling clients	Range = 14 to 66	Structured lifestyle interview	Psychological position, sex	More firstborns and youngest borns saw themselves as favored by their fathers	Final decision about birth-order position determined by the client's therapist
Lester (1987)	NA		Reexamined data from a number of previous studies	NA	Found an excess of first and middleborns among suicide completers; excess of middle and last-borns among suicide attempters	Limited number of studies drawn on Most cited studies were pre-1975
Lieberman, Shaffer, & Reynolds (1985)	374 physical anthropologists (sex NS)	NS	Nine-item author-designed measure	Sex	Oldest, last, and only borns more likely than intermediate borns to support race concept	Limited number of females in intermediate, only born, and last-born positions
Lohman, Lohman & Christensen (1985)	70 families from Champaign–Urbana, IL area	NS	Psychological position questionnaire Adlerian Clinical Instrument Semantic Differential instrument	Psychological position, sex, siblings' sex, sibship size, age spacing, and SES	Found support for the importance of "psychological" birth-order position over ordinal position	Nonclinical sample

Study	Sample	Age	Instrument	Controlled	Results	Comments
McCann & Stewin (1988)	63f, 43m undergraduate students	NS	Asked to indicate birth position and what percent of their dreams had been frightening	None	Tend firstborns to report more frightening dreams than youngest and middleborns; results contradict Brink & Matlock (1982)	Had just four "only" subjects two-item questionnaire used
McCann, Stewin, & Short (1990)	45f, 51m undergraduate psychology students	25.4	Author-developed questionnaire	Sex, sibship size	Firstborns found to have greater frequency of frightening dreams than last-borns	Age and tendency to remember dreams controlled for five-item questionnaire used
Melillo (1983)	174 female academics	Range = 26 to 68	Author-developed questionnaire	Psychological position, sex	Only borns and oldest more greatly represented among female doctoral degree holders; perceived birth order not found to be more important than ordinal position	Three-item questionnaire Sample came from three universities and one professional school
Nystul (1981)	139f, 81m Australian undergraduate students	Above 17	Personal Orientation Inventory	Sex, sibship size	Oldest male in a three-child family lower self-actualizer than siblings	Cross-cultural study Subjects all white

(Continued)

TABLE 24.1 Characteristics of Birth-Order Research Studies (*Continued*)

Authors	Sample Characteristics	Age (Years)	Assessment Methods Used	Variables Controlled For	Primary Results	Comments
Perlin & Grater (1984)	75f, 15m under-graduate psychology students	Range = 18 to 22	Interpersonal Check List	Sibship size, Age spacing	Oldest borns obtained higher scores on scales measuring dominance and aggression	Limited number of male subjects
Phillips, Bedeian, Mossholder & Touliatos (1988)	835 public government and industrial accountants	NS	Biodata questionnaire Regular and special purpose scales of the California Psychological Inventory (CPI)	None	Firstborns scored higher than last-borns on dominance, good impression, and achievement via conformity; no differences found between groups on four other CPI scales	Only first and last-borns studied
Phillips, Long, & Bedeian (1990)	551f, 531m accountants	NS	Special purpose scale of the California Psychological Inventory	Sex; subjects randomly selected	First/only borns scored higher than later borns on Type A characteristics	First/only borns combined for analysis All other birth-order positions grouped under "later" born

Study	Sample	Age	Instrument	Variables	Findings	Comments
Pulakos (1987)	100f, 100m undergraduate psychology students	Most 17 to 25	Author-developed questionnaire	Psychological position, sex, siblings' sex, sibship size	Oldest born seen as being in Responsible role, most often middle born in the Popular role, and youngest in the Spoiled role	Birth-order scheme of Jordan et al. (1982) used. Most subjects single, probably Caucasian, middle-class
Schierbeek & Newlon (1990)	32f, 16m inpatients 20f, 27m high school students	Range = 12 to 18	One-page birth-order form	Psychological position	Majority of in-patients perceived themselves in an inferior psychological position; psychological birth order explained about 10% of the difference between samples	Just 3 "Only" subjects in sample. Males/females grouped together for data analysis
Shouval, Shouval, Kau-Venaki, & Sharabani (1984)	153f, 167m Israeli school children of Eastern and Western ethnic origin	11 to 13	Autonomy Multiple Choice Measure	Sex, sibship size, tried to control SES	Ordinal position effects found for two and three-child Eastern (but not Western) families; study showed effects of ethnicity on birth order	Cross-cultural study. Subjects from middle socioeconomic families. Families with two or three children only included in analysis

(Continued)

TABLE 24.1 Characteristics of Birth-Order Research Studies (*Continued*)

Authors	Sample Characteristics	Age (Years)	Assessment Methods Used	Variables Controlled For	Primary Results	Comments
Singh (1990)	120f, 20m Indian high school students	13 to 15	Punjabi version of Junior Eysenck Personality Questionnaire	Sex, sibship size	Last-born males more tough-minded than firstborn males and firstborn/last-born females	Cross-cultural study
Snell, Hargrove, & Falbo (1986)	1074f, 875m university students	NS	Work and Family Orientation Questionnaire	Sex	Women's and men's achievement motivation profiles associated with different birth orders	Subjects all Caucasian
Stein, DeMiranda, & Stein (1988)	25f, 48m substance abusers	25.4	Modified birth-order scheme (Jordan et al., 1982)	Sex, sibship size	About half of male substance abusers were firstborns	Subjects all Caucasian

Note: f = females, m = males; NS = not specified; NA = not applicable.

sex, siblings' sex, sibship size, age spacing, and socioeconomic status (SES). In the table, a "Comments" column is included to identify other study characteristics of importance.

Results

The following observations or conclusions emerged:

1. the samples varied widely, ranging from university students to counseling clients to married couples;
2. sample sizes ranged from 73 to 1,949, with about half of the studies having at least 200 subjects;
3. when providing age information, 14 studies provided only an age range, and eight studies did not specify any age characteristics at all;
4. most studies used only one assessment method in the data-gathering process;
5. 10 studies used assessment methods developed by the article authors for these particular investigations;
6. in half of the studies, subjects' race went unspecified;
7. four studies were cross-cultural in nature;
8. the primary birth-order positions studied were first, middle, and last or youngest;
9. psychological position was examined in only five of the studies; and
10. subjects' sex and sibship size were controlled for in 19 and 11 studies, respectively, but siblings' sex, age spacing, and SES appeared to be controlled for in only two or three studies.

Considering the limitations of these studies, the primary conclusions suggested by these data could be stated as:

1. firstborns often manifest characteristics consistent with the "firstborn profile" described in the Adlerian literature, e.g., being more dominant, responsible (see Table 24.1);
2. achievement motivation patterns vary according to birth-order positions;
3. birth order when combined with the variable of sex (e.g., subjects' sex) relates to selected achievement variables and locus of control;
4. studies support the importance of "psychological position" in birth-order research; and
5. some evidence suggests that birth-order effects vary as a result of ethnicity.

Discussion

In reflecting on these findings, several issues merit comment. First, that age and race often went unmentioned or were not well specified is easily correctable and need to be better addressed for replication purposes.

Second, with 10 of the 25 studies relying on self-developed questionnaires that had as few as one, three, or five items, we must wonder about (a) instrument reliability and validity and (b) this continued creation of assessment methods vis-à-vis birth order. If a reliable/valid method already exists, then let us use it so that cumulation of findings can occur. If it is necessary to develop a new assessment method, then it is also necessary to present information about its reliability and validity. This reliability/validity information seems to have been lacking in several of the studies reviewed here.

Third, "psychological position" received some empirical support, but still how do we best assess this important concept? Of the studies to assess psychological position (Kiracofe & Kiracofe, 1990; Lohman, Lohman, & Christensen, 1985; Melillo, 1983; Pulakos, 1987; Schierbeek & Newlon, 1990), each used a different way to determine it. To insure consistency of measurement across studies, it seems important that one theoretically sound, valid method or a small set of such methods be identified for assessing psychological position. The studies of Lohman et al. (1985) and Kiracofe and Kiracofe (1990) provide good examples for thinking about this issue.

Fourth, such variables as siblings' sex, sibship size, age spacing, and SES were not controlled for in the majority of studies. If birth-order research is to produce viable results, at a minimum it should control for subjects' sex, siblings' sex (e.g., Jordan, Whiteside, & Manaster 1982), and sibship size (see Schooler, 1972). Where this is not done, results can only be seen as highly tentative at best.

Fifth, the clearest results emerge for the first-born position. But if we consider previous critiques (see Ernst & Angst, 1983), to what extent are these results real or artifactual? Studies showing first-born effects fared no better in controlling for intervening variables. We must regard these results as highly tentative as well; they neither confirm nor disconfirm Adler's views, providing only suggestive possibilities about what could be.

From this review, we see that intervening variables in birth-order research have yet to be adequately dealt with. These variables must be confronted if birth-order research is to produce meaningful results and can best be handled by greater experimental manipulation and control. These comments are not new, but their message has yet to be heeded. If this continues to be the case, further inconsistent or questionable research findings will result, we will have to remain highly tentative over what significant findings do emerge, and the promise of birth-order research (in supporting Adler's theoretical formulations) will continue to be only minimally fulfilled.

References

Allred, G. H., & Poduska, B. E. (1988). Birth order and happiness: A preliminary study. *Individual Psychology, 44*, 346–354.

Brink, T. L, & Matlock, F. (1982). Nightmares and birth order: An empirical study. *Individual Psychology, 38*, 47–49.

Bryant, B. L. (1987). Birth order as a factor in the development of vocational preferences. *Individual Psychology, 43*, 36–41.

Ekstein, D., & Driscoll, R. (1983). Leadership, popularity, and birth order in women. *Individual Psychology, 39*, 71–77.

Ernst, C., & Angst, J. (1983). *Birth order: Its influence on personality.* New York: Springer-Verlag.

Fraser, R., & Nystul, M. S. (1983). The effects of birth order and sex on locus of control. *Individual Psychology, 39*, 63–65.

Gold, S. B., & Dobson, J. E. (1988). Birth order, marital quality, and stability: A path analysis of Toman's theory. *Individual Psychology, 44*, 355–364.

Ivancevich, J. M., Matteson, M. T., & Gamble, G. O. (1987). Birth order and the Type A coronary behavior pattern. *Individual Psychology, 43*, 42–49.

Jordan, E. W., Whiteside, M. M., & Manaster, G. J. (1982). A practical and effective research measure of birth order. *Individual Psychology, 38*, 253–260.

Kiracofe, N. M., & Kiracofe, H. N. (1990). Child-perceived parental favoritism and birth order. *Individual Psychology, 46*, 74–81.

Lester, D. (1987). Suicide and sibling position. *Individual Psychology, 43*, 390–395.

Lieberman, L., Shaffer, T. G., & Reynolds, L. T. (1985). Scientific revolutions and birth order. *Individual Psychology, 41*, 328–335.

Lohman, J. F., Lohman, T. G., & Christensen, O. (1985). Psychological position and perceived sibling differences. *Individual Psychology, 41*, 313–327.

McCann, S. J. H., & Stewin, L. L. (1987). Frightening dreams and birth order. *Individual Psychology, 43*, 56–58.

McCann, S. J. H., Stewin, L. L., & Short, R. H. (1990). Frightening dream frequency and birth order. *Individual Psychology, 46*, 304–310.

Melillo, D. (1983). Birth order, perceived birth order, and family position of academic women. *Individual Psychology, 39*, 57–62.

Nystul, M. (1981). The effects of birth order and family size on self-actualization. *Journal of Individual Psychology, 37*, 107–112.

Perlin, M., & Grater, H. (1984). The relationship between birth order and reported interpersonal behavior. *Individual Psychology, 40*, 22–28.

Phillips, A. S., Bedeian, A. G, Mossholder, K. W., & Touliatos, J. (1988). Birth order and selected work-related personality variables. *Individual Psychology, 44*, 492–499.

Phillips, A. S., Long, R. G., & Bedeian, A. G. (1990). Type A status: Birth order and gender effects. *Individual Psychology, 46*, 365–373.

Pulakos, J. (1987). The effects of birth order on perceived family roles. *Individual Psychology, 43*, 319–328.

Schierbeek, M. L., & Newlon, B. J. (1990). Substance abuse and attempted suicide: The role of perceived birth position in adolescents. *Individual Psychology, 46*, 358–364.

Schooler, C. (1972). Birth order effects: Not here, not now! *Psychological Bulletin, 78*, 161–175.

Shouval, R., Shouval, E., Kau-Venaki, S., & Sharabani, R. (1984). Ethnic and cultural variations in children's independence by ordinal position and gender. *Individual Psychology, 40*, 3–21.

Shulman, B. H., & Mosak, H. H. (1977). Birth order and ordinal position: Two Adlerian views. *Journal of Individual Psychology, 33*, 114–121.

Shulman, B. H., & Mosak, H. H. (1988). *Manual for life style assessment.* Muncie, IN: Accelerated Development.

Singh, K. (1990). Toughmindedness in relation to birth order, family size, and sex. *Individual Psychology, 46,* 82–87.

Snell, W. E., Jr., Hargrove, L., & Falbo, T. (1986). Birth order and achievement motivation configurations in women and men. *Individual Psychology, 41,* 428–438.

Steelman, L. C., & Powell, B. (1985). The social and academic consequences of birth order: Real, artifactual, or both? *Journal of Marriage and the Family, 47,* 117–124.

Stein, S. M., DeMiranda, S., & Stein, A. (1988). Birth order, substance abuse, and criminality. *Individual Psychology, 44,* 500–506.

IX
Inferiority

CHAPTER 25

The Movement from "Felt Minus" to "Perceived Plus": Understanding Adler's Concept of Inferiority

AL MILLIREN, FERN CLEMMER, WES WINGETT, and
TONY TESTERMENT

One of the basic tenets in Adlerian theory is the dynamic of inferiority. Adler often wrote of it as one's "sense" of being in a "minus" position. As the individual comes into this world, the child is in a position of being helpless and incapable. Although this is common for all newborns and infants, the nature of the situation contributes to a sense of being "less than." The inferiority feeling is a self-comparison (Adler, 1956, 1964; Dreikurs, 1954, 1967) made from the time infants are able to interact with those around them (Adler, 1956). Inhabiting the infant's world are "creatures" with greater skills and resources. It appears to the child that everyone is bigger, better, faster, smarter, or more adept. Thus, the individual begins life dependent on everyone else for mere survival; "to be a human being means to possess a feeling of inferiority which constantly presses towards its own conquest" (Adler, 1964, p. 116). Therefore, we begin life from a position of "felt minus."

Adler postulated that the early circumstances of human life contributed to producing feelings of inferiority; these continue to develop as children compare themselves with an unattainable ideal of perfection depicted by their parents (Adler, 1956) and recognize their powerlessness in the face of nature (Adler, 1964). Compounding this may be the condition of neglect, pampering, disability, or disfigurement (Adler, 1964). It was Adler's belief that these specific conditions escalated a sense of feeling inferior. However, being in a "felt minus" position is not necessarily negative. The sense of inferiority, though it may not be consciously felt (Adler, 1956), contributes to the motivation for normal development (Adler, 1969). It creates a striving—a striving to overcome, to achieve significance, to master our life situation(s).

Adler identified two kinds of inferiority feelings. First was a universal feeling of inferiority. The second was exaggerated feelings of inferiority (Adler, 1958). Both types of feelings of inferiority lead to a striving to overcome—a striving to achieve significance. Adler labeled this the "perceived plus"—a kind of fictional view of how things might improve. It is our adopted plan, if you will, for how things could be better or different. Each individual generates in early childhood (and usually before age 6) his or her unique and specific view of self, others, and the world and how one should be to move through the world. The majority of this plan is formed at a time when we do not have the means for processing the conclusions we are reaching.

As we grow and develop through a process of trial and error, we begin to acquire or create behaviors that, as we see it, will take us to these fictional successes. It is our map for getting to how it is to be "when we grow up." Some behaviors we adopt will be useful and will take the path of social interest—they will serve to help us move toward, and with others, in a spirit of community. Other behaviors might be viewed as useless, although we might not have that awareness, and serve to move us away from, and against, others. Either way, these behaviors are of our own creation and, from a personal perspective, contribute to how we move in the world from the "felt minus" to the "perceived plus." These behaviors become our vehicle to becoming "better than," or "smarter than," or "more capable than," or "more important than." However, although the final goal is always positive, the means we adopt for reaching it may not be.

The inferiority feeling is a motivating force that can be focused in a positive or negative direction (Adler, 1956, 1964; Dreikurs, 1957) and that can be viewed as useful or useless (Manaster & Corsini, 1982) depending on the development of social interest (Adler, 1964). Mosak spoke of three areas of perceived inferiority: (1) a discrepancy between the self-concept and an ideal self-image including physical characteristics; (2) a discrepancy between self-concept and environmental evaluations including social environment; and (3) a discrepancy between the self-concept and the moral code. Dreikurs (1967), too, spoke of the assumption of being inferior physically, socially, or in comparison to one's own goals and standards.

Adler is credited as being the creator of the term *inferiority complex*. It has been suggested (Powers, 2004, personal communication) that Adler may have offered up this terminology as a sort of "tongue-in-cheek" kind of joke. Although we may never know for sure, it has a ring of possibility. In the early 1900s, psychologists were busy labeling groups of behaviors as "complexes." Sigmund Freud had his Oedipus and Electra complexes and Carl Jung was busy creating others, and Adler might have decided it would be quite fun to identify a complex of his own. It is easy to imagine Adler, in a mode of mischief, with a twinkle in his eye, thinking, "… and now I have the inferiority complex!"

A second possibility occurs in this regard. Adler was not one for labels or typologies, so the question becomes one of, "Why did he create this particular 'complex'?" Often, in teaching, Adler would use labels to describe certain classes of behaviors or personality types solely for convenience of discussion and not as categories or typologies. It could just be that the "inferiority complex" was solely one of these teaching metaphors. A third hypothesis may simply be that *he* never created the term at all. Adler might be the recipient of a gift from some reporter or other observer at one of his lectures. Against a backdrop of the times when complexes were in vogue, someone else may have used the term in recording one of Adler's lectures.

We may never know the truth behind the origin of the inferiority complex, yet it does serve as a useful descriptor. Most folks, in some area of life or another, possess *feelings of inferiority*. These are natural and normal aspects of living, and they motivate us to achieve. Maddi (1978) sees people from Adler's perspective as striving toward ideals (rather than being pushed by drives) with universal feelings of inferiority as part of our human nature necessitated by our physical vulnerability. The social units we must form, and the striving within those units against man's inferiority to nature, enable us to survive (Darwin, 1915, Kropotkin, 1914; Leakey & Lewin, 1977; Montagu, 1966). Kopp (1982) calls it "socially interested compensatory striving." If we are trying to do something together, we will be showing a sense of worth and the courage to be imperfect. We will be choosing to focus on the future.

> Compensating for universal feelings of inferiority generates a striving for perfection, significance, and security in harmony with other fellow human beings in order to overcome shared problems. Yet the particular expression of the striving in an individual

depends on (a) a sense of identification with others; (b) personal self-ideals toward which the individual strives; (c) personal definition of security, significance, and success; (d) specific cooperative behavior patterns in which the individual has trained him/herself; and (e) conjunctive attitudes and feelings toward others which facilitate this movement. Each of these factors ... reflect choices (often unconscious). (p. 184)

To be stuck in one's personal inferiority space is a totally different situation. Some people become discouraged in their efforts to overcome inferiority or improve their situation. These individuals may lack the courage to approach life tasks or even entertain a pathological life style (Manaster & Corsini, 1982). This latter instance has been labeled "inferiority complex" and describes the attitude of a person who is expressing that he or she feels incapable of solving an existing problem (Adler, 1935). It is the difference in the "felt minus" that generates movement to the "perceived plus"—of having a sense things could be better—and "believing" one is inferior, thus stuck in the "felt minus."

From this position we focus on protection from being proven worthless (Adler, 1956). The motivation is not toward significance by overcoming one's sense of inferiority, but toward achieving significance by living one's inferiority! Alexandra Adler, psychiatrist, practitioner of Individual Psychology, and daughter of Alfred Adler writes:

We say that a person is suffering from "an inferiority complex" when he reacts fatalistically to a crippling situation without attempting to correct or improve it. This should not be confused with the "feeling of inferiority" which is present in everyone in certain situations, particularly in every child—a feeling which normally incites an individual to achieve future successful development. (1938, p. 3)

Bickhard (1978) states that inappropriate inferiority feelings come from mistaken goals, being self-centered instead of feeling connected to humanity. The root mistake, then, when inferiority feelings are the response to a certain situation, is a lack of social interest. The only way to allay either kind of inferiority feeling is contribution to the common welfare (Adler, 1956).

The discussion can be illustrated by the above figure or visual model. The base of the model depicts the movement from "felt minus" to "perceived plus." This is the motivation sequence for most of us, yet there is

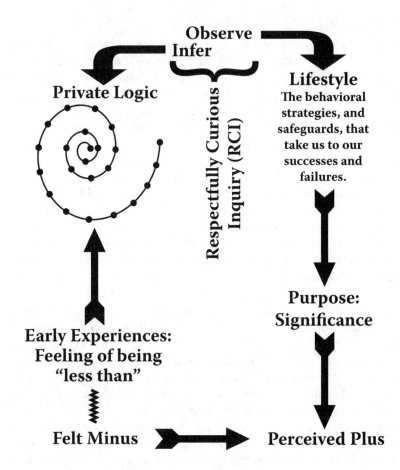

Fig. 25.1 Felt Minus to Perceived Plus. Copyright © 2005, Al Milliren.

more to it than this simple sequence. Going up the left side of the model, we see the notion of "felt minus" derives from our early life experiences and these are the building blocks for a developing "private logic."

At the top of the model and parallel to one's private logic is the concept of "life style"—a system of behavioral strategies and safeguards. Thus, the private logic is the belief system counterpart to the behavioral system or life style we use to implement our private logic (Kern, 2004, personal communication). Our life style is what carries us to our various goals (of significance) or "perceived plus." The arrows in the center top of the model, drawn in opposite directions, bring our attention to the fact that we can observe behavior, but can only infer private logic. A further examination of these various elements follows.

Private Logic

Inferiority feelings depend on perceptions of self and surroundings, that is, on one's private logic. The logic in private logic should be considered as plural. It is comprised of the totality of our beliefs about who we are, how others are, and how we think the world should be for us. The spiral or coil was borrowed from a little booklet on self-concept theory (Purkey, 1968), where it was used to represent the person's self-concept(s). It is our thinking that some of the conclusions drawn about self, others, and the world are more surface or peripheral to the system while others are deep and at the core. It seems likely that core beliefs will be those to which we are tenaciously committed and, therefore, will be harder to change, whereas those on the surface may be more transient or fleeting, thus easier to modify. Regardless, all beliefs in the system are interconnected. This represents the principle of holism. Although the downside of this view is the complexity of the system, the upside is the encouraging thought that change in any part of the system will effect changes in the entire system.

The private logic represents our conceptual "plan" for negotiating successfully through life. It provides us with the guidelines for how we view ourselves, how we relate to others, what to expect from those around us, how the world should treat us, and so forth. These may be accurate reflections of how things really are, or they may be totally erroneous conclusions, or they may be some degree of both. Regardless, they are all our creation based on information we received in the very early years of life. For example, Mosak has talked about the deaf child's inferiority feelings. As life style convictions emerge, it is possible for some dissonance to occur between the child's self-concept and the self-ideal formed from experiences with hearing people. This often leaves deaf people with an impaired sense of self-esteem (Craig, 1965; Elser, 1959; Emerton, 1978; Reich, Hambelton, & Holdin, 1977; Schlesinger & Meadow, 1972).

Quite often, we may be making decisions about life challenges as a 30- or 40-something adult based on conclusions drawn as a 3-year-old. And these conclusions may be nonverbal, intuitive impressions, through which we instinctively know something may either "feel" okay or not okay! Bernard Shulman (1973) describes "private logic" in this way:

> It is an Adlerian axiom that a man acts according to the way he perceives it; that his private reality is subjective. Furthermore, if there is cognitive dissonance between his private reality and the consensual view of others, he will prefer his private reality to the latter and will act according to it. (p. 366)

Life Style

As defined in the model, life style is the totality of the behavioral strategies and safeguards that take us to our successes and failures. Although we believe everything we do is aimed at achieving a positive sense of significance, not everything we do will manifest positively. *Self-handicapping* is a term introduced by Jones and Berglas (1978) to denote protection of self-image. They suggest self-handicaps may be acquired (e.g., consumption of alcohol) or claimed (e.g., report of physical symptoms). Self-handicaps may be internal (e.g., withdrawal of effort) or external (e.g., choice of distracting performance settings). Rhodewalt and Davison (1986) studied the application of self-handicaps by people who had received inferiority-inducing news about test performance and were not sure how to ensure a better subsequent performance. Negative feedback elicits feelings of inferiority and self-handicapping alleviates the fear of confirming self-conceptions of inferiority (Adler, 1930; Snyder & Smith, 1982). People chose to self-handicap following failure because, in doing so, they reduce inferiority feelings. Rhodewalt and Davison (1986) found that self-handicapping after reported failure occurs when there is an uncertainty about the cause of the initial poor performance, which would be clarified by a second poor performance, and the individual was unclear about how to avoid failing again.

No one gets up in the morning with the purpose of making his or her life miserable—we do not set out to behave in self-defeating ways. Our intent is to make things better for ourselves. However, we do not always make the most appropriate choices in our behaviors and we do things detrimental to our welfare. One student of our acquaintance constantly notices every little (as well as big) thing that is going awry in her life. She remembers the exact dates and times when negative (for her) events occurred in her life; as a result, she is miserable and has trouble identifying the good around her. She does not set out to make her day-to-day life feel crummy. In fact, these events serve to remind her of what she does not want out of life. Unfortunately, the memories and experiences get in the way of her noticing what is going well. Thus, even when she does notice those things, she is always on the lookout for the possibility that nothing can be that good.

Measures of Inferiority

Measures that attempt to describe inferiority feelings fall short of addressing a normal universal feeling of inferiority. Most measures that aim at a description of the inferiority feeling start with the self-concept construct. This construct was influenced by the branch of sociology know as Symbolic

Interactionism. Cooley's "looking-glass self," the imagined perception of self in the mind of another (Cooley, 1902) starts with the imagination of one's appearance or behavior to another person, evaluates the other person's appraisal of the appearance or behavior, and continues the process with a responsive self-evaluation and accompanying feeling. Mead (1934) says people come to see themselves as they believe others see them, and become what they believe people expect them to become.

Ashby and Kottman (1996) noted a lack of research on the feeling of inferiority. Dixon and Strano (1989) reviewed research related to inferiority feelings and found little empirical research. They characterized attempts to measure inferiority as inadequate and emphasized the need for a reliable and valid measure of inferiority independent of measures of self-concept and self-esteem. They prescribed that such a measure would utilize a comparison of self with family members relative to perception of physical characteristics, social characteristics, and personal goals and standards as subjective rather than objective evaluations.

Heidbreder (1927) constructed a rating scale of 137 traits thought to be characteristic of an "inferiority complex." Subjects indicated the degree to which they possessed each trait. She reported test/retest reliability of .72 to .75. The approximate normal distribution of the scores in a norm group suggested to Heidbreder that the "inferiority complex" is present in different degrees in different individuals. Her discussion of the "inferiority complex" focused on the degree of presence or absence of this "pathological characteristic" in "normal" individuals. Later researchers (Festinger, 1954; Kemper, 1966; Sherwood, 1965; Ziller, Hagey, Smith, & Long, 1969) take family relationships more into account in the formation of self-identity.

Some investigators (Calvin & Holtzman, 1953; Dymond, 1949; Miejamota & Dornbush, 1956; Reeder, Donohue, & Biblarz, 1960) obtained self-ratings from group members using an index of six traits, such as the Dymond-Cotrell method (Dymond, 1949). They required group members to rate (1) themselves, (2) other members, (3) how others would view them, and (4) how others would view themselves. The purpose was to measure group member empathy. Other researchers (Berger, 1952; Phillips, 1951) developed scales that provided correlations between attitudes toward self and others. Secord and Jourard (1953) developed a scale to measure body cathexis—a person's feeling about their body—and related the feeling to a measure of anxiety. They found that body cathexis was associated with insecurity.

Self-efficacy is the self-expectation that one can successfully perform a behavior. This sense of capability is influenced by past experiences and perceptions of those experiences (Bandura, 1982) and is part of a person's private logic. When a person lacks self-efficacy, the person is blocked from doing something, even if knowledge of how to proceed is apparent, by virtue of self-perceptions of incapability. Research in the area of self-efficacy points to its effect on reactions to stress, coping ability, interactions with authority, overcoming failures, independence, goal orientation, pursuit of one's own interests, and pursuit of career (Bandura, 1982). If a child has a sense of self-efficacy about a behavior, the child may have overcome the feelings of inferiority related to the behavior (Dinter, 2000).

Dinter (2000) attempted to investigate the feelings of inferiority of college-aged students by examining life style patterns correlating with a feeling of self-efficacy. She found that people who scored high on the Belonging/Social Interest scale and high on the Striving for Perfection scale on the BASIS-A Inventory, as well as people who scored high on the Belonging/Social Interest scale and low to moderate on the Wanting Recognition scale, tended to have a greater sense of self-efficacy compared with those who did not fit this combination. Ashby and Kottman (1996) identified a distinction between normal and neurotic perfectionism. Adler said striving for perfection was a common way for people to try to overcome feelings of inferiority and, as long as this striving was socially useful, it could be thought of as a positive trait (Adler, 1956). Other researchers (Ashby & Kottman, 1996; Kottman & Ashby, 1999; Rice, Ashby, & Preusser, 1996; Rice, Ashby, & Slaney, 1998) point out that perfectionism may have a positive, adaptive component.

Respectfully Curious Inquiry

"Respectfully Curious Inquiry" (RCI) is our label for the process of understanding the individual (Milliren & Wingett, 2005). This process provides a means for exploring an individual's private logic and identifying the "perceived plus" or the "felt minus." Included in RCI are such skills as: setting mutually agreed upon goals; attending to the client; employing the use of "directed reflections"; reflective listening; empathic creativity; and Socratic questions.

One tool that we employ to understand the individual's unique and creative movement, developed by Wes Wingett, is to ask the person to tell us the story of how he or she learned to ride a bicycle. As the individual tells his or her story, we listen for how the individual moves from the "felt minus" involved in not being able to ride a bicycle to the "perceived plus" of mastering this activity.

> All the methods of Individual Psychology for understanding the personality take into account the individual's opinion of his goal of superiority, the strength of his inferiority feeling, the degree of his

social interest, and the fact that the whole individual cannot be torn from his context with life—or, better said, from his context with society. (Adler, 1964, p. 327)

We listen for how the person learns to acquire a new skill, the social context involved, and indications of any of Adler's (1964, p. 328) five entries to understanding the life style.

As an example, we include a short interview with a woman in her early 40s who related the following story:

> It was a purple bike with training wheels and it had a pink and purple and white basket. Mom started me out, she pushed me around on the concrete in front of the house. Then I rode up and down the gravel lane and the gravel made the training wheels lose their grip. So Dad took them off and he would run beside me and then he just let go and I thought he was still hanging on. I went quite a ways and told Dad that I was putting on the brakes. I turned around and he was about a quarter of a mile behind me. I was a really bad tomboy so I had a lot of confidence.

When asked what she experienced before she could ride, she stated, "I couldn't keep up with anybody and I felt lonely." When asked how it was after she learned, she said, "I could be with my friends and I felt accepted and comfortable."

As helping professionals, it is our task to help our clients (students) discover and understand what it is that they "are up to." We are then in a position to help them consider alternative beliefs and behaviors. In this case, the woman began to realize that part of her frustration with being overwhelmed in her job was built on having to learn everything that everyone else already knew. She could not stand not knowing something, and consequently, spent considerable time while away from work trying to be as skilled as her coworkers—even when it wasn't necessary for her to be involved. Her "felt-minus" or position of inferiority was based on not knowing as much as others. When she discovered herself in this position of inferiority, she went out of her way to learn what she thought she needed to know—her "perceived plus." As a result, we set a goal of helping her discriminate between what was important for her to know and what wasn't.

Summary

So we ask, "What is inferiority?" Simply stated, inferiority is an enduring awareness (either conscious or unconscious in thought) of inadequacy, often accompanied by the affinity to devalue one's self, sometimes pursuing markedly aggressive behavior by way of overcompensation. This overcompensation is the instigator of both exceptional achievements and unsociable conduct. In other words, feelings of inferiority are the source of all human motivation directed towards a goal of significance.

From our first breath of air at birth, we begin our journey with inferiority feelings as our compass to guide us down paths for the exploration of life. It is true that on some paths an intensified sense of inferiority, along with a lack of ability to endure, may bring into existence repressed and exaggerated feelings of superiority, thus giving rise to arrogance. More often, inferiority feelings lead us to compensate in useful, problem-oriented ways that benefit others as well as ourselves. Though at first glance inferiority appears to be negative in nature, a felt minus, it may lead the individual on the positive path of striving for competence in meeting nature's challenges (not just superiority over other people)—the perceived plus of movement toward self-improvement to reach a personal apex and contribute to a better society in the process.

Private logic represents our conceptual "plan" for negotiating successfully through life, the belief system counterpart to life style. Conclusions drawn about self, others, and the world are peripheral or at the core, and core beliefs will be harder to change. Life style is the totality of the behavioral strategies and safeguards that take us to our successes and failures. Through a process of "respectfully curious inquiry" we are able to help our students and clients examine their concepts and beliefs about who they are, how others are, and what they expect from the world.

Measures that attempt to describe inferiority feelings fall short of addressing a normal, universal feeling of inferiority. Most measures that aim at a description of the inferiority feeling start with self-concept or self-esteem constructs and do not take into consideration the "more than" or "less than" feelings that arise from the family constellation. Dinter's (2000) research concerned people who scored high on the Belonging/Social Interest scale and the Striving for Perfection scale on the BASIS-A Inventory. It also concerned people who scored high on the Belonging/Social Interest scale and low to moderate on the Wanting Recognition scale, and tended to have a greater sense of self-efficacy compared with those who did not fit this combination. These results seem to demonstrate the most promising direction for research concerning inferiority.

References

Adler, Alexandra (1938). *Guiding human misfits.* New York: Macmillan.
Adler, A. (1930). *Problems of neurosis.* New York: Cosmopolitan.

Adler, A. (1964). Complex compulsion as part of personality and neurosis. In *Superiority and social interest: A collection of later writings* (pp. 71–80; H. L. Ansbacher & R. R. Ansbacher, Eds.) Evanston, IL: Northwestern University Press. (Original work published 1935.)

Adler, A. (1956). *The individual psychology of Alfred Adler: A systematic presentation in selections from his writings* (H. L. Ansbacher & R. R. Ansbacher, Eds.). New York: Harper & Row.

Adler, A. (1958). *What life should mean to you.* New York: Capricorn Books.

Adler, A. (1964). *Superiority and social interest: A collection of later writings* (H. L. Ansbacher & R. R. Ansbacher, Eds.). Evanston, IL: Northwestern University Press.

Adler, A. (1969). *The science of living.* Garden City, NY: Anchor Doubleday.

Ashby, J. S., & Kottman, T. (1996). Inferiority as a distinction between normal and neurotic perfectionism. *Individual Psychology, 52* (3), 237–245.

Bandura, A. (1982). Self-efficacy mechanism in human agency. *American Psychologist, 32* (2), 122–147.

Berger, E. M. (1952). The relations between expressed acceptance of self and expressed acceptance of others. *The Journal of Abnormal and Social Psychology, 47,* 778–782.

Bickhard, M. H. (1974). A response to Crandall's "reply" and alternative "formulation." *Journal of Individual Psychology, 34* (1), 27–35.

Calvin, A. D., & Holtzman, W. H. (1953). Adjustment and the discrepancy between self-concept and the inferred self. *The Journal of Consulting Psychology, 17,* 39–44.

Craig, H. (1965). A sociometric investigation of the self-concept of the deaf child. *American Annals of the Deaf, 110,* 456–478.

Cooley, C. G. (1902). *Human nature and the social order.* New York: Charles Scribner's Sons.

Darwin, C. (1915). *The ascent of man.* London: Murray.

Dinter, L. D. (2000). The relationship between self-efficacy and lifestyle patterns. *The Journal of Individual Psychology, 56*(4), 462–474.

Dixon, P. N., & Strano, D. A. (1989). The measurement of inferiority: A review and directions for scale development. *Individual Psychology, 45* (3), 313–323.

Dreikurs, R. (1954). The psychological interview in medicine. *American Journal of Individual Psychology, 10,* 99–102.

Dreikurs, R. (1957). *Psychology in the classroom.* New York: Wiley.

Dreikurs, R. (1967). *Psychodynamics, psychotherapy and counseling.* Chicago: Alfred Adler Institute.

Dymond, R. F. (1949). A scale for the measurement of empathic ability. *The Journal of Consulting Psychology, 13,* 127–133.

Elser, R. (1959). The social position of hearing handicapped children in regular grades. *Exceptional Children, 25,* 304–309.

Emerton, M. (1978). Mainstreaming: Some social considerations. *Volta Review, 80,* 21–30.

Festinger, L. (1954). A theory of social comparison process. *Human Relations, 7,* 117–140.

Heidbreder, E. F. (1927). The normal inferiority complex. *The Journal of Abnormal Social Psychology, 22,* 243–258.

Jones E. E., & Berglas, S. (1978). Control of attributions about the self through self-handicapping strategies: The appeal of alcohol and the role of underachievement. *Personality and Social Psychology Bulletin, 4,* 200–206.

Kemper, T. (1966). Self-conceptions and the expectations of others. *Sociological Quarterly, 7,* 323–343.

Kopp, R. R. (1982). On clarifying basic Adlerian concepts: A response to Maddi. *Journal of Individual Psychology, 38*(1), 80–900.

Kottman, T., & Ashby, J. S. (1999). Social interest and multidimensional perfectionism. *The Journal of Individual Psychology, 55* (2), 176–185.

Kropotkin, P. (1914). *Mutual aid.* Boston, MA: Porter Sargent.

Leakey, R., & Lewin, R. (1977). *Origins.* New York: Dutton.

Maddi, S. (1978). Existential and individual psychology. *Journal of Individual Psychology, 34,* 182–190.

Manaster, G. J., & Corsini, R. J. (1982). *Individual psychology, theory and practice.* Itasca, IL: Peacock.

Mead, G. H. (1934). *Mind, self and society from the standpoint of a social behaviorist.* Chicago: University of Chicago Press.

Miejamota, F., & Dornbush, S. (1956). A test of the symbolic interactionist hypothesis of self-conception. *The American Journal of Sociology, 61,* 339–403.

Milliren, A., & Wingett, W. (2005). *In the style of Alfred Adler: Respectfully curious inquiry.* Handout presented to the West Texas Institute for Adlerian Studies. Unpublished.

Montagu, A. (1966). *On being human.* New York: Hawthorn.

Phillips, E. (1951). Attitudes toward self and others: A brief questionnaire report. *The Journal of Consulting Psychology, 15,* 79–81.

Purkey, W. W. (1968). *The search for self: Evaluating student self-concepts.* Gainesville, FL: Florida Educational Research and Development Council.

Reeder, L., Donohue, G., & Biblarz, A. (1960). Conceptions of self and others. *The American Journal of Sociology, 66,* 153–159.

Reich, C., Hambelton, D., & Holdin, B. (1977). The integration of hearing-impaired children in regular classrooms. *American Annals of the Deaf, 122,* 534–543.

Rhodewalt, F., & Davison Jr., J. (1986). Self-handicapping and subsequent performance: Role of outcome valence and attributional certainty. *Basic & Applied Social Psychology, 7* (4), 307–322.

Rice, K. G., Ashby, J. S., & Preusser, K. J. (1996). Perfectionism, relationships with parents, and self-esteem. *Individual Psychology, 52* (3), 246–260.

Rice, K. G., Ashby, J. S., & Slaney, R. B. (1998). Self-esteem as a mediator between perfectionism and depression: A structural equations analysis. *Journal of Counseling Psychology, 45*(3), 304–314.

Schlesinger, H., & Meadow, K. (1972). *Sound and sign.* Silver Springs, MD: National Association of the Deaf.

Secord, P., & Jourard, S. (1953). The appraisal of body-cathexis; body-cathexis and the self. *The Journal of Consulting Psychology, 17,* 343–347.

Sherwood, J. (1965). Self-identity and referent others. *Sociometry, 28,* 66–81.

Shulman, B. (1973). Encouraging the pessimist: A confronting technique. *The Individual Psychologist.* xiv (1), 7–9.

Snyder, C. R., & Smith, T. W. (1982). Symptoms as self-handicapping strategies: The virtues of old wine in a new bottle. In G. Weary & H. Mirels (Eds.), *Integrations of clinical and social psychology.* New York: Oxford University Press.

Ziller, R., Hagey, J., Smith, M., & Long, B. (1969). Self-esteem: A self-social construct. *The Journal of Consulting and Clinical Psychology, 33,* 34–95.

CHAPTER 26

The Measurement of Inferiority: A Review and Directions for Scale Development

PAUL N. DIXON and DONALD A. STRANO

Introduction

Many of the constructs prominent in current applications of Individual Psychology have their foundation in an older, more fundamental construct: the feeling of inferiority. For example, the currently applied construct of an individual's striving is dependent on a feeling of inferiority, whether that is goal striving, striving for superiority, or striving for perfection (Adler, 1964). Thus, the feeling of inferiority is key to the understanding of other constructs such as individual striving. Yet, there is little empirical support for the existence of a feeling of inferiority. This lack of empirical evidence is, at least in part, due to the absence of any sound measure of an inferiority feeling.

That there is no adequate measure of inferiority is particularly surprising given the construct that an inferiority feeling forms the foundation for much of Individual Psychology. It is one of the most popularized Adlerian concepts, having been incorporated into general knowledge (Loevinger, 1966). However, this construct remains unclear in the literature. The clarification of the nature of the inferiority feeling will provide some guidelines for development of a measure of inferiority proposed in a later section.

Defining the Feeling of Inferiority

Existing definitions of an inferiority feeling seem inconsistent with Adler's own definition. Further, in direct contrast to the wholistic nature of Individual Psychology, the attention paid to this construct frequently fails to take into account its interconnectedness with other aspects of the theory of Individual Psychology. Although the Ansbachers (Adler, 1964) state that Adler's later writings place the inferiority feeling as secondary to striving (i.e., for superiority, overcoming, perfection, etc.), they also point out a change in focus in his theory at this time. He moved toward a conceptualization of the feeling of inferiority as a result of a comparison with the goals toward which the individual strives (Adler, 1956, 1970). It does not seem possible that one can strive to overcome unless there is something one is seeking to overcome. Adler's writings support this. He does not deny the existence nor the importance of the inferiority feeling although he devotes more space in later writings to striving and social interest.

In Adler's last book, *Social Interest: A Challenge to Mankind* (1938), he lists the three basic assumptions of Individual Psychology: (a) a universal sense of inferiority, (b) it is characteristic of life that the individual will struggle to overcome his inferiority, and (c) the individual's and society's adjustment depends on the development of social feelings. The evolution of Adler's assumptions is the construct of the life-style (Rotter, 1962). Thus, it can be argued that at the basis of the individual's life-style is a feeling of inferiority.

An inferiority feeling has often been defined as a low self-concept or self-esteem. Frequently, researchers deal with an abnormal inferiority feeling or an inferiority complex. Yet, "to be human means to have inferiority feelings" (Adler, 1964, p. 54). A feeling of inferiority is universal, not a disease. Instead, it is a motivator for normal development (Adler, 1969). The inferiority feeling is seen in terms of a self-comparison (Adler, 1956, 1964; Dreikurs, 1954, 1967; Mosak, 1977) which is made from the moment infants are able to interact with those around them (Adler, 1956). Thus, from the first instant children can differentiate themselves from the environment, they begin making comparisons. For Adler, the first social interaction of the infant is feeding at the mother's breast (Adler, 1956). This involves a necessary cooperation from which both participants benefit. Other developmental theorists have presented similar views of this interaction (Bower, 1977; Bowlby, 1969).

At an early age, children, through their small physical size and dependence on others for nurturance and protection, realize their inferiority (Adler, 1956; Dreikurs, 1967). This feeling of inferiority continues to develop in the children's comparison of themselves with an unattainable ideal perfection defined for them by their parents (Adler, 1956). Children also recognize their own powerlessness in the face of nature (Adler, 1964). Thus, children have a feeling of inferiority (Dreikurs, 1954), although this may not be consciously felt (Adler, 1956).

The inferiority feeling becomes the motivating force for each individual and can be directed in either positive or negative directions (Adler, 1956, 1964; Dreikurs, 1957, 1967; Mosak, 1977). The direction this takes will depend on the degree to which the individual's social interest is developed (Adler, 1964) and will determine whether the individual's behavior is useful or useless (Manaster & Corsini, 1982). Adler suggests that the development of an inferiority feeling results in large part from childhood comparisons with other family members. Therefore, the measurement of inferiority should utilize a comparison with other family members. In addition, a proper measurement of the inferiority feeling should make this comparison relative to personal characteristics germane to the overall self-perception.

Mosak (1977) also stressed the comparative nature of the inferiority feeling. He first defined self-concept as attitudes referable to the self and then based each area of the inferiority feeling on a comparison with the self-concept. The first area of perceived inferiority is a comparison of the self-concept with an ideal self-image which includes physical characteristics. The second area is seen as the discrepancy between self-concept and the individual's environmental evaluations, which includes the social environment. The final area, which he identified as a form of guilt, is defined as the discrepancy between the self-concept and the individual's moral code. Similarly, Dreikurs (1967) saw the inferiority feeling as an assumption of being inferior physically, socially, or in comparison to one's own goals and standards. These three areas of comparison are suggested for a comprehensive measure of inferiority.

A comprehensive measure of inferiority must also consider that although the inferiority feeling may involve some real inferiority such as organ inferiority (Adler, 1956), the subjective perceptual nature is of primary importance. Dreikurs (1967) emphasizes that there is a major difference between real inferiority and a perceived inferiority. While objective phenomena do exist (i.e., organ inferiority), it is the subjective evaluation of this relative to others that results in a feeling of inferiority (Adler, 1956). Thus, a measure of the inferiority feeling should require comparison of oneself to others; a reflection of the subjective evaluation.

As with early recollections (Adler, 1937; Mosak, 1977; Olson, 1979), a measure of inferiority should utilize the individual's current biased apperception. The person's subjective perception rather than any objective reality is central to the understanding of the inferiority feeling. Individual's recollections consist of the few memories recalled of all the possible combinations of memories available (Dreikurs, 1967; Olson, 1979). Thus, a measure of inferiority can be interpreted as having meaning in the responses themselves rather than as a second best representation of some underlying real comparison made by the individual in his or her childhood. This interpretation is consistent with Meehl's (1967) suggestion for interpreting scales of this nature.

Current Measurement of Inferiority

Self-Concept vs. the Feeling of Inferiority

Measurement of a feeling of inferiority typically relies on various self-concept scales. The pitfalls of this approach are associated with a subtle but nevertheless important distinction between the inferiority feeling and self-concept.

While reviewing studies of inferiority, Goldfried (1963) chose articles measuring self-concept because none had a measure of an inferiority feeling. Worchel and Hillson (1958), in a study of the inferiority feeling in the criminal, take a self-concept measure and assume a similarity with an inferiority feeling. A visual inspection of a self-concept scale such as the SEI (Coopersmith, 1967), or the Tennessee Self-Concept scale (Fitts, 1964), shows that the items predominantly refer to "I" with little or no comparison to others in an attempt to get a self/other evaluation.

Loevinger and Ossorio (1958) note a weakness in many self-concept scales because they often measure stereotyped conventional self-concept responses (i.e., social desirability) as highest. This method ignores what they consider to be important: a realistic self-accepting self-concept. Although much of the literature on self-concept relates to a striving for social status and social approval (Coopersmith, 1967), this is seen as an effort to maintain a level of self-esteem. This would be in conflict with the Adlerian view of man as continually striving from a felt minus to a plus, as growth oriented and not static (Adler, 1956). Individual Psychology conceptualizes the neurotic character as pursuing a goal of enhancing self-esteem. This behavioral attempt to overcome the inferiority feeling is seen as arising out of a learned self-boundedness (Adler, 1956). Loevinger and Ossorio (1958) see many self-concept scales measuring neurotic striving, a stereotyped contemporary social contention that everybody who is not superior is necessarily inferior (Dreikurs, 1967). In this sense, self-concept can be seen as tied to the behavioral expression of a deeper construct (i.e., the inferiority feeling), but falling short of the construct.

Of particular relevance in the present discussion is a social definition of self-concept, which must start with Cooley's (1902) "looking glass-self." This can be defined as the imagined perception of self in the mind of another. This perception is thought to have three elements: (1) the imagination of one's appearance to the other person, (2) the imagination of the other person's appraisal of the appearance, and (3) some kind of self-valuing feeling.

Extending from this conception of self comes the social interactionist perspective. Mead (1934) outlines an approach to self-concept which stresses that individuals will conceive of themselves as they believe significant others conceive of them and will tend to act in accord with these expectations projected to significant others. It should be noted here that the subjective perception, rather than any objective reality, is of importance. Thus, individuals will try to act the way "people like them" should act.

Measuring Inferiority Feelings

Heidbreder (1927) attempted a study of the "normal inferiority complex." Using the definition of inferiority complex outlined by Adler, particularly the existence of this in "normal" individuals, she constructed a rating scale consisting of 137 traits that would be characteristic of an inferiority complex. Subjects were to indicate the degree to which they possessed each trait. She reported retest reliabilities of +.72 to +.75 for the scale and an approximate normal distribution of the scores in a norm group. Heidbreder uses this last finding to indicate that the "inferiority complex" is something present in different individuals in different degrees with no one possessing all or none of the characteristics. She conducted an early version of a t-test (i.e., the amount of difference between two groups in proportion to the probable error of the difference), between the upper and lower quarters of the distribution for each item. Of the 137 items tested, only two (those relating to sex roles) did not show the expected difference.

This attempt at measuring the Adlerian notion of "normal inferiority complex" falls short of addressing a normal universal feeling of inferiority. Heidbreder restricted herself to a discussion of the "inferiority complex" and the degree of presence or absence of this pathological characteristic in "normal" individuals. This is evident when she identified Adler's definition of the core of the inferiority complex as a "disorder in the self-regarding attitudes" (Heidbreder, 1927, p. 248). Thus, she failed to step beyond a definition of the inferiority feeling as a low self-concept or self-esteem.

Heidbreder hinted at a comparative component in one of the characteristics she listed. This points to an individual's "relative inferiority or superiority" to others. However, it is a minor component and lost in relation to a large number of other characteristics reportedly measured. The self-concept approach of her scale is also apparent in the wording of individual items.

This shortcoming stands out further when she discussed the presence or absence of the inferiority complex. Although she noted that the presence of the traits in her scale to a slight degree is normal (i.e., as is apparent in the lower quarter of her distribution), she was seeking a cut-off point at which to dichotomize the presence or absence of the inferiority complex. Heidbreder raised a question herself as to the validity of the scale, (i.e., Is the self-report of the traits objectively more frequent or subjectively more striking?). However, in line with Dreikurs's (1967) discussion of the inferiority feeling and several authors' positions on interpreting personality measures (Crown & Marlow, 1964; Meehl, 1967), it is the subjective "biased apperception" (Adler, 1956) that may well be the essential source of variation in the scale.

Finally, in discussing the response style of the groups at the extremes of the distribution, Heidbreder concluded that "individuals who are insecure in their self-regarding sentiments are peculiarly sensitive to any particulars in which they differ from most people" (1927, p. 255), and they also will tend to exaggerate these differences. Although she pointed to an acute awareness of interpersonal comparison in the group containing the inferiority complex, she doesn't see any comparison in the low group.

Later researchers (Festinger, 1954; Kemper, 1966; Sherwood, 1965; Ziller, Hagey, Smith, & Long, 1969) stress the importance of the individual's relations with others in the formation of a self-identity. A common approach to studying the social interactionist approach and thus, the influence of referent others on self-concept has been within a small group setting. Several investigators (Calvin & Holtzman, 1953; Dymond, 1949; Miejamota & Dornbush, 1956; Reeder, Donohue, & Biblarz, 1960) have done this by obtaining self-ratings from each group member and in addition had each member rate all other members of the group. However, these data were not used to compute a self-other discrepancy as is suggested by the nature of the inferiority feeling. Instead, a composite of others' attitudes toward the individual is computed to more closely match Cooley's (1902) or Mead's (1934) concept of self-concept as the imagination of the other person's assessment of one's self.

The studies mentioned above used an index of self-conception similar to the Dymond-Cotrell method (Dymond, 1949). This method requires that each individual in a group do four ratings: (1) themselves, (2) each other member of the group, (3) their belief of how others will view them, and (4) how others will view themselves. This is done for each of six traits. The original intent in this methodology was the measurement of empathic ability. Thus, the purpose of this scale is very different from that expected of an inferiority measure. That is, the ratings are utilized to determine how accurately individuals could predict other individuals, self-perception, and perception of them. This accuracy is utilized to discuss the individual's empathic ability rather than a feeling of inferiority.

Along this same line, other authors (Berger, 1952; Phillips, 1951) have developed scales to measure the relationship between attitudes toward the self and others. Again, however, the interest here is the correlation between self and other ratings, not the relationship between a self-other discrepancy and other personality variables. Berger (1952) references Adler's early work on self-other comparisons only in terms of the abnormal behavioral extreme of overcompensation (Adler, 1956).

Ziller, Hagey, Smith, and Long (1969) developed a scale to measure self-evaluation in relation to significant others. The respondents were asked to place symbols representing themselves and significant others in a set of six horizontally arranged circles. They argue that avoiding verbal self-report has advantages. The authors discuss this as a self-social construct which presents self-other orientations. Although there may be a relationship between this measure and the feeling of inferiority, the measurement of a discrepancy between self and other evaluations (particularly self as a child and family of orientation) seems likely to tap a different construct.

Two other scales can be found that have some relationship to the measurement of inferiority. Beloff and Beloff (1959) utilized a stereoscope to measure unconscious self-evaluation. The subjects were presented a picture of themselves and a stranger on each side of the stereoscope. They were than asked to rate this picture for degree of attractiveness. This was then compared with a rating made on a control composite. Their results indicated that the self-composite was rated higher than the control. They see the results as supporting the theory that individuals hold favorable unconscious self-judgments. Although this could be seen as counter to Adler's theory, the results are based on an evaluation of the self in comparison to strangers rather than with significant others (i.e., the family of origin). Further, it is not clear to what extent the presence of the picture of the stranger paired with the individual's picture influenced the rating.

Finally, Secord and Jourard (1953) developed a scale to measure body cathexis, or the feeling of an individual toward his or her body. They related this scale to a measure of anxiety and found it to be useful in discussing personality. They also conclude that low body cathexis is associated with insecurity. Although this scale addressed one aspect of Dreikurs's (1967) definition of the inferiority feeling (i.e., physical characteristics), it does it in a unidimensional manner rather than in the comparative approach reflective of the mechanisms underlying the development of the inferiority feeling.

Conclusion

The development of an individual's life-style (Adler, 1956) is believed to be formed by an early age and develops in response to the comparative feeling of inferiority through the individual's biased apperception (Adler, 1936, 1956). These early comparisons resulting in the individual's unique, biased approach to the world (i.e., life-style) are made in relation to the child's first society, the family. Thus, the individual's perception of themselves and their families of origin could form the basis for an enduring comparative feeling of inferiority. Further, the feeling of inferiority, developed by approximately age five, is seen as a relatively stable, enduring trait; a foundation for the life-style.

There is little empirical research of this construct so central to Adlerian Theory, and attempts to measure inferiority are inadequate. This lack of an appropriate scale may explain in part the paucity of research related to inferiority, and certainly emphasizes the need for a reliable and valid measure of inferiority independent of measures of self-concept and self-esteem. The review of the development and motivational qualities of the inferiority feeling offers some guidelines for the development of a valid measure of inferiority as does the review of a variety of existing measurement efforts.

A scale designed to measure the feeling of inferiority should consider the use of comparison, in particular: (1) the comparison of self with family members, (2) this comparison relative to the perception of physical characteristics, social characteristics, and personal goals and standards, and (3) the comparison of self to family members as a subjective evaluation rather than an objective reality. The resulting scale with physical characteristics, social characteristics, and goals and standards subscales, with appropriate reliability and with some initial empirical validation, could provide an impetus for increased research related to the feeling of inferiority.

References

Adler, A. (1936). Compulsion neurosis. International Journal of Individual Psychology. 2, 3–22.
Adler, A. (1937). The significance of early recollections. International Journal of Individual Psychology. 3, 283–287.
Adler, A. (1938). Social interest: A challenge to mankind. London: Faber & Faber, Ltd.
Adler, A. (1956). The individual psychology of Alfred Adler: A systematic presentation from his writings. H. L. Ansbacher & R. R. Ansbacher (Eds.). New York: Basic Books.
Adler, A. (1964). Superiority and social interest: Collection of late writings. H. L. Ansbacher & R. R. Ansbacher (Eds.). Evanston, IL: Northwestern University Press.
Adler, A. (1969). The science of living. New York: Doubleday.

Adler, A. (1970). Fundamentals of individual psychology. The Journal of Individual Psychology, 26, 36–49.

Beloff, H., & Beloff, J. (1959). Unconscious self-evaluation using a stereoscope. The Journal of Abnormal and Social Psychology, 59, 257–258.

Berger, E. M. (1952). The relations between expressed acceptance of self and expressed acceptance of others. The Journal of Abnormal and Social Psychology, 47, 778–782.

Bower, T. G. R. (1977). A primer of infant development. San Francisco: William Freeman.

Bowlby, J. (1969). Attachment and loss, Vol I. Attachment. New York: Basic Books.

Calvin, A. D., & Holtzman, W. H. (1953). Adjustment and the discrepancy between self-concept and the inferred self. The Journal of Consulting Psychology, 17, 39–44.

Cooley, C. H. (1902). Human nature and the social order. New York: Charles Scribner's Sons.

Coopersmith, S. (1967). The antecedents of self-esteem. San Francisco: William Freeman.

Crown, D., & Marlow, D. (1964). The approval motive. New York: Wiley.

Dreikurs, R. (1954). The psychological interview in medicine. American Journal of Individual Psychology, 10, 99–102.

Dreikurs, R. (1957). Psychology in the classroom. New York: Wiley.

Dreikurs, R. (1967). Psychodynamics, psychotherapy, and counseling. Chicago: Alfred Adler Institute.

Dymond, R. F. (1949). A scale for the measurement of empathic ability. The Journal of Consulting Psychology, 13, 127–133.

Festinger, L. (1954). A theory of social comparison process. Human Relations, 7, 117–140.

Fitts, W. (1964). Manual: Tennessee Self-Concept Scale. Nashville, TN: Counselor Recordings and Tests.

Goldfried, M. R. (1963). Feelings of inferiority and the deprecation of others: A research review and theoretical reformulation. The Journal of Individual Psychology, 19, 96–109.

Heidbreder, E. F. (1927). The normal inferiority complex. The Journal of Abnormal Social Psychology, 22, 243–258.

Kemper, T. (1966). Self conceptions and the expectations of others. Sociological Quarterly, 7, 323–343.

Loevinger, J. (1966). The meaning and measurement of the ego development. The American Psychologist, 21, 195–206.

Loevinger, J., & Ossorio, A. G. (1958). Evolution of therapy by self-report: A paradox. The American Psychologist, 13, 366.

Manaster, G. J., & Corsini, R. J. (1982). Individual psychology, theory and Practice. Itasca, IL: F. E. Peacock.

Mead, G. H. (1934). Mind, self and society from the standpoint of a social behaviorist. C. W. Morris (Ed.). Chicago: University of Chicago Press.

Meehl, P. E. (1967). The dynamics of structured personality tests. In D. N. Jackson & S. Messick, (Eds.). Problems in human assessment. New York: McGraw Hill.

Miejamota, F.; & Dornbush, S. (1956). A test of the symbolic interactionist hypothesis of self-conception. The American Journal of Sociology, 61, 339–403.

Mosak, H. H. (1977). On purpose: Collected papers. Chicago: Alfred Adler Institute.

Olson, H. A. (1979). Early recollections. Their use in diagnosis and psychotherapy. Springfield, IL: Charles C. Thomas.

Phillips, E. (1951). Attitudes toward self and others: A brief questionnaire report. The Journal of Consulting Psychology, 15, 79–81.

Reeder, L, Donohue, G., & Biblarz, A. (1960). Conceptions of self and others. The American Journal of Sociology, 66, 153–159.

Rotter, J. B. (1962). An analysis of Adlerian psychology from a research orientation. The Journal of Individual Psychology, 18, 3.

Secord, P., & Jourard, S. (1953). The appraisal of body-cathexis; body- cathexis and the self. The Journal of Consulting Psychology, 17, 343–347.

Sherwood, J. (1965). Self identity and referent others. Sociometry, 28, 66–81.

Worchel, P., & Hillson, J. S. (1958). The self-concept in the criminal: An exploration of Adlerian theory. The Journal of Individual Psychology, 14, 173.

Ziller, R., Hagey, J., Smith, M., & Long, B. (1969). Self-esteem: A self-social construct. The Journal of Consulting and Clinical Psychology, 33, 34–95.

X
Overcompensation

CHAPTER 27

Overcompensation in Adlerian Theory

TREVOR HJERTAAS

The paradox is that the poorly equipped man, the man who starts behind the line, has the greatest advantage. Progress and achievement result only from the conquest of difficulties. (Adler, 1927/2004, p. 7).

The purpose of this essay is to trace the development of Adler's concept of overcompensation, offer a clear definition of it, and to note some strengths, limitations, and possible directions for research in this area.

Development of the Concept of Overcompensation

The concepts of compensation and overcompensation are among Adler's earliest ideas. Adler (1907/2002) initially presented them in his 1907 work, "A Study of Organ Inferiority." Here Adler noted how weakened or damaged organ systems could compensate, sometimes becoming even stronger than the average organ through these compensatory efforts (one kidney, for example, growing larger and more efficient to compensate for the inadequacy of the other). Adler also described in this work how psychological processes could be utilized to aid this process of compensation, writing of a "greater activity on the part of the psyche" (p. 123).

"A Study of Organ Inferiority" may be read as an early example of psychosomatic medicine. In this study, Adler examines the interplay between biological and psychological factors, giving as an example a young girl with "a functional inferiority" of the digestive organs, who would vomit or get diarrhea when emotionally upset. Adler also noted that some individuals with similar difficulties would compensate through their choice of profession, becoming cooks, for instance.

As Ansbacher and Ansbacher (1956) state, however, Adler was initially concerned with the overcompensation for inferior organ systems, not overcompensation for inferiority feelings, a development that was to come three years later. At this later point, Ansbacher and Ansbacher (1956, p. 44) explain, subjective "attitudes and opinions" became the core of Individual Psychology, and, thus, it is only for that which the individual personally feels to be inferior that must be compensated. When Adler's thought did evolve to this point, however, it remained parallel to his original formulation:

> The mechanism of the striving for compensation with which the soul strives to neutralize the torturing feeling of inferiority has its analogy in the organic world. It is a well known fact that those organs of our body which are essential for life produce an overgrowth and over-function when through damage to their normal state their productivity is lessened. ... Similarly, under pressure of the feeling of inferiority, of the torturing thought that the individual is small and helpless, the soul attempts with all its might to become master over this [painful feeling of inferiority]. (Adler, 1927/2004, p. 15)

Adler (1956) also stated:

> Children who have an organ inferiority, who are weak, clumsy, sickly, retarded in growth, ugly or deformed, or who have retained infantile forms of behavior are very prone to acquire through their relations to the environment a feeling of inferiority [later revision: increased feelings of inferiority]. This feeling rests heavily upon them, and they aim to overcome it by all means. (p. 53)

Shulman and Klapman (1981) presented some illustrations of psychological compensation in line with Adler's original formulation:

> When a spastic child develops strong intellectual interests, when a homely girl trains herself to be charming and pleasant, when

a physically weak boy becomes a diplomatic persuader of others, we all recognize that the child is compensating for a deficiency along courageous and useful channels. (p. 94)

From a biopsychosocial perspective, one can see the true value of Adler's idea. For example, an individual's propensity toward depression, acquired through a combination of heredity and unfortunate early-life experiences (which themselves influence the formation of the person's neural substrate), could be compensated for through the active and courageous seeking of new means of coping and of viewing life and self. Adler, being a true holistic thinker, discerned almost 100 years ago how psychology could impact biological and social factors, and that the individual need not remain forever a "prisoner" of such early or unavoidable conditions.

Ansbacher and Ansbacher (1956) explain that Adler's thinking, in developing a dynamic principle of compensation for a subjective inferiority, evolved from compensating for an organ inferiority, to the aggressive drive, to the masculine protest, and later into various manifestations of the striving for superiority, culminating in the striving for perfection. All of these conceptualizations include the idea of striving to overcome a felt lack or disadvantage. Overcompensation, therefore, can be seen as one variant of the striving for perfection. It is most apparent as something distinct when an individual has an exaggerated or strongly felt sense of inferiority, for which "normal striving" is inadequate to compensate.

In his essay "The Feeling of Inferiority and the Striving for Recognition" (1927/ 2004), Adler also makes it clear that any efforts at compensation will be in the direction of the final, fictive goal. Ansbacher and Ansbacher (1956) state:

> The fictional goal is, in many ways, a device of the individual to pull himself up by his bootstraps, as it were.... [I]t serves two compensatory functions. (1) It initiates compensation, and (2) it creates positive feelings in the present which mitigate the feelings of inferiority [since the individual reassures him or herself that success can be achieved in the future]. (pp. 97–98)

That compensation will be in the direction of the final, fictive goal is an important point, since it implies that overcompensation is another fictional "as if." A suffering individual may say to him- or herself something like: "I may be very ugly, but if I learn to paint lovely pictures, then the beauty of my spirit will be revealed and my physical limitations will not matter." This is a useful fiction, a conviction (and one that is often only vaguely conscious) and, as such, may be difficult to measure in direct ways, but may be understood phenomenologically.

Adler also stated that the desire to compensate could become "over-driven" and manifest, on the useless side of life, as the "striving for power:"

> Where the feeling of inferiority is so intensified that the child believes that he will never be able to compensate for his weakness, the danger arises that in his striving for overcompensation, he will aim to overbalance the scales. The striving for power and dominance may become exaggerated and intensified until it must be called pathological. The ordinary relationships of life will never satisfy such children. Well adapted to their goal, their movements must have a certain grandiose gesture about them. They seek to secure their position in life with extraordinary efforts, with greater haste and impatience, with more intense impulses, without consideration of any one else.... They are against the world, and the world is against them. (Adler, 1927/2004, p. 15)

Adler noted that the clinician can discern this exaggerated striving for power in numerous psychopathological conditions, including delinquency and antisocial personality, neurotic conditions (including many anxiety states, depression, and personality disorders), psychosis, alcoholism, and drug abuse. A few less-than-useful attempts at compensation can be seen in some of Seidler's (1947) case histories, included in this volume (chapter 28). However, if the individual felt he or she had a good relationship with other people and felt equal to others (through the compensatory efforts), then, Adler believed, the person would find a solution to the difficulties of life on the useful side.

Adler also believed that the child could be encouraged toward useful compensation through the active intervention of the parent or teacher. If such people pointed out what the child had done correctly, emphasized his or her ability to persevere, learn, and accomplish even more, and thus imparted the sense that the child was capable, then the child would likely find the courage to overcome any difficulties. Such interactions would later be called "mirroring" and "assuming a self-object function" by Heinz Kohut (Ornstein, 1991), who also viewed them as essential for the development of a healthy sense of self.

Definitions of Compensation and Overcompensation

Backman and Dixon (1992) state that "Adler's conceptualization of compensation provides a broad framework within which various types of compensatory behaviors prompted by biological or psychological shortcomings can be analyzed" (p. 271). They also cite the definition of compensation in the English and English (1958) dictionary of psychological terms as "action that aims to make amends for some lack or loss in personal characteristics or status; or action that achieves partial satisfaction when direct satisfaction is blocked" (p. 101). Backman and Dixon (1992) further state:

> According to English and English, these efforts to compensate for losses can take several directions: (a) the development of a different or substitute activity ... (b) pursuing the original goal with an unusually zealous effort ... or (c) modifying or denying value in the original goal. (pp. 259–260)

The latter would be equivalent to the "sour grapes" strategy noted by Mosak and Maniacci (1998, pp. 161–162). Although it is interesting to think of this as a psychological compensation, it would likely not be considered as such by most Adlerians.

In another text, Mosak and Maniacci (1999) explain that compensatory efforts can take place directly, within the area of felt deficiency; indirectly, in another area; or through overcompensation. They define *direct compensation* as

> compensation within the area [that] typically involves coping with the task despite what appear to be severe challenges. For example, if I break my arm, I learn to function with the cast; if I become blind, I learn to navigate my way around with a cane, a seeing-eye dog, and the like. Text-books often cite Helen Keller, Teddy Roosevelt, and Demosthenes in this regard. (p. 83)

Indirect compensation is defined as "Compensation in another area [that] entails working to build up one area if another is deficient. For instance, I may be poor in school, but I can become an excellent athlete" (p. 83). Seidler (1947) noted that in some cases indirect compensation may be an avoidance:

> It is reasonable to assume that shy, fearful, hesitant individuals will not adjust themselves to failures by attacking the difficulty, but will evade the issue, and therefore will be driven into another field for overcompensation. We find individuals who compensate for physical inferiority by wit, or the ability to recite well, or other similar achievements. (p. 192)

Overcompensation, as described by Mosak and Maniacci (1999),

> occurs if people overexcel in an area despite having a setback.
> Specifically, someone who is deficient in one area works hard to
> become not only proficient but better than what would normally
> (typically) be expected from someone who started out without the
> deficiency. An example might be someone with a foot problem who
> becomes not only a "normal" walker but a great dancer. Thus,
> overcompensation, if directed toward constructive goals, may
> culminate in excellent achievements. (pp. 83–84)

Although Mosak and Maniacci imply that overcompensation must be
direct (in the same area where the inferiority is felt), I would argue that
overcompensation may also be indirect. What distinguishes it from compensation is its more ambitious goal—to become greater than the norm,
which Seidler (1947) also suggests.

Also of importance to the definition is that Adler, at least in his later
conceptions, strongly emphasized the subjectivity of inferiority feelings
which could lead to compensatory efforts. Shulman and Klapman (1981)
explain this as follows: "The subjective perception of a defeat and the subjective conviction that it is important to compensate for the defect are
required before the child initiates a psychic compensation" (pp. 93–94).
Thus, a subjective feeling of inferiority for which the individual believes he
or she can and should compensate is necessary. Similarly, Seidler (1947)
stated: "The deliberate decision to make a continuous effort in order to
overcome a definite difficulty is found so often that it can be considered as
an essential characteristic of overcompensation" (p 189).

It should be noted that a strong feeling of inferiority will not automatically lead to overcompensation. Grey (1998) stated: "It should also be
emphasized that for the tiny number of individuals who overcame a physical handicap to achieve greatness, there were millions with other similar
handicaps who unfortunately did not" (p. 14). Grey (1998) also observed
that Adler "commenced using the term 'inferiority complex' to describe
those people who, for whatever reason, were unable to compensate for
their feelings of inferiority in a positive and cooperative manner" (p. 16).
These discouraged individuals make a display of their inadequacy to help
excuse their failures or limitations. This view is also shared by Shulman
and Klapman (1981), and implies that "courage, confidence, and optimism" are necessary to initiate overcompensation.

In sum, the five essential characteristics of compensation that have to be
considered in research are that:

- both compensation and overcompensation can be either direct (in the area of felt deficiency) or indirect (in another area);
- overcompensation is distinguished from mere compensation by the more ambitious goal to become greater than the norm;
- the area of perceived deficiency is subjective;
- a decision is made to overcome the felt deficiency in some way (although the person is sometimes not entirely conscious of having done so); and
- the individual takes appropriate steps to do so (rather than merely dwelling in the realm of fantasy or attempting to excuse oneself because of the perceived inadequacy).

Proposals and Recommendations for Research

Included in this text is the elegant research of Coleman and Croake (1987), designed to assess compensation in visibly handicapped children. This research utilizes the California Test of Personality (in particular the subscales of "self-reliance," "sense of personal worth," and "feeling of belonging") with a group of children with visible handicaps and a matched control group, where they find evidence consistent with Adler's theory of overcompensation.

It should be noted that the subscales on the California Test of Personality, as is true of all "objective" personality inventories, are only approximate measures of the underlying construct and, thus, lack perfect validity, being unable to be entirely accurate measures of what they attempt to gauge. Finding instruments that can fully measure an underlying construct is a difficulty in Adlerian research (see Mosak, 1991). This limitation must be accepted in much of psychological research, but this does not necessarily decrease its value. As Kelly and Main (1978) noted:

> An issue which may pose a potential stumbling block to the Adlerian researcher lies in the behaviorist's emphasis upon overt, observable behavior as the only valid unit of study. The Adlerian would certainly reject this assumption and point to the importance of such internal states as self-conception, world view, and fictive goals as legitimate for psychological investigation.… It must be pointed out that the researcher need not look for direct causality, but only for probability relationships between events and outcomes. Such a position places the Adlerian researcher back on firm theoretical ground. For when considering probabilities, one must also assume that "everything can be something else as well.…" In addition, Individual Psychology ascribes to a position of "soft determinism" which

recognizes the inner nature of life as well as the pressures of external reality. (p. 224)

If the researcher is willing to accept the limitations that "soft determinism" imposes, and values the results that can be derived from measurement with well-constructed, if imperfect, instruments, then much can be accomplished with "quantitative" research, as Coleman and Croake (1987), for example, have shown.

Backman and Dixon (1992) in their article on psychological compensation, review the literature in four broad areas: sensory handicaps, cognitive deficits, interpersonal losses, and compensation for brain injury. They cite numerous results that either suggest that psychological compensation has occurred or—as in the Coleman and Croake study—strongly support its occurrence.

As well, they cite numerous strengths of Adler's model of overcompensation for research, including the distinction between automatic and deliberate compensation, the distinction between objective and subjective deficits, a psychological origin of compensation (feelings of inferiority), and Adler's uniqueness in recognizing that certain compensatory strategies can have negative consequences. As well, they perceive some limitations in Adler's model, primarily due to their goals as empirical investigators. Although Backman and Dixon recognize the importance of evaluating whether a compensatory behavior has positive consequences both for the individual and for other people in his or her environment, as does Adler, they criticize Adler for being somewhat arbitrary in his judgment concerning this issue. They call for strict criteria by which such a judgment would be made. From the Adlerian perspective, such criteria may be helpful but cannot be absolute, since what is "useful" and what is not can only be judged sub specie aeternitatis, and is thus somewhat uncertain and ever-changing, depending on the needs of a situation. This may be contrary to the requirements of empirical research, but is ultimately more respectful of reality.

Another concern raised by Backman and Dixon (1992) is their questioning of the feeling of inferiority (stating that it lacks empirical validation) and noting that it is difficult to differentiate it from overcompensation itself (since, in Adlerian theory, "normals" also engage in some form of compensatory behavior). These are valid concerns. The feeling of inferiority may be fully comprehended only qualitatively and may be somewhat beyond the scope of the scientific method. Phenomenological approaches or indirect empirical "support" may be all that can be achieved in this area (although creative means such as that of Dixon and Strano (1989) have been attempted). Discriminating normal striving from overcompensation involves differentiating points along a continuum, because Adler recognized that the original dynamics he observed at work in overcompensation were identifiable in all human beings in one form or another. Thus the criteria the researcher must decide on is not so much what constitutes overcompensation and what constitutes "normal" striving, but rather how much striving should still be considered within the normal range before it is termed overcompensation. Any decisions about this matter will, of course, be somewhat arbitrary.

Backman and Dixon (1992) also present certain guidelines that they believe will further research in the area of overcompensation. They stress the importance of gathering data on the origins, mechanisms, and forms of compensatory behavior. They state that attempts should be made to devise research strategies that enable the objective assessment of the origin of compensatory behavior as well of as the behavior itself. They advise using a control group so that it can be demonstrated that individuals in an experimental group differ from controls in use of compensatory behavior (as noted, this being an important point from the Adlerian perspective, as Adler believed that all people strive to move from a position of a felt "minus" to one of a felt "plus"). They also recommend gathering information regarding an individual's subjective perception of a deficit and if he or she was consciously aware of initiating a compensatory effort; how the person compensated; and whether the compensatory effort had positive benefits for both the person and others in the environment. They state that such efforts would illustrate the "real life" applications of the research. The results of such an approach would certainly be valuable and would also provide a bridge to more "qualitative" research.

In fact, Regine Seidler (1947), in her paper, "The Phenomenon of Overcompensation," presents a classical example of qualitative research —the case study. In a sensitive and thorough explication of numerous early recollections, Seidler is able to show how the dynamics of overcompensation unfold and to explain why they manifest as they do in various instances. Seidler then hypothesizes some principles from her findings.

In terms of other areas of qualitative (descriptive) research, the phenomenological method, the exploration of mental states (Nissim-Sabat, 1995); hermeneutic research, a related approach, where an attempt is made to make clear the meaning of a particular lived experience, often through a narrative (Packer & Addison, 1989); and protocol analysis, where an attempt is made to identify cognitive processes involved in performing a task (Ericsson & Simon, 1993) may also prove useful methods in future research in this and other areas of Individual Psychology.

Conclusion

Further research in this area along either quantitative or qualitative lines would be useful. Numerous areas could be explored. In addition to continued work in the areas of sensory handicaps, cognitive deficits, interpersonal losses, and compensation for brain injury (all noted by Backman and Dixon, [1992]), compensatory strategies seen in individuals with moderate or severe psychological problems could be examined through both objective and subjective methods.

The foundation of the past has been firmly established. We now need to wait to see what structure the future will erect on it. I have no doubt that many of the ideas of Adler will survive this test of time.

References

Adler, A. (1956). *The individual psychology of Alfred Adler: A systematic presentation in selections from his writings* (H. L. Ansbacher and R. R. Ansbacher, Eds.). New York: Basic Books.

Adler, A. (2002). A study of organ inferiority. In H. Stein (Ed.), *Journal Articles: 1898–1909* (pp. 115–192). San Francisco: Classical Adlerian Translation Project. (Original work published 1907.)

Adler, A. (2004). *Journal articles: 1927–1931* (H. Stein, Ed.). Bellingham, WA: Classical Adlerian Translation Project.

Ansbacher, H. L., & Ansbacher, R. R. (1956). Comments. In A. Adler, *The individual psychology of Alfred Adler: A systematic presentation in selections from his writings* (pp. 44, 97–98). New York: Basic Books.

Backman, L., & Dixon, R. (1992). Psychological compensation: A theoretical framework. *Psychological Bulletin, 112*(2), 259–283.

Coleman, R., & Croake, J. (1987). Organ inferiority and measured overcompensation. *Individual Psychology, 43*(3), 364–370.

Dixon, P., & Strano, D. (1989). The measurement of inferiority: A review and directions for scale development. *Individual Psychology, 45*(3), 312–322.

English, H., & English, A. (1958). *A comprehensive dictionary of psychological and psychoanalytical terms.* New York: Longmans, Green.

Ericsson, K., & Simon, H. (1993). *Protocol analysis: Verbal reports as data.* New York: Bradford Books.

Grey, L. (1998). *Alfred Adler: The forgotten prophet.* Westport, CT: Praeger.

Kelly, D., & Main, F. (1978). Idiographic research in Adlerian psychology: Problems and solutions. *Journal of Individual Psychology, 34*(2), 221–231.

Mosak, H. (1991). "I don't have social interest": Social interest as construct. *Individual Psychology, 47*(3), 309–320.

Mosak, H., & Maniacci, M. (1998). *Tactics in counseling and psychotherapy.* Itasca, NY: Peacock.

Mosak, H., & Maniacci, M. (1999). *A primer of Adlerian psychology: The analytic-behavioral-cognitive psychology of Alfred Adler.* New York: Bruner/Mazel.

Nissim-Sabat, M. (1995). Toward a phenomenology of empathy. *American Journal of Psychotherapy, 49*(2), 163–170.

Ornstein, P. (Ed.). (1991). *The search for the self: Selected writings of Heinz Kohut.* Madison, CT: International Universities Press.

Packer, M., & Addison, R. (1989). *Entering the circle: Hermeneutic investigation in psychology.* New York: State University of New York Press.

Seidler, R. (1947). The phenomenon of overcompensation. *Individual Psychology Bulletin, 6*(4), 185–194.

Shulman, B., & Klapman, H. (1981). Organ inferiority and psychiatric disorders in childhood. In *Contributions to Individual Psychology* (pp. 21–104). Chicago: Adler School of Professional Psychology.

CHAPTER **28**

The Phenomenon of Overcompensation

REGINE SEIDLER

Individual Psychology considers the attitude of an individual toward the experience of failing as a decisive factor in his personality development. The experience of failure may discourage the individual, and consequently lower his élan, his zest for accomplishment. He may withdraw in an attempt to avoid further failing. Put to a test, the recurrence of failure is only natural. However, for the discouraged individual this renewed experience of failing will serve as a confirmation of his feared inability, and thus lead to further withdrawal. On the other hand, there are individuals who, in the case of failing, not only do not give up, but try the harder. They are untiring in their attempts to reach their goal, and in the end find their efforts rewarded. They may not only reach their goal, but go even farther and show exceptional achievements. Demosthenes is a classic example.

According to this hypothesis there seem to be mainly two ways of adjustment to the experience of failure: attack or withdrawal, and their various modifications.

Forty-four college students were examined, and autobiographical compositions were used to determine the kind of the reported failures, the attitude toward the experience of failure and the reactions to it in the subjects involved. A thorough analysis of a number of cases which showed the phenomenon of overcompensation led to the postulation of a hypothetical theory, which may contribute to the understanding of the dynamics of overcompensation.

Subject 23 reports of his early stammering:

> Early in my life I was the object of ridicule by my father because of stammering and a general lack of fluency in oral expression. His mimicking and laughter were, at times, infuriating, and served to shake further my confidence in my speech, to precipitate emotional expectancy manifested in anxiety to express myself favorably. The fact that he too stammered (which explains his pleasure in belittling others) provided only slight consolation for the humiliation.

What became of this stammerer?

"I majored in speech, engaged in considerable extracurricular dramatics and radio, and, after graduation, worked in the field of speech correction."

All childhood recollections of S 23, as well as later incidents in his life, have one characteristic in common: belligerence. He is a fighter, and he cannot take defeat. He fights mentally with arguments, and he fights actually with his fists. In case of defeat, he still wins through rationalizing:

> A female class mate, Susie, had been throwing snow balls at me. She and I were straightway ordered upon the green carpet of the principal's office. Susie's only defense was that I had "dared" her to do it. She was sternly reproved for the unseemly act and told not to throw snowballs, even if someone did "dare" her. Then she was told to go home. I remained to explain why I had urged such a well-behaved girl to be guilty of such flagrant misbehavior. Teacher was using the third switch when I "broke down and cried." I explained to my waiting comrades, "She wouldn't have made me cry, only I knew she wouldn't stop until I cried."

Thus the boy rationalized his defeat into a victory over the teacher; it was in his power to make the teacher stop.

There are, however, incidents when he adjusted himself to difficulties by withdrawal, e.g., by "playing hookey." But he turns such a withdrawal into a victory over his mother:

> Because I disliked walking two miles to school, and had been in a fight with a different boy each day of the first week in defense of my "city ways" and was progressing toward bigger adversaries instead of smaller ones, and because the teacher "had it in for me,"

I heeded nature's beckoning finger one bright morning and spent the day listening to her silent teachings in preference to Miss Baker's shrill voice. My mother discovered my truancy in the afternoon, and as a result of the ensuing argument, it was decided that I need not return to school until the next month, when Father planned to move back to the city. I was secretly proud of my victory over Mother, and for years afterwards, I managed to "play hookey" from school by some means or other.

His fighting attitude does not disappear after his return to the city:
"After we moved to the city, I continued my budding pugilistic career by qualifying as an enemy of the 'Third Street Gang.' Now, my status reversed, I was fighting because the gang called me a 'country jake.' "
It fits well into the picture of overcompensation that the initial experience of this fighter was extreme fear. The following is a report of his very first childhood recollection:

I remember being pecked by a belligerent rooster and reacting with extreme fright. Several times after that I had nightmares which were probably related to the experience. I was frightened by an owl at about the same time, so it is understandable why I dreamed of being pursued by an enormous bird, eight or ten feet tall.

Why does this fear not lead into discouragement, withdrawal, introversion?
It is easy to see from the reports of S 23 that his environment set a premium on his fighting spirit. His belligerent attitude was encouraged by his father, who always admired his victories:

I vaguely remember, at the age of five, hearing a conversation between Mrs. Foster, a neighbor, and my mother. I was at that particular time resting underneath a davenport in an adjoining room. Mrs. Foster related that she had witnessed the bouncing of a rock from the head of her son, Junior. At the same time she saw me heading homeward at a rate of speed which I had never been known to attain when leaving a game of "cowboys and Indians." It seems there had been a difference of opinion as to who should be the leader of the cowboys. Mother was sincerely shocked and assured her neighbor that a severe punishment was in store for her erring boy. I remained under the davenport until my father came home from the office. A lengthy argument between Father and Mother ensued, but in the end Father patted my head and proudly asserted, "he did right in taking his own part." Mother went into the bedroom with a headache.

S 23 describes the attitude of his parents toward him in the following statements:

"Father continually defended me and evinced considerable pride in his offspring's belligerence and 'independence.' Mother continually strived to teach me the principles of brotherly love, cooperation and Christian living."

He expressed in his reports warm admiration and affection for his mother—but he calls Father "a great pal with whom I have always gotten along beautifully (except for a few arguments which don't count now) and who has always 'stuck up' for me."

However, we remember that this same father made fun of the boy's stammering, and we read more about Father's belittling and scornful attitude in a report on debates, in which the whole family found much pleasure:

> Early in life, I confined my debates to discussions with my siblings and my mother, but as verbal facility grew and my own opinion of my fund of knowledge inflated itself, I graduated to debates of increasing warmth with my father. Increased speaking facility and fluency would logically have been the result of that experience; but another factor asserted itself here. Father enjoyed arguing. He also enjoyed the self-elevation that comes with winning an argument. Most of the time he did win. However, as I grew older, there were occasional discussions in which there was a question as to whether the parent was the victor. When Father was not sure that he was winning an argument, his favorite conclusion was to accuse me of having 'crazy ideas,' to say I stammered, and then he proceeded to mimic my hesitating speech. Considerable decrease in my confidence in my speech resulted. I tended to withdraw from expression of my ideas in class and social situations, because I feared that I couldn't express myself without hesitation and that the reaction would be the same that my father had often given.

S 23 reports repeatedly of similar experiences, distinct failure experiences, which discouraged him and hindered his progress. Such relapses, however, were always only temporary. They operated as a challenge, led to harder efforts, to more effective training and, therefore, in the end to higher results—to overcompensation.

We see, then, that overcompensation, which without doubt was established in this case where the stammerer became a speech expert, did not

Fig. 28.1

come about in a line which led straight upward, but rather in a movement which ran like this:

It is, however, doubtful whether the repeated failure experiences would have had a challenging effect if the individual in question had not possessed the trait of aggression, and had not been encouraged by the fundamentally trustful relationship between his parent and him. Furthermore, it seems that the individual must necessarily reach a point where he deliberately decides whether to continue his efforts or to give up.

An incident which I feel definitely affected the choice of a life occupation, which fate made for me, and consequently affected my personality, occurred in an English class. I was called on to deliver an oral report. It seemed simple enough; I had only to read it. I had told myself for days that it was nothing to worry about, no sense in getting nervous. But the more I lectured on the non-importance of oral reports, the more important they became. By the time the teacher said, 'And now, *The Social Implications in George Eliot's Novels*,' the physiological changes that occur with emotion happened with full force, I stood before the class, my knees quaked, the paper shook in my hand, and my voice cracked. It was not until the end of the report that the outward manifestation of fear became less noticeable.

> The self-anger and humiliation, the debates with myself that followed, brought forth the conclusion that one of two alternatives must be taken. I must either give up speaking before groups, or I must overcome my fear of speaking situations. Here, the influences in my previous life that contributed to a favorable adjustment exerted an influence on my decision. I had had enough successes in previous speech situations to convince me that it was possible to overcome the fear of speech situations. Anger at my poor performance was sufficient to provide a drive to remedy the personal fault. From then on I forced myself into public speaking. I majored in

speech, engaged in considerable extracurricular dramatics, and radio, and after graduation worked in the field of speech correction.

To be sure, not in all cases of overcompensation is such a crucial point for the development of this phenomenon reported. However, the deliberate decision to make a continuous effort in order to overcome a definite difficulty is found so often that it can be considered as an essential characteristic of overcompensation.

S 23 overcompensated in the field of his failure, in speech; he overcompensated directly. We may assume that individuals who overcompensate directly will be personalities who are unable to face defeat. They have no other way out of a difficulty than to attack it, and to work hard on it; they crave for superiority, for power. If this assumption is correct, we should be able to trace this desire for power also in other expressions of their personality pattern. Thus we expect S 23 to display this drive for power, when called upon to make three wishes. He writes:

> Being given three wishes with no reservations places upon us, who have become aware of our social obligations, a grave responsibility. We naturally want to satisfy our selfish desires, but if we can at the same time benefit our fellow human beings it behooves us to do so. As a means to the end I would desire, these are my three wishes:
>
> 1. Immunity to death for a period of one hundred years. This would give me the means toward a number of personal desires—money, a woman, power to help free the world from oppression, and establish democratic government throughout the world.
> 2. That I find a woman who would always love me. All of the worldly ends that the first wish would grant would not insure that essential to my complete happiness.
> 3. That I retain all the human characteristics I now have. The 'superman' role, which the first wish would give me, must not deprive me of the simple joys, sorrows, sympathy and understanding that human beings are endowed with.

There is no doubt indeed that someone who wants to defeat death, to be loved forever, and to combine with his superman role the ability to enjoy the simple joys of daily life, is striving for power and superiority all around. He has to get everything he wants, he is unable to sacrifice anything. As he cannot face defeat, it is obvious that he will compensate in the field of his original failure. He is bound to attack the difficulty directly.

In another case, Subject 30, we see that such attacks can lead to pseudo-successes. The girl experienced a social defeat, and soon afterwards she learned, by chance, of the deep impression she could make by displaying a wild temper. Although this impression was certainly not a favorable one, it gave her the deep satisfaction of being noticed, of gaining a social reputation, even if it was the reputation of being a "wildcat." She attempted to live up to this reputation to the best of her abilities. She reports:

> In the fifth, sixth and seventh grades, I became known as the 'wildcat,' and organized a girls' club to fight physically with the boys of our grade. We developed a secret code, rules for our gang, officer positions, strategy, etc. I was the chief fighter, even going so far as to cut notches in my fingernails, the better to scratch the boys with.

As might be expected, this "overcompensation" did not serve its purpose when the girl grew up. However, her "trained temper" had become habitual, and it was not easy to change into a calm controlled person. Thus, S 30 rationalizes:

> I find that I enjoy the company of people who are sensitive enough to become emotional once in a while. They are more interesting to me than the people who always try to remain calm and undisturbed.

S 30 is perfectly aware of her rationalization, and, in fact, tries hard to reach her true goal: genuine social achievement. Again, we find in this case those crucial points in the development of overcompensation, where the girl deliberately tries to change herself and to continue her efforts with all her strength. Such crucial moments repeat themselves, and seem to lead to increasing successes. Returning to the line, picturing the movement in the development of overcompensation, we find these to be the starting points of the upward strokes. (The periods indicate the crucial points.)

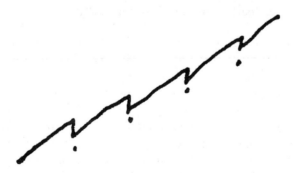

Fig. 28.2

> Upon being graduated from grammar school I vowed to myself that I would change. A new school, different boys and girls, new teachers—all represented a chance to turn over a new leaf. I wanted, desperately, to be nicer, not to get angry so quickly, to be sweet to people even if I detested them, and perhaps to find some friendships that would last a life-time. That was my goal. I must have felt the need for more social approval to try to change so drastically. As it turned out, I did not change very much. True, I joined a sorority and many clubs, became an officer of two of them, but even so, I knew I still was never considered a 'sweet' girl. I had friends, but I knew that I was hard to get along with occasionally. Strangely enough (it seems strange to me now that I should have wanted so much to change) upon being graduated from high school, I vowed the same thing. College would be another chance to redo myself.

The belligerence, which had been a significant trait in the personality of S 23, is found again in the "wildcat." The desire for power and superiority, which characterized S 23, is well matched by S 30's drive for perfection. Even after an influential college teacher got her to accept her limitation in the academic field, she was still not able to accept being less accomplished in social matters than her friend.

"I'll never be satisfied until I prove myself as successful as she, yet I am quite sure I will be able to do so some day."

It can be stated that aggressiveness, or even belligerence, is a significant trait of individuals who overcompensate for their shortcomings directly, since it is found in all cases of this kind.

Subject 35 reports how she reacted after being told by the head of the physical education school, whom she had consulted on her future plans, that she was not "particularly good teaching material":

> Ever since I can remember I was going to be a "gym teacher like Dad." After much weeping and self-pity, I decided that what I wanted was Physical Education, and that I was going to teach in spite of the head of the department. It was a great satisfaction to me when, at the end of my senior year, I was first in my class academically for five semesters, and had received an A in my practice teaching. I am exceedingly glad that I got "fighting mad," for I am really interested in my teaching and in my summer camp work.

In this case, we see again that challenging the ability of the individual produced the urgent and continuous drive for achievement which led to overcompensation in the end. The girl reports of a similar challenge with respect to her camp work:

> My first year I followed a very remarkable woman, and being young, I tried very hard to live up to her reputation. She has a state-wide reputation, is very well known in the National Red Cross, and had a creative talent, which I never possessed. Many times that first year I got so discouraged and so tired of hearing people say, "Pop used to do it this way," that I wanted to leave. But, being afraid of the disapproval of my parents and of myself, I stuck it out. The next year I was asked back. By that time, I was establishing my own rep-utation. Besides running a waterfront, I could call square dances, run off game contests, and plan rainy day programs (all things I learned in physical education courses). The memory of my prede-cessor was fading, so I didn't have that to combat. The director told me that I was adding much to camp life, and my self-confidence began to increase. Again my contract was renewed. This last sum-mer at the end of two and a half weeks I left camp for an emergency appendectomy. The director, knowing I couldn't come back as waterfront director, asked me back as assistant director.

These essential characteristics of aggression and of challenging discour-agement pertain only to the phenomenon of direct overcompensation. It is reasonable to assume that shy, fearful, hesitant individuals will not adjust themselves to failures by attacking the difficulty, but will evade the issue, and therefore will be driven into another field for overcompensation. We find individuals who compensate for physical inferiority by wit, or the ability to recite well, or other similar achievements.

Subject 41 is a fearful individual who suffers from episodes of melan-cholia. All her childhood recollections indicate fear: an unfortunate expe-rience with dogs, which led to a phobia of dogs; a severe whipping at the age of three for taking some pennies; a bad car accident, resulting in a fear of driving. During her early adolescence, she was overweight and was very unhappy about it. However, she did not attack the assumed cause of her unhappiness directly, but used it for compensation in another field:

> I suffered from spasms of melancholia and had deep feelings of depression. This was all due to a physical handicap which turned out to be within my control. I was definitely overweight—being five feet one inch tall and weighing one hundred ninety-two pounds.... Although I was aware of my figure, I didn't try to make myself as inconspicuous as possible.... I used my fatness as the butt

of my joking, calling myself a two-ton-truck, or as I walked by, saying "Here comes the charge of the light brigade." Because of this, I was considered the "life" of the party, and I was never left out of group gatherings.

Such "overcompensation" could have only a temporary value. This fearful girl needed the extended and efficient help of an older sister in order to attack her feeling of social inferiority. Part of this attack involved losing weight. The loss of weight did not solve the problem immediately, but encouragement followed by social success, linked with an improved appearance, improved her status.

This one week was a turning point in my personality development. There were boys there from another city who didn't know of my past obesity. I was surprised and pleased to find myself attractive to boys, where it never had happened before. I wouldn't believe that I was the girl I had always wanted to be.

Subject 39 is another case of an overcompensating perfectionist. This is well demonstrated in her reports on dancing, and on skating. By careful, deliberate training, she became an excellent dancer; typically, she uses the words: "I became known as one of the best dancers." However, she did not master skating to perfection, and, consequently, she considers her skating performance as a failure, "feeling like the proverbial cow on ice"—while her friends find that she skates as well as anyone. A remark in a report on her fear of accidents strikingly reveals her "perfectionist" attitude. The same girl, who was unable to stand the sight of an accident, overcompensated for this by efficiency in emergency situations, and remarks with respect to the other members of her family: "I am the best one to handle them."

Summary

The analysis of those cases that adjust to failures by overcompensation shows that they have certain common characteristics:

1. Overcompensation does not develop in a movement which follows a straight line toward the goal, but occurs following challenging situations which block the development temporarily and which lead into a more urgent and more effective striving toward the goal.
2. These challenging situations are crucial moments in the development of overcompensation, in which the individual considers the

situation with profound seriousness, and decides to put all his efforts into reaching his goal.

3. Individuals, compensating directly, show the trait of aggression, or even of belligerence.
4. Individuals who overcompensate are frequently perfectionists.
5. There is always some encouraging influence in the environment of such individuals.

CHAPTER 29

Organ Inferiority and Measured Overcompensation

RICHARD L. COLEMAN and JAMES W. CROAKE

Adler (1979) believes that to be human is to feel inferior. Humans strive toward superiority to overcome this feeling of inferiority. The specific direction of this striving is unique to the individual. Those with an organ inferiority place upon themselves an additional burden and strive with greater urgency. They tend to overcompensate for their defective organs. Examples of these phenomena are Demosthenes, who had a speech impediment and became known for his great oration, and Franklin Roosevelt, who was crippled by poliomyelitis, and became president of the U.S. It is the purpose of this study to determine whether children with a visible physical handicap demonstrate overcompensation compared to controls.

Goldberg (1974) and Henderson and Bryan (1984) report that children with invisible disabilities receive more positive reactions from others than children who have visible handicaps. Tavormina (1975) studied diabetes, asthma, cystic fibrosis, and hearing handicapped children and found them to be quite normal on personality measures. Stewart and Rossier (1978) found an increased intensity of depression, anxiety, and guilt in those with spinal cord injury. Larter (1982) found no differences in self concept in physically handicapped children compared to nonhandicapped peers. There is evidence that children with cerebral palsy and those with cleft palate demonstrate more social withdrawal than control groups (Quay and Peterson, 1967). Steinhausen (1981) reported similar results for a group of mixed visibly handicapped children. None of the above studies measured self-reliance and only indirectly were there inferences to feelings of personal worth.

Method

Twenty-six children were randomly selected from the Bureau of Crippled Children rolls. They ranged in age from 9 through 15 years with visible physical handicaps. The physical handicaps included 22 children with mobility problems involving leg or back braces or amputations, and four had suffered severe burns or other disfiguring accidents. This sample was matched with 26 controls by age, sex, race, IQ, socioeconomic status, and family constellation, and were drawn from the schools in the same county.

The matching for age in the control child was within six months of the indexed child. There were 17 males and 9 females, and 15 blacks and 11 whites in each group. Each subject was matched within 10 points on the Nam/Powers Socioeconomic Scale (Nam and Powers, 1968). Similarly, all subjects were matched within 10 IQ points. Each subject was also matched by family constellation: oldest brother, middle brother, youngest brother, oldest sister, middle sister, or youngest sister. All sibling matches were within four years by family position, e.g., to be considered an oldest the subject had to have a sibling who followed within four years or to be a youngest one had to have a sibling who was no more than four years older.

The California Test of Personality (CTP) was individually administered to each child. Data were analyzed using the Wilcoxon Matched-Pairs, Signed-Ranks test for comparisons between handicapped children and their matched controls. For comparisons between subgroups within the handicapped sample, a median test was used to test the significance of the difference between the two groups.

Results

The subscales on the CTP that differentiated the handicapped children from the control group were "self-reliance" (handicap mean = 47.7, S.D. = 29.2; control mean = 34.8, S.D. = 27.4; $Z = 1.84$; $p < .03$) and "sense of personal worth" (handicap mean = 52.7, S.D. = 31.0; control mean = 37.5, S.D. = 28.3; $Z = 1.96$; $p = .03$). The CTP Manual (Clark, Tiegs, & Thorpe, 1953) describes children scoring high on "self-reliance" as being independent and able to handle situations for themselves. Such children tend to be emotionally stable and responsible in their behavior. Children scoring high on the "sense of personal worth" have a feeling of being well thought of by others, having faith in their future success, and believing that they are average or better than average in ability.

Comparisons by sex

Handicapped male children scored higher on "self-reliance" than the male control group (handicap mean = 51.9, S.D. = 25.0; control mean = 39.1, S.D. = 25.1; Z = 1.85; p = .03). Female handicapped children scored higher on "sense of personal worth" than female controls (handicap mean = 64.0, S.D. = 34.6; control mean = 40.0, S.D. = 32.1; z = 1.57; p = .058).

Comparison by race

Like the total sample and the subsample, sex, when race is considered, black handicapped children also scored higher on "self-reliance" than the black normal controls (handicap mean = 45.8, S.D. = 32.1; control mean = 35.7, S.D. = 32.3; Z = 1.53; p = .06). And like the total sample, black handicapped children scored higher on "sense of personal worth" (handicap mean = 64.9, S.D. = 27.1: control mean = 42.4, S.D. = 34.3; Z = 2.13; p = .02).

White control children scored higher on "feeling of belonging" than did white handicapped children (handicap mean = 21.0, S.D. = 29.9; control mean = 47.3, S.D. = 28.3; Z = 2.09; p = .02). The CTP Manual (1953) describes children scoring high on this subscale as feeling that they are loved by their family, encouraged by good friends, and generally accepted by people.

Comparisons Within the Handicapped Group

Within the handicapped sample, two scales differentiated males from females. Males scored higher on "self-reliance" than did handicapped females (male handicap mean = 51.9, S.D. = 25; female handicap mean = 34.1, S.D. = 34.4). Using the median test, this difference was found to be significant (p = .05). Handicapped males also scored higher on "withdrawing tendencies" (male handicap mean = 40.9, S.D. = 27.3; female handicap mean = 19.0, S.D. = 20.6; p = .03). There were no other significant differences between subsamples on the CTP.

Discussion

The overall findings suggest that handicapped children tend to be self-reliant, independent, able to handle situations for themselves, emotionally stable, responsible, feel well thought of by others, have faith in their future success, and believe that they are capable. There was evidence that the white handicapped children, but not the blacks, felt less loved by their families, less encouraged by friends, and less accepted by people.

The handicapped group's higher scores on "self-reliance" and "sense of personal worth" are consistent with Adler's theory of overcompensation and in accord with the ideas of Crookshank (1936) and Shoobs & Goldbern (1942), who state that people may overcompensate for a physical defect. These results are not in agreement with Bowe (1980), who found handicapped children to be generally timid and withdrawn. Nor do they agree with Kammerer (1940), who noted feelings of social and personal inferiority in his sample. However, the Baker and Kammerer studies can be criticized for their lack of reliability, validity, and control groups.

The handicapped males' higher scores on "self-reliance" and "withdrawing tendencies" suggest that they are more confident of their abilities with a greater acceptance of reality than their normal controls. These findings agree with those of Meissner, Thoreson, and Butler (1967).

Summary

The higher scores on those scales of the CTP for children with obvious organ inferiorities indicate that Adler's notion of overcompensation for felt inferiority is present. The other scales of the CTP did not differentiate this sample of children with obvious deformities from the normal control group.

The studies of Gates (1946), Carter and Chess (1951), and Watson and Johnson (1958) indicate that the individual's reaction to the organ inferiority is more important than the specific defect. This idea is consistent with Adler's "psychology of use": It is not what one has but what one does with what one has that is important (Adler, 1956). Those with organ inferiorities can choose to surrender and retreat from the additional challenge posed by the defect or through encouragement can compensate, or overcompensate, and attain greater success. Both compensation, as evidenced by those CTP scales where there were no differences, and overcompensation, as seen in higher scores on some CTP scales for the group with disabilities, would seem to be in evidence in the present study.

References

Adler, A. (1956). *The individual psychology of Alfred Adler.* H. Ansbacher & R. Ansbacher (Eds.). New York: Harper and Row.

Adler. A. (1979). *Superiority and social interest.* H. Ansbacher & R. Ansbacher (Eds.). New York: W. W. Norton.

Bowe, F. (1980). *Rehabilitating America.* New York: Harper and Row.

Carter, V., & Chess, S. (1951). Factors influencing the adaptations of organically handicapped children. *American Journal of Orthopsychiatry*, 21, 837.

Clark, W., Tiegs, E., & Thorpe (1953). *California test of personality.* Monterey, CA: McGraw-Hill.

Crookshank, F. (1936). Organ inferiorities. *Individual Psychology Medical Pamphlet*, 16.

Gates, M. (1946). A comparative study of some problems of social and emotional adjustment of crippled and non-crippled girls and boys. *Journal of Genetic Psychology*, 68, 219–244.

Goldberg, R. (1974). Adjustment of children with invisible and visible handicaps: Congenital heart disease and facial burns. *Journal of Counseling Psychology*, 21, 428–432.

Henderson, G. and Bryan, W. V. (1984). *Psychosocial aspects of disability.* Springfield, IL: Charles C. Thomas.

Kammerer, R. (1940). An exploratory psychological study of crippled children. *Psychological Record*, 23, 35–54.

Larter, S. (1982). *The physically handicapped and health impaired children: Do they prosper in regular elementary schools.* Toronto: Toronto Board of Education.

Meissner, A., Thoreson, R., & Butler, A. (1967). Relation of self-concept to impact and obviousness of disability among male and female adolescents. *Perceptual and Motor Skills*, 24, 1099–1105.

Nam, C., & Powers, M. (1968). Changes in the relative status level of workers in the United States 1950–1960. *Social Forces*, 47, 158–170.

Quay, H., and Peterson (1967). Manual for the behavior problem checklist. Champaign, IL: University of Illinois.

Shoobs, N., & Goldbern, G. (1942). *Corrective treatment for unadjusted children.* New York: Harper.

Steinhausen, H. (1981). Chronically ill and handicapped children and adolescents: Personality study in relation to disease, *Journal of Abnormal Child Psychology*, 9, 291–297.

Stewart, T., & Rossier, A. (1978). Psychological considerations in adjustment to spinal cord injury. *Rehabilitation Literature*, 39, 75–80.

Tavormina, J. (1975). *Chronically ill children: A psychologically and emotionally deviant population?* Washington, D.C.: National Science Foundation.

Watson, E., & Johnson, A. (1958). The emotional significance of acquired physical disfigurement in children. *American Journal of Orthopsychiatry*, 28, 85–87.

XI
Phenomenological Approach

CHAPTER 30

Phenomenology and the Qualitative in Individual Psychology

CHRISTOPHER SHELLEY

As clinicians and practitioners, Adlerians employ narrative as a tool to facilitate psychological growth and healing. Whether it is parents using Adlerian parenting methods, counselors and therapists in the consulting room, teachers in the classroom or Adlerian writers drawing on the rich texts of their diverse literature, it is tacitly recognized that language and narrative are pinnacle to an *understanding* psychology. This essay examines the philosophical ideas that underpin the use of narrative and qualitative methods.

Adler was a psychological practitioner of extraordinary method. His client base, especially in Vienna, was often drawn from the lower economic classes (Hoffman, 1994). The material conditions of everyday life and the pragmatics of offering psychological services to the less financially endowed necessitated an approach that allowed for faster resolution of psychic distress. This contrasted with the upper-class and leisurely psychoanalytic method from which Adler famously diverged. Moreover, Adler's social idealism and his attention to history and context rendered him a complex thinker who fashioned techniques that, nonetheless, appeared elementary to some. For example, the ideas and concepts Adler put forward were frequently railed against by orthodox Freudians and their later supporters, dismissed as superficial, and decried as mere ego psychology (Kaufmann, 2003). Some critics, moreover, still contend that Adler's is not a depth psychology but rather one that panders to "platitudes," a shallow system seeking "to make a virtue of being simplistic" (Kaufmann, 2003, p. 263). Even those whose systems closely approximate that of Adler accused him of having taken an insufficient journey into the depths, as Karen Horney charged (Paris, 1994). Such criticisms, however, fail to grasp the inherent complexity of Adler's field psychology and of the centrality of intersubjective understanding to which Individual Psychology (IP) adheres. Certainly, some of Adler's concepts hold an initial digestibility and this "common sense" ease of entry into Adlerian thinking is appreciated, especially by lay adherents. However, connecting these concepts to the overall doctrine is, as the advanced Adlerian knows too well, a challenging yet invigorating project. This epistemological and methodological complexity is implicit in Adler's (1956) own summary that

> all the methods of Individual Psychology for understanding the personality take into account the individual's opinion of his goal of superiority, the strength of his inferiority feeling, the degree of his social interest, and the fact that the whole individual cannot be torn from his context with life—or better said, from his context with society. (p. 327)

Understanding the person means understanding his or her context and the ways in which the surrounding milieu is interwoven with one's unique subjectivity. Lewis Way (1950), in discussing Adler's adoption of the neo-Kantian philosophy of Vaihinger, draws attention to the subjectivistic orientation of Individual Psychology: "It is therefore never possible to suppose the human being capable of anything in the nature of a 'pure perception' or apprehension of reality undistorted by the nature of his own mental world" (p. 65).

Method in Psychology

The subjectivistic, context-dependent presuppositions of Adlerian psychology necessarily pose problems of method. The embeddedness of the human psyche in its object imparts inevitable challenges of representation for psychologists. Psychology as a discipline, especially as it developed over the 20th century in Anglo-American contexts, generally esteems quantitative truth claims predicated on operationalism (Danziger 1997; Deese, 1972). Such claims elevate the abstract, numeric, and reified findings of especially laboratory-based research over and above the generally subjectivistic, narrative, and meaning dimensions yielded by qualitative research.

The development of psychology as a discipline, forming as it did from a 19th-century split with rationalistic and often introspective philosophy, carved out an experimental and empirical niche. The 19th-century importation of the German Wilhelm Wundt's objectivistic laboratory methods (while disregarding his subjectivistic *völkerpsychologie*) into Anglo-American psychology, placated psychology's penchant for representing itself as unbiased and empirical, a rigorous scientific psychology. This objectivist niche has been defended diligently by academic psychology through its historic adoption of *positivism* as the proper means for generating truth claims about the reality of human subjects and their individual psychological processes. This general adherence to positivism differs markedly from Adler's adoption of Vaihinger's *idealistic positivism* in ways that will become apparent.

Some Adlerians, recognizing the psychological grounding of Individual Psychology qua psycholog*y* have understood the necessity of generating quantitative research in order to retain a place in psychology as a discipline. Adler was, however, more of a practitioner, interdisciplinarian, and, indeed, philosopher than a classical academic psychologist. His conscious celebration of philosophers such as Vaihinger, Smuts, the social philosophy of Marx, and aspects of Nietzsche are clearly woven into his overall doctrine (Lehrer, 1999).

Adler never followed the rigorous quantitative dictates of the developing discipline of psychology. Such a psychology veered relentlessly to the "hard" truths of the human psyche as object. On the contrary, Adler retained the concept of the self, with its holistic, synthetic, subjectivistic *and* objectivistic features intact. Empirical psychology, in contrast, disavowed the self and solidified around mechanistic, deterministic, and measurable constructs (Danziger, 1997). Hence academic psychology generally espouses *nomothetic* laws while Adlerian psychology largely clusters toward *idiographic* ones, with limited nomothetic exceptions (Adler, 1956).

However, William Stern, famous in psychology for introducing the concept of Intelligence Quotient, noted that nomothetic and idiographic aspects in psychology are not clear-cut; they may represent two positions but not two distinct fields (1911/1996). A differentiation of the nomothetic from the idiographic point of view should not be considered as a binary separation into separate scientific disciplines. Gordon Allport, who studied with Stern in Germany, subsequently abandoned behaviorist and laboratory methods with which he had previously concurred, to develop Stern's notion of *real individuality*. Stern's idea of real individuality and Allport's subsequent *personalistic* psychology represent a break with the subject/object divide in experimental psychology (Nicholson, 2000). This break represents an exception to the rule by which academic psychology continues to be interested in the object often at the expense of the subject.

Much of the research that academic psychology generated over the 20th century was nomothetic and actually strikes one as a subset of physiology or, at least on the borderland thereof. Such aggregate representations resulting from experimental settings reduce the self to component features lacking in agency, a series of elemental chains devoid of the existential or spiritual aspects that make a life worth living. Hence, Anglo-American psychology also repudiated aspects of another founding figure, William James (1842–1910), who, like Adler, argued a similarly conceptualized holistic self that intertwines material, social, and spiritual dimensions (e.g., biological embodiment, sociological factors, and existential aspects, respectively). All three tiers are viewed by James as equally significant in understanding human selves, although James personally favored the spiritual self as "supremely precious" (1955/1890, p. 203).

Especially in America, retaining a place in academic psychology required Adlerians to produce quantitative data. However, the kinds of quantitative data that Adlerians produce are predicated on notions of soft (as opposed to hard) determinism (Adler, 1956). In a classic article, Ansbacher argued for the generation of quantitative data. Yet, citing a brief paper that Adler wrote on the issue of quantitative methods, Ansbacher noted the proviso that Adler understood experimental results as limited, representing "a shadow of reality" (Ansbacher, 1941/1994, p. 477). Ansbacher nevertheless concluded that a detailed book referencing quantitative data in order to support the presuppositions of IP would be welcome. In remarking on Adler's commonsense approach, he stated that

> [I] regret that it is based entirely on the case history method. Valid truths can in many cases be stated in quantitative terms. Such a book would reveal that the original Adlerian tenets are exceedingly well supported by subsequent quantitative research. ... It would also show that the general trend is much more in accord with Individual Psychology than is usually assumed by the Adlerians themselves. (p. 477)

Although Ansbacher regrets the exclusivity of the case study approach, this method is a narrative one that has, nevertheless, served all depth psychologies well. It is certainly not without its insufficiencies (e.g., cultural and ecological validity) and needs to be viewed as part of the qualitative genre, a particular thread of method amongst an array of possibilities. Its strengths rest in potentially capturing the paradoxical complexity and interpretational richness that strictly quantitative methods lose. I would agree, however that its one-sidedness as method is problematic. However, for a number of reasons that beg investigation, Ansbacher's call for quantitative research results to substantiate Adlerian truth claims remains a complex one. First, Adler was not, as we have seen, opposed to experimental methods (usually producing quantitative results). The dilemma for Adlerians is what to do with such results, since they pose an inevitable interpretational problem. Second, Adler's own positioning of quantitative results as casting a "shadow" of reality suggests the incompleteness of such data. Thus, the problem is not necessarily the generation of quantitative data but its subsequent interpretation and use. Clearly, the philosophical requirement is to make use of such data synthetically. Synthesis is posed as a means to unite the "shadow" with its object and this necessarily means to represent an account that does not negate the subject. Such an approach, when synthesized contextually, will solve problems of ecological validity and static reification.

Another problem with generating quantitative truth claims in IP rests with Adler's philosophical commitments. Smuts (1926/1973) was scathing toward the psychology of his day for its penchant to produce a collection of reductionist, atomistic, and quantitative representations. In contrast, Smuts viewed personality as among the highest expressions of holism, which is compromised when rendered asunder through reductive analysis. He wrote that

> each human individual is a unique personality; not only is personality in general a unique phenomenon in the world, but each human personality is unique in itself, and the attempt at "averaging" and generalising and reaching the common type on the approved scientific lines eliminates what is the very essence of personality, namely, its unique individual character in each case. (p. 279)

In rendering personality unique and indivisible, an exemplary manifestation of holism, Smuts repudiates the positivist epistemology and associated methods of psychology: "the province of psychology is much too narrow and limited for the purpose of personality; and both its method and procedure as a scientific discipline fail to do justice to the uniquely individual character of the personality" (p. 280). According to Smuts, and adopted by Adler, a key aspect to the unique individual character is its distinctive phenomenology. This proposition celebrates personality not as an aggregate of traits but one that colors and shades human experiences with an underlying creative force.

Phenomenology

The philosopher most identified with phenomenology is Edmond Husserl (1859–1938). Husserl's phenomenology is not concerned with abstract or objective events independently of how such events are *experienced*. Hence, Husserl focuses on how phenomena are experienced by a knowing subject (Bowie, 2003). In turning to the subject, he was not averse to objectivity, but rather concentrated on the subject's *knowing* of objects. The "I" experiences by means of reflection and by its ability to hold within the mind mental representations. If I look into someone's eyes, I can strive to see them as an ophthalmologist might (as objects: cornea, pupils, iris, crystalline lens, and so on), and subjectively experience them as warm, alluring, bright, beautiful, cold, calculating, defective or even menacing. Yet, my experience of striving to see eyes objectively will also be biased by my very act of looking (previous knowledge, intention, hypotheses, and assumptions). Though I may be able to see eyes as objects, I do so by willfully repressing or ignoring an indivisible subjectivity. I do not have a wholly objective access to the object.

Bowie (2003) argues that "for there to be consciousness at all it must have an object to be conscious of ... and it must be connected to a subject that thinks" (p. 63). Hence, phenomenology concerns itself with describing consciousness, the consciousness of a subject that thinks. Husserl's[1] concentration is focused on what he called *evidenz*, cognitive comprehensions or *encountering* that concerns itself with how objects are known at all. The presumptions of phenomenology are generally drawn from the premises of German Idealist philosophy (e.g., Fichte, Schelling) which ultimately concerns itself with wholes. Bowie furthermore notes that subject and object are intertwined in ways that cannot be artificially separated, as evidenced in the claim that since nature produces subjectivity, nature's objective products are also inherently subjective.

Martin Heidegger (1889–1976), in developing a *hermeneutic* stream of phenomenology, emphasizes *understanding* (Heidegger, 1953). His perspective is holistic in as much as phenomena are embedded in temporal and situational contexts. Understanding requires an ongoing interplay between whole and parts in order for phenomena to be both knowable and intelligible. Bowie (2003) summarizes Heidegger's point of view: "Why should seeing the sunset as an object of physics have priority over the everyday apprehension of it as an object of beauty, given that this is the way the phenomenon is initially manifest?" (p. 203).

A core issue to surface in the hermeneutic stream of phenomenology rests with the fact that we are diachronically rooted in the world; that is, our *being* is within and not outside of the world. Heidegger's magnum opus,

Being and Time (1953), connotes the embeddedness of human subjects in a world that, when experienced, contains temporal boundaries that cannot be wholly transcended. Heidegger's pupil Hans-Georg Gadamer (1900–2002) extended this thesis by speaking of the historical force of *tradition* (1960), a somewhat inadequate translation of the German *Überlieferlung,* which carries no exact English counterpart. Tradition in the Gadamerian sense means both what is handed down from the past and the ongoing conversation that gives force and movement to what the past carries forward. Like language, one's tradition preexists. By being born into a particular time, one inherits (introjects) the traditions (values, beliefs, ideologies, and customs) that already exist and move dialectically in ways that cannot be wholly grasped. The best one can do is to try and foreground the prejudices one (unconsciously) carries, to strive for glimmers of truth through dialogue and the generation of new, perhaps more comprehensive questions.

Truth Claims

Like Heidegger, Gadamer privileges language over mathematics and puts into question the whole idea of method as a means to substantiate absolute truth claims. Indeed, it is argued that "rule-bound methods … predetermine how the world can appear in them" (Bowie, 2003, p. 253). Methods, whether quantitative, qualitative, or a mixture of the two, are themselves reflective of a prejudice inherited from the traditions of 19th- and 20th-century modernity, laden with beliefs drawn from the Enlightenment. In contrast, Gadamer (1960) places his faith in Art, which, he believes, is uniquely poised to transcend the limitations of a scientific method that projects the hard truth of the object independently of the contingency of the subject. Indeed, as Stones (1985) points out, quantitative methods especially prioritize method rather than phenomena. If one thinks of the violinist as object, one might consider measuring and quantifying the tendon movements, number of breaths, vibratic motion of the finger(s), calibration of bow and string, firings of the eardrum, blood flow, and attention to meter. An indeterminate number of empirical approaches may attempt to understand the structural and physiological mechanics of the violinist's effect, yet nowhere are the experience, meaning, creativity, or holistic features of the artist and the music apparent. Such an approach in this instance is hollow, bereft of those intrinsically linked features that make art and creativity a force in human subjects, contributing to those experiential dimensions that make a life worth living.

The evisceration of subjectivity and experience are what Husserl disputes, the appropriation of logic into empirical psychology. Like Gadamer,

Adler too recognized the transcendent and creative power of art, claiming that "Some day soon it will be realized that the artist is the leader of mankind on the path to the absolute truth" (1956, p. 329). In addition, like Gadamer, Adler concedes that we are not "blessed with the possession of absolute truth" (1956, p. 142). This metaphysical statement points to Adler's unique synthesis of both the metaphysical and the dialectical traditions in philosophy. Without direct access to absolute truth, one of the things that Adler turns to is dialogue. This is akin to Gadamer's (1960) emphasis on Art and the necessity of dialogue to reveal the glimmers of truth that Art may yield. Likewise, one can see it in Stein's (1991) emphasis on Socratic exchange and Maddox's (2001) insistence that IP be founded ideally on "open dialogue and debate" (p. 45). These positions harmonize with Gadamer's "to and fro" of dialogue.

Individual Psychology and Phenomenology

Phenomenology has long been acknowledged as fundamental to IP and is a crucial aspect to an Adlerian epistemology. Mosak (1989) notes that "The *Journal of Individual Psychology* (now *Individual Psychology*) referred to itself as being, 'devoted to a holistic, phenomenological, teleological, field-theoretical, and socially oriented approach'" (p. 81). As well, Ansbacher and Ansbacher (1956) argue that IP holds similarities with Husserl's *phenomenology* although Adler did not use the term. Indeed, several points of convergence unite IP with both the hermeneutic and existential streams of phenomenology. In order to comprehend Adler's use of phenomenology better, it is necessary to engage in further philosophical unpacking.

Adler's subscription to the post-Kantian philosophy of Vaihinger (1911/ 1965), specifically the somewhat obscure doctrine of *idealistic positivism*, cleverly counters ordinary positivism. Idealistic positivism is actually a repudiation of the more familiar positivism sourced to Auguste Comte (1798–1857) or the later views of the *logical positivists* (1920s) of the Vienna school, a stream of positivism that has abated over time. Adler's use of Vaihinger's ideas are predicated on the notion of truth *as if* truth. The statement resonates more clearly with Nietzsche, whose ideas Vaihinger admired and credited in *The Philosophy of As If*.

The distinction between idealistic and other forms of positivism is manifest in the concept of the *fiction*. Adler (1956) clarifies:

> *Fictio* means, in the first place, an *activity* of *fingere*, that is to say, of constructing, forming, giving shape, elaborating, presenting, artistically fashioning, conceiving, thinking, imagining, assuming,

planning, devising, inventing. Secondly, it refers to the *product* of these activities, the fictional assumption, fabrication, creation, the imagined case. Its most conspicuous character is that of unhampered and free expression. (p. 78)

Ansbacher and Ansbacher distinguish between the idealist and the positivist:

> Whereas idealism regards ideas as the ultimate reality, and positivism recognizes only observable facts, Vaihinger's system regards ideational constructs, even when in contradiction to reality, of great practical value and indispensable for human life. This is what Vaihinger means when he calls his philosophy "Idealistic Positivism" or "Positivist Idealism." (Adler, 1956, p. 87)

Ansbacher and Ansbacher outline Adler's use of the fiction as a means to substantiate the theory of IP. The theoretical core posits subjectivity as being fictional in nature. Fictions cannot be causally linked to objective matter. Rather, fictions are drawn from the inventive aspects of the mind and resonate with the fundamentally creative spirit of the human subject. Moreover, fictions are formed in the unconscious, a point of divergence with phenomenology's emphasis on consciousness. This aspect actually differentiates Adler's use of phenomenology from the "knowing subject" or the detailed descriptions of consciousness that Husserl sought. We are not the *all*-knowing subject. Hence, the contents of consciousness are, for Adlerians, subject to the interpretative dialogue necessary to unpack their unthought meanings. This premise tends to place Adler's IP on the hermeneutic side of the phenomenological stream. It also differentiates IP's connection to phenomenology from cognitive psychology's exclusive phenomenology of consciousness.

However, Adler cannot be located solely in the hermeneutic stream of phenomenology. He also resonates with key aspects opened up by the *existential* stream (based on Merleau-Ponty, Arendt, Sartre, and de Beauvoir). This stream focuses more on *description* than the hermeneutic preference for interpretation. The existentialists concentrate on complex issues such as freedom, choice, and the conscious knowledge of the inevitability of death (ontological temporality).

Also akin to the existentialists, in his method of psychotherapy Adler unites subject and object. This is evidenced in the clinical uses of (a) empathy, and (b) taking an objective stance similar to the concept of *bracketing*. This ostensibly produces the ingredients necessary for an *understanding psychology*. To empathize with the client while simultaneously observing from an "objective" point of view (bracketing-out presuppositions) draws attention to the *existential index*. Giorgi (1997) explains:

> to enter into the attitude of the phenomenological reduction means to (a) bracket past knowledge about a phenomenon, in order to encounter it freshly and describe it precisely as it is intuited (or experienced), and (b) to withhold the existential index, which means to consider what is given precisely as it is given, as presence, or phenomenon. (p. 238)

Adler did not use the terms *bracketing* or *existential index*, but a consonance with these concepts is apparent under aspects of idealistic positivism, which again is concerned with truth *as if* truth. To bracket out one's presuppositions or biases is an important technical aspect of Adlerian therapy. From a clinical point of view in IP, the attempt constitutes a stance of neutrality, a conscious awareness not to infect the clinical environment with one's own material as best as one consciously can. The hermeneutic stream of phenomenology disputes the subject's ability to achieve this fully, hence the emphasis on stance (*as if*). To completely extinguish the prejudices of the self is to stand outside of time and space, an impossibility (Shelley, 2000).

The hermeneutic rationale that disputes bracketing stems from the unconscious force of prejudices—one cannot extinguish what one does not know. Gadamer (1960) ascertains that "language is more than the consciousness of the speaker; so also it is more than a subjective act" (p. xxxvi). Moreover, the potential for countertransference and the necessity of supervision for good therapeutic practice emphasize the impossibility of a totalizing bracketed stance. This leads to a final point of confound with phenomenology in Adler's system, the question of a dynamic unconscious. IP acknowledges the force of unawareness in human life and is correctly positioned as a modality of *depth psychology* that connects the here and now with the fictions formed in childhood that point to future goals (constructed teleologies).

Phenomenology's concern with the precise detailing of conscious experience is important to Adlerians but such material is limited, subject to the necessity of interpretation. The force of one's unconscious goals can distort the products of consciousness. Therefore, pure experiencing becomes a near impossibility (e.g., see Adler's concept of *private logic* and his use of the Kantian-based *biased apperception*). Our task is to minimize the intrusiveness of unaware biases, to become aware of unconscious projection as manifested in transference and other safeguarding tendencies.

This is something that good supervision, reflexivity, and self-knowledge ideally imparts to the therapist/counselor.

Qualitative Methodologies

Psychology's overreliance on positivism and, subsequently, a near one-sidedness regarding the elevation of quantitative methods, have left the *subject* of psychology in the shadow of its embedded object. Holloway (2005) suggests that some Adlerians have acquiesced to this dominant trend by similarly pursuing the operationalization of concepts such as *social interest* in order to produce objective and quantitative studies to substantiate the concept. He notes that some Americans seem to prefer a measurable conception while Europeans favor a philosophically based orthodoxy to the concept's German root *Gemeinschaftsgefühl*. The Europeans, he argues, are more likely to view it as existentially or spiritually grounded and less likely to pursue reified characterizations of the so-called manifestations of social interest. If Americans have tended to pursue quantitative studies on social interest (something that Slavik and Croake [1997] argue is conceptually unquantifiable), they have done so in ways that are consistent with the overall research program of North American psychology. North American psychology remains staunchly committed to quantitative results regardless of challenges posed by third-wave psychology (e.g., humanistic and existential). This retention of a near methodological monopoly is also regardless of the fact that other disciplines, such as sociology, education, and anthropology long ago dropped the exclusivity of the quantitative in favor of a diversity of methods.

In IP specifically, I do not oppose quantification projects so long as they do not trump qualitative attempts or remain as reified representations (e.g., unsynthesized findings that succumb to frozen, calcified abstractions devoid of dynamics and lacking in a holistic, ecological validity).

Rennie, Monteiro, and Watson (2002) have conducted an extensive quantitative study on the minor rise of qualitative methods in psychology. In their analysis, they note that qualitative methods such as grounded theory, discourse analysis, phenomenological methods and so on have enjoyed a recent surge. The study examined published articles in psychology from 1900 to 1999. Defining qualitative methods, the authors remark on its status:

> The term "qualitative research" refers to a variety of approaches to enquiry in the health and social sciences that address the meaning of verbal text in verbal rather than numeric terms. More fundamentally, qualitative research is more subjective than quantitative

research; more exploratory than confirmatory; more descriptive than explanatory; more interpretive than positivist. Thus, in many ways qualitative research cuts across the grain of accustomed research practice. Accordingly, there is resistance to accepting it in many quarters. (p. 179)

Qualitative research projects published in psychology during the 1990s, the authors note, amount to an overall yield of 9% of the whole. This is a very small yield, yet far greater than in previous decades.

One wonders why there has been so little qualitative inquiry in psychology. Wood-Sherif (1987) and, separately, Kidder and Fine (1997), note that the formalization of psychology as discipline was conducted almost entirely by men who imported their biased worldview, including elevating objectivist and abstract tenets (patriarchal values), that have had the effect of silencing the voice of women. Freud belied the trend, however, and, with all his noted flaws, gave "hysterical" women a way to voice repressed suffering. Some feminists have argued that, historically, women needed to become hysterical in order to be heard. Hence feminists' paradoxical celebration of psychoanalysis, disdaining its misogyny (theoretical intrusiveness of, for example, the "electra complex" in interpreting excavated voice) and celebrating its commitment to emancipate repressed narrative (Kurzweil, 1995). Moreover, the historic exclusion of women from the academy is traced back over a millennium with philosophical justifications appearing from time to time, such as the Baconian notion of men as rational "knowers" and women as the irrational mystery to be "known" (Westmarland, 2001). In the claim to the real and the universal, "man" continued to constitute women as "other."

If women were to have formalized the foundations of psychology, one speculates that it would not be so one-sided toward positivism and quantitative data (which provocatively suggests not a neutral representation of statistical scores but an androcentric phenomenology masked as objectivity). Instead, through social movements, women were eventually permitted into the academy yet socialized and compelled to master and reproduce the foundations of a "male" epistemology. Feminists draw vexed attention to the continued dominance of quantitative methods as a sustained epistemological aspect of psychological institutionalization, again traced to its foundations that were constructed entirely by men. This is an essentialized reading, however, in a world where sex/gender binaries are now considerably more muddled. The effect of the object/subject split is to maintain Cartesian dualism, which feminists also describe as disembodying (Smith, 1999). Perhaps to attest to the feminist claim, it is noteworthy that traditional female disciplines such as nursing do not privilege quantitative over qualitative knowledge production (Rennie, Monteiro, & Watson, 2002).

The aims of qualitative methods in psychology are often different from quantitative ones. Qualitative accounts tend to render data derived from information-rich interviews, to lend voice to experiences, or reflexive accounts garnered from detailed participation in groups (e.g., as an observer or reflexive participant such as in ethnography). Henwood (1996) notes that psychology, by and large, is a nonreflexive discipline and so may find the concept of self-reflection and foregrounding of bias *as part of the research process* simply too foreign. Nevertheless, famous psychologists have, on occasion, traversed qualitative practices. For example, Kidder and Fine (1997) note,

> In the 1940s and 1950s, Muzafer Sherif and his collaborators immersed themselves in the rivalries of a summer boy's camp to write about conflict and cooperation. In the 1950s, Leon Festinger and colleagues infiltrated a doomsday sect to observe what happens when prophecies fail. In these classic studies social psychologists entered their subject's lives without structured questionnaires, pre-determined variables or research designs and no one doubted that they were doing psychological research. (p. 35)

Finally, how do we know the accurateness or truthfulness of a qualitative, narrative-based account? A hermeneutic standpoint suggests that truth is something to strive for and yet the best one can hope for is to yield only glimmers. This begs the question, how does one prove the proof to which ensuing facts are constructed? Skultans (2005) suggests that, in reflecting the philosophical premises of Richard Rorty,

> we have a duty to listen to narrative simply because the narrator is a human being. And if the told story diverges from the lived story, it may well be that the told story tells us more about the values and aspirations of the narrator than might the lived story. (p. 73)

Skultans' point resonates with the fictive constructivism at the core of IP (Slavik, 2002). Layers of meaning may be garnered through the use of narrative, the stuff of interpretation. That truths can be bent and distortions conjured gives psychologists some reasonable pause for thought in accepting narrative generated from qualitative accounts. On the other hand, there are also, as the perennial saying goes in quantitative research, lies, damn lies, and statistics.

Conclusion

It is my concluding contention that IP requires little philosophical substantiation for the use of qualitative methodologies. On the other side of the coin, Adlerians are free as always to pursue quantitative knowledge production. I certainly would not wish to obstruct such efforts. The results of quantitative studies are, however, argued to produce incomplete data, a "shadow" of reality. In IP, such results philosophically demand synthesis in order to be intelligible in the manner that I believe Adler (1938) intended. Otherwise, quantitative data succumbs to reification and falls on the wrong side of positivism. Finally, Adler's late period, which turned in part to existentialism, finds common ground with phenomenological approaches to the detailed descriptions of conscious experience. Qualitative methods that employ an existential/phenomenological approach are, however, in danger of producing their own variety of incompleteness. The unconscious force of the fictional goals that populate unawareness demand space in struggling for the glimmers of truth to which we strive. Phenomenology provides an excellent entry point into the quest for intelligibility of such conceptions as style of life and social interest. However, phenomenology has yet to prove itself comprehensive enough to plumb and capture the depths and paradoxes that a depth psychology such as IP proposes. Nevertheless, it is through narrative and intersubjective exchange that voice can be lent to explicate the concealed aspects, one's unthought movement, purpose, intentions, to garner insight into the forms of one's style of life. In this regard, phenomenology can prove valuable as a beginning but cannot, I counter, embellish itself as an end.

Acknowledgments

I am grateful for comments received on drafts of this chapter from Steve Slavik (Vancouver) and Dr. Henry Stein (Bellingham, WA). Moreover, my ongoing work as an Adlerian has been actively supported by my colleagues in the Adlerian Society (UK) and Institute for Individual Psychology, especially Paola Prina (London), Anthea Millar (Cambridge), and Dr. Karen John (Bath, Avon). Without such support, I doubt that I could muster the courage to put pen to paper and fingers to keyboard. Finally, I am inspired by my students at the University of British Columbia and the Adler School of Professional Psychology (BC) who never fail to teach me exactly what it is that I need to know.

References

Adler, A. (1938). *Social interest: A challenge to mankind* (J. Linton & R. Vaughan, Trans.). London: Faber & Faber.

Adler, A. (1956). *The individual psychology of Alfred Adler: A systematic presentation in selections from his writings* (H. L. Ansbacher & R. R. Ansbacher, Eds.). New York: Basic Books.

Ansbacher, H. L. (1994). The future progress of individual psychology. *Individual Psychology, 50*(4), 476–477. (Original work published 1941.)

Ansbacher, H. L., & Ansbacher, R. R. (1956). Individual Psychology in its larger setting. In A. Adler, *The individual psychology of Alfred Adler: A systematic presentation in selections from his writings* (pp. 1–18; H. L. Ansbacher & R. R. Ansbacher, Eds.). New York: Basic Books.

Bowie, A. (2003). *Introduction to German philosophy: From Kant to Habermas.* Cambridge, UK: Polity.

Danziger, K. (1997). Historical formation of selves. In R. D. Ashmore & L. Jussim (Eds.), *Self and identity: Fundamental issues* (pp. 137–159). Oxford: Oxford University Press.

Deese, J. (1972). *Psychology as science and art.* New York: Harcourt, Brace, Jovanovich.

Gadamer, H. G. (1960). *Truth and method* (J. Weinsheimer & D. G. Marshall, Trans.). New York: Continuum.

Giorgi, A. (1997). The theory, practice, and evaluation of the phenomenological method as a qualitative research project. *Journal of Phenomenological Psychology, 28* (2), 235–261.

Heidegger, M. (1953). *Being and time.* (J. Stambaugh, Trans.). Albany, NY: State University of New York.

Henwood, K. L. (1996). Qualitative inquiry: Perspectives, methods and psychology. In J. T. Richardson (Ed.), *Handbook of qualitative research: Methods for psychology and the social sciences* (pp. 25–39). Leicester, UK: British Psychological Society.

Hoffman, E. (1994). *The drive for self: Alfred Adler and the founding of individual psychology.* New York: Addison-Wesley.

Holloway, J. (2005). The good, the bad, and *Gemeinschaftsgefühl.* In P. Prina, A. Millar, K. John, & C. Shelley (Eds.), *Adlerian yearbook—2005* (pp. 11–34). London: Adlerian Society (UK) and Institute for Individual Psychology.

James, W. (1955). *The principles of psychology.* Mineola, NY: Dover. (Original work published 1890.)

Kaufmann, W. (2003). *Freud, Adler, and Jung: Discovering the mind,* Vol. 3. London: Transaction Publishers.

Kidder, L., & Fine, M. (1997). Qualitative inquiry in psychology: A radical tradition. In: D. Fox and I. Prilleltensky (Eds.), *Critical psychology: An introduction* (pp. 34–50). London: Sage.

Kurzweil, E. (1995). *Freudians and feminists.* San Francisco, CA: Westview Press.

Lehrer, R. (1999). Adler and Nietzsche. In J. Golomb, W. Santaniello, & R. Lehrer (Eds.), *Nietzsche and depth psychology* (pp. 229–246). Albany, NY: State University of New York Press.

Maddox, C. (2001). Individual psychology, logotherapy and the challenge of the 21st century. In P. Prina, C. Shelley, & C. Thompson (Eds.), *Adlerian yearbook—2001* (pp. 44–58). London: Adlerian Society (UK) and Institute for Individual Psychology.

Mosak, H. H. (1989). Adlerian psychotherapy. In R. J. Corsini & D. Wedding (Eds.), *Current psychotherapies* (pp. 64–116). Itasca, IL: Peacock.

Nicholson, I. A. (2000). A coherent datum of perception: Gordon Allport, Floyd Allport, and the politics of personality. *Journal of the History of the Behavioural Sciences, 36* (4), 463–470.

Paris, B. J. (1994). *Karen Horney: A psychoanalyst's search for self-understanding.* New Haven, CT: Yale University Press.

Rennie, D. L., Monteiro, A. M., & Watson, K. D. (2002). The rise of qualitative research in psychology. *Canadian Psychology, 43* (3), 179–189.

Shelley, C. (2000). Epistemology and methods in individual psychology: Towards a fusion of horizons with hermeneutics. [Special issue]. *Journal of Individual Psychology: Year 2000, 56* (1), 59–73.

Skultans, V. (2005). Narratives of displacement and identity. In P. Prina, K. John, A. Millar, & C. Shelley (Eds.), *Adlerian yearbook—2005* (pp. 72–94). London: Adlerian Society (UK) and Institute for Individual Psychology.

Slavik, S. (2002). The subject matter of Individual Psychology. In K. John, A. Millar, P. Prina, & C. Shelley (Eds.), *Adlerian yearbook—2002* (pp. 124–136). London: Adlerian Society (UK) and Institute for Individual Psychology.

Slavik, S., & Croake, J. (1997). Social interest is not altruism. In P. Prina, C. Thompson, & C. Shelley (Eds.), *Adlerian yearbook—1997* (pp. 46–56). London: Adlerian Society (UK) and Institute for Individual Psychology.

Smith, D. E. (1999). *Writing the social: Critique, theory, and investigations.* Toronto, ON: University of Toronto Press.

Smuts, J. C. (1973). *Holism and evolution.* London: Macmillan. (Original work published in 1926.)

Stein, H. T. (1991). Adler and Socrates: Similarities and differences. *Individual Psychology, 47* (2), 241–246.

Stern, W. (1996). *Die Differentielle Psychologie in Ihren, Methodischen Grundlagen.* Leipzig: Barth. (Original work published in 1911.)

Stones, C. R. (1985). Qualitative research: A viable psychological alternative. *Psychological Record, 35*(1), 63–75.

Vaihinger, H. (1965). *The philosophy of "as if."* London: Routledge & Kegan Paul. (Original work published 1911.)

Way, L. (1950). *Adler's place in psychology.* London: Allen & Unwin.

Westmarland, N. (2001). The quantitative/qualitative debate and feminist research: A subjective view of objectivity. *Forum Qualitative Sozialforschung / Forum: Qualitative Social Research.* [Online journal], *2*(1). Retrieved September 15, 2003 from http://qualitative-research.net/fqs/fqs-eng.htm.

Wood-Sherif, C. (1987). Bias in psychology. In S. Harding (Ed.), *Feminism and methodology* (pp. 37–56). Bloomington, IN: Indiana University Press.

Note

1. See Husserl's work *Logische Untersuchungen* (1900–1901).

CHAPTER 31

Community Feeling, Empathy, and Intersubjectivity: A Phenomenological Framework

FRED J. HANNA

Ansbacher and Ansbacher (1979) considered social interest, or Gemein-schaftsgefühl, to be "probably Adler's most significant concept" (p. 41). O'Connell (1991) referred to it as "Adler's most penetrating and basic concept" (p. 26). Nevertheless, the concept remains difficult to understand in its fullest sense and remains in need of greater clarification and acceptance (Manaster, 1991). The purpose of this article is to shed a ray of experiential light on Gemeinschaftsgefühl by exploring it in the context of Husserl's (1931, 1970) phenomenological philosophy, which is grounded in human consciousness and experience.

The central theme is that Gemeinschaftsgefühl, as community feeling, is ultimately experiential and may be a characteristic of the nature and structure of human consciousness itself. In addition, the suggestion will be made that the social interest that results from community feeling might be enhanced by certain modes of inquiry such as Husserl's phenomenological method or certain forms of relevant meditative practice. The discussion will begin with definitions of Gemeinschaftsgefühl, and then proceed to an examination of it in the context of phenomenology. Along the way, various

Buddhist and Hindu ideas will be compared with Gemeinschaftsgefühl so as to provide a transcultural perspective. Community feeling can be understood to be as experientially real as phenomena such as anger, grief, or the sense of one's own existence.

Social Interest and Community Feeling

Gemeinschaftsgefühl is usually translated as social interest. However, this translation has been criticized for decades as being superficial, limited, and culturally bound (see, for example, O'Connell, 1991). Other English alternatives have been social feeling, community feeling, fellow feeling, sense of solidarity, communal intuition, community interest, social sense, and feeling of belongingness. O'Connell (1991), dissatisfied with these translations, suggested that the term humanistic identification be used.

Ansbacher (1992) clarified much of this confusion by pointing out that the translation and use of Gemeinschaftsgefühl as social interest has become a pervasive error in the Adlerian literature. Ansbacher (1992) clearly demonstrated that the original and proper translation of the term is community feeling, and that community feeling and social interest are different concepts and not synonyms at all. In the present article, Ansbacher's suggestion to use community feeling as a translation of Gemeinschaftsgefühl will be followed. The term social interest, or soziales Interesse, will also be referred to but in accord with Adler's original intent as an activity-oriented manifestation of community feeling. Ansbacher (1992) quoted Adler as defining social interest as "the action line of community feeling" (p. 405) as in the sense of cooperation and helping. He pointed out that social interest derives much of its meaning and strength from the deeper sense of community feeling.

In its more simple definition, community feeling is a natural capacity to identify oneself with a greater community and eventually all of humanity, considering the struggles of the many to be nothing other than one's own. Here the nature and boundaries between self and other begin to become a bit fuzzy. "Self-boundedness," Adler (Ansbacher & Ansbacher, 1956) said, "is an artifact thrust upon the child during his education and by the present state of our social structure. The creative power of the child is misled toward self-boundaries" (p. 138). Part of the process of a person's moving beyond the boundaries of self lies in the identification of the self with another or others (Ansbacher & Ansbacher, 1956). Adler (Ansbacher & Ansbacher, 1956) observed that empathy is the key through which this transformation of identity occurs. His now famous description of empathy was in terms of seeing through another's eyes, hearing with another's ears, and feeling with another's heart. Empathy, he said, was at the core of Gemeinschaftsgefühl (Ansbacher & Ansbacher, 1956).

However, community feeling "can go even further," Adler said, "extending itself to animals, plants, and inanimate objects and finally, even to the cosmos" (Ansbacher & Ansbacher, 1956, p. 138). In fact, Ansbacher (1991) referred to Gemeinschaftsgefühl as a "general connectedness" among beings and things. He quoted Adler as having stated that "community feeling is actually a cosmic feeling, a reflection of the coherence of everything cosmic that lives in us ... and which gives us the ability to empathize with things that lie outside our body" (Ansbacher, 1992, p. 403). Although there seems to be some uncertainty as to whether this is innate (see Mosak, 1991), Adler nevertheless often characterized it as such (see Ansbacher & Ansbacher, 1956; Ansbacher, 1991) and as being present in some form in virtually all human beings.

Adler (Ansbacher & Ansbacher, 1956) was also clear in acknowledging all of this as metaphysics but also said that metaphysics was a part of Individual Psychology (Ansbacher, 1992). This bold but accurate view was quite unlike views taken by the vast majority of personality and psychotherapy theorists (see Hanna, 1994). In this same vein, Mosak (1991) pointed out that Gemeinschaftsgefühl is a hypothetical construct. But the author will attempt to point out that Gemeinschaftsgefühl is more than mere metaphysics or a hypothetical heuristic. It is eminently experiential and phenomenologically accessible. To begin this approach, it will be helpful to examine the work of one of Adler's contemporaries, Edmund Husserl.

Phenomenology and Intersubjectivity

Edmund Husserl (1859–1938), in Germany, founded a highly influential philosophical movement called phenomenology around 1906. This approach proved to be a pervasive influence on twentieth-century philosophy, especially existentialism—which is closely aligned with Adlerian psychology (Ansbacher, 1931; Johnson, 1977; Maddi, 1936; Stern, 1970; Van Dusen, 1959). As nearly as can be determined, neither Husserl nor Adler appear to have had an influence on the other's work, although Husserl is occasionally mentioned in an Adlerian context, for example, by Ansbacher and Ansbacher (1956) and Landsman (1958).

Phenomenology is essentially the study of consciousness, and of human experience in the context of consciousness (see Husserl, 1931/1977, 1936/ 1970). It is probable that no Western philosopher examined consciousness more thoroughly or rigorously than did Husserl. As a philosophy, phenomenology distinguished itself by approaching the understanding of world and self through an actual methodology for conscious, experiential, intuitive understanding rather than logical analysis or metaphysical speculation. The method was based on suspending intellectual theories, judgments, preconceptions, and assumptions so that pure, unbiased observation of phenomena could take place as much as possible. With practice and discipline, the method allowed the phenomenologist to arrive at the essential structures of virtually any aspect of human experience. Of this method, experimental psychologists Herrnstein and Boring (1965) said that it was "the most primitive kind of observation of experience that it is possible for man to achieve" (p. 611).

Consciousness remained the chief focus of Husserl's philosophy and methodology and he sought to arrive at its essential structure. Husserl (1931/1977) was clear in stating that one of the purposes of phenomenology was to disclose the ultimate nature of the human self. His explorations eventually took him to the core of consciousness. What he ultimately discovered there may have implications for understanding Adler's conception of Gemeinschaftsgefühl.

Intersubjectivity and Empathy

When Husserl arrived at the roots of consciousness he found the core or kernel of human individuality which he called the transcendental ego. But as he continued he found much more. Husserl found others. He found that human beings are united by a common framework of consciousness. He termed this intersubjectivity. Intersubjectivity for Husserl is consciousness beyond the level of the individual. Husserl (1936/1970) observed that "there is a sole psychic framework, a total framework of all souls, which are united not externally but internally … through the intentional interpenetration which is the communalization of their lives" (p. 255). Along these same lines, Husserl (1936/1970) observed that "souls themselves are external to one another [only] in virtue of their embodiment" (p. 228); and are internally understood, recognized, and interpenetrated by each other through what he called transcendental empathy (see Husserl, 1929/ 1975, 1931/1977; also see Elliston, 1977). Husserl (1929/ 1975) said that the individual ego expands into an "*intersubjective transcendental community [Gemeinschaft] which, in turn, is the transcendental ground for the intersubjectivity of nature and of the world in general*" (p. 35, italics in original). It appears that Adler's Gemeinschaftsgefühl or community feeling was of the same flavor and character as Husserl's intersubjective transcendental community.

Even though they utilized differing descriptive categories and language, it seems highly possible that Adler and Husserl were in some manner plumbing the same depths. Of crucial importance, however, is the fact that unlike Adler, Husserl (1913/1931) utilized a method. He often stressed that "phenomenology is not a theory" (p. 13) but an experiential, discovery-oriented mode of research that reveals the essential nature and structure of phenomena. In other words, intersubjectivity is no more a theoretical entity than are phenomena such as mental images or emotional pain. The term itself, of course, is merely a descriptive symbol but what the term represents is experienceable in its immediacy and immanence. Like community feeling, it can accommodate a wide variety of descriptors which in no way change its original nature.

Asian Perspectives

Intersubjectivity is not confined to phenomenology. What Husserl discovered had been documented in India, China, and other Asian cultures, long before the birth of Christ. In fact, there are an extraordinary number of parallels between Husserl's phenomenology and Asian psychologies that were also built upon a framework of experiential knowledge (see Hanna, 1993). In an Adlerian context, Leak, Gardner, and Pounds (1992) noted distinct elements of social interest (in the general use of the term) in Buddhism. Similarly, there are significant parallels between the Buddhist idea of compassion and Gemeinschaftsgefühl (Croake and Rusk, 1980).

In both Hindu and Buddhist worldviews self-boundedness is less rigidly individual and closer to being universal (Radhakrishnan & Moore, 1957). Schools of Buddhism, especially the Theravada school, go as far as to deny the existence of any kind of self whatsoever (Rahula, 1978). Once again, this is based not on mere theory born of speculation and logic but rather of experience born of contemplative methods of inquiry. Such perspectives are based on relentless, rigorous, and disciplined phenomenological inspection and reflection. Scores of volumes have been written on Asian views of self (e.g., Buddhadasa, 1989)—so many that there is no need for elaboration here. The focus of this discussion is on the potential for such deep and intense inner experience to lead directly to a more communal view of life and humanity.

Conclusion

From a Husserlian perspective, Adler's Gemeinschaftsgefühl is directly accessible phenomenologically and thus can be experientially discovered in one's inner experience. Community feeling and intersubjectivity may well be part of the woof and warp of human consciousness itself. Social interest, as "the action line of community feeling," derives its power and impetus from the underlying vital, dynamic, intersubjective nature of the human community—which appears ultimately to be the community of life and the world as a whole.

In addition, the ability and capacity to identify and empathize with others —to consider the bounds of self to extend beyond a narrow skintight conception—may be made possible by the ontological substratum of intersubjectivity that has been experienced by many human beings across cultures and throughout history. In other words, empathy itself springs from that underlying intersubjectivity, just as Adler and Husserl said.

In light of the evidence presented here, experiential methods such as Husserlian phenomenology or Buddhist mindfulness meditation have the capacity to contact this intersubjective domain within the human being. It is not surprising that each of these methods involves the recognition, generation, and enhancement of empathy. Such methods have direct implications for the clinical task of enhancing awareness of community feeling and inspiring social interest in clinical settings. Adler (Ansbacher & Ansbacher, 1956, 1979) often stated that psychotherapy was of utility in this regard. Perhaps there are other means as well.

It might, therefore, behoove a therapist to incorporate such methods as meditation to assist in developing social interest. Although meditative practice is clearly not enough in itself (see Kornfield, 1993), its practice seems to have a tendency to allow a person to reach depths of empathic experience not usually accessed by conventional therapies. This is an approach that would make use of and enhance awareness of the community of life in general. Further, given the nature of the transcultural, psycho-spiritual, and mystical reports of such experience (see Eriksson, 1992), it may be that when people do experientially contact such intersubjective domains, social interest—as the action line of community feeling —may tend to spontaneously increase as a result (as possible evidence, see Smurthwaite & McDonald, 1987).

Consciousness, long bypassed by psychological researchers, is now among the most important avenues of research (Sperry, 1993). At this point in the history of psychology, due to the decline of once dominant reductionistic paradigms such as positivism and behaviorism, the stage has been set for allowing consciousness to reenter the playing field. Of course, consciousness has always been important in Individual Psychology (Maddi, 1978), and as he did with so many other aspects of effective psychotherapy, Adler was the first to recognize its value. For the purposes of research, one need not limit inquiry into the nature of community feeling and social interest to psychometrics and statistics. Researchers can ascertain and receive rich qualitative descriptions of community feeling or social interest in select people, through qualitative research designs (see Hanna & Shank, 1995; Polkinghorne, 1989).

The question of whether Gemeinschaftsgefühl is innate still remains. Mosak (1991) outlined the confusion that Adler himself seems to have had on this topic. Mosak (1991) noted that Gemeinschaftsgefühl is a hypothetical construct and not a thing that one possesses like jewelry or a credit card. Mosak is entirely accurate in his assertion that social interest is a conceptual abstraction much like depression. However, the purpose here has been to take a slightly different approach. Gemeinschaftsgefühl is indeed a construct but what the construct represents is also, paradoxically, at the very core of those human entities which create and designate constructs.

Reports from across culture, class, gender, and education indicate that community feeling is experienceable and identifiable by a person phenomenologically. The phenomenon that Adler labelled Gemeinschaftsgefühl, and that Husserl labelled intersubjectivity is bigger than psychology, deeper than philosophy, and surpasses the limits of language bound by subject/object or self/other categories. Curiously, this characteristic of consciousness may itself be the source of, and the motivation to pursue, each of these disciplines as modes of inquiry. Hindus tell the story of how Brahman, the ultimate reality, manifests or fragments itself into all living and nonliving beings and then plays a game with itself of attempting to come to know or understand its true, original nature (Venkatesananda, 1984).

Whatever the case, Gemeinschaftsgefühl is there, at or near the core of human consciousness. Experiential awareness of it may naturally lead to social interest as a potential to be developed, aspired to, and put into practice. To those not so experientially oriented, however, community feeling will tend to remain little more than a product of Adler's intellect, to be argued, modified, qualified, negated, or redefined as the case may be. As Mosak said, it is, in any case, not something that can be possessed. Gemeinschaftsgefühl is ontological. It cannot be possessed any more than space, time, or being. It can, however, be phenomenologically discovered and explored.

References

Ansbacher, H. L. (1959). A key to existence: Editorial. *Journal of Individual Psychology, 15*(2), 141–142.

Ansbacher, H. L. (1991). The concept of social interest. *Individual Psychology, 47*(1), 28–46. (Original work published 1968.)

Ansbacher, H. L. (1992). Alfred Adler's concepts of community feeling and of social interest and the relevance of community feeling for old age. *Individual Psychology, 48*(4), 402–412.

Ansbacher, H. L., & Ansbacher, R. R. (Eds.). (1956). *The individual psychology of Alfred Adler.* New York: Basic.

Ansbacher, H. L., & Ansbacher, R. R. (Eds.). (1979). *Superiority and social interest.* New York: Norton.

Buddhadasa, B. (1989). *Me and mine.* Albany, NY: SUNY Press.

Croake, J. W., & Rusk, R. (1980). The theories of Adler and Zen. *Journal of Individual Psychology,* *36*(2), 219–226.

Elliston, F. (1977). Husserl's phenomenology of empathy. In F. Elliston & P. McCormick (Eds.), *Husserl: Expositions and appraisals* (pp. 213–231). Notre Dame, IN: University of Notre Dame.

Eriksson, C. (1992). Social interest/social feeling and the evolution of consciousness. *Individual Psychology, 48*(3), 277–287.

Hanna, F. J. (1993). The transpersonal consequences of Husserl's phenomenological method. *The Humanistic Psychologist, 21*(1), 41–57.

Hanna, F. J. (1994). A dialectic of experience: A radical empiricist approach to conflicting theories in psychotherapy. *Psychotherapy, 31*(1), 124–136.

Hanna, F. J., & Shank, G. (1995). The specter of metaphysics in counseling research and practice: The qualitative challenge. *Journal of Counseling and Development, 74*(1), 53–59.

Herrnstein, R. J., & Boring, E. C. (Eds.). (1965). *A sourcebook in the history of psychology.* Cambridge, MA: Harvard University Press.

Husserl, E. (1931). *Ideas: General introduction to pure phenomenology.* New York: Collier. (Original work published 1913.)

Husserl, E. (1970). *The crisis of European sciences and transcendental phenomenology.* Evanston, IL: Northwestern University Press. (Original work published 1936.)

Husserl, E. (1975). *The Paris lectures.* The Hague: Martinus Nijhoff. (Original lectures given 1929.)

Husserl, E. (1977). *Cartesian meditations.* The Hague: Marinus Nijhoff. (Original work published 1931.)

Johnson, E. L. (1966). Existential trends toward individual psychology. *Journal of Individual Psychology, 22*(1), 33–42.

Kornfield, J. (1993). *A path with heart.* New York: Bantam Books.

Landsman, T. (1958). Four phenomenologies. *Journal of Individual Psychology, 14*(1), 29–37.

Leak, G. K., Gardner, L. E., & Pounds, B. (1992). A comparison of Eastern religion, Christianity, and social interest. *Individual Psychology, 48*(1) 53–64.

Maddi, S. R. (1978). Existential and individual psychologies. *Journal of Individual Psychology, 34*(2), 182–190.

Manaster, G. J. (1991). Editor's comments. *Individual Psychology, 47*(1), 1–3.

Mosak, H. H. (1991). "I don't have social interest": Social interest as a construct. *Individual Psychology, 47*(3), 309–320.

O'Connell, W. E. (1991). Humanistic identification: A new translation for Gemeinschaftsgefühl. *Individual Psychology, 47*(1), 26–27. (Original work published 1965.)

Polkinghorne, D. E. (1989). Phenomenological research methods. In R. S. Valle & S. Hailing (Eds.), *Existential-phenomenological perspectives in psychology* (pp. 41–60). New York: Plenum.

Radhakrishnan, S., & Moore, C. A. (Eds.). (1957). A sourcebook in Indian philosophy. Princeton, NJ: Princeton University Press.

Rahula, W. (1978). *What the Buddha taught.* London, Gordon Fraser.

Smurthwaite, T. J., & McDonald, R. D. (1987). Examining ecological concern among persons reporting mystical experiences. *Psychological Reports, 60,* 591–596.

Sperry, R. W. (1993). The impact and promise of the cognitive revolution. *American Psychologist, 48*(8), 878–885.

Stern, A. (1958). Existential psychoanalysis and individual psychology. *Journal of Individual Psychology, 14*(1), 38–50.

Van Dusen, W. (1959). The ontology of Adlerian psychodynamics. *Journal of Individual Psychology, 15*(2), 143–156.

Venkatesananda, S. (1984). *The concise Yoga Vasistha.* Albany, NY: SUNY Press.

Permissions

Index